CAPITALISM AFTER POSTMODERNISM

INTERNATIONAL COMPARATIVE SOCIAL STUDIES

VOLUME V

CAPITALISM AFTER POSTMODERNISM

Neo-conservatism, Legitimacy and the Theory of Public Capital

BY

H.T. WILSON

BRILL
LEIDEN · BOSTON · KÖLN
2002

This book is printed on acid-free paper.

Library of Congress Cataloging-in-Publication Data

Wilson, H.T.
Capitalism after postmodernism : Neo-conservatism, Legitimacy and the Theory of Public Capital / by H.T. Wilson.
p. cm. — (International comparative social studies, ISSN 1568-4474 ; 5)
Includes bibliographical references and index.
ISBN 9004124586 (alk. paper)
1. Capitalism. I. Title. II. Series.

HB501 .H567 2001
330.12'2—dc21 2002019573

Die Deutsche Bibliothek – CIP-Einheitsaufnahme

Wilson, Hall T. :
Capitalism after postmodernism : Neo-conservatism, Legitimacy and the Theory of Public Capital / by H. T. Wilson. – Leiden ; Boston; Köln : Brill, 2002
(International comparative social studies ; Vol. 5)
ISBN 90–04–12458–6

ISSN 1568-4474
ISBN 90 04 12458 6

PRINTED IN THE NETHERLANDS

For Rudolf Meidner

CONTENTS

For the common people had believed that he would bring about a complete redistribution of property, while the nobles had hoped he would restore the old order or at least make only insignificant changes. Solon, however, set himself against . . . both factions, while saving the country and giving it the laws that were best for it, under the circumstances.

Aristotle, *The Constitution of Athens*

Where production is directly oriented toward use, and only the excess product is exchanged, the costs of circulation appear only for the excess product, not for the main product. The more production comes to rest on exchange, the more important do the physical conditions of exchange—the means of communication and transport—become for the costs of circulation. Capital by its nature drives beyond every spatial barrier. Thus the creation of the physical conditions of exchange—of the means of communication and transport—the annihilation of space by time—becomes an extraordinary necessity for it. Only in so far as the direct product can be realized in distant markets in mass quantities in proportion to reductions in the transport costs, and only in so far as at the same time the means of communication and transport themselves can yield spheres of realization for labor, driven by capital; only in so far as commercial traffic takes place in massive volume—in which more than necessary labor is replaced—only to that extent is the production of cheap means of communication and transport a condition for production based on capital, and promoted by it *for that reason.* All labor required in order to throw the finished product into circulation—it is in economic circulation only when it is present on the market—is from capital's viewpoint a barrier to be overcome—as is all labor required as a *condition* for the production process (thus e.g. expenses for the security of exchange etc.).

Karl Marx, *Grundrisse*

Co-opt: to elect into any body by the votes of its members.

Chambers 20th Century Dictionary
New Edition, 1983, p. 276

PREFACE

This book quite purposely addresses a number of interrelated issues in old and new political economy and its critique around several key themes. Emphasis throughout on deficits, debt and the so called 'public debt', apart from a chapter devoted specifically to the topic, implies that (allegedly) more positive developments, like globalization and the new competitiveness, for example, however important, have not superseded these concerns in the writer's mind. Indeed, a focus on globalization in particular often appears to have the effect (if not the intent) of taking the mind of the reader or listener off questions of debt and indebtedness altogether.

This is because the debt is not really a partisan political issue at all, when addressed historically and in terms of critique, as I attempt to show in this book. The left has often been opposed to it and its increase and the right, in particular neo-conservatism today, absolutely requires a certain, guaranteed amount of it in order to justify its policies, programs and practices. Debt, in the form of the 'public debt', is what provides neo-conservatism with most of its raison d'etre, however incapable of eliminating it or bringing it down substantially those governments espousing its policies seem to be. Indeed, contracting out and privatization often have quite the opposite result, no matter how difficult it may be to discover the many and varied 'sleights of hand' involved in these practices.

In this sense neo-conservatism is a negative politics, not because it constructively criticizes and posits real alternatives but because it is a regressive political philosophy in practice which cannot sustain close analysis of the relation between what it says and what it does. Society has more than enough room for such regression, however; its very complexity allows its (alleged) traditional lessons from the past to be brought to the surface with a chastening effect, if little else. The public debt continues to be a major justification for all forms of downsizing, contracting out and privatizing government functions, programs and services and deregulating the economy, a less direct way of accomplishing the same thing. The fact that the real purpose of these policies is not to bring down or eliminate the debt is the best place to begin a critique of neo-conservatism.

Apart from its role in justifying these policies, many corporate and other institutional entities make a good, and often even honest, living off the 'public debt' of numerous nation-states. Little wonder they oppose fiscal and related attempts by governments to improve their economies by trying to grow out of their debts through spending and related incentives. These policies are inflationary, and will therefore lessen the value of the debt held by these entities. Alongside NAFTA we now have the WTO, backed up by central banks and bond rating agencies, to stop recovery from happening by these means. Controlling inflation, instead of being one policy among many, to be used when appropriate, has become the dominant premise against which all other 'interventions' must justify themselves. Besides, governments cannot go bankrupt, and therefore can be tapped interminably, along with the public capital that ultimately makes this worthwhile.

This is a serious limitation on states and their governments since it leaves mainly devices favoring the institutions of capital and their further extensive and intensive growth as ways of coming out of slumps, recessions and slow downs. The essence of these policies, what makes them quintessentially neo-conservative, is their root assumption that recovery depends upon controls and restrictions on the institutions of the people, that is public and social institutions, particularly the latter. The result is a serious institutional imbalance within capitalist democracies, apparently all the more necessary as capital seeks to move to a higher, more supranational or global level of aggregation. In this endeavor, capital now has such a decided institutional edge that its legitimacy in capitalist democracies, and in the developed world as a whole is, or soon will be, coming under threat in fundamental ways.

Addressing constructively, as well as defending, this line of argument has required extensive and very specific referencing of sources read and used in each chapter, and in the text as a whole, in order for it to function as a teaching device and not just as a theoretical treatise. That this often includes citations without pagination directs the reader's attention to the index and/or elaborated table of contents in the sources cited. Sources are not necessarily cited and discussed solely, or even mainly, because they agree with the writer's point of view on the matters under consideration. Many take a different tack to arrive at the same view, while others may employ similar reasoning to a quite different conclusion. Sources that disagree with the writer are regularly cited and discussed, and readers are encouraged to consult them in concert with the text.

Having said this, I hope nevertheless that I have made it clear in what follows why I believe that present developments seriously jeopardize the balance between capital, public and social institutions on which the progress and welfare of the developing world, as well as capitalist democracies themselves, depends. At the present time, the institutions of capital, admittedly with a modicum of continuing citizen tolerance, if not support, are racing far too fast and too far ahead of those of the public and society, creating thereby a dangerous imbalance. It is this series of events over the past twenty-five years to which progressive forces representing general and specific public and social interests are presently attempting to respond.

The surprising convergence of interests between neo-conservatism and postmodernism, especially the latter's nihilistic tendencies, however unintended and unexpected, has set the boundaries of this text's attempt to return to both the labor theory of value and the idea of the wealth of nations in pursuit of a theory of public capital and its co-optation. The theory of public capital builds on the concept of value extraction from political economy and its critique, but seeks to address its more recent institutional manifestations, including those in the public and social spheres, as sources of the most significant legitimations of capitalism that we now have. That these sources of legitimation have been taken far too much for granted in recent years, and may not be so available to capital in the future for the reasons indicated, is the overriding argument of this text.

H.T. Wilson
Toronto and Thornhill, Ontario

CHAPTER ONE

INTRODUCTION

No one who acknowledges the many cultural and historical forms that capitalism has taken, and continues to take, can really believe that present and emerging changes in its composition and direction justify the claim that it is being superseded by something that is fundamentally different. Even if globalization were a recent development, its reality would hardly warrant extrapolating qualitative difference of the magnitude implied from mere growth in complexity and scale.

This, among other things, serves to bring to mind two controversial arguments. One sees technology as a factor of production independent, or potentially independent, of both capital and labor. The other assumes (with Engels) that at a certain point changes in quantity, scale, complexity and scope transcend old forms and create something that is qualitatively new. The first is categorically mistaken, while the second is conditionally correct, but without the consequences for their analysis of capitalism that many postmodernists assume.[1]

Compare, for example, present realities not only with Marx's still relevant intensive definition of capitalism in *Grundrisse, Capital* and *Theories of Surplus Value* but with Max Weber's detailed and comprehensive extensive definition in 'Sociological Categories of Economic Action' and elsewhere in *Economy and Society*.[2] Together, they provide

[1] See Jacques Ellul, *The Technological Society* (New York: Alfred Knopf, 1964), and later in Ellul, *The Technological System* (New York: Continuum, 1980), and my critique in H.T. Wilson, 'The Sociology of Apocalypse', *Human Context*, Volume 7, No. 3 (Autumn 1975), pp. 474–494; Langdon Winner, *Autonomous Technology*. Technics Out of Control as a Theme in Political Thought (Cambridge, Mass.: MIT Press, 1977); and Wilson, 'Science, Technology and Innovation', *Methodology and Science*, Volume 15, No. 3 (1982), pp. 167–200. The reference to Engels is in Friedrich Engels, *The Dialectics of Nature* (Moscow: Progress Publishers, 1972).

[2] Karl Marx, *Grundrisse*. Introduction to the Critique of Political Economy (Harmondsworth: Penguin, 1973); Marx, *Capital*. A Critique of Political Economy, 3 Volumes (Moscow: Progress Publishers, 1953–1959); *Theories of Surplus Value*, Parts I–III (Moscow: Progress Publishers, 1963–1971). Max Weber, *Economy and Society*,

support for the view that ours is indeed a capitalist system, a view that is only reinforced by present 'globalizing' practices when these practices are looked at from an institutional perspective.[3]

Thus, while organizational structures may differ from the start and change in various ways in response to the exigencies of historical time and the spaces of cultural practice and social and political reality, institutions are more than capable of accommodating the diverse, even conflicting, means undertaken in pursuit of maximization. All that is required is that the basic conditions stated in the conceptual and practical formulations of Marx, Weber and others come into being and continue to persist. It is in the process of creating this institutional configuration, one which includes, but is not exhausted by capitalism, that capitalism begins to develop into a world system.[4]

It is the fact that many to most of the features of this configuration have persisted through world wars and depressions that provides further support for the notion that capitalism as a set of practices must be embedded in a wider and more complex set of institutional interdependencies. This observation is confirmed by the work of Clegg and Redding, among many, many others.[5] Once this matter has been addressed critically, then the idea that post-modernity is synonymous with or includes a post-capitalistic (as opposed to a post-industrial) economic reality becomes difficult to accept.

Volume I, Part I, especially pp. 63–226, 284–355; Volume II, especially Chapters VIII and XI (Berkeley: University of California Press, 1978); Weber, *General Economic History* (London: George Allen and Unwin, 1968, 1927).

[3] Alfred Chandler, *Strategy and Structure* (Cambridge, Mass.: MIT Press, 1962); Chandler, *The Visible Hand* (Cambridge, Mass.: Belknap Press, 1977); Peter Mathias and M.M. Postan (general editors), *Cambridge Economic History of Europe* (Cambridge: Cambridge University Press, 1983), particularly Volume 7, 'The Industrial Economies: Capital, Labour and Enterprise', Chapter 2, Part 2 'The U.S., Japan and Russia', pp. 70–133, 503–504, 561–564, including the contribution by Chandler; Immanuel Wallerstein, *Historical Capitalism* (London: Verso, 1983); Wallerstein, *The Modern World System*, 3 Volumes (New York: Academic Press, 1974).

[4] Thus Weber's interest as 'a product of modern European civilization' in capitalism, science and science-based technology, law and legal institutions, bureaucracy, and the relation between political economy, economics and the social sciences. This is still the essence of the institutional configuration that we call advanced industrial societies, or capitalist democracies, today. See *Economy and Society, op. cit.* and especially the initial and summary statements at the beginning and the end of Weber, *The Protestant Ethic and the Spirit of Capitalism* (New York: Charles Scribner's Sons, 1952).

[5] Stewart Clegg and S. Gordon Redding (eds.) *Capitalism in Contrasting Cultures* (Berlin and New York: Walter de Gruyter, 1990); Mathias and Postan, *Cambridge Economic History of Europe*, Volume 7, *op. cit.*

Better to argue, with Calinescu, Jameson and numerous others, that postmodernism is a movement within modernity and/or the cultural logic of late capitalism.[6] This revision would also serve to accommodate the thinking of Lash and Urry, who define their view of Marx's theory of circulation as one in which, to quote Berman quoting Marx, 'all that is solid melts into air'.[7] In Volume II of *Capital*, titled *The Process of the Circulation of Capital*, Marx does allude to the various circuits of capital, and the fact that spatial and temporal considerations do render sensible the idea that circulation processes will vary and will impact back upon production.[8]

But to argue that as a consequence of this 'commodities are cast adrift and acquire mobility to flow through changing spaces at shifting times', even if true, in no way challenges the fact that the institutional matrix within which capitalism is (or is being) embedded persists, even as elements of it change internally.[9] As the authors themselves point out in *Economies of Signs and Space*, this contradicts the claim that organized capitalism is in the process of coming to an end. Indeed, much postmodern writing on the subject of an allegedly vanishing capitalism calls to mind Twain's apocryphal claim that 'recent reports of my death in the press have been greatly exaggerated' more than anything else.

It suggests that we acknowledge in its place the fact that *some* forms of organized capitalism are coming to an end or changing in important ways while *others* more compatible with new institutional demands and requirements are coming into being. The reasons for this may include globalization, the web and information technology,

[6] Matei Calinescu, *Five Faces of Modernity* (Durham, N.C.: Duke University Press, 1987), especially pp. 263–312, 356–363 and 381–385; Frederic Jameson, *Postmodernism* (Durham, N.C.: Duke University Press, 1991), especially the introduction, chapters 1, 2 and 7–10.

[7] Scott Lash and John Urry, *Economies of Signs and Space* (London: Sage Publications, 1994); Marshall Berman, *All that is Solid Melts into Air*. The Experience of Modernity (London: Verso, 1983). Note that this citation/book title is taken from the early pages of Karl Marx and Friedrich Engels, *The Communist Manifesto*, written in 1847–1848. It is therefore not just from the so called 'early' Marx, but from one of the most rhetorical parts of a revolutionary call to arms very short on analysis compared to the sources cited above, which address 'all that is solid'. Cited from Lewis Feuer (editor), *Marx and Engels: Basic Writings* (Garden City, New York: Doubleday, 1959), p. 10.

[8] Marx, *Capital*, Volume II, *op. cit.* But see Marx, *Grundrisse*, pp. 524–525 for the location of the headnote excerpt that anticipates much of this discussion.

[9] Lash and Urry, *op. cit.*, p. 1.

international and supranational agreements and the so-called 'new economy' generally. However, they may also include *the reality of competition itself*, as well as changes in consumer taste and interest, however 'engineered' or spontaneous they may be. Ongoing activities and processes like these cannot help but generate some continuous level of 'disorganization' if the system is working as its supporters and its detractors alike say it should.

For 'all that is solid to melt into air' on a continuous, or even an intermittent basis, there must be institutional capacities and functions operating through various organized structures and processes that *keep producing the solidity, or the solidity that replaces what has already melted into air*. Marx and Weber both took this general observation for granted in their own respective efforts to address the relationship between history, society, economy and culture in time, space and circumstance. Indeed, the power and persuasiveness of their analyses rests to a considerable extent on the way they display this emerging and/or established institutional configuration that includes, but is not exhausted by, capitalism at different points in its development. This is especially the case for Weber, for the obvious reason that he observed and discussed the emergence and development of this increasingly complex configuration half a century after Marx, when it was already well established in its industrial or financial form in many social and cultural settings.

Since disorganized capitalism often reflects the role of market activity, however restricted its openness and however interdependent it is on state and other institutions, we need to see *the market itself as an institution* rather than evidence of the absence of an institution. This is particularly necessary given both modernist and postmodernist tendencies to treat institutions themselves as a throwback to traditional social formations that have at best a residual role to play today. As an institution, the market is a key element in the very system of institutions so central to the configuration that I have alluded to, one that is itself being increasingly traditionalized, even as new cultures participate in its practices and give pride of place to its values and interests.

Even (or especially) in the high technology, high value added sphere of business, commerce and finance, companies come into being, undergo significant changes and go out of business with considerable, though not predictable, regularity, and do so for very different reasons. This does not necessarily mean that capitalism in any given case is disorganized and/or coming to an end, except in the ways suggested, ways that refute such a notion altogether because they usually are, after all, part of its very dynamic, not something alien to it. Indeed, many 'in house' critics of capitalism continue to bemoan the fact that in given sectors capitalism is too solid, too structured and organized, too uncompetitive and unchanging, and support policies more friendly to entrepreneurial and small business activity, especially in an age of 'global reach'.

Thus, far from acknowledging the claim that organized capitalism is coming to an end, almost everyone on either side of the issue, from economists positive or neutral toward globalization and the 'new economy' to investigative journalists highly critical of it, would make just the opposite assertion. Change in line with what would be expected of capitals in general under given circumstances is certainly to be expected, and occasionally even praised, but this hardly constitutes evidence of a disorganized capitalism spinning mindlessly out of control. Indeed, in *Economies of Signs and Space*, Lash and Urry suggest that the very emergence of these new economies provides evidence for the claim that a new, albeit interdependent, capitalism, aspects of which are decidedly 'post industrial' is emerging.[10]

Nevertheless, these new economies, far from eliminating their need for commodities requiring industrial production and subsistence and other labor, actually displace these activities either internally or to other parts of the globe under new technologies and new cultural, political and economic rules. Far from melting into air, 'dirty' factory and sweatshop production and the labor on which it depends all too regularly turns up either in less developed countries or the less developed sectors of our own, alongside service functions often performed under conditions of wage slavery, if not slavery itself.[11] In what follows, several trends are addressed that give substance to these developments. Instead of looking at them as evidence for the emergence of a postmodern society beyond capitalism because the present institutional matrix or configuration seems less organized and coherent, or just plain different, than it was in the relatively recent past, this study reaches a different conclusion.

[10] Compare to Scott Lash and John Urry, *The End of Organized Capitalism* (Cambridge: Polity Press, 1987) as the authors suggest. But see Claus Offe, *Disorganized Capitalism* (London: Hutchinson, 1984) for essays that reach back to the origins of this claim.

[11] Lash and Urry, *Economies of Signs and Space*, pp. 1–7, 145–170.

For reasons put forward in early chapters, it argues that, far from being secure in their legitimacy, even in the most successful sectors and countries, neo-conservative governments, national and international financial institutions and those capitals they represent are doing serious, even irreparable institutional damage to their respective societies. This in spite, and perhaps even because, so much of the 'new economy' is concerned with people devoted to generating a 'fast capitalism' which consumes objects, signs and spaces at an exponential rate, even by comparison to what was the case a decade ago.[12] Economies of signs and space will always have to acknowledge the unavoidable priority that capitalism necessarily gives to time—its capture, redefinition and control everywhere it operates, or intends to operate—as a precondition for the existence of markets and the preeminence of exchange over use values.[13]

Present policies are damaging not only the public and social infrastructure that neo-conservatives often think is optional given their commitment to more and more direct forms of co-optation of human, public and social resources in their effort to reach higher levels of aggregation in the search for markets and profits. Indirectly, they are also damaging the capital sector itself because their actions gravely upset the balance that is so necessary between capital, public and social sectors in all capitalist democracies. While it is clear that capital often to usually has an advantage because its institutions are the oldest and best established relative to the later to emerge institutions of the public, and thereafter society, serious imbalances between them will not be something that citizens and publics will long endure.[14]

By exploring the discourses that signal the return of so much of the rhetoric of 'old fashioned' capitalism in the guise of neo-conservatism and the 'new economy', we are able to realize more than ever before how vast society's capacity for regression to earlier forms really is. Its very complexity as *a socially and culturally specific form* of collective

---

[12] Ben Agger, *Fast Capitalism* (Urbana and Chicago: University of Illinois Press, 1989).

[13] H.T. Wilson, 'Time, Space and Value', *Time and Society*, Volume 8, No. 1 March 1999), pp. 161–181. For a different analysis more in the tradition of Thorstein Veblen, see the indictment of many of these new economies of signs and space as wasteful and waste-making in Herschel Hardin, *The New Bureaucracy: Waste and Folly in the Private Sector* (Toronto: McClelland and Stewart, 1991).

[14] H.T. Wilson, *Bureaucratic Representation: Civil Servants and the Future of Capitalist Democracies* (Leiden and Boston: Brill, 2001); Wilson, 'The Downside of Downsizing', *The New Public Management: International Developments*, edited by D. Barrows and H.I. Macdonald (Toronto: Captus Press, 2000), pp. 55–80.

life rather than a synonym for it is what makes it possible for it to reach so far back and so deeply into its structure as a false totality in order to dredge up these earlier forms.[15] Of course, this is not achieved in reality but only in rhetoric. Its achievement would imply that capitalism really had shed those institutions on which it today depends more than ever before, and we should know, if we do not already know, that this is not, and never can be, the case.

Like the market itself, and the priority and legitimacy its values presently give to private greed, consumption and display, these earlier forms include discourses around individualism and competitiveness, as well as globalization, privatization, free trade and the dangers of debt, especially the 'public debt'. These discourses presently provide the grounding in legitimacy for the most exponentially increased extraction of value—much of it in the form of public capital—from public and social labor and resources that has taken place in capitalist democratic nation states for over seventy years. Whatever reality inheres in discursive references to globalization and the new economy it has allegedly spawned, the capitalist democratic state is and will remain the major basis for the extraction and co-optation of the labor power and public capital on which capitals depend for the foreseeable future. That this extraction and co-optation is backed up by supranational and international bodies and national banks and bond rating agencies representing the interests of increasingly external debt holders only underscores the point rather than disputing it.

My use of the term 'co-optation', as well as extraction, to address this phenomenon in these countries is offered in the most literal sense, because it relates capitalism to representative democracy and the congeries of political and governmental institutions on which capitalism depends in the most direct possible way. To 'co-opt' is 'to elect into any body by the votes of its members', when one and one's associates are part of this membership in another capacity.[16] The co-optation of public capital from the labor of other citizens of these nation states thus goes on inside them in a way that is thoroughly compatible with consent, political parties and the electoral

[15] Theodor Adorno, 'Society', in *The Legacy of the German Refugee Intellectuals*, edited by Robert Boyers (New York: Schocken Books, 1969), pp. 144–153; H.T. Wilson, *The American Ideology* (London: Routledge, 1977).

[16] *Chambers 20th Century Dictionary* (Cambridge: Cambridge University Press, 1983), p. 276.

process. Indeed, this is the only way that the process of extracting surplus value can acquire legitimacy from most of the citizens of these societies who participate in it, often actively and enthusiastically.[17] Nothing more readily characterizes the movement from a capitalist economy in a pre capitalist collective form to a capitalist society embedded in a wider matrix of institutional supports than the process by which extraction is both legitimized and concealed by the co-optation of public capital to private uses.

The attempt in what follows to update the labor theory of value as it expresses itself in the extraction of labor power and the creation of surplus value from this labor by capitals is thus to focus on the co-optation of public capital, also (but not only) by capitals. This co-optation of public capital is built atop and, consequently, thoroughly dependent upon, the extraction of labor power and the surplus value that follows from it. Nowadays, this occurs in institutional settings where infrastructural as well as material values and resources are co-opted alongside such extraction and value creation. Since the institutions of capital are the oldest and best established element in this institutional matrix relative to the later to emerge institutions of the public, and, later, society, it is indisputable that these institutions have had, and continue to have, a central role in creating and sustaining this infrastructure.

Thus the preference here for calling the value and resources of this institutional infrastructure public *capital*, however dependent their co-optation remains on the extraction and creation processes cited, and however much of it (too much at present) is employed for private uses by capitals. Nevertheless, it is a different basis for power in the market and the state, especially nowadays. Indeed, co-optation often either hides (or seeks to hide) capital's dependence on the extraction and value creation process, or in fact creates less or no value of any kind through extraction and creation relative to what it trades on in and through institutional co-optation. This would be the basis for the not-unreasonable claim that entrepreneurs, inventors and small businesspersons can and often do make against organized, corporate, transnational capitals in particular. Without in any way endorsing their behavior, it is precisely the latter's influence over and effective control of state and extra-state social and economic

[17] Wilson, *Bureaucratic Representation*, especially chapter 3.

resources and values that often limits the former's access to and use of these institutional resources and infrastructure.

Capitals, in effect, extract surplus value, either in this way or by reference to earlier modes whenever and wherever possible, while pointing to the *institutional* as well as material value that these societies and cultures have accumulated in the form of infrastructure as evidence of *capital's* reliability and good faith. What makes the capital *public* (and *social*), in addition to being the surplus value provided by individual and collective labor, is the institutional, historical and cultural reference that capitals trade on in any and all markets, however open or restricted, that they enter.[18] The reason they can do this, as noted, is that the institutions of capital are the oldest and best defended legally and politically relative to the later-to-arrive public, but especially social institutions. At the same time that this is happening, we are told that objective forces—for which the major mantras are globalization and the new economy—are making it even less possible to govern our societies democratically than was the case before.[19]

Discourses favoring heightened extraction and co-optation come to one another's assistance to the extent that the concepts cited above encourage us to treat these two occurrences as distinct, if not mutually exclusive, events rather than elements of an interrelated phenomenon. Thus our continuing collective delusion that globalization, deeply understood, is a competition between countries and capitals rather than between classes. While it is true that aspects of this process have clear, objective properties, many are nevertheless regressive in ways which society alone makes possible for the reasons indicated. It is an awareness of these latter properties that helps us in our efforts to disentangle the negative from the positive tendencies of capitalism in the interests of balanced institutional development and the democratic and social control of extraction and co-optation that alone makes such balanced development possible.

[18] Although what I am really addressing here is *both* public *and* social capital, paralleling the second and third institutional sectors of capitalist democracies respectively, discussed in 'The Downside of Downsizing', *op. cit.* and in *Bureaucratic Representation*. However, I have had to respond to the 'co-optation' of the term 'social capital' (like 'public choice') by groups on the whole sympathetic to the neo-conservative agenda. Thus by 'public capital' I mean both public and social institutional forms.

[19] See especially Linda McQuaig, *The Cult of Impotence: Selling the Myth of Powerlessness in the Global Economy* (Toronto: Viking, 1998).

CHAPTER TWO

CAPITALISM AND LEGITIMACY

It is more than reasonable to ask why anyone would want to carry out a scholarly study on the question of the legitimacy of capitalism in the present circumstances. Even more understandable to question the sense of someone who feels that such a study is necessary, if not imperative, today. With the former Soviet Union and much of Eastern Europe in tatters, China determined to continue with market reforms, and many of the most powerful Western and Asian economic powers supporting one or another version of the neo-conservative agenda, is it not indisputable that capitalism is triumphant? Furthermore, is it not on the basis of an objective assessment of the economic performance of these nation-state systems that this conclusion has been reached?

In one sense this appears clearly to be the case. It is difficult to dispute the fact that general publics constituting a clear to an overwhelming majority in Western capitalist countries support, either actively through the electoral process or more passively by their apparent consent, policies and regimes committed to what is somewhat euphemistically called 'the new political economy'.[1] Even though the vast majority of the citizenry in these countries are rarely if ever what we would call capitals (or capitalists) in the strict sense, they appear to be clearly supportive of the form that capitalism has taken in their respective nation-states. Even in capitalist societies with deep and long-standing class divisions and/or strong labor, socialist or communist party traditions this generalization is defensible, though perhaps less so than in countries like the United States and Canada.

But this has not really answered the question just posed, since public support through the ballot box and in other ways is hardly

[1] But see Ankie Hoogvelt, *Globalization and the Postcolonial World: the New Political Economy of Development* (Baltimore: John Hopkins University Press, 2000); Harry Dahms (editor), *Transformations of Capitalism: Economy, Society and the State in Modern Times* (New York: New York University Press, 2000); Will Hutton and Anthony Giddens (editors), *Global Capitalism* (New York: New Press, 2000); Ingrid Rema (editor), *The Political Economy of Global Restructuring* (Aldershot, U.K.: Edward Elgar, 1993); Joyce Kolko, *Restructuring the World's Economy* (New York: Pantheon, 1988).

synonymous with an objective assessment of economic performance, and may even be contrary to it. All that this public support may mean is that publics have been persuaded to question the so-called Keynesian consensus around technical progress, social welfare and a liberal-socialist agenda by those who advocate a more fiscally and monetarily responsible approach to government expenditure. In this case, responsibility requires them to treat the nation-state as a 'household-writ-large'.[2] Thus re-conceptualized on the basis of a revived and resuscitated Nineteenth Century liberalism and fitted out with the thoroughly inaccurate moniker of 'neo-conservatism', this agenda seeks to stabilize and cut back public expenditure, deficits and the 'public debt' that has allegedly been the result of such profligacy.

Somewhat ironically, this is being attempted while a parallel process, in which the private indebtedness of real individual, family and group households has gone through the proverbial ceiling, has not only been tolerated but encouraged through advertising, the mass media and low interest loans from banking and financial institutions. Thus we are to seek to reconcile consumer capitalism with public and social sector 'downsizing' and government withdrawal from established public, social and economic functions and responsibilities. The major exception to this is a heightened governmental presence in all jurisdictions concerned with the collection of regressive sales and goods and services taxes, often collected by businesses themselves, alongside various forms of 'clawback' and the attempt to supplant universality with disbursement systems based on means testing. The incompatibility between these two views is often reconciled, somewhat artfully, by the claim that the latter is needed in order to stimulate the private sector economy.[3]

Yet one of the most glaring weaknesses of the neo-conservative agenda is precisely its refusal to really commit to economic growth

---

[2] Robert Kuttner, *The Economic Illusion: False Choices between Prosperity and Social Justice* (Boston: Houghton Mifflin, 1984); Fred Block, *The Mean Season: the Attack on the Welfare State* (New York: Pantheon Books, 1987); Block, *Revising State Theory: Essays in Politics and Postindustrialism* (Berkeley: University of California Press, 1990).

[3] H.T. Wilson, 'The Downside of Downsizing: Bureaucratic Representation in Capitalist Democracies', in *The New Public Management: International Developments* (Toronto: Captus Press, 2000). The full panoply of neo-conservative techniques and strategies for co-opting the state in capitalist democracies in an even more direct way than has been the case for 75 years is discussed in Wilson, *Retreat from Governance* (Ottawa: Voyageur International, 1989) and, more comprehensively, in *Bureaucratic Representation* (Leiden and Boston: Brill, 2001).

and innovation in the countries where it holds sway, often under the banner of socialist, social democratic or labor parties. This refusal has taken many forms, including the absence of any real interest in generating adaptive infrastructure and retraining schemes and a consistent preference for 'free trade' models instead of those which seek to generate more active 'industrial policy' approaches to economic activity and business-government relations.[4] None of this should come as a surprise, since this particular refusal is ideologically consistent not only with the established, even traditional, preferences of anti-Keynesian conservatives but with the philosophy of contemporary capitalism and with capitals themselves.

Having said this, the present neo-conservative agenda is very consciously directed to using state power to directly co-opt public capital and the legitimacy on which both it and subsequent extractive value can be realized. And it does so in ways that go beyond virtually anything that we have seen under the so-called Keynesian consensus, ideology to the contrary notwithstanding.[5] Under this consensus, capitals had to content themselves with more indirect methods of co-optation, partly because of public and social concerns coming out of the Great Depression of the 1930's and 40's. But it was also because they themselves had lost confidence in their capacity as capitals to co-opt directly using sympathetic or comprador governments and parties without paying the price of economic collapse and social instability. That this perception has changed substantially owes much to the nature of the Keynesian consensus that was achieved in the 1950's and 60's.

This changed perception was achieved by building on the very policies, practices, structures and relationships that are now so roundly condemned by the present and emerging 'conventional wisdom'. Those supportive of the neo-conservative agenda which originated in Great Britain with Margaret Thatcher and The Conservative Party were able to make their case to publics disillusioned with something and ready, with proper prodding, to blame labor, social democracy and socialism. This was particularly true when adherents of the lat-

---

[4] The idea that the 'free market' itself could constitute a major vehicle of 'industrial policy' is something that numerous countries, most prominently Japan, picked up from the United States. See Jerome Davis, *Capitalism and its Culture* (New York: Farrar and Reinhart, 1936); and Thurman Arnold, *The Folklore of Capitalism* (New Haven: Yale University Press, 1937).

[5] Discussed in chapter 8, this study, 'Public Capital and its Co-optation'.

ter parties and groups could not (or would not) make a case against this agenda.[6] Failure or refusal to point out what is wrong with this agenda by showing how far short of its goals its results fall is an extremely serious harbinger of a failure of nerve, one with significant consequences for progressive forces in capitalist democracies.

Thus, for example, the Soviet collapse, far from demonstrating the poverty of Marx's analysis of Western capitalist development, clearly vindicates his argument. It does this by suggesting that one cannot go directly from a pre-capitalist feudal social formation into socialism without a long and drawn out 'intervening' period of capitalism. Analysis of some unique features of Russian and greater Russian development, relying on established authorities and accepted knowledge, effectively puts to rest the view that the Soviet Union really was a socialist or communist power as Marx would have understood it.[7] While it is doubtless true that this is what the Soviet leadership has claimed since Lenin, it is ironic that this is virtually the only thing it said which those espousing the neo-conservative agenda agree with because it now suits their purposes to do so.

One is therefore warranted in arguing that there is an essential compatibility, however unintended, between the assessment of the Soviet Union as a pre-capitalist rather than a post-capitalist society and the neo-conservative agenda in key Western and Asian countries. After all, is it not clear that the former USSR in particular will be required to return to ground zero in order to begin the long trek through the very entrepreneurial capitalism based on 'free markets' that it believed it had either gone through already or circumvented altogether? Since key Western and Asian economic powers appear to be reviving the values and virtues of old fashioned capitalism, doesn't this make a case for precisely these values? The short answer is that neo-conservatism is a far greater problem for Marx's theory of economic development than any set of events in the former Soviet Union and the rest of Eastern Europe, *but only if it is doing what it says it is doing.*[8]

---

[6] See for example, John Kingdom, *No Such Thing as Society* (Buckingham, U.K.: Open University Press, 1992).

[7] H.T. Wilson, 'Non Identity, Causation and Culture: the Essential Marx', to appear as chapter 5 in Wilson, *The Vocation of Reason. Studies in Critical Theory and Social Science in the Age of Max Weber*, edited with a Foreword by Thomas M. Kemple (forthcoming).

[8] Theodor Adorno, 'Society' in *The Legacy of the German Refugee Intellectuals*, edited

After all, the Marxian theory of development argues that something quite different from this apparent return to earlier doctrine and earlier values should occur with extended capitalist development. In the circumstances, one would be justified in viewing the linear conception of development that Marx is supposed to have espoused with considerable suspicion, to say the least. A quick response would argue that Marx's theory of development has been misunderstood and present events seriously misinterpreted. Indeed, the utter poverty of the neo-conservative agenda will eventually be revealed by its failure to deliver on its promises without compromising fundamentally the hard and harsh medicine it says is absolutely necessary if the patient is to be cured.

In addition, the process by which capitals seek continuing social and political legitimation while participating in an increasingly direct co-optation of public capital and the values, capacities and institutions on which it depends is becoming more and more tenuous. Capitalism's legitimacy is, or soon will be, under threat in ways that will no longer allow it to displace the blame from the economy to public administration, to social welfare and social administration, or to labor, as has been the case for the past twenty-five years.[9] The hypocritical practice of attacking the social and economic functions of governments, while using anti-government parties in power to facilitate even more direct forms of the co-optation of public capital to private uses, is thoroughly bankrupt. This suggests that capitals will find themselves increasingly exposed, particularly when publics become aware of what they, through their governments, *actually do for capital!*

There are two specific counterclaims to the new political economy that critics of one or another version of the neo-conservative agenda make which, though different, are not incompatible. One argues that the 'public debt' is not really a problem at all, that some of the most impressive spurts of economic growth occurred (for example) in the midst of a substantial per capita indebtedness in a num-

by Robert Boyers (New York: Schoken Books, 1969), pp. 144–153 and elsewhere. Adorno would argue that it is the very complexity of society as an historically and culturally produced 'form of life' that increases exponentially its capacity for the sort of regression to earlier forms and discourses that is evident in contemporary neo-conservatism.

[9] Gary Teeple, *Globalization and the Decline of Social Reform* (Toronto: Garamond Press, 1995).

ber of Western countries after World War II. This argument stresses how central to overcoming indebtedness economic growth is, and assumes that governments committed to growth must actively assist in generating the infrastructure which will solve the problem. Here there is a largely unstated assumption that indebtedness based on deficit spending is inevitable, and that the solution, far from trying to lower the debt through contraction and household management, is to *grow out of it* by creating new economic activity.[10]

Neo-conservatives have responded by arguing that this solution, so central to a Keynesian assessment of the problem and how to solve it, is no longer available to us. Reasons for this, apart from ideology, include the sheer size of the debt, the number of public and social structures within a country which depend upon deficit financing, and the international and global nature of those to whom the debt is owed. Alongside this is the ideological belief that such growth involves governments in too prominent a role, thereby allegedly subverting the process of 'real' growth itself. Better to deregulate the economy and to privatize, downsize, curtail, cut back or withdraw public and social sector activities, benefits and services. This to the end of maximizing the utilities of 'free trade', and, with it, an increasingly unrestricted dependence on the 'free market' of international debt holders. This provides a thoroughly self-serving rationale for the private sector that is only masked by its apparent concern for frugality on the part of the national household.

It also legitimizes to an even greater extent than was already the case the mobility of capital, something much more difficult to justify where an 'industrial policy' approach to business-government relations prevails within a given country or supranational entity. As a consequence, capitals are simultaneously able to support downsizing, deregulation and related neo-conservative policies addressed to the public and social sector and 'free trade' postures over those required for an industrial policy approach to trade. They do this while using the power position of these very anti-government parties to guarantee both a more direct and continuous co-optation of

[10] Francois Crouzet, *Capital Formation in the Industrial Revolution* (London: Methuen, 1972); Casper van Ewijk, *On the Dynamics of Growth and Debt* (Oxford: Clarendon Press, 1991). See especially Jeffrey Cantor and Donald Stabile, *A History of the Bureau of the Public Debt: 1940–1990, with Historical Highlights from 1789–1939* (Washington: Bureau of the Public Debt, 1990).

public capital for private uses and a spirited defense of the right of capital mobility. The major restriction on such mobility only indicates how willing neo-conservatives are to resort to anti-democratic and anti-social forms of government and politics to achieve their goals. The *Free Trade Agreement*, and its successors the *North American Free Trade Agreement* and the emerging *Free Trade Agreement of the Americas*, are user-friendly devices for containing capital flight. They simultaneously legitimize flight within the Western Hemisphere and defend the application of neo-conservative deregulatory and downsizing measures, while providing a legitimate basis for discriminating against trade with countries beyond their reach.[11] The result has been a consequential narrowing of the public's perceived realm of choice, combined with intergenerational forgetfulness about the feasibility and possible viability of past (and present) solutions.

The second counterclaim to advocates of the new political economy focuses not so much on past solutions and the consequences of ignoring them as upon who or what is responsible for the present situation of indebtedness itself. While all agree that interest on the debt is a major, even dominant, factor, it is on the matter of which expenditures, investments or other activities have created and continue to sustain both the debt and interest payments on it that disagreement ensues. Neo-conservatives, not surprisingly, blame organized labor, social welfare and allied disbursements and the costs of public and social sector programs for the debt. In contrast, those who oppose this agenda focus on incentives, subsidies, contracts and subcontracts, tax exemptions, so called 'tax expenditures', selective protectionism and even privatization itself, alongside government backed loans and investments from banks and the private sector to foreign governments and corporations to make their case.[12]

Present critics of capital, particularly in its neo-conservative variant, claim that these latter examples are merely the tip of the iceberg in accounting for public handouts, loans, gifts and non-financial

[11] John Cuddington, *Capital Flight: Estimates, Issues and Explanations* (Princeton: Department of Economics, Princeton University, 1986); Donald Lessard, *Capital Flight: the Problem and Policy Responses* (Washington: Institute for International Economics, 1987); Benu Varman-Schneider, *Capital Flight: A Critique of Concepts and Measures* (Hamburg: Verlag Weltarchiv Gmbh, 1989).

[12] H. Chorney, J. Hotson and M. Seccareccia, *The Deficit Made Me Do It* (Ottawa: Canadian Centre for Policy Alternatives, 1992); Wilson, *Bureaucratic Representation*, especially introduction and chapters 1, 5.

means of legitimation, support and assistance to the private sector. What is almost always overlooked in discussions of business-government relations in mature capitalist societies is the unavoidably symbiotic relationship between public and private sectors, and the continuing dependence of business, industry, and commercial and financial institutions on governments for both legitimation and real tangible support and acknowledgement.[13] That this operates at numerous levels and takes many forms is something whose consequences will be discussed further on.

For now suffice it to say that strong support from the private sector for a model of government activity based on lobbying and related forms of private initiative is tied directly to its continuing dependence on public capital and public sector legitimation for its success. The neo-conservative agenda, with its preference for more direct methods and processes of co-opting public capital, and the good faith on which this capacity rests, is even more dependent than its Keynesian predecessor on reversing public sector initiatives in favor of private sector lobbying and related activities.[14] This suggests that we are deluding ourselves when we claim to believe that capitals exist independently of sovereign legal and political entities, particularly in the form of the contemporary nation-state.

Wherever this state is discovered to be the institutional, legal, political and organizational basis for the economy, it is necessary to look to its human and non-human resources, its historical values and traditions and its contemporary infrastructure. They are the key to understanding its 'good faith' status and 'carrying capacity' for the deficits, debts and indebtedness generally which international and supranational financial institutions are willing to sustain. To be sure, these financial institutions are themselves directly and indirectly legitimized by the good faith status and carrying capacity of the nation state(s) in which they are located, as well as by those who acquiesce in their dictates. This means that the argument for a global, regional or domestic capitalist system independent of states in both tangible and symbolic ways becomes impossible to take seriously.

[13] Charles Lindblom, *Politics and Markets* (New Haven: Yale University Press, 1977); Herschel Hardin, *Privatization Putsch* (Montreal: Institute for Research on Public Policy, 1989).

[14] Robert Went, *Globalization: Neo-liberal Challenges, Radical Responses* (London: Pluto Press, 2000); Teeple, *op. cit.*

Yet it is a necessary feature of the rhetoric, ideology and folklore of capitalism in all its forms and variants that government activity be understood to be either in the public interest if capital desires it, or an unwarranted 'intervention' if it does not. Analysis of the central role of sovereign states in the nurturing and sustenance of capitalism must focus on the human resources of unorganized publics, as well as on territory and natural resources, in any effort to understand the relationship between the labor theory of value and public capital co-optation.[15] Indeed, it is precisely the way that this co-optation of public capital by private interests updates, complements and vindicates the labor theory of value extraction in an age of capital mobility which will be central to the argument of this study.

The agencies of primary, but particularly secondary, socialization are an essential societal element sustaining the legitimacy of capitalism in advanced industrial societies. In addition, as noted, are various forms of mass media, often openly supportive of the new political economy, but always supportive, even if occasionally critical, of capitalism in general. Admittedly, public understandings of capitalism rarely if ever include the sorts of issues and questions cited here. At the same time it is necessary to point out the mass media's role, alongside more formal and continuous modes of secondary socialization, in defending capitalism even while criticizing one or another capital. More often, however, especially where the neo-conservative agenda holds sway, these agencies are engaged in displacing difficulties or problems in 'the economy' to other sectors, groups and individuals in order to blame or implicate government, politicians, social welfare, or unions.[16]

When this is combined with 'news' from other parts of the world, particularly from the former Soviet Union or the so-called 'Third World', publics are left with very little to go on apart from a comparison between the conditions as reported, and the now apparently minor problems 'at home'. The distance between the stark realities

---

[15] Arnold, *op. cit.*; Michael Storper, *The Capitalist Imperative: Territory, Technology and Industrial Growth* (Oxford: Basil Blackwell, 1989); H.T. Wilson, 'Time, Space and Value', *Time and Society*, Volume 8, No. 1 (March 1999), pp. 161–181.

[16] David Lewis, *Louder Voices: Corporate Welfare Bums* (Toronto: James Lewis and Samuel, 1972); Laurence Kallen, *Corporate Welfare* (New York: Lyle Stuart, 1991); Ernest Lieberman, *Unfit to Manage* (New York: McGraw Hill, 1988); Stanley Aronowitz, *False Promises* (Durham, N.C.: Duke University Press, 1992); and Chris Philippson, *Capitalism and the Construction of Old Age* (London: Macmillan, 1982).

from abroad so often featured in daily and nightly newscasts, and the immediate concerns of members of the general population in capitalist democracies, make the latter rather than the former seem vague, remote and decidedly academic when compared to conditions elsewhere. Ironically, it is the very collapse of the USSR, and the ascendancy of Yeltsin and Putin as defenders of private property, markets, privatization and international capitalist investment, which has made the 'transition' there so devastating. Yet it and Third World troubles presented in a surreal fashion by the nightly media has the effect of persuading publics that their problems are not only miniscule by comparison, but totally unconnected to these troubles.

The September 11, 2001 terrorist attack on the World Trade Center and the Pentagon using American commercial aviation may only temporarily alter this observation, since analysts predict that the Federal government's response will help turn the U.S. economic recession around, or at least contribute to minimizing its impact. Since the rationale for the American government response will be to 'provide for the common defense' and protect private as well as government property, the massive expenditures required can be fully justified under neo-conservatism's doctrine of 'limited government'. The only likely casualty, from their perspective, will be its consequences for the panoply of neo-conservative schemes presently in place in U.S. airports, like the downsizing, contracting out and privatization of security functions, backed up by an economic atmosphere favoring deregulation generally. It is almost inevitable that expert analysis will reveal these schemes in operation to be at least partly to blame for the lax security measures that contributed to the subsequent highjackings and their consequences. On the other hand, some commentators have already addressed this question in such a way as to turn it against government rather than the private sector, stating that commercial providers cannot be blamed when they follow security regulations that are themselves lax or inadequate.

A high percentage of members of these audiences are employed in secretarial, administrative, managerial and professional and semi-professional capacities for private sector business, industrial, commercial and financial organizations. They continue to constitute what is probably the most significant segment of the non-capitalist general public who support one or another version of neo-conservatism. Not only do they depend for their wages, salaries or fees (and often status) on private sector economic activity. Their socialization process, however subtle, is continuous and often intense by comparison with other segments of the population supporting neo-conservatism.[17] They cannot help but develop something of a 'vested interest' in the system as it is generally understood. This is all the more likely to be true in countries and cultures where socialization stresses, even fetishizes, the distinction between public and private sector activity and employment, implying that the second is more valuable and worthwhile than the first.

A major consequence of this fragmentation of the population into types of employment is to submerge the fact that virtually everyone is a person who is participating in the creation of surplus value either through work outside the home or 'shadow work'.[18] In its place is put the idea that external status hierarchies comport with an objective conception of 'merit', *particularly in the private sector.* Even Max Weber, ambiguous about many features of capitalism, allowed his common sense and theoretical understanding of class to be fragmented into 'status groups' in the name of sociology and the disciplined but unreflective observer. This point addresses not only the continuing reality of class but the way that allegedly empirical distinctions cover over similarities and differences that are more essential, and perform an indirect (when not a direct) form of legitimation in the process.[19]

It has been necessary for neo-conservatives and their supporters to use explicit techniques of socialization and status legitimation in order to bring on board so many occupationals engaged in private bureaucratic management in the medium and large corporations. While one might justifiably wonder why such an effort was necessary in the face of capitalism's crying need for and dependence upon

---

[17] See Ronald Glassman, *The New Middle Class and Democracy in Global Perspective* (New York: St. Martin's Press, 1997).

[18] Juliet Schor, *The Overworked American* (New York: Basic Books, 1991); Schor, *The Overspent American* (New York: Basic Books, 1998). Ivan Illich first coined the term 'shadow work' in *Shadow Work* (London: Marion Boyars, 1981) and *Gender* (New York: Pantheon, 1982) to describe the unpaid work of women in the home and elsewhere. Also see H.T. Wilson, *Sex and Gender* (Leiden: Brill, 1989), especially chapters 1–3; and Hannah Arendt's discussion of labor and consumption in *The Human Condition* (Chicago: University of Chicago Press, 1958).

[19] Max Weber, *Economy and Society*, Volume I, Part 1, chapter 4, pp. 302–307; Volume II, chapter 9, 6, pp. 926–940. See Kees van der Pijl, *Transnational Classes and International Relations* (London: Routledge, 1998); and Leslie Sklair, *The Transnational Capitalist Class* (Oxford: Basil Blackwell, 2001).

these individuals, one only needs to look at the most salient characteristics of these 'private bureaucrats' to understand.[20] Weber's discussion of the ideal-typical 'bureaucracy', applicable with equal facility to public and private sector large scale work organizations, makes it apparent that these individuals are in the main non-capitalist supporters of capital. As such, they are very much in need of status legitimation because of their bureaucratic and managerial functions and orientations. Even their increasing participation in the stock market can be seen as a way of legitimizing their work activity while attempting to recover from the consequences of neo-conservatism's preference for contractual work and hostility to pension and related contributions.

Weber's discussion of the properties of a functional formal bureaucracy reduces to three clusters of factors: *authority* (hierarchy, discipline, rules and procedures, seniority), *competence* (specialized knowledge, formal certification, performance assessment); and *occupation* (separation of legal ownership from management; full-time salaried career; no right of appropriation).[21] Of the three, the cluster most significant for my purposes here is occupation, because it reinforces the clear distinction between entrepreneurial and managerial orientations, as against public and private sectors, especially where *de facto* tenure is built into a given position. In addition, technological developments and forms of knowledge and training occuring outside work organizations have created serious stresses and strains for managers, while indicating a heightened dependence on specialized expertise from the outside. In effect Weber's bureaucrat, once putatively a technical specialist, is now usually a generalist by comparison, no matter whether this expertise is contracted in the market or internalized on a more permanent basis in the structure of the organization.

That this has led to status anxiety on the part of many managers cannot gainsay the way in which the private sector has attempted to respond. The indispensability of managers in general was quickly comprehended by boards and chairs, which sought to shore up and further legitimize the hierarchical systems of authority even as they were overlaying them with a line-staff model. While this model would accommodate specialists, it would do so mainly by treating them as

---

[20] Herschel Hardin, *The New Bureaucracy* (Toronto: McClelland and Stewart, 1991).

[21] Weber, *Economy and Society*, Volume I, Part 1, chapter 3, pp. 212–226; and especially Volume II, chapters 10, 11, pp. 941–1005.

second class employees, particularly in private sector employment.[22] This eventually came to include stock options for upper level managers, coupled with support for the managerial role as a synthesizer and integrator of group activity and, consequently, as a function possessed of a different type of specialized expertise from that possessed by technically and professionally trained personnel. The final indicator, perhaps more responsible than we are willing to admit for the decline of *organizational* (as opposed to *organized*) capitalism, was the development of, and subsequent dependence upon, the professional MBA by the private sector.[23]

A final point, which cannot be too highly emphasized, is the process by which women and visible minorities variously neutral or opposed to capitalism are being integrated into the private (as well as the public) sector work world as full time occupationals. While this process occurred much earlier for both groups in the lower reaches where the majority in each case continues to be found, it is now occurring in managerial-bureaucratic, professional and executive functions as well, though rarely as quickly as their members and supporters would like.[24] Both groups are beginning to invest in their own assets by taking advantage of educational and training opportunities formerly not (or less) available to them, often with the assistance of pro-active government programs like affirmative action and pay equity.

The result is the emergence of a group of individuals sufficiently integrated into and dependent upon the capitalist system in private and public sector work organizations to be further socializable as non-capitalist supporters of this system, whether from necessity, conviction or a combination of both. To say this, however, is not to argue that this process is occurring in an amorphous way that leaves class distinctions behind or reduces them to nothing; on the contrary. One of the most significant points to be made about programs

[22] Victor Thompson, *Modern Organization* (New York: Alfred Knopf, 1961); Thompson, *Bureaucracy and Innovation* (University, Alabama: University of Alabama Press, 1968).

[23] H.T. Wilson, 'The Dismal Science of Organization Reconsidered', *Canadian Public Administration*, Volume 14, No. 1 (Spring 1971); Charles Perrow, *Complex Organizations* (New York: McGraw Hill, 1972); Luis Suarez-Villa, *Invention and the Rise of Technocapitalism* (Lanham: Rowman and Littlefield, 2000).

[24] See the bimonthly publication *Women in Management*, published by the School of Business at the University of Western Ontario, London, Ontario, Canada for evidence of this continuing concern.

like pay equity and affirmative action is that their class specific basis is to be found in the very structures of the programs themselves, as well as by a comparison of the jobs to which each program is addressed.

Pay equity rates and compares different jobs performed by men and women on a points basis, and adjusts salaries upward where the female job is found to be at least equal in difficulty, skills required or hardship. The resulting rating and comparing is something that is feasible mainly where the jobs being assessed lack discretion and/or can be broken down into task-specific components. Affirmative action, in contrast, seeks to represent the surrounding community in microcosm by preferring members of under-represented groups if their qualifications are 'substantially equal' to over represented, mainline groups, usually white males. Affirmative action applies in the main to groups above the 'class ceiling' whose qualifications include university and subsequent professional or academic training and whose job preferences are managerial-bureaucratic, professional or executive in nature.[25] Nothing that has been said here suggests that individuals fully incorporated into the occupational system of capitalist societies will become active advocates of capital, much less capitals themselves. Nevertheless, they do perceive themselves to be dependent on its healthy functioning in ways that others, who may in reality be more dependent, often do not. They can therefore be counted on to be passive supporters wherever they are found, particularly if they equate a viable capitalism with neo-conservative values and policies.

Even unionized personnel in capitalist democracies can frequently be counted on to take a position which is at best neutral toward neo-conservatism and/or displaced onto other allegedly causative agents including, not infrequently in recent times, the leaders of the socialist, social democratic and labor parties they once supported. In effect, the gradual inclusion of more and more adults into the working society as full-time occupationals can be expected to increase neutrality toward or support for capitalism by the non-capitalist working majority and deflect hostility and criticism onto other institutions or processes.[26] Whether this will generate an increased tendency to

---

[25] Wilson, *Sex and Gender*, chapters 1 and 2; Wilson, *Bureaucratic Representation*, chapter 6.

[26] Arendt, *op. cit.*; Aronowitz, *op. cit.*; Schor, *The Overspent American*; Teeple, *op. cit.*

defend neo-conservative values and policies on the grounds that they represent the only viable basis for capitalism is another matter altogether. This is especially true because of the movement toward part-time and contractual work already cited, one that these full-time occupationals can readily identify with, albeit negatively, because it is an ever-present threat. This can be expected to have a rather different result, even in the absence of evidence of neo-conservative hypocrisy, double standards and corruption. This is because such an outcome is usually not voluntarily chosen and almost always entails a significant change in standard of living and quality of life.

Here we come face to face with one of the most serious contradictions of late capitalism, one captured nicely in the conflict between a fiscally responsible, frugal national-state 'household' and fiscally irresponsible real households up to their necks, and often over their heads, in consumer debt. The fact that contemporary capitalism in all its forms has no choice but to support and actively seek to work through this contradiction only underscores the important role that various forms of socialization, alongside the mass media, will have to continue to perform on their behalf. Much has to do with what legitimizes capitalist development from the standpoint of what neo-conservatism says its goals are, much with the already largely socialized human being it works with and on in these societies. Before addressing some of the major points and issues raised here, however, it will be necessary to engage in a more sustained discussion of legitimacy and its relationship to capitalism as an institution.

CHAPTER THREE

LEGITIMACY AND CAPITALISM

The first chapter operated with a commonsense conception of 'legitimacy', on the assumption that its general meaning was unambiguous and could be taken for granted. Now, however, we need to go into greater detail about the special sense and concerns that reliance on this concept conveys. Voegelin made the point with great force in a number of his writings that it is always necessary to distinguish between commonsense and specialist senses of a concept, and to be clear about which sense one is employing when writing or speaking.[1] We need to be a great deal more self-conscious about the meaning we intend when we make reference to legitimacy and legitimation as concepts. This is not because there is any inconsistency between the two senses but because one necessarily complements the other and is required for a more thorough exposition of the problems and concerns with which it is associated.[2]

Whereas in the first chapter legitimacy as a concept was bounced off capitalism as the more holistically concrete point of reference, here capitalism will be bounced off legitimacy as the more concrete concept. The purpose is to develop in a more concerted manner the theory of public capital and its relation to both the process and the forms of co-optation and Marx's labor theory of value. This theory, and others from Marx with which it is intertwined, provides an indispensable platform for discussing the theory of public capital and its co-optation. This latter theory both supplements and complements Marx's thinking while implying the possibility of a more specific lineage and immediate derivation from Marx.[3] An analysis of the process by which public capital is accumulated, co-opted and invested is precisely what gives added significance to the labor theory of value at a point in the capitalist development process when capital seems to

[1] Eric Voegelin, *The New Science of Politics* (Chicago: University of Chicago Press, 1952), pp. 27–106.

[2] See Italo Pardo (editor), *Morals of Legitimacy: Between Agency and System* (New York: Berghahn Books, 2000).

[3] H.T. Wilson, *Marx's Critical/Dialectical Procedure* (London: Routledge, 1991).

have supplanted labor as the primary factor of production in every sense. That this claim is groundless requires reference not just to ongoing processes in space and time, but past and contemplated future value extraction, and the continuous utilization by capital of legitimated institutions grounded in a country's people and their labor.

That it is the sovereign national state that explains and renders sensible both the reality of capitalism and its claim to legitimacy will be a major argument of this study.[4] Legitimacy in all cases is clearly referenced to institutions, in the sense that it is institutions which both convey legitimacy while being the object of values, beliefs, practices and relationships seeking legitimation. While institutions often utilize formally organized structures and processes, they are always more than and different from them. There is clearly an aspect of persistence and continuity that is elemental to defining something as an institution, rather than simply a value, belief, practice or relationship *per se*.[5] Institutions are expected, approved or prescribed patterns of behaviour found in (or across) given countries and cultures, and may or may not be directly or immediately legal, juridical or political in nature.

The idea that capitalism itself is an institution is defensible because capitalism is a set of culturally ingrained patterns of behavior that have persisted on a continuous basis in some Western societies for over two hundred years. Even where this has not been the case, values and beliefs conducive to capitalism have been present and have eventually led (or are leading) to the emergence of a capitalist economy and thereafter the likelihood of a capitalist society in other countries. The distinction between economy and society is important inasmuch as it addresses our attention to the important, but segmentally distinct, function of the economy as such in capitalist democracies.[6] Historically, it is from the economy, and the monopoly of technology that its ascendancy makes possible, that capitalism has

[4] Sigrid Quack, Glenn Morgan, Richard Whitley (editors), *National Capitalisms, Global Competition and Economic Performance* (Philadelphia: John Benjamin Publishers, 2001); Gordon Smith and Moises Naim, *Altered States: Globalization, Sovereignty and Governance* (Ottawa: International Development Research Centre, 2000).

[5] Rogers Hollingsworth and Robert Boyer (editors), *Contemporary Capitalism: the Embeddedness of Institutions* (Cambridge: Cambridge University Press, 2001).

[6] For a careful delineation of the distinction, see Weber, *Economy and Society*, Volume I, Part 1, chapter II, pp. 63–211; Part 2, chapters I, II and VII, pp. 311–355, 635–640; and Volume II, chapter VIII, pp. 641–900.

branched out to influence, and often to control, other areas of a country's society and culture. Obviously, the process by which elements of 'Third World' countries and cultures are integrated into multinational and global capitalism are different in specific senses, yet on the priority of the economy and technology to other sectors in this developmental process the generalization would appear to hold.

The legitimacy of capitalism as an institution, alongside those values, beliefs, practices and relationships elemental to it (the market, private property, private profit, contracts, individualism, 'liberty' *etc.*) depends directly and continuously on state, governmental and public and social sector support. Even though we say that its legitimation is completely assumed and taken for granted, capitalism continues to need this support in order to underscore, modify, shift or extend its influence, power or control over other areas, issues or concerns where it wishes its actions to be legitimated.[7] By tying novel activities and undertakings in areas not formerly part of its established repertoire of actions to already existing values, beliefs, practices and relationships, capitalism is able to justify present conduct and concerns on the basis of past legitimations. While it would be irresponsible to imply that this process is a one way street, significant challenges to capital in capitalist democracies, even in the form of sustained criticisms of neo-conservative policies, are difficult to find.

MacIver argued that success for all institutions of a society was to be discovered in the process by which they tie themselves to its overarching 'myth of authority'.[8] It is the monopolistic role of states, governments and their public and social sectors in what Easton called 'the authoritative allocation of values for society' that helps explain why capitals turn, or endeavor to turn, states and governments into 'the executive committee of the dominant class'.[9] A major issue relates to the role of representative democracy and popular sovereignty, as well as public and social institutions of governments, as possible

[7] Jonathan Boswell and James Peters, *Capitalism in Contention* (New York: Cambridge University Press, 1997). Habermas' claim in several studies that capitalism is unique in not depending mainly on legitimation from above, like all past regimes and systems, but only needs to meet objective criteria of 'economic performance' will be addressed critically further on.

[8] Robert MacIver, *The Web of Government* (Glencoe: Free Press, 1947).

[9] David Easton, *The Political System* (New York: Alfred Knopf, 1953), and subsequent studies by Easton based on this definition of the functions of states and governments.

problems for and breaks on this process of co-optation. Another relates to the degree to which we can presume, or need to presume, a harmony of interest on the part of capitals as they seek to steer or manage governments in ways conducive to their perceived interests.

One can make a strong case, for example, for the claim that differences on specific details between capitals regarding both means and concrete objectives should not be used to hide a larger order consensus on the state's role in capitalist democracies. Thus, though differences may lead to interest group jockeying and conflicts, most agree that the system as a whole is preferable to other alternatives. In public policy analysis this agreement is reflected in the increased tendency to treat 'interest group pluralism', even in the United States but certainly elsewhere, as at best ideology and rhetoric. In contrast stands the reality of corporatist, concertationist and even more institutionalized approaches based on constitutions, legislation and permanent state institutions of capital found in, of all places, the bureaucracy itself. Linkages between institutions possessing one or another form of legitimacy, particularly those tying law and politics to the economy (commerce, finance, industry and business), turn out to be indispensable to capitalism as an institution in its own right.[10]

Max Weber's study of legitimate authority concluded that there are three basic types that can be distinguished in the pre-modern, modern and contemporary period, and that this tripartite distinction holds across cultures as well as epochs. Weber hastened to add that these 'ideal types' were never found in pure and unmixed form in actual societies and cultures. Reality would always be a composite of all three with one or another dominant. While the same institution might change over time in its relative admixture of the three types, it was much rarer, and often of world-historical significance, when the dominant form changed drastically from the preponderance of one form to that of another. Weber distinguished traditional, charismatic and what he called 'legal-rational' types of authority and bases of legitimacy as his most salient ideal types, and stressed how

[10] See Wilson, 'The Downside of Downsizing', *op. cit.*; and *Bureaucratic Representation*, chapters 2, 3, 5. Both employ a sectoral approach to the analysis of these political-economic relationships, with capital the first sector and the public and social the second and third, in terms of longevity, persistence and what Lindblom, *op. cit.* calls capital's 'privileged position'.

important the rise of legal-rationality was in understanding modern Western civilization.[11]

At the same time, and more significantly, he insisted that legitimacy could as often (and as justifiably) be seen to inhere in the two non-rational bases as in the one he called legal-rational. It was Weber's ambiguous and ambivalent attitude to the form of reason manifested in legal-rational authority that helps explain and make sense of his conception of legitimacy. Legitimacy for Weber was clearly both social and sociological, in the sense that it was based on the acknowledgement, acceptance, perhaps even acquiescence of many or most elites and a majority or significant plurality of the general population in governance by a given person, group and/or institution.[12] Legitimacy thus carried with it no moral sense apart from a very narrow conception of recognition. It was simply a property of whatever institutions existed in a given country or culture, usually political, legal and juridical institutions but economic and social institutions as well, particularly with the modern emergence of economy and society.

The fact that legitimacy derived from the latin for law and lawful (*lex, legis*) can be explained by the earlier reference of institutional values, beliefs, practices and arrangements to *natural* law (*ius naturale*) rather than to either the law of nations (*ius gentium*) or civil law (*ius civile*). That both traditional and charismatic types emerge as distinct forms of authority apart from legal-rationality in Weber's schema is explained in part by the need to find new bases for asserting legitimacy following the collapse of natural law in the Eighteenth Century.[13] The new approach, based on historical and social research, thus viewed traditional and charismatic forms of legitimacy in the light of the legal-rational form that had become so indispensable in

[11] On the ideal type and concept formation, Weber, *Economy and Society*, Volume I, Part 1, chapters I, III, pp. 3–62, 212–226; Weber, *Methodology of the Social Sciences* (Glencoe: Free Press, 1949), pp. 89–112. On types of authority and their legitimacy, *Economy and Society*, Volume II, chapters X, XI, pp. 941–955, but especially pp. 956–1005.

[12] See *Economy and Society*, Volume I, Part 1, chapter III, pp. 212–215. For Weber determinations of legitimacy do not privilege legal-rational over traditional and charismatic forms, and apply to non political and non governmental agencies as well as state bodies.

[13] Norman Kemp Smith, *The Philosophy of David Hume* (London: Macmillan, 1941); Pauline Westerman, *The Disintegration of Natural Law Theory* (Leiden: Brill, 1998).

legitimizing the secular national state itself over the past two to three hundred years.

Weber's understanding is more complex than a standard legal or social rendering precisely because of the way that he challenges the moral superiority of legal rationalism while extolling its technical indispensability in modern Western societies. This type of authority, is, after all, the basis for the emergence of that secular, functionally rational bureaucracy on which capitalism will increasingly depend as it solidifies and matures, extending itself outward from the economy to society as a whole. It is certainly not a coincidence that these two institutions, along with experimental science, constituted the key to understanding the uniqueness of modern Western civilization for Weber. The fact that for him capitalism and the nation-state were intertwined and interdependent from the very dawn of modern Europe led him to concentrate on the form of rationality, broadly speaking, that they (and science) shared, and how it related to religion and religious transformations in a secular direction.[14]

The resulting institutional complex was successively legitimated as a whole, with one or another institution depending on the other for its justification. Throughout most of modern Western history it has been the national state and its claim to sovereignty, power and legality which has provided the basis for legitimating both capitalism and science. Ironically, it can be argued that it is the rise of representative democracy, first restricted, then extended to virtually all adults, which, alongside sovereign power and legality, has been instrumental in turning this formerly asymmetrical process of legitimation around.[15] In place of a theory like natural law, which was available to legitimize many types of institutional values, beliefs, practices and arrangements, a conception of legitimacy emerges which goes beyond the very limited basis of sovereign power and legality found in early national states. It reasserts, from the other side as it were, the idea that legitimacy can both inhere in and be conveyed by economic, social, cultural *etc.* institutions as well as by political and legal ones.[16]

---

[14] Weber, *Economy and Society*, Volume I, Part 1, chapter II, pp. 164–211; Part 2, chapters I and II; Volume II, chapters VIII and XI.

[15] But see Wilson, *Bureaucratic Representation*, which argues that public and social sector bureaucrats often represent the weak, poor, needy, elderly and otherwise disadvantaged far better than democratically elected representatives.

[16] Weber, *Economy and Society*, Volume I, Part 1, chapter III, pp. 212–216; Volume II, chapter X, pp. 941–948. Compare Jurgen Habermas, *Legitimation Crisis* (Boston:

It is therefore Weber's typology, itself indicative of the same 'rationalistic bias' he found in capitalism, science and the sovereign national state's 'rule of law', which is central to his claim to have produced a value-free sociology. Though the basis of legitimacy had shifted away from those institutions partaking in and sanctioned by the moral content of natural law, the concept of institutions to which the idea of legitimacy was referenced stays essentially the same in Weber's typology. In the process of doing this, it takes account of a different approach to discovering those institutions whose authority is legitimate. For Weber legal-rationality could not possibly be the only (or even necessarily the best) authoritative basis for claiming legitimacy, given the historical emergence of that most central institutional complex of modern Western civilization—capitalism, science and the secular national state.[17] At the same time, Weber did distinguish rational from non-rational forms of authority and bases of legitimacy, as noted, but did so in a way that was at best ambiguous and ambivalent and that at worst challenged the reasonableness of such rationality in fundamental ways.

When people criticize Weber's schema for the absence of any moral or ethical basis for preferring one type of legitimacy to another, they are often ignoring not only his theory of institutions but also his goal of a 'value free' sociology itself. In addition, they fail to acknowledge the impact of his criticism of the narrow norms of Western (formal, instrumental, functional) rationality, even in the face of his inclusion of non-rational forms of legitimation in this typology. It is considerations like these that account for both the resulting schema and disappointment with it by those desirous of a moral or ethical basis for assessing the legitimacy of various types of authority. Weber's point was to try to put himself in the place of the historic individual brought up to value given institutions as legitimate, his/her tendency or disposition to what Hume called the 'habit of obedience'. What made Weber's claim to the absence of a deep rationalistic bias in his preference for typologies persuasive is precisely his preoccupation with understanding from the actor's point of view.[18]

Beacon Press, 1973), to 'Technology and Science as Ideology', in Habermas, *Toward a Rational Society* (London: Heinemann, 1971), pp. 81–122.

[17] Weber, *Economy and Society*, Volume II, chapter XI, pp. 963–965, 969–975, 980–985, 987–994, 998–1005.

[18] *Ibid.*, Volume I, Part 1, chapter IA 1–10, pp. 3–19.

In the event, ideal type conceptions of forms of authority and bases of legitimacy would have to be unreal not only because they were formally 'pure' and functioned as a vehicle for *comparing* the social, economic, political, legal or cultural reality to which they were addressed. The role of such concepts in the hands of the disciplined observer indicated the price paid theoretically for such formal approaches to knowledge and knowing precisely because it was only a more disciplined version of everyday life human practices. At the same time, it served to underscore what else must be done to compensate for one's inability to experience directly the events or phenomena in question. *Verstehen* for Weber means empathic understanding of the actor's experience, achieved less by focusing on the actor's biography and psychological states as on the situation and context of meaning in which he/she participated, no matter how different the values, beliefs, practices and relationships discovered differed from his own.[19] Weber's method has a direct bearing on his understanding of legitimacy, and constitutes a major point of departure and conceptual basis for the analysis of the legitimacy of capitalism that follows.

This becomes particularly evident when we compare Weber's approach to conceptualizing and understanding the phenomenon of legitimacy with that of Jurgen Habermas. In many respects Habermas has taken Weber's work on the subject as his own point of departure for the analysis of legitimacy and its relation to the key institutions of modernity.[20] Habermas has been concerned to study the ways that capitalism and capitals have sought to legitimize their activity, values and institutions, both on their own and relative to the rest of the institutional complex that Weber believed was so central to any adequate understanding of modern Western civilization. Not surprisingly, this effort at legitimation has sought to affirm the very formal, instrumental and functional types of rationality also found in the rule of law and modern experimental science by extolling the objective and impersonal nature of the process of assessment. That the basis of such legitimation is in a fundamental sense 'legal-rational'

[19] *Ibid.*, chapter IA, 5–9, pp. 8–14.

[20] Jurgen Habermas, *The Theory of Communicative Action* (Boston: Beacon Press, 1984–1989), especially Volume I, *Reason and the Rationalization of Society* and Volume II, *Lifeworld and System: A Critique of Functionalist Reason*; and Habermas, *The Philosophical Discourse of Modernity* (Cambridge, Mass: MIT Press, 1987).

as Weber understood it is clear from the position of the disciplined observer that such a rationalistic bias both expresses and defends.

The form that the legal-rational conception of authority has taken in assessing the legitimacy of capitalism is objective in the sense that it points to the 'performance' of the economy under capitalist management as an impersonal indicator and ultimate point of reference.[21] This is part and parcel of the very meritocratic concept of 'rational domination' that Weber disputed while being caught up in it as a central prop of the ideology of modernity in all of the latter's many institutional guises. Rational domination expresses the central assumption of meritocracy and technocracy itself. It assumes that the institutional matrix found in capitalism, the national state and experimental science and expressed in the market, the rule of law, methodical discipline and a specifically technical bias is itself impersonal and objective, and therefore superior to all earlier institutional systems.[22]

Weber's point, addressed by Habermas, is that the criteria for assessing this vaunted superiority, far from being objective and impersonal, are produced, sustained and even legitimized by the very institutions and activities for which they are supposed to constitute objective and impersonal indicators. The incomprehensibility of rational domination for Weber is nowhere more clearly justified and made sense of than in his scepticism toward such institutionally generated acts of self-satisfaction and *hubris*. First generation critical theorists (Adorno, Horkheimer, Marcuse) and, more recently Habermas, have criticized both Marx and Weber for failing to anticipate and take account of the way that 'science' has supplanted political economy as the central ideology, legitimating both capitalism and the secular national state. However, the fact remains that it is alleged to be the actual performance of the capitalist system as a whole, based on an impersonal and unbiased method of assessment, which continues to legitimize this system. This is not to say that therefore legitimation from below is the only vehicle that the system and its supporters *actually employ* to successfully legitimize its preferences, values and outcomes.[23]

[21] See Habermas, 'Technology and Science as Ideology', *op. cit.*, pp. 96–100.

[22] On the idealized relationship between merit and the market see Weber, *Economy and Society*, Volume II, chapter 11, pp. 963–990; Volume I, Part 2, chapter VII, pp. 635–40; and Wilson, *Bureaucratic Representation*, chapter 6, pp. 128–134.

[23] Habermas, 'Technology and Science as Ideology', *op. cit.*, pp. 96–99 and *supra*. H.T. Wilson, 'Science, Critique and Criticism: the "Open Society" Revisited', in

Since 1989, if not before, this process has focused on how the failure of the so-called 'socialist' economies of the USSR and other Eastern European countries proves the objective superiority of the institutions of Western capitalist democracies, particularly capitalism itself. Many have argued against this, asserting that it is the system's putative commitment to individual rights and liberties far more than capitalism that accounts for this failure and resulting collapse. Ironically, it may be the very refusal of capitalist democracies to enforce rigid adherence to meritocratic values in favor of the irrationality of the market, for example, alongside political and legal values, that best accounts for their success and persistence. Thus, far from it making sense for defenders of capitalism to attempt to displace 'system problems' from the economy onto other institutions, it is perhaps these institutions, alongside the irrationalities of the market, that deserve the credit, such as it is. Having said this, we must acknowledge that these processes of displacement have themselves become even more institutionalized in our discourses than has been the case since the 1950's as a consequence of the ascendancy of neo-conservatism after 1975. This is especially evident in attacks on bureaucracy, regulation and the public and social sectors as a whole, but occasionally even in criticisms of the processes and structures of representative democracy itself.[24]

In effect, analysis of the actual operation of capitalist systems has been ignored by appealing to a superficial reading of Marx sponsored by those so fundamentally opposed to him. Since there has been no institutional crisis so serious as to portend economic or social collapse on the order of that which took place in the USSR, the idea that the bases of legitimacy on which capitalism rests may be under challenge or threat appears little less than nonsensical. Others, however, would argue that present transformations of capitalism away from shared responsibility for the society toward a more traditional focus on 'the economy' and 'the market', and on privatization and

---

On Critical Theory (editor) John O'Neill (New York: Seabury Press, 1976), pp. 205–230 at pp. 219–224.

[24] Wilson, *Bureaucratic Representation*, chapter 1. See also Stephen Craig (editor), *Broken contract?: Changing relationships between Americans and their Government* (Boulder, Colorado: Westview Press, 1996); Nicholas Kittrie, *The War against Authority: from the Crisis of Legitimacy to a New Contract* (Baltimore: Johns Hopkins University Press, 1995); and John Dryzek, *Democracy in Capitalist Times* (New York: Oxford University Press, 1996).

deregulation, are leading to precisely such challenges and threats to its legitimacy.[25] The present illusory thinking that has resulted from this consequential tendency to see a causal relationship between capitalism as a system and the decline of the USSR has only served to reinforce the self-congratulatory rhetoric and hyperbole of supporters of the neo-conservative agenda. As noted, it has also led them to view the USSR as proof of the failure of Marx's analysis rather than a *pre-capitalist* society whose post-1989 path will doubtless vindicate more than it will disprove Marx's theory of capitalist development.[26]

Habermas addressed the issue of the legitimacy of capitalism from a perspective which argued, in the period between 1968 and 1973, that the old capital-labor basis for asserting class struggle had been rendered obsolete by the apparent institutionalization of 'scientific-technical progress'. Such progress, aided and abetted by 'technocratic consciousness' and agencies of secondary socialization and mass media, had largely overcome the split between the truncated rationality of work and labor settings and the heretofore independent processes of talk, discussion and criticism formerly outside and beyond these settings. It is as a consequence of this alleged development that Habermas argues that both ideology and repression have been overcome in favor of socialization and persuasion. Forms of communicative behaviour either independent or critical of the kind of talk, thinking, decisions and actions sanctioned by the systems of 'rational-purposive action' found in work and labor settings have, he argues, been successfully repressed and/or reconstituted without the need for either ideology or repression.[27]

---

[25] Pippa Norris (editor) *Critical Citizens: Global Support for Democratic Government* (New York: Oxford University Press, 1999); Jorge Valadez, *Deliberative Democracy, Political Legitimacy and Self Determination in Multicultural Societies* (Boulder, Colorado: Westview Press, 2001); Daniel Hellinger and Dennis Judd, *The Democratic Façade* (Belmont, California: Wadsworth Publishing Co., 1994). Note that it is precisely the present neo-conservative ascendancy in capitalist democracies that has made *the legal and political legitimacy* of these governments, as well as the legitimacy of the capitalist system, such a central issue today.

[26] Clark Everling, *Social Economy, the Logic of Capitalist Development* (London: Routledge, 1997); David Marquand, *The New Reckoning: Capitalism, States and Citizens* (Malden, Mass.: Polity Press, 1997).

[27] Habermas, 'Technology and Science as Ideology', *op. cit.*; Habermas, *Legitimation Crisis*. Whereas in the first study, Habermas employs a substructure-superstructure metaphor, in the second he moves away from political economy toward phenomenology by speaking of the 'life world' and the 'systems world'.

However correct or incorrect this characterization of 'advanced industrial societies' may have been between 1968 and 1973, the emergent reality over the past thirty years of a retrenching capitalism has sought to extend and intensify its privileged access to the state. This has been carried out in order to realize a more direct and immediate co-optation of public capital and the value, resources and institutions on which it is based by undercutting its shared responsibilities for other areas of the institutional matrix first fully articulated and understood by Weber. This process of retrenchment, and the withdrawal from shared responsibilities that goes with it, includes attacks on small business and entrepreneurs, as well as on the social safety net, regulation, the public sector and even representative democratic processes. It suggests that a form of national and trans-national concentration of capital is occurring alongside an increasing polarization of the middle class into an updated, global version of Marx's capital-labor distinction.[28]

What is becoming increasingly apparent, apart from the actual effects of the neo-conservative agenda on capitalist democracies over the past thirty years, is that its 'stern medicine' is often prescribed by governments whose members are more than willing to embrace a double standard. The point, however, remains that whether these individuals, groups and parties do or do not believe what they are prescribing is largely moot, if only because there is no deficit and debt-free market economy run by independent, private capitals at the end of the 'cure'.[29] If all else fails, their continued devastation of the public and social sectors in pursuit of a more direct process of co-opting public capital can be justified by pointing to the WTO and the IMF, to central banks in national states and to the bond markets in major world cities.

This so called 'global restructuring' is an opportunity to take advantage of the superior mobility of capital in order to rearrange production processes and investment possibilities and to benefit from low labor costs and beneficial guarantees from national state gov-

[28] Sklair, *op. cit.*; Pijl, *op. cit.*; Stephen Haseler, *The Super Rich: the Unjust New World of Global Capitalism* (New York: St. Martin's Press, 2000); Hans Peter Martin and Harald Schumann, *The Global Trap: Globalization and the Assault on Prosperity and Democracy* (Montreal: Black Rose Books, 1998); and William Kreml, *America's Middle Class: from Subsidy to Abandonment* (Durham, N.C.: Carolina Academic Press, 1997).

[29] Ewijk, *op. cit.*; Chorney, Hotson and Seccareccia, *op. cit.*

ernments.[30] That this in no way contradicts, but rather complements, the process of an increasingly direct co-optation of public capital is clear from the fact that under globalization the pressure on governments from their respective capital sectors has *increased* dramatically. This suggests that 'free trade', far from being anathema to an industrial policy where the state and capitals are directly and continuously concerted, is the most successful form of industrial policy of them all. This is because its conception of free trade is always external, never internal, to the state in question.

Shifting the terrain to the international arena allows capitalism to legitimize itself anew, on the assumption that capitals are simply responding to inevitable events or preordained realities in an effort to maximize their utilities. They are doing this while attempting to overcome the lassitude, malevolence or incompetence of governments and some international organizations that insist on standing in their way. This rendition contrasts strikingly with capital's actual reliance upon national treasuries, currencies, metals and the 'full faith and credit' promise of their present and future human and non-human resources in order to finance directly or back up private investments. In the process, they are able to distribute and further socialize risk and uncertainty, thereby producing a 'we win, you lose' scenario in international trade and commerce that is only reinforced by appeals to the debt and globalization as *cause celebres*.[31] This only compounds and extends and intensifies further processes of co-optation within states, however different the particular form and combination they take. During the last thirty years we have seen the collusion of anti-government parties in power under a neo-conservative agenda that reasserts what is nothing less than an ideological function for the state apparatus, one thoroughly at variance with the model of 'rational purposive action'. Its threat to supplant altogether the tie between fiscal policy, technical progress and social welfare so central to the Keynesian consensus can no longer be ignored because it is now a

[30] Ernest Lieberman, *Unfit to Manage: How Mismanagement Endangers America and What Working People Can Do About It* (New York: McGraw Hill, 1988); Aronowitz, *op. cit.*

[31] Linda McQuaig, *Shooting the Hippo: Death by Deficit* (Toronto: Viking, 1995); McQuaig, *The Cult of Impotence: Selling the Myth of Powerlessness in the Global Economy* (Toronto: Viking, 1998) on the 'public debt' and 'globalization' as mantras.

dominant discourse, working below the level of institutions like representative democracy and the promise of formal elections.[32]

Habermas argued that the emergence of a market economy based on private property, fair exchange and the right of capital accumulation allows pre-modern forms of legitimation 'called down from the lofty heights of cultural tradition' to be supplanted by legitimations 'summoned up from the base of social labor'. Legitimation of the institutional framework is thus dependent on the base of social labor, which means that even though the agencies that provide it are independent of all non-economic concerns, they in turn must rely on the performance of the economy to a greater extent than ever before.[33] Apart from the fact that the dependencies cited refer only to state agents, and not to capitals, the effect is to modify the state's role so that it becomes a mouthpiece extolling the virtues of the system while displacing blame to other sectors. The difficulty for state agents is always that system failure becomes their problem, and consequently is judged to be their failure.[34] The triumph of neo-conservatism as the dominant discourse not only puts in jeopardy the public's capacity to decide 'rationally' on the contours of the system of 'rational purposive action'. It allows the illusion of 'self-sustaining economic growth', albeit with more than the odd bump in the road, to justify continued devastation of the public and social sectors.

While modifications of the productive forces always lead to 'structural modifications of the institutional framework', Habermas claims that these forces have never before been able to produce their own performance-based legitimacy in a way that is not only independent of traditional and charismatic modes, but threatens these modes directly. The result is that the state's own justification for its actions can now *only* be legitimated from below rather than above, thereby

---

[32] Allan Engler, *Apostles of Greed: Capitalism and the Myth of the Individual in the Market* (London: Pluto Press, 1995); and James Gee, Glynda Hull and Colin Lankshear, *The New Work Order: Behind the Language of the New Capitalism* (Boulder, Colorado: Westview Press, 1996).

[33] Habermas, 'Technology and Science as Ideology', *op. cit.* pp. 96–98.

[34] In the process of displacing blame, neo-conservative governments and the state and international bodies that support their policies also displace risk. See Ulrich Beck, *Risk Society: Towards a New Modernity* (London: Sage Publications, 1992); Beck, *What is Globalization?* (Malden, Mass.: Polity Press, 2000); Beck, *The Brave New World of Work* (Malden, Mass.: Polity Press, 2000); and Barbara Adam, Ulrich Beck and Joost van Loon, *The Risk Society and Beyond: Critical Issues for Social Theory* (London: Sage Publications, 2000).

reversing the pre-capitalist pattern which favored the subordination of productive forces to those of 'the cultural tradition'.[35] One response is that even legitimation from below has to be carried out, at least in part, from 'above'. Legitimation *means* system justification by agencies external to the institutions being legitimized, wherever we find them.

Even when the general population, or significant elements therein, are neutral or supportive towards a given institutional system combining capitalism, science and the secular national state, parallel and super-structural agencies continue to be instrumental to the need for both continuous and contingent legitimations. Reducing the field of contingent responsibility by focussing the public's mind on a particular government or individual limits the blame, and makes it possible for it to have a perceived effect without jeopardizing the system as a whole. A problem only occurs when these mechanisms fail to provide even this piecemeal effect because now things are believed to be beyond the public control of citizens and amenable only to the individual choices of consumers and spectators. Neo-conservatism, far from encouraging citizens to believe in their political function through the mechanism of formal elections, has significantly narrowed the 'realistic' options allegedly available to them.

System legitimation, and the legitimation of capitalism in particular, requires that this be provided *independent of* the system's productivity and growth in subtle ways that nevertheless seem factual and objective. In addition, the very activity of taking the system and its benefits so much for granted produces not simply stable expectations, but *heightened* ones. These expectations support a permanent expansion of the system of rational-purposive action, in the form of the substitution of capital for labor, precisely because citizens know that this expansion cannot be total, and are correct to believe this. Even the worst failures of this system do not serve to indict it, but merely require state agents to backtrack and retrench, in order to 'negatively' legitimize by displacing blame for the system's 'temporary' setbacks onto other sectors of society and the institutional framework.[36] Present developments since the late 1970's are justified as

[35] Habermas, 'Technology and Science as Ideology', *op. cit.* p. 97.

[36] See Adorno, 'Society', *op. cit.* It is in these circumstances that the very complexity of Society as a false totality provides it with an exponential capacity for regression to earlier, more primitive forms and justifications, thereby reconstituting

necessary restructuring in response to the emergence of the high technology and service sectors, as well as globalization itself. Both unanticipated events and the need to displace blame in response to them have thus seriously compromised the claim that the system legitimizes itself by its performance, its ability to 'deliver the goods'. But neo-conservatism has never made such a claim; indeed, its raison d'etre is to provide ideological aid and comfort to state agents in the ways suggested *regardless of system outcomes.*

Meantime, neo-conservative state agents have begun to detach themselves from those parts of the institutional framework that are not amenable to contracting out and privatization, while extending and intensifying those functions of the nation-state which support an accelerated co-optation of public capital. It is no accident that in what are alleged to be 'lean and mean' times requiring the downsizing and cutting back of the public and social sectors, only the capital sector in these societies continues to grow.[37] Public and social functions that cannot be privatized, contracted out or cut loose to float in a market setting for whose problems they were intended to be a solution are subjected to more and more restrictions on eligibility, access and duration.

This portends a significant change in the perceived *space* of capital, as it assures itself that the system is sufficiently stable to deal with, displace onto other institutions or deflect onto the Third World any economic consequences that might have issued from such activity in the past. At the same time, it directs the process of the extended and intensified co-optation of public capital more and more into the international arena where comparative advantage for the higher value-added industries and businesses, alongside essential financial and banking services, is still to be found.[38] Far from having to accept the scope and limits of trade, commerce and production either within or between nation-states, capitals so disposed turn the demands, exigencies and risks inherent in international and cross-cultural trade back on the nation-state itself. They do this by objectifying globalization as an irresistible process that requires us to seriously rethink

---

the old institutional framework of legitimation in new guise. The most recent result of the operation of this process is neo-conservatism.

[37] Wilson, *Bureaucratic Representation*, chapters 2 and 5.

[38] Eric Sheppard, *The Capitalist Space Economy* (London: Unwin, Hyman, 1990); Wilson, 'Time, Space and Value', *op. cit.*

not only the role of private sector regulation and public and social institutions in capitalist democracies, but even representative democracy itself.

Though no one could call these changes a return to 'old style politics', as both Offe and Habermas have pointed out, they clearly do sunder the Keynesian bond between fiscal policy, technical progress and social welfare. This suggests that the neo-conservative agenda does replace the technocratization of politics and the consequent reduction of politics to administration with a more, rather than less, ideological politics.[39] Instead of the depoliticization of politics and its displacement by a plebiscitary system mainly concerned with technical means and system rationality, the period since 1975 has been characterized by heightened recourse to an ideology standing in opposition to those parts of the institutional system we would call rational. The latent class antagonisms noted by Habermas in 1973 have been activated and made manifest in many capitalist democracies that expected never to see them, or ever to see them again. This is not because the system is no longer delivering the goods, but rather because it is reaching the limits of the very consumer confidence that constitutes one side of the central bargain between capitalism and the apolitical citizen as consumer and spectator.

When citizens no longer see a direct connection between technical progress and their own welfare, as well as that of their society, some form of indirect repression supplemented by displacement to other institutions, other countries and other ideologies is required. Capitals, backed up by neo-conservative rhetoric and ideology, have come to believe that these processes are required and justified in order to co-opt public capital more directly, even at the risk of resuscitating class antagonisms while enforcing social and economic discipline. It is in the light of this that one has to ask whether they themselves believe they are under the sway of the very objective and impersonal forces which they took Marx so much to task for addressing. Retreat from responsibility for the rest of the institutional system, including most prominently public, social and regulatory functions, indicates *both* increased self confidence in the resilience of capitalism as a national and trans-national system *and* an emerging dilemma

[39] Engler, *op. cit.*; Gee, Hull and Lankshear, *op. cit.*; Kreml, *op. cit.*; Martin and Schumann, *op. cit.*

from the standpoint of its legitimacy under the guidance of neo-conservatism. The question now is whether capital would *even be capable* of returning to the Keynesian consensus if it was required to do so, or whether forces within it favoring greater capital mobility will collide with its need to co-opt public capital more efficiently in response to these very forces.

CHAPTER FOUR

SOVEREIGNTY AND LEGITIMACY

The discussion thus far has sought to challenge directly some of the most salient assumptions accepted and taken for granted about capitalism's legitimacy by denizens of advanced industrial societies. At the same time my focus on *institutions*, as distinct from organizations, groups and other relationships and arrangements, has drawn attention to the central role of the modern national state in every aspect, phase and function of the emergence and development of capitalism and capitals. This was done in order to suggest how thoroughly inadequate many or most renditions of this established relationship are. Addressing this relationship as the essence of the most central institutional matrix of modern Western civilization is a way of updating Weber's analysis and assessment. Indeed, this matrix in all its permutations and combinations, including its present neo-conservative form, can itself be treated as an institution in its own right.[1]

The question of sovereignty, what precisely it is and where it is alleged to be vested, is fundamental to the issue of the legitimacy of capitalism and its tie to the modern secular national state. That this is the case whether or not sovereignty is a real or a 'fictive' concept is evident from the fact that people act upon and make both everyday and long-term assumptions on the basis of it. To say this is not to reduce the issue and its resolution, ongoing or settled, to mere ideology, but rather to point once again to the relationship between specialist and commonsense concepts, while acknowledging that central concepts like sovereignty can have, and invariably will have, both usages and functions.[2] Sovereignty, it turns out, has replaced legitimacy as a strictly legal and juridical basis of defence and justification applied to the nation-state in international law and diplomacy.

[1] Adorno, 'Society', *op. cit.*; Wilson, *The American Ideology*.

[2] Voegelin, *op. cit.* See also Daniel Philpott, *Revolutions in Sovereignty: How Ideas Shaped Modern International Relations* (Princeton: Princeton University Press, 2001); Bernard Gilson, *The Conceptual System of Sovereign Equality* (Leuven: Peeters, 1984); Robert Klein, *Sovereign Equality among States: the History of an Idea* (Toronto: University of Toronto Press, 1974).

In contrast, legitimacy has been popularized as a commonsense concept addressed to almost any person, group, relationship or arrangement in virtually all institutional settings in advanced industrial societies.[3]

Blackstone put the matter simply and succinctly in his *Commentaries on the Laws of England* when he stated that: 'There is and must be in every state a supreme, irresistible, absolute and uncontrolled authority, in which the right of sovereignty resides.' Though the term is of modern derivation, it has been applied retrospectively to ancient and medieval authorities in order to assert continuity and thereby underscore legitimacy. In some cases the concept of sovereignty has itself been viewed as a more appropriate way of addressing and assessing legitimacy. 'Sovereignty' draws attention to formal aspects of legitimacy while reducing to one or a few the number and type of institutions in the position to claim principal (sovereign) legitimacy.[4] The result has been the creation of a system of legitimations proceeding outward and downward from those institutions that are considered to be sovereign, or principally legitimate.

On the other hand, there are institutions in all capitalist democracies whose legitimacy rests upon and is accounted for by reference to factors independent from, and often in conflict with, that of the sovereign institution or power. Stability within nation states, and occasionally between them, depends very much on how powerful such independent institutions are, particularly if they are able to aggregate and concentrate their forces and influence against the sovereign. Often this will take the form of an effort to either take (or retake) control of the sovereign institution(s), or displace them by harking back to or reinstating older forms.[5] This latter action is particularly evident in modernizing countries and cultures. On the other hand, a relationship more akin to 'peaceful coexistence' normally prevails in established capitalist democratic societies where earlier institutional forms, still considered residually legitimate, complement or actively assist those institutions which are tied directly to the sov-

---

[3] Hendrik Spruyt, *The Sovereign State and its Competitors* (Princeton: Princeton University Press, 1994).

[4] William Blackstone, *The Sovereignty of the Law: Selections from Commentaries on the Laws of England* (Toronto: University of Toronto Press, 1973).

[5] See Weber's discussion of the ties between economic development and older forms in *Economy and Society*, Volume II, chapters 3, 10–14, pp. 1094–1110.

ereign power and are thoroughly interdependent with it. It is these institutions which form the remainder of the central institutional matrix of advanced capitalist societies, the point of central value reference for modern Western civilization in these countries.[6]

We need to view capitalism not as an institution whose legitimacy is apparently unassailable in these societies, but one whose values, practices, relationships and arrangements are sufficiently intertwined with those of other central institutions, including the state, that it is part of the central institutional matrix of these societies. In effect, capitalism itself may not be sovereign, but it partakes in a direct and continuing way with the state, the government and the capital, public and social sectors in ways which guarantee it legitimacy and continuous aid and support.[7] Similarly, individual capitals, or cabals of capitals, may attack the central institutional matrix in which capitalism consistently finds itself, but this is usually only temporary 'sour grapes'. Nevertheless, a significant realignment of state-capital relations in pursuit of a more direct co-optation of public capital than was possible under the Keynesian consensus is occurring, one that goes beyond the concerns of individual capitals periodically distressed with the system.[8]

Jockeying for sovereign power, especially in democratic societies, is not only problematic for all contenders but the official state authority. It is wasteful and senseless inasmuch as the ideal arrangement for capitals in particular has always been to take the credit or lay the blame for collective outcomes in which joint actions either succeed or fail. Attempts to challenge this pattern, as, for example, in claims over the past thirty or more years that the multi-national corporation had successfully supplanted the sovereignty of the national state were quickly dropped. This was less because capitalism would now, for the first time, be held directly responsible for its decisions and actions than because of the emergence of supra-national aggregations of states (EU, NAFTA/FTAA) attempting to reassert their own sovereignty (and that of their members) over economic activity. Nothing captures the sense of these latter responses to the multinational

[6] Peter Cameron, *Property Rights and Sovereign Rights* (London: Academic Press, 1983); Terry Pickett, *Inventing Nations: Justifications for Authority in the Modern World* (Westport, Conn.: Greenwood Press, 1996); Hollingsworth and Boyer, *op. cit.*

[7] Wilson, *Bureaucratic Representation*, chapters 2, 5.

[8] Marquand, *op. cit.*; Boswell and Peters, *op. cit.*; Dryzek, *op. cit.*

corporation and globalization better than the observation that they are defensive retrenchments against, rather than guarantors of, international free trade. This is especially true for the EU, with its greater emphasis on political, social, labor and human rights and its greater willingness to formally acknowledge international covenants setting out and defending these rights.[9]

Weber's analysis of the modern nation state at a high point in its earlier development, though dated in some respects, captures the essence of the argument offered here.

> Since the concept of the state has only in modern times reached its full development, it is best to define it in terms appropriate to the modern type of state, but at the same time, in terms which abstract from the values of the present day, since these are particularly subject to change. The primary formal characteristics of the modern state are as follows: It possesses an administrative and legal order subject to change by legislation, to which the organized activities of the administrative staff, which are also controlled by regulations, are oriented. This system of order claims binding authority, not only over the members of the state, the citizens, most of whom have obtained membership by birth, but also to a very large extent over all action taking place in the area of its jurisdiction. It is thus a compulsory association with a territorial basis. Furthermore, today, the use of force is regarded as legitimate only so far as it is either permitted by the state or prescribed by it . . . The claim of the modern state to monopolize the use of force is as essential to it as its character of compulsory jurisdiction and of continuous operation.[10]

While one would be warranted in noting exit and mobility between states, the component of a state's population comprised of immigrants and refugees, and recent challenges to total internal jurisdiction, virtually everything that Weber says is directly germane to the issue of what makes a state a sovereign entity in international law. Legal jurisdiction over territorial space, duties and responsibilities as well as rights concurrent with citizenship, a monopoly in the *legitimate* use of force in 'internal' matters and the power to establish and determine forms of economic, political and legal-juridical arrangements are the

---

[9] See Thomas Banchoff and Mitchell Smith (editors), *Legitimacy and the European Union: the Contested Polity* (London: Routledge, 1999); Percy Lehning and Albert Weale (editors), *Citizenship, Democracy and Justice in the New Europe* (New York: Routledge, 1997); and H.T. Wilson, 'The Challenge of Participatory Democracy in an Emerging Supranational Europe', *The European Legacy*, Volume 3, No. 4 (1998), pp. 86–95.

[10] Weber, *Economy and Society*, Volume I, Part 1, chapters 1, 17 (3), p. 56.

definitive properties of the state as we know it.[11] What is of more than passing interest, however, is the fact that the state, or 'municipality', is thereby legitimated as a sovereign entity by and through a body of law which has *no binding force*, in the sense that a state functioning within its acknowledged territorial jurisdiction has.

This means that sovereign legitimation is only euphemistically carried out by a higher and more inclusive authority. One cannot even say that it occurs *de jure*, in contrast to the reality of *de facto* legitimation by other states functioning through either comity or necessity as an international 'peer group' of colleagues and friends.[12] When one adds to Weber's formulation those properties that would make it representatively democratic, committed to civil and human rights and liberties and often comprised of two or more 'official' ethnic, cultural or linguistic groups, one has the skeletology of a working definition of the contemporary capitalist state. The early modern understanding of the state as a *nation-state* comprised of one ethnic, cultural and linguistic group has been challenged over the past century by the emergence and persistence of states either cobbled together from past empires or the result of arbitrary territorial divisions by former colonial powers.[13] Add to this globalization and internationalization in the economic, commercial, trade and financial arenas and one has a minimally adequate conception of the tensions, stresses and strains placed upon claims to sovereign legitimacy in the contemporary world.

Before turning to an analysis of types of sovereign legitimacy, based on a discussion of forms of government, it will be necessary to point out in an initial way the *economic* functions that sovereign states perform for private parties within and across their respective domains of legitimate jurisdiction. Weber itemized these activities in a way which allows us to see what the bare minimum is that the state must do for capital in what was, when he wrote, the only form of state—the capitalist state. Apart from the delegation to capitals of the right

[11] *Ibid.*, Volume I, Part 1, chapters 2, 32, pp. 166–174.

[12] Sarah Owen Vandersluis (editor), *The State and Identity Construction in International Relations* (New York: St. Martin's Press, 2000); Scott Pegg, *International Society and the De Facto State* (Aldershot, U.K.: Ashgate Press, 1998).

[13] See Valadez, *op. cit.*; and D. Archibugi, D. Held and M. Kohler, *Re-imagining Political Community: Studies in Cosmopolitan Democracy* (Stanford: Stanford University Press, 1998).

to run central aspects of its economy, and the consequences that follow from this series of past and present ongoing decisions, there are those activities that are directly relevant to taxation and the accumulation, investment and co-optation of public capital. Speaking of the modern capitalist state, Weber noted:

> It is . . . here that we find public credit in the form of issues of government securities, the legal form of the business corporation, the issue of securities, and financing carried on as the business of rational [sic] enterprises, trade in commodities and securities or organized exchanges, money and capital markets, monopolistic associations as a type of economically rational organization of the production of goods by profit making enterprises as opposed to the mere trade in them.[14]

Weber drew specific attention in his initial catalogue of functions that the state performs for capital to the state's 'mode of regulation of the monetary system' and 'commercialization of bills of exchange and securities'. He did this because he was aware that a purely capitalist system, the parameters of which he had set down earlier in the text, was impossible and utopian. In reality, capitalism depended directly and continuously on the state as a sovereign entity capable of enforcing its laws throughout its legitimate jurisdiction with force, or, more often, the threat of force.[15] That this would have to include those features of the state which underscored its interdependence with and loyalty to capitalism and capitals goes without saying, particularly when one realizes how comprehensive these functions and activities carried out on behalf of capital were and are. What is involved is a radical transformation in collective life, even in the earliest periods of capitalist economic development, but particularly once the system is established and its ties into the rest of collective life, beginning with governments and the public sector, are increased, extended and intensified.[16]

Sovereignty, or principal legitimacy, is absolutely essential to the prosecution of all phases of this process of development. Indeed, there is no process of capitalist development *anywhere*, past, present or to come which does not directly and continuously involve the state, governments and the public sector. It is, after all, hardly a

---

[14] Weber, *Economy and Society*, Volume I, Part 1, chapter 31, 6, pp. 165–166.

[15] *Ibid.*; Lindblom, *op. cit.*, chapters 5, 6, 11–13, 22, 25.

[16] Wallerstein, *The Capitalist World System*, Volumes I and II; Wilson, *The American Ideology*.

coincidence that the movement of commercial capitalism backward and thereafter outward into an international manufacturing mode awaited the full emergence of the state as a legal and administrative entity. Further movement into society, the unique form of collective life which capitalism has almost single-handedly fashioned, continues and intensifies this dependence, to the point where the more appropriate term for describing the resulting relationship is interdependence.[17] This should not be taken to mean that there is real reciprocity between the state and its capitals, for the reality is that sovereign power and protection, regardless of who promotes and supports it, continues to be the *sine qua non* without which capitalism is destitute, puerile, impotent.

It needs the laws it often helps make in order to encourage acquiescence in the state's legitimate authority within its own territorial jurisdiction to enforce, execute, administer and implement its policies and interests. It needs the recourse it has to the state's legitimate right to use force to back up these laws, particularly those which pertain to property and contract rights, but in a vast number of other areas as well. These would include most prominently those elements of the institutional structure of capitalism that Weber cited as central to any appreciation of capitalism as a national (and trans-national) *system*. To be sure, with subsequent development capitals are able to count increasingly on secondary (even primary) socialization, backed up by the mass media of communication and popular culture. This effects a more comprehensive and long-lasting internalization of those values, beliefs and attitudes on which continual support for, or neutrality toward, capitalism depends absolutely.[18] Looked at as an internally generated and/or imposed power, sovereignty is the single most indispensable property that the state possesses for capitals and capitalism.

That Blackstone's definition of sovereignty raises at least as many issues as it settles is evident from its reference to 'a supreme, irresistible, absolute and uncontrolled authority' which must be present

---

[17] Contrary to Margaret Thatcher. See John Kingdom, *No Such Thing as Society* (Buckingham, U.K.: Open University Press, 1992), the book title being a shorthand from one of her most infamous remarks on the subject.

[18] Gee, Hull and Lankshear, *op. cit.*; Hellinger and Judd, *op. cit.*; and Stephen Nathanson, *Should We Consent to be Governed?* (Belmont, Calif.: Wadsworth Publishing Co., 1992).

'in every state'. Along with this is the fact that at any given time, as noted, institutions possessed of equal (or greater) legitimacy may be challenging whoever or whatever is considered legally sovereign in a given jurisdiction. Indeed, it has even been argued that sovereignty lies elsewhere than in the 'sovereign' itself, as, for example, in the case of the United Kingdom, where the monarch may be sovereign, but can only participate in actual sovereignty when it is shared with Parliament. Rather than treat such a controversy as proof that sovereignty is a fictive concept, it is essential that we stay with its sense, as suggested earlier. It is then possible to take account of specific problems in its conceptualization and understanding, while not letting them detract from the function sovereignty really performs, particularly in capitalist nation states.[19]

In the case of the United Kingdom, as in others where newer institutions have emerged, or governing functions have been institutionally separated, it is the impact of representative democracy and subsequent extensions of the state's legal and administrative structures into society and economy which often accounts for confusion over sovereignty. Here one must distinguish external from internal sovereignty, the idea of the state acknowledged as a 'municipality' in international law from the state as the principally legitimate institution responsible for the maintenance of domestic civil order. In the first case some institutional entity must represent the state in its relations with other states and supranational or international bodies, or at the very least function as a symbol of its sovereign status in these arenas. In the second case, however, there may well be a split jurisdiction on the matter of sovereignty resulting from the need to take account of political developments that have substantially altered the method and processes of governance in capitalist states.

The idea of popular sovereignty, sovereignty expressed in and through the people by voting and participating in public life, provides an important counterpoint to the more monistic and monocratic view of sovereignty operative in international affairs, where states (or municipalities) are presumed to constitute single sovereign units. In most cases the pattern has been to maintain a monarch or its secular equivalent as the sovereign representative in a symbolic

[19] Compare Stephen Krasner, *Sovereignty: Organized Hypocrisy* (Princeton: Princeton University Press, 1999) to Jeremy Rabkin, *Why Sovereignty Matters* (Washington, D.C.: AEI Press, 1998).

sense while conferring 'real' sovereign power on the government of the day and its leadership. The government and its leaders are presumed to be the representatives of the people, who retain ultimate sovereignty in a representative democracy.[20] Because the government of the day, particularly its executive arm, is often freer from supervision and monitoring when it deals in international matters, it has frequently negotiated and even formalized arrangements on behalf of capitals with little or no effective control by legislative and judicial bodies. It is the capacity of these agencies of government to bind future regimes and legislatures that has been of particular concern to groups defending the right of subsequent governments to undo past arrangements if this is the policy of the winning party or coalition.[21] Where internal sovereignty is at issue, particularly since World War II with the increased role of the state and its law in society and economy, there have been attempts to extend controls on capitals through legislation and the courts. These were complemented by an exponential increase in social, public service and regulatory functions until recently, when the accession of neo-conservatism to political power in these countries began to reverse this trend significantly.

But this has been more than balanced by increases over the same period in activities and functions that the state carries out in a direct or indirect way for capitals. As Aitken has pointed out, the state in North America was the first to become specifically responsible for economic development, alongside the traditional maintenance of civil order with which European (and other) states have always been concerned.[22] The effect of this joint responsibility has been the development, virtually unopposed, of that panoply of institutions supportive of capitalism and its infrastructure needs, discussed by Weber, which

[20] Jens Bartleson, *A Genealogy of Sovereignty* (New York: Cambridge University Press, 1995); F.H. Hinsley, *Sovereignty* (Cambridge: Cambridge University Press, 1986). On the clash between sovereignties in England, Edmund Morgan, *Inventing the People: the Rise of Popular Sovereignty in England* (New York: Norton, 1988).

[21] The *North American Free Trade Agreement*, which (like its predecessor) may be renegotiated each time it is reopened when new states join, but never revoked or abrogated by signatory governments, is a case in point. But note that American courts have stated that Congressional statutes cannot be overruled by any supranational or international body on matters within Congress' legitimate jurisdiction.

[22] H.G.J. Aitken, 'Defensive Expansionism: the State and Economic Growth in Canada', in W.T. Easterbrook and M.H. Watkins (editors), *Approaches to Canadian Economic History* (Toronto: McClelland and Stewart, 1967).

are now found in all capitalist states. Where traditional or other parallel institutions either fail to assist, or actively resist, the requirements of continuing capitalist legitimation, it is all the more necessary for this infrastructure, and the political, legal and administrative structures comprising the rest of the institutional matrix, to actively respond to such ongoing threats. Only in this way can the responsibility for economic development try to walk the fine line between supporting private capitals and dealing with the social effects of capitalism.[23]

The shift away from responsibility for society and the retreat towards a more strict understanding of 'the economy' by capitalists in recent years must always be related to the tension between the two notions of duty which emerge from the state's obligation to encourage and support economic development. From the standpoint of the concept of sovereignty looked at internally, the split between 'the sovereign' and the people as sovereign is serious enough to threaten capitals who do not attend adequately to the need for sustained legitimations through the mass media, buttressed by agencies of secondary socialization. This is only underscored by the globalization of capital and its demand for even greater actual and potential mobility than was the case in the past. This is increasingly seen to require that the people's representatives, operating supranationally or internationally, have the ability to effect arrangements on behalf of capitals with the conviction that they are fully backed up at home by the people whom they formally represent.[24]

No matter how problematic for capitals a given regime may be when it is functioning domestically as the agent of civil order in a representative democracy, they cannot afford to turn away from their continuing need for its support and assistance. This is even true where it is not willing or able to provide any form of symbolic legitimation for them. A case in point for many years was Sweden, which operated a social welfare and service state based on the popular sovereignty of a consistent majority, while providing optimum conditions which would allow capitals to compete in the international market largely unfettered by other constraints. It was the *social* contribution that these capitals made, through taxation and employment,

[23] Thomas Dye (editor), *The Political Legitimacy of Markets and Governments* (Greenwich, Conn.: JAI Press, 1990); Mattei Dogan (editor), *Comparing Pluralist Democracies: Strains on Legitimacy* (Boulder, Colorado: Westview Press, 1988).

[24] Norris, *op. cit.*; Marquand, *op. cit.*

which in large part sustained this arrangement until the lifting of exchange controls in 1992. The accession to power of a party more directly supportive of the interests of capital foundered almost immediately, even given the changed economic situation, because it ceased to believe, mistakenly as it turned out, that the public any longer wished to contain and control the behavior of capitals.

Any typology of sovereignty would have to focus on the same phenomena, historically and today, that Weber did in addressing the issue of what constitutes legitimate authority. Sovereignty, unified or divided, must inhere in some person, family, body, system of offices or document that is claimed to be beyond the purview of any authority external to it. Speaking technically and legalistically, that which is sovereign is not subject to legal or judicial challenge, at least not once it has acted (or been employed) with finality in its acknowledged sphere of jurisdiction. While there are always issues of both due process and substance in rule of law representative democracies bearing on the legitimate exercise of sovereignty, it becomes particularly significant in war, depression or emergency. Indeed, many have argued that states come the closest to suspending, if they do not actually suspend, many democratic, civil and human rights and liberties in these circumstances. It is the appeal to sovereignty that ultimately justifies this action by governments in such states, and the fact that such action is acquiesced in by most, if not all, citizens bears significant testimony to the reality of the idea and practice of sovereignty, or principal legitimacy.[25]

When Weber states that his three bases of legitimacy and forms of authority are to be found mixed together in all capitalist industrial societies, he addresses directly the issue of different, competing and conflicting kinds of legitimate institutions, including the sovereign power, or that which is principally legitimate.[26] At the same time, he points to national state differences as the product of distinct cultures and traditions from the past. These differences persist, even in the face of their participation in the general culture that is the institutional matrix of capitalist democracies, what Weber meant by modern Western civilization. The important thing to keep in mind

[25] See Edward Corwin, *Total War and the Constitution* (New York: Alfred Knopf, 1947); and Clinton Rossiter, *Constitutional Dictatorship: Crisis Government in the Modern Democracies* (New York: Harcourt, Brace and World, 1963).

[26] Weber, *Economy and Society*, Volume I, Part 1, chapter 3, pp. 212–216.

when comparing Weber's typology of legitimate authority to the places where sovereignty in such states can be vested is that each type, form or location may be *institutionalized*, and thereby come to constitute more than a value, practice, relationship or arrangement on its own. To say this is simply to underscore once again the fact that institutions may (and usually do) comprehend one or more of these properties while yet possessing a permanence, continuity and taken-for-grantedness which makes them more than merely a group, association or organization.

As it turns out, it is precisely the combination of the three bases for the exercise of legitimate authority in a state, with the legal-rational form normally dominant, along with the locus or site of sovereign power, which provides the institutional foundation of sovereignty. Legitimate authority may be exercised by institutions, in whatever area of collective life, which are not themselves sovereign, and which may only participate peripherally in the institutional matrix which includes the sovereign power, or its representative. Similarly, the locus or site of sovereignty, or principal legitimacy, only provides us with the organizational 'bare bones' of the actual institutional structure in the absence of an understanding of the specific 'mix' of the three bases in each individual case. The insufficiency of the locus or site on its own requires us to take account of ongoing socialization processes in a given society generated by and dependent upon its central myths. Attention must also be given to the social psychology of peoples living in societies with different specific cultures, but similar understandings of and supports for capitalism, science, the national state and the rule of law, complemented by representative democracy and civil and human rights and liberties.[27]

One would be warranted in presuming that capitals would prefer whatever institutional matrix would guarantee maximum stability consonant with consistent state support for their overall interests in a continuous extraction of value from labor and other factors of production, including the co-optation of public capital. While this is generally the case, one must be careful not to attribute too much support on the part of capitals for the idea that stability and continuous extraction is best realized solely or mainly by institutions of legitimacy and principal legitimacy whose basis is legal-rational as

[27] See Clegg and Redding, *op. cit.*

Weber understood it. Indeed, it would be more accurate to argue, on the basis of historical and contemporary practice, that capitals are prepared to adopt strategies that seek to utilize all three bases of legitimacy in varying combinations. The preferred mix depends on the political-economic and social circumstances, the locus or site of sovereignty or principal legitimacy in question and whether it is an issue that bears on the internal or external expression or manifestation of sovereignty.

Thus, while there are occasions when reference to the values, practices, relationships and arrangements provided by institutions and structures of legal-rational authority would be most relevant and helpful to the perceived interests of capitals, this may not always be the case. As Weber suggested, the fact that the three forms are only 'ideal types' and that reality is always some combination of the three means that the reasoning, argumentation and justification required will have to combine elements of charismatic and traditional types with legal-rationality. For example, a legal-rational basis would be provided for in any claim which stated that there are facts that are objectively true and 'correct' in the sense that they are not put forward to serve anyone's perceived or real interests at the cost of other elements of society. Recent concern about deficits and the public debt by neo-conservative governments has made just these sorts of appeals to the objective and disinterested nature of their claims, and in particular, the 'dire straits' to which failure to enforce rigid social and economic discipline will lead.

Given the 'matter of fact' nature of our culture and the status and value which we accord to facts, it is hardly surprising to discover that this is a very powerful and convincing basis on which to anchor preferences and justify courses of action.[28] On the other hand, our very tendency as a general culture to *prefer* this basis of justification, what Weber called formal reason based on analysis of causes and effects, has by now come to constitute the key point of value reference in capitalist democracies themselves. It thus becomes an indispensable element central to our institutional *tradition* of invoking

[28] Thorstein Veblen coined the phrase 'matter of factness' to describe what he believed was the core value of the Western institutional matrix in 'The Place of Science in Modern Civilization', *American Journal of Sociology*, Volume 11 (1906), pp. 585–609, as well as in later studies.

legitimacy, or principal legitimacy, in a particular way, often independent, or relatively independent, of the locus or site.[29] In contrast, the traditional basis for claiming legitimacy, or principal legitimacy, focuses on habit, custom, the taken for granted, and continuity and permanence (often including a 'tradition' of legal-rationality) as the preferred values to be maximized or honored in a given country or culture.

Even apart from the fact that the preference for a traditional basis is so often mixed with legal-rationalism in the ways suggested, capitals will occasionally support this basis on its own independent of the tie to legality. Thus, institutions and practices, values and beliefs, even prejudices, will be appealed to on grounds that they are, after all, essential elements of a given society or culture. Reference will also frequently be made (or presumed) to the view that settled and tried and tested ways of doing things are best, and that particular interests or goals of capitals are thoroughly compatible, if not in perfect harmony, with *both* individual and family interests and community values. A good example here is the idea that the state must once again be viewed as a 'household' which must be frugal, disciplined and fiscally responsible for its debts. The claim to be a taken-for-granted element of the central institutional matrix is appealed to explicitly or subliminally in order to encourage a view which sees capitalism and capitals not only as agents of needs and interests but as defenders of established understandings of what constitutes community well-being.

The exercise of internal sovereignty, while often necessary for the realization of those interests and goals of capitals dependent in the main on legal-rational and traditional bases of justification, is virtually indispensable where one or both are complemented or supplemented by a charismatic basis of authority. Though this form is rarely, if ever, supported by capitals, save in the most extreme cases, and then only when combined with legal-rational and/or traditional modes, it is an essential component of any effort to justify significant real or apparent changes in doctrine or practice. Weber's claim that charisma was inherently unstable cannot gainsay its clear indispensability where the purpose is to generate support for non-violent

[29] See H.T. Wilson, *Tradition and Innovation: the Idea of Civilization as Culture and its Significance* (London: Routledge, 1984), for discussion of Western civilization itself as an institutional 'form of life' or general culture.

change in society's ways of doing things political, economic or social. This means that the charismatic mode must operate residually or surreptitiously, and be embedded in the firmament of other forms and institutions that are perceived to be legitimate. Only then can capitals use the charismatic form to seek changes more conducive to their perceived interests in and through governments, agencies of secondary socialization and the mass media.[30]

While charisma usually attaches to a person, and residually to the immediate family or associates of this person, it can (and is) readily merged with legal-rational authority. Here its embeddedness in continuous structures complements personal characteristics and qualities with occupancy of a position whose discretionary, leadership and creative component completely dominates, and informs, the specific tasks or functions that are required of this position. Charisma can then be understood to constitute a property of that individual whose incumbency is 'spirited' in the sense of being committed to change and innovation, albeit through activity that meets a 'legal-rational' standard.[31] Leadership as a change-agent requires at least some consistent support from human and institutional others. This is not only because it must be given effect in a way that is 'rational' from the standpoint of accepted norms, but because charisma itself is a product of social interaction that is only sensible by reference to values, not a property of some isolated individual.

Roughly the same point can be made, albeit to a lesser extent, for the relationship between traditional and charismatic bases of legitimacy. In this case change is necessary, but only if it happens gradually and from time to time in response to the needs of individuals in specific group, interactive and collective networks and settings who are its immediate agents. The English colloquialism that stresses the need to 'move with the times' captures this sense quite precisely. Of central importance to this understanding is the view that change and innovation, however dependent on the leadership qualities of an individual, should ideally be incremental within the established system. Even if fundamental changes in values, thinking and practice are (allegedly) entailed, this should take place, at least for the most part,

[30] Weber, *Economy and Society*, Volume I, Part 1, chapter 3, iv–v, pp. 241–254.

[31] On 'charisma in microcosm' in capitalist democracies, see H.T. Wilson, 'Space and Place as Convergent Sources of Political Identity', *History of European Ideas*, Volume 21, No. 4 (1995), pp. 496–504.

within formally existing frameworks of action. Charismatic authority, whether from the public or private sector, must often be *formally*, as well as substantively, combined with legal-rationality and tradition in rule of law representative democracies undergoing fundamental changes, as the present worship of businesspeople and entrepreneurs demonstrates.

Turning to the sites where legitimacy, and principal legitimacy or sovereignty, are generally found, we find ourselves strongly tempted to compare and contrast them to Weber's three forms of legitimate authority in order to discover the real-world empirical 'mix'. As noted, executives in capitalist democratic states are less constrained in their exercise of sovereignty viewed externally as a necessary feature of international relations than in the exercise of sovereignty viewed internally as the power (and obligation) to maintain civil order. From the standpoint of the obligation of the modern state to promote and support economic development by and on behalf of its capitals, *both* internal and external expressions and manifestations of sovereignty are essential, given the rise of international trade and globalization.[32] At the same time, it is in the expression of external sovereignty, for the reasons cited above, that individual political leaders are most likely to be the immediate (and interim) locus of sovereignty, whether they are acting in foreign affairs in matters economic or non-economic.

Charisma, however embedded and situated, and subject to incremental criteria and the obligation to 'report back', thus has its primary repository in the individual as the representative of sovereign power, the moreso when this person, with or without colleagues, is operating in the international arena. Charisma must be organized and managed if it is to be a basis for the claim to legitimacy in rule of law representative democracies. This means that it must at one and the same time be sedimented in legal-rationalism and tradition and viewed as an expression of *agency* functioning on behalf of the sovereign people and *their* state.[33] This function is mainly symbolic for monarchs, presidents and chancellors, tangible, albeit through legislatures and governments for prime ministers and premiers in parliamentary-cabinet systems, and a combination of the two for the

[32] Thomas Franck, *The Power of Legitimacy among Nations* (New York: Oxford, 1990).
[33] Wilson, 'Space and Place as Convergent Sources of Political Identity', *op. cit.*

American and French presidents. Charisma, in short, must never be allowed to establish claims to sovereignty or principal legitimacy—even in crises or emergencies—that are too independent of either legal-rational or traditional modes. It is paramount that sovereignty be understood to be *delegated* to such agents on a temporary basis and as a *trust* through their representative, governmental and legal institutions.

One of the most important ways that charisma in all its forms and manifestations is contained in its long-term effects, given the inherent instability which derives from its personal, individual aspect, is through its routinization. In effect, institutions already possessed of legitimacy or residual legitimacy, or interdependent with such institutions, *absorb and channel* the residual effects of this charisma in either a legal-rational or a traditional direction, or, as is more likely for the reasons suggested, into institutions which combine both forms. Weber did compare and contrast the routinization of charisma in a traditional direction with the process of its rationalization into legal-rational and constitutional expressions of authority. Yet he placed far less emphasis on the extent to which the emerging institutional web of relations between the state, its laws and administration and capitals was producing a *general culture* which would require an *increasing* number of *tradition-based* forms of legitimation.[34] Nevertheless, (and in contrast to his brother Alfred, writing at a later date) Weber did maintain some skepticism toward the claims to objectivity inherent in the occidental preference for formal rationality, legal rationality, bureaucracy and meritocracy. Far from making a case for the objective superiority of civilization over mere 'culture', these institutional practices only served to underscore the *greater* capacity for domination and mobilization that were inherent in this preference.

A look at potential and actual repositories of sovereignty from the standpoint of the interests of capitals reveals a not surprising preference for stability, order and other values conducive to 'fair exchange' in society. This is particularly the case once the political-economic infrastructure that Weber discussed in such detail has come into being. Only when capitalism is battling against remnants of feudal, aristocratic or agrarian institutions using whatever class, economic

[34] Weber, *Economy and Society*, Volume I, Part 1, chapter 3 (9a), (12a); Part 2, chapter 1 (2), chapter 4 (2); Volume II, chapter 14, i (1–5), ii (1–13), iii (1–3); chapter 15 (1).

and political leverage it can find is there an interest in macro-level change that shakes central structures and processes to their foundations. Significantly, capitals often reach accommodations with such institutions because the latter can aid them in establishing and maintaining legitimacy, alongside their ongoing quest for influence with the sovereign or its representatives. In this case, it will frequently be argued that the resulting relationship leaves the pre-capitalist or pre-industrial institution in question as a mere shell, form without substance. Such accommodations once again underscore the fact that capitalism, however central to an emerging (or established) general culture, still has to establish and maintain commodius relations with those elements of a country's traditional culture(s) still revered by its people and by those non-capitalist elites which continue to be influential.

The historical record will bear out several observations of a general nature which, however, must be conditioned by specific country analysis and comparisons because of the persistence of cultural differences and the ongoing requirement that capitals adapt to them. This is even, or rather especially, true in an age when capital's greater mobility as a factor of production is leading to its *apparent* internationalization and globalization.[35] First, capitals normally prefer monarchs if they possess only symbolic sovereignty, in contrast to the actual sovereignty held by a popularly elected legislature in countries where monarchy is still considered desirable (if not necessary) by the people and various elites. Here and in other instances, legal-rationality and tradition are intertwined and have a dominant influence as bases of legitimate authority and control over the monarch. The United Kingdom is the most prominent example of a powerful, albeit still mainly symbolic and constitutional monarchy, while The Netherlands, Belgium, Sweden and Spain are almost totally of the latter type.

In France, in clear contrast, the excesses of the *ancien regime*, with the pre-revolutionary judiciary as its handmaiden, led to the French Revolution of 1789, which in turn culminated in the installation of Bonaparte at a key point just prior to the emergence of early industrial capitalism. He brought back the aristocracy for stability, and made

[35] See Saskia Sassen, *Losing Control?: Sovereignty in an Age of Globalization* (New York: Columbia University Press, 1996).

serious improvements in the legal and judicial system which were instrumental to capitalist development after his demise in 1815. While Bonaparte was obviously preferable to either phase of the Revolution for capitals, particularly during the period of his command of the Republican Armies, his military campaigns following on his self ordained Emperorship (including the status of 'Sovereign') created after 1808 a very unstable situation for French capitals. No doubt this was aggravated by the fact of a two front war, massive ordinance requirements and overextended supply lines, particularly after the invasion of Russia in 1812. During the period that followed Napoleon's defeat, a pseudo-monarchy with strong legislative assemblies and his legal and judicial innovations guaranteed a suitable setting for the development of industrialization by a new breed of capitals.

Germany in many ways represents the most intriguing case of all, because it challenges the claims of both the political economists and Marx regarding the relationship between the economic 'substructure' and the political and cultural 'superstructure' throughout the Nineteenth and early Twentieth centuries. Prior to the Franco-Prussian war of 1870, Germany was a patchwork of duchies and principalities, with only Prussia politically and militarily pre-eminent. Preference for a monarchy which combined symbolic with considerable tangible power and influence was more than complemented by a strict commitment to a formal legal-rationalism and the political leadership of Bismarck, particularly after the victories of 1870. Bismarck introduced the first social legislation because of his fear of the kind of violent revolution which he believed he had observed in France after 1848 and 1871, and was supported by most established large and small capitals in doing so. Created a prince in 1871, he viewed himself as both sovereign and as an instrument of the German nation, but lacked the temperament for party politics, which led to his demise at the hands of Kaiser Wilhelm Hohenzollern in 1890.

Kaiser Wilhelm was a symbolic source of sovereignty, alongside the Prussian institutions of legal-rationalism that had emerged. Most large capitals in Germany supported his war aims in 1914, as well as Hitler's in 1939, because they believed that each leader could win. In addition there was, and still is, much money to be made and credit built up through warfare, even (or especially) in a situation in which the country where capitals are headquartered loses the war. Even devastation of a country's productive infrastructure can be seen to have a bright side, in that it clears the way for newer, more technologically advanced industrial facilities which a country might otherwise be tempted to protect through tariffs, quotas *etc.* The post World War II contrast between the United Kingdom and Western Germany and Japan is a case in point. Hitler, uniquely amongst all totalitarian dictators, made himself sovereign and attempted, with less success than is generally believed, to destroy the system of Prussian legal-rationalism that had been put in place after 1870. German capitals, some of whom traded with their American counterparts throughout World War II, used Switzerland, Sweden and Portugal as their intermediaries. Indeed, they had little choice if they remained in Germany after 1933 but to adapt themselves to the new Behemoth, however skeptical they might have been (or eventually became) about their post-war fate.[36]

The United States Marshall Plan, which constitutes the most massive example of industrial and economic reconstruction in world history, was instrumental in putting Western Europe on its feet. A parallel, albeit very different, program did the same thing for Japan. In both cases it was the fear of communism, coupled with the need for friendly alliances with Western Germany and Japan, which motivated capitals to support programs of such scope and scale during and after their respective military occupations. Apart from the resources of the United States, there was the reality of an 'arms race' which provided many large capitals with a continued, or even heightened, opportunity to participate in what has since come to be known as 'Pentagon Capitalism'.[37] Capitals involved in this system of non-competitive contracts and subcontracts reacted with considerable dismay to the so-called 'peace dividend' which descended on the United States in particular with the collapse of the USSR and the Warsaw Pact as a whole. Thankfully, China and three or four 'rogue' states have now come to their rescue, and promise to fill the void that this collapse has created, either because of the threat they are alleged to pose in their own right, or because they function as staging bases for paramilitary terrorist groups.

Capitals in contemporary nation-states characterized by the rule of law and representative democracy normally prefer a division of

[36] Franz Neumann, *Behemoth: the Structure and Practice of National Socialism*, 1933–1944 (New York: Oxford University Press, 1944).

[37] Seymour Melman, *Pentagon Capitalism: the Political Economy of War* (New York: McGraw Hill, 1970).

symbolic and actual sovereignty, alongside the opportunity to lobby and a settled combination of legal-rationalism and tradition, particularly if the home 'captive' market is substantial. Charisma is useful only if harnessed and embedded in the ways indicated. The rule of law must enfranchise, if not grant outright, explicit constitutional and/or traditional protection to the right to lobby alongside well-enforced property and contractual rights. There must be recognition of the right to pass on 'social' costs and other 'externalities' to *both* taxpayers and customers, for example, in the case of human rights, affirmative action, pay equity and environmental legislation. The other side of Lindblom's observation that business has a 'privileged position' in capitalist democracies because it is 'delegated' the power to 'run the economy' is thus that this power includes passing on these costs to taxpayers and ratepayers, as well as customers, by charges to the 'public debt'.[38] If legal-rationalism and tradition provide strong enough bases of stability and guarantees of incremental change, separated, divided and competing systems of political legitimacy are preferable to a single fused structure like the Parliamentary-Cabinet system, particularly under conditions of majority government. This is because access points are multiplied in systems of separated and divided sovereignty and institutional legitimacy, thus the desire for, and constitutional protection of, lobbying in the American system of government. Only where governing parties are committed to an integrated 'industrial policy' approach, rather than one which favors 'free trade', is there a substantial likelihood that capitals, particularly large capitals, will prefer a Parliamentary-Cabinet system over one which separates and divides both sovereignty and the institutions of political legitimacy.

Another locus of sovereignty, besides a person, a family, a body or a system of offices, is itself a highly symbolic as well as tangible source of legitimacy—a written constitution or other fundamental document. When such a document has the status of a 'higher law' than that of the legislature in a representative democracy, and is therefore available to judge and assess legislation, the high judiciary can be expected to acquire a substantial political role. Since courts are effectively insulated from the type of lobbying that capitals usually like to engage in, it is only the fact that judges and justices are

[38] See Lindblom, *op. cit.*, chapters 13, 22.

appointed, not elected, that makes the situation bearable for capitals. This does not mean that constitutional questions are always, or even usually, settled in a way which is favorable to their perceived interests, just that there usually are compensatory devices available to them in the overall system which can compensate for judicial opinions and their possible consequences.[39] In addition, of course, are the legal resources available to capitals, alongside their lobbying power, in order to achieve a legislative override of the high judiciary when it acts as the final interpreter of a written constitution or other basic document in ways inimical to their interests.

The next chapter focusses on the tension and uneasy equipoise between capitals and the established system of capitalism in a given nation-state or supranational entity and representative democracy. By the latter is meant a method of organizing and expressing popular sovereignty in such states through systems of government, political parties, interest groups, elections and agencies of capital, public and social administration. Recent discussions about what makes capitalism safe for democracy and democracy safe for capitalism will be of particular importance, as will arguments from the 'private sector' that allege a causal relationship between productivity and innovation and the capacity to provide public and social benefits, services and functions. Finally, a significant split in interests and perspective has occurred within the capital, public and social institutions of capitalist democracies as a direct consequence of the neo-conservative agenda in practice. These sectors now are increasingly viewed in a zero-sum fashion as belonging either to capitals or to the people, with less and less perceived space in between for overlap and the exploration of mutual interests.[40] This latter development is extremely problematic for capitals, because the pressure being placed on public, but especially social, institutions by this agenda is beginning to affect more and more people.

---

[39] Michael Mandel, *The Charter of Rights and the Legalization of Politics in Canada* (Toronto: Thompson Educational Publishing, 1994).

[40] Wilson, *Bureaucratic Representation*, chapter 2.

CHAPTER FIVE

CAPITALISM AND DEMOCRACY

Many have claimed that the uneasy equipoise between capitalism and democracy over the past century or more is the wonder of modernity. Lindblom has pointed out that representative democratic institutions have only taken root in nation-states that already possess, or are in the process of developing, 'market-oriented systems'. However much we may regret the precise ways that 'the market is harnessed to democratic purposes', democracy is to be found in no other economic system. While 'every democratic system is also a market-oriented system', this is not to say that 'all market-oriented systems are democratic', however.[1] Nevertheless, the presence of a consistent and continuous institutional linkage between capitalism and democracy, with the market emerging prior to subsequent democratic arrangements where the two are found together, is of central significance for this study.

A number of questions present themselves for consideration for anyone trying to explain this phenomenon. (1) Is there a causal relationship between capitalism and democracy? (2) Or is the relationship rather more complementary and cultural in nature? (3) What are the implications of the neo-conservative agenda, in particular its continuing reliance on the 'debt crisis' for this relationship? (4) Is it a relationship that capitals consciously defend, or is it supported and maintained as a 'lesser evil'? (5) What are the future implications of a neo-conservative politics committed to one or another form of 'free trade' for both capitals and representative democracy in the new international and global economy?[2] This chapter examines the implications of each of these questions, but in no particular order. In the process, it addresses the distinct likelihood that capitals are acting

---

[1] Charles Lindblom, *Politics and Markets* (New York: Basic Books, 1977), p. 116 and *supra*.

[2] Jeff Gates, *Democracy at Risk: Rescuing Main Street from Wall Street* (Cambridge, Mass.: Perseus Publishing, 2000); Ian Gough and Gunnar Olafsson (editors), *Capitalism and Social Cohesion: Essays on Exclusion and Integration* (New York: St. Martin's Press, 1999); Dryzek, *op. cit.*

precipitously when they retreat backward into 'the economy' and away from responsibilities to public and social institutions. This coincides with, and is often justified by the need for, a parallel retreat outward into the new international and global system in order to take advantage of the opportunities presented by greater capital mobility. Far from being an 'objective' process, globalization can be seen as a rationale for a set of choices made by capitals in an economic, financial and political environment that encourages them to forget or ignore their continuing dependence on public capital and the legitimation that its institutional auspices provide.

Nevertheless, this latter point does raise the issue of whether capitals really have any option but to respond in this way, in which case the neo-conservative agenda may pose a serious problem for the present and future legitimacy of capitalism itself. Capitals would appear to have opted for a combination of both of the strategies cited above. They believe that existing institutional modes of public control and manipulation, including the mass media, processes of secondary socialization and agencies of representative democratic government, are more than sufficient to sustain their agenda of social discipline and public and social sector devastation. Indeed, there is now a sustained effort in a number of capitalist nation-states to terminate the tacit alliance between democratically elected governments and the public sector bureaucracies on which program implementation, and experienced advice and expertise, have consistently depended.[3]

'Downsizing' and 'restructuring' are concepts that refer to the public and social sectors far more pointedly than they do to business, commerce, finance and industry. The only elements of the public sector administrative system which capitals now say can be fully justified are those agencies concerned with law enforcement, private sector economic support and advocacy, and manipulation and 'fine tuning' of the economy of a given nation state or sub-unit therein. In effect, we are beginning to see the emergence of a *market* system of political democracy, in which horror stories and dire warnings produce the desired effects among general publics.[4] Included, increasingly, among these effects is support for the devastation of many

[3] Wilson, *Bureaucratic Representation*, chapters 1–3, 7, 8.

[4] Anticipated to some extent by Lindblom, *op. cit.* Also see Robert Kuttner, *Everything for Sale: the Virtues and Limits of Markets* (New York: Alfred Knopf, 1997); and Dye, *op. cit.*

functions of (not just programs in) the public and social sectors, in whatever jurisdiction one finds them and by whatever means. Health care, education and higher education, housing, social welfare, psychiatric counselling and public transportation are some of the best known examples in recent years.

This is more than supplemented by what is happening to collective bargaining rights and labor-management relations generally. Four of the most important functions which members of capitalist democratic societies perform are as citizens, workers, consumers and clients. Public and social sector devastation, alongside a 'see no evil' approach to labor-management relations, possesses clear legal and constitutional implications which governments supportive of the new social gospel may not be able to escape. Meanwhile, those elements of the governmental apparatus supported by capitals are in the process of being transformed into a system which not only supports, but is thoroughly dependent upon, private sector initiatives. These initiatives include lobbying, consultation, concertation and corporatism, alongside downsizing, contracting out, hollowing out, privatization and 'reverse privatization'. The resulting 'lean and mean' public administration is not only more costly, but also constitutes a device for transforming the system of bureaucratic representation away from its public and social responsibilities toward the interests of capitals.[5] It is worth noting that instead of this restructuring activity having a negative impact on the growth of subsidies, contracts and subcontracts for the private sector, these outcomes are now understood to be a necessary consequence of the 'new partnership'.

Any claim like the one made twenty years ago that the public sector was 'overcrowded' with actors must reflect on the emerging and intended impact of the neo-conservative agenda on the public and social sectors.[6] Alongside a market system of political democracy run by anti-public and anti-social sector political parties, we are beginning to see the emergence of a market concept of public and social administration. These activities are increasingly being justified or condemned on the basis of whether they meet *private sector criteria*

[5] Wilson, *Bureaucratic Representation*; Aronowitz, *op. cit.*; Kreml, *op. cit.*

[6] See Claus Offe, *Contradictions of the Welfare State* (London: Hutchinson, 1984); and 'The Risk Analysis Controversy', special issue of *Policy Sciences*, Volume 15, No. 3 (April 1983) devoted to the tension between capitalist and democratic institutions and the relation between risk, governance and public sector 'overcrowding'.

of what constitutes a proper public and social function, rather than on whether the performance of this function is effective. Since 'the market' for many of these functions is one which the private sector either claims it can serve better, or one which it believes should be eliminated, cutback or transferred to other jurisdictions, this initiative by neo-conservatives constitutes nothing less than a direct take-over of the governmental system.[7] This is most obvious when 'reverse privatization' occurs, that is, when the form of a public agency or bureau is retained, but its function is transformed into one of promoting a deregulated private sector activity while relying on voluntary compliance. In effect, the agency or bureau becomes a de facto part of the capital rather than the public sector through a sleight of hand of which citizens are completely ignorant and of which they may not approve. That these initiatives are occurring with the apparent consent of majorities of voters in these countries is precisely what emboldens capital while at the same time crying out for careful analysis.

A point not lost on many capitals is the fact that governmental institutions actively or tacitly supportive of capital are frequently older, better established and more secure, given the early imperatives of capitalist development, than newer public, key sector and social welfare programs, benefits and services. This is only underscored in the present context by the fact that those most supportive of these newer functions frequently affirm this point in their own critical analyses of the neo-conservative agenda in practice. This observation is well defended on both sides of the issue, and states that there are governmental institutions that belong to capital and governmental institutions that belong to the public and society respectively.[8] This tripartite distinction, long present but only recently acknowledged publicly, was first announced formally in the United Kingdom, largely in response to Margaret Thatcher's destruction of unions and public and social sector institutions after 1980. It speaks to a *further* fragmentation of the political and administrative infrastructure in capitalist democratic societies.

What it also speaks to is the division already cited between those governmental agencies that are dispensable, for one reason or another, under allegedly 'objective' downsizing or restructuring requirements,

[7] See Wilson, *Bureaucratic Representation*, p. 26 and *supra*.

[8] This has long been the perception in the United Kingdom. See David Bull, 'Anti-Discretion Movement in Britain: Fact or Phantom?', *Journal of Social Welfare Law* (1979), pp. 65–83; and Kingdom, *op. cit.*

and those which continue to be necessary, or even indispensable, to capital in given nation-states. What is really taking place as a combined result of this retreat from public and social responsibilities, embrace of a narrow definition of 'the economy' and flight into the global arena to take advantage of greater capital mobility is nothing less than a *total restructuring of the state apparatus itself.* While this shift in the direction of what is clearly a more direct and continuous co-optation of public capital may indeed constitute a response to what capitals and their supporters believe to be 'objective conditions', there is an element of purposefulness evident in these actions as well. The now-standard form that this neo-con con takes is as follows: first, cut back funding to some agency or bureau; second, observe a (not surprising) decline in its performance; third, recommend one or another strategy to take it partly or fully out of the public or social sector. The result is to de-legitimize the public and social sectors of government while legitimizing its capital sector and capital itself.[9] These actions and initiatives make it clear that past doubts about capitalism's legitimacy have faded, not only in the memory and thinking of most capitals themselves, but in the minds of members of general publics and society as well.

An intimation of this perhaps came to capitals in both the United Kingdom and the United States (and elsewhere) when successive intrusions into established Keynesian arrangements, as well as relationships not yet imbued with institutional status and legitimacy, were accepted, and even well received, by general publics. In effect, neo-conservative elements used their very lack of intellectual credentials to press an economic, political and social agenda during the 1980's which was far more ideological than anything being practiced by liberal and social democrats in these countries. Capitals were emboldened even more when they discovered to their delight that general publics, and increasingly even the mass media and 'unattached' intellectuals, were acquiescent in the reasons provided by capitals and their neo-conservative supporters as to why their own policies had failed. This was followed by the collapse of any effort on the part of defenders of the Keynesian consensus to challenge the new interpretations and explanations.[10]

[9] See Wilson, 'The Downside of Downsizing: Bureaucratic Representation in Capitalist Democracies', *op. cit.*; Wilson, *Bureaucratic Representation.*

[10] In Canada, this took the form of what I call a 'retreat from governance'. See

Either explicitly or by their silence on these matters, supporters of the Keynesian consensus acknowledged responsibility for deficits and debts, along with their inability to rectify the situation using their own policy arsenals. This constituted one of the most serious instances of what in constitutional law is called a 'vacating of the field' of responsible discourse and analysis that we have seen in capitalist democracies in recent memory. Far from being 'overcrowded', this particular arena of concern relating social values and their rank-ordering to public and social policies and their effective implementation now became decidedly one-sided in a way that was directly opposite to what happened between 1933 and the mid 1970's in these same countries. Public acceptance of the neo-conservative gospel on debt, deficits and appropriate public and social functions owes much more to this failure of nerve and subsequent acquiescence of media and intellectual elites than it does to the presence of any objectively correct 'facts' about the economies in question.[11]

This in turn generated the perception that it was public and social sector involvement *per se* unrelated to the functions it served and the interests it promoted that was the real problem. Complementing this mistrust of government, both in terms of bureaucratic competence and political integrity, was disillusionment with the normal processes of representative democracy.[12] This disillusionment justified the process by which all elites, including those who wish to occupy high office, supported the narrowing, downsizing and restructuring not only of public and social institutions but of the democratic role of citizens as well. That this all appears to be taking place with the tacit, if not explicit, consent of general publics indicates their apparent disappointment with what are now termed 'non-market' solutions for political and governmental problems. Solutions to these problems, it is argued, now need to be reformulated using criteria more sympathetic to the market and to capital.

Wilson, *Retreat from Governance* (Hull: Voyageur Publishing Co., 1989). On the central role of 'unattached intellectuals', see chapter 13, this study.

[11] See Colin Hay, 'The Invocation of External Economic Constraint: A Genealogy of the Concept of Globalization in the Political Economy of the British Labour Party, 1973–2000', *The European Legacy*, Volume 6, No. 2 (April 2001), pp. 233–249 at pp. 234–235; Gordon Clark and Michael Dear, *State Apparatus: Structures and Language of Legitimacy* (Boston: Allen and Unwin, 1984); Gee, Hull and Lankshear, *op. cit.*

[12] Kreml, *op. cit.*; Dryzek, *op. cit.*

This takes on an aura of urgency and immediacy that only the recourse to poor 'household' management and resulting fiscal irresponsibility can capture. In the most radical case, general publics have now been persuaded that unemployment, already denied as a serious problem when compared to inflation and interest rates, can now be increased exponentially and still remain 'tolerable' by downsizing or eliminating altogether the public and social agencies and functions cited.[13] Perhaps an even more significant element complementing this most recent act of emboldenment by capitals and their supporters in governments has been their willingness to speak directly to an issue which until now could not be discussed without much equivocation and hesitation, if at all. Neo-conservatives now assert that taxes on corporate income, capital gains and other forms of wealth acquisition are counter productive in the present and emerging circumstances. All that may now be justifiable and 'fiscally responsible', apart from significant cuts in public and social sector spending, are consumption taxes on goods and services, supplemented by real property tax increases to individuals and families.

One needs only to note how regressive such forms of taxation are, how much they skew the tax load downward toward those less able to pay, to see how far we have fallen from the post-war informal contract between the people and their representatives and capitals. What has transpired over the past thirty years in many capitalist democracies has been the collapse of any meaningful general consensus around the idea that capitals and their politically elected governments have a reciprocal obligation to the public and society. While this sense of reciprocal obligation is more clearly the case for capitals, they have been grouped together here for a reason that should be evident in what follows, if not in what has already been said.

A dominant feature of the emerging situation addresses directly the problems raised by this new alliance between corporate and state structures. One is the refusal of both to support positive and affirmative responses to deficits and debts by installing training and retraining programs directed to helping the economies in question grow out of this very indebtedness.[14] Since at least 1945 responsible political

[13] Linda McQuaig, *Shooting the Hippo: Death by Deficit* (Toronto: Viking, 1995).

[14] I. Diwan and D. Rodrik, *Debt Reduction, Adjustment Lending and Burden Sharing* (Cambridge, Mass.: National Bureau of Economic Research, 1992); Mary Janigan, 'A Debt Handbook', *MacLeans*, September 27, 1993, pp. 34, 36–38.

leaders have understood that one does not address and deal constructively with debts incurred through borrowings by nation-states and sub-units therein by going into an economic holding pattern. This is precisely *because* it constitutes a passive rather than an active response and is unlikely to be effective on its own. Today, however, publics are persuaded not only that the cost of such programs is too prohibitive for capitals to undertake given the state of 'the economy', but also that they will only increase the debt further if undertaken by governments. The issue here is less whether these claims are true and more what present and emerging conditions in and between capitalist democracies increasingly make them appear to be a credible assessment of the situation.

The difficulty with this line of reasoning is that it ignores national state experiences since 1945 in addressing problems of indebtedness, in many cases more extensive as a *per capita* measure than is the case today. In addition, it treats all debt the same, looking at it only when aggregated and treating it as inherently undesirable, when neoconservatives really do not believe this at all, if their actions rather than their ideology is to be given any credence.[15] More detailed arguments as to why debt is often desirable and who is responsible for much or most of it today are provided in chapter nine, where the refusal to employ past experience and distinguish between different forms and causes of indebtedness is discussed. In addition to the fact that capitals only rarely support the resuscitation of apprenticeship training, there is an alliance between them and neo-conservative governments which argues that governmentally supported training and retraining schemes will only create more debt, not decrease it.

This reasoning is not dissimilar to what has been employed to justify devastating only those functions of the public and social service infrastructure which are of no direct or indirect use to capital, while leaving intact (or expanding) those that are. In addition, public and social sectors are obliged to act like a family household of *forty to fifty years ago* rather than today at the same time that they must honor market criteria in determining which functions are appropriate ones for them to carry out. These are not only conflicting requirements, but ones that make no sense when addressed to the proper performance of these functions. Having said this, there is a reason why

[15] Janigan, *op. cit.*; Chorney *et al., op. cit.*

the public is subtly persuaded, and often blatantly propagandized, to treat their individual and family households as entities which can (and must) run a continual debt. Owing money or its equivalent to private capitals sustains massive parasitic employment while it reflects capitalism's obscene dependence on consumer indebtedness even (or especially) in the face of the so-called public debt of which it is so significant a part.[16] This constitutes one of the gravest problems that capitalist democracies will have to face, and ultimately resolve. While this contradiction appears to be serving the interests of capital in the short run, it is incompatible with the long-term interests of capitals in the creation and distribution of the public capital on which they continue to depend for both their material success and their ongoing legitimation.

Even more problematic than the hypocrisy about nation-states and their sub-units behaving like households is the patent fiction that the private sector operates with either a surplus or a balanced budget, or that they rectify their absence independently of governments once they get into a deficit position.[17] As it turns out, capitals and their supporters are not only appealing to what is at best an historical (if not imaginary) household with their demands for discipline, restraint and 'the bottom line'. They are also appealing to what is clearly an historical (if not an imaginary) corporation, company, association or partnership when they make such claims. However serious the lies, deceptions, manipulations, and plain hypocrisies cited in the text thus far, they pale by comparison to what has been done to persuade general publics and their representatives that the present state of indebtedness precludes any reliance whatsoever on positive and affirmative governmental responses. Training and retraining schemes that would help us decrease the debt by *growing out of it* are precluded, like other government fiscal and industrial policy measures,

[16] See Andrew Hurley, *Diners, Bowling Alleys and Trailer Parks: Chasing the American Dream in the Postwar Consumer Culture* (New York: Basic Books, 2001); Mark Gottdiener (editor), *New Forms of Consumption: Consumers, Culture and Commodification* (Lanham, Maryland: Rowman and Littlefield, 2000); Kimberly Lau, *New Age Capitalism: Making Money East of Eden* (Philadelphia: University of Pennsylvania Press, 2000); Richard H. Robbins, *Global Problems and the Culture of Capitalism* (Boston: Allyn and Bacon, 1999); Sandra Vandermerwe, *Customer Capitalism: the New Business Model of Increasing Returns in New Market Spaces* (London: Nicholas Brealey, 1999).

[17] Lewis, *Louder Voices: Corporate Welfare Bums* (Toronto: James Lewis and Samuels, 1972); Laurence Kallen, *Corporate Welfare* (New York: Lyle Stuart, 1991).

because they create inflation, thereby decreasing the value of the debt held by offshore interests.

The major culprits, aided and abetted by the mass media and professional and technical 'experts' and consultants, are the World Trade Organization (WTO), the International Monetary Fund (IMF), central banks in capitalist nation states, and the bond rating companies in major U.S., European and Japanese cities. Large segments of the general public have been persuaded that these institutions are objectively correct in every injunction and demand that they make on our allegedly profligate use of public and social services and benefits, alongside key public sector functions they wish to see downsized, contracted out or privatized. Indeed, it would not be out of order to argue that these institutions have acquired, or are now in the process of acquiring, a legitimacy that seriously threatens to undermine popular sovereignty and the institutions which represent and express it, both internally and externally.[18] The implications of this, in concert with those developments already cited which help us see the reasons for such an allegation, will require us to address once again the uneasy equipoise between capitalism and democracy.

If this equipoise is as indispensable to capitals as Lindblom and others think, then the possibility that the co-optation of representative democratic institutions must occur as a consequence of the more direct and continuous co-optation of public capital promises to generate even more serious problems for capitalism. The collapse of that political-economic equilibrium so central to the earlier Keynesian consensus is one that more and more capitals would now justify on grounds it really was no equilibrium at all, but rather an imbalance favoring the public and social sector.[19] Elemental to this process, they would argue, was the view that party competition in most instances would favor the party that wished to spend more for public and social purposes. Even conservative parties of restraint would have little choice in these circumstances but to try to slow down such profligacy when in power, while accepting as given the existing level

---

[18] In particular, bureaucratic public and social (as opposed to capital) institutions and regulatory bodies not already (or ever) 'captured' by their clienteles. See Wilson, *Bureaucratic Representation*, chapters 1–3, 5, 7.

[19] David Coates, *Models of Capitalism: Growth and Stagnation in the Modern Era* (Malden, Mass.: Polity Press, 2000); Alexander Hicks, *Social Democracy and Welfare Capitalism: A Century of Income Security Politics* (Ithaca: Cornell University Press, 1999).

of expenditure and involvement by government and the public sector in the economy and society.

What is forgotten is that it was during the post Depression and post World War II periods that virtually all of the present day mechanisms and processes were put in place to improve, if not to formalize, state initiatives, instruments, arrangements and relationships for and on behalf of capitals themselves. Thus the massive undertakings, including in an indirect way even those public and social services, benefits and programs which capitals now seek to cut back, eliminate or transfer, were carried out with an eye to preserving capitalism from its own excesses, that is, from itself.[20] This was understood by many leading capitals in key Western countries after World War II, and accepted as a necessary evil, given the threat to social stability and public order that an unregulated capitalism had once posed. The fact that this threat arose in the absence of the very public and social services and regulations which neo-conservatives now wish to eliminate, downsize, contract out or privatize only underscores the need to reassert the tie between the bureaucratic representation of public and social interests and the ballot box.

That the large majority of these interventions justified a wide range of promotive and protective functions for capital is something that neo-conservatives conveniently ignore. One reason among many which helps explain why they do this bears on conflicts among capitals themselves which arise out of the fact that points of power, influence, bargaining and leverage with governments are inherently scarce. Since a given policy is likely to be in the interests of some capitals and against those of others, it means that capitals must compete with one another in non (or even anti) market ways through parties, governments and the public sector generally. Capitals secured an indirect basis for public capital co-optation built atop the extraction of surplus value from labor, while using the state as a vehicle to create the very mass consumption society that they can now only reconcile with a more direct co-optation by destroying public and social institutions.[21]

---

[20] Claus Offe, *Contradictions of the Welfare State*; and the other papers in the special issue of *Policy Sciences*, Volume 15, No. 3 (April 1983), pp. 191–305, titled 'The Risk Analysis Controversy'.

[21] Gottdiener, *op. cit.*; Robbins, *op. cit.*; Lau *op. cit.*

The simple arithmetic of consumer capitalism is that social welfare and public subsidization *always* function as vehicles which allow those who are not working, and/or who are infirm, sick, injured, marginal or less economically able, to continue to purchase the goods and services of those who are working. To devastate the public and social infrastructure in the ways presently envisioned, while seeking to maintain the form of consumer capitalism presently in place, runs so contrary to the logic of the present system that one is tempted to try to discover the function served by this apparent incompatibility. Could it be that in its retreat to the economy, narrowly defined, capitals are seeking to base the process of value extraction, and now public capital co-optation, more and more on exploitative production and trade relations with developing countries and on financial activities and transfers of a global nature?[22] So-called global institutions of capital could then be seen as a way of building on value extraction in developing countries by basing the present and future co-optation of public capital there on these institutions without having to support the public and social infrastructure found in capitalist democracies. Or do capitals really believe in 'the market' in its present and emerging form as a vehicle which can be globalized successfully once we readjust structurally the public and social sectors in advanced capitalist societies in the ways indicated?

A tentative answer is that both possibilities are likely because they are thoroughly compatible with one another. 'Downsizing' and 'restructuring' are devices to realize in a non-military way goals very similar to those which wars accomplish through the imposition of the instruments of violence and mass destruction on the populations and capital infrastructures of both 'winners' and 'losers'. This suggests why use of the term *devastation* may be appropriate when discussing the projected, emerging or actual impact of the neo-conservative gospel of social discipline and household fiscal responsibility on public and social institutions. Refusal to support more progressive forms of taxation, and publicly sponsored training and retraining schemes which seek to actively transform these economies in a higher value added direction, speaks volumes to the continued good health of the (no longer) traditional theory of capitalist motivation.[23]

[22] See especially Richard Harris and Melinda Seid (editors), *Critical Perspectives on Globalization and Neoliberalism in the Developing Countries* (Boston: Brill, 2000).

[23] David Reisman, *Conservative Capitalism: the Social Economy* (New York: St. Martin'

The illusion in the first case is that no one must interfere with the maximum possible mobility of capital lest capitals get jittery and move to greener pastures elsewhere. This value preference is central to the policies of all those who defend the neo-conservative agenda's alleged concern with deficits and debt. Somewhat ironically, this approach has now become the basis for an unseemly competition between countries at different levels of development, one which virtually guarantees precisely the result it was intended to preclude. Even the presence of supranational trade agreements cannot hide the chagrin that neo-conservative governments most strongly supportive of mobility rights feel when their own capitals act on this right and relocate facilities or liquid assets to other countries.[24] The illusion in the second case is that the new 'unseen hand'—the global marketplace—can be counted on to eventually generate an equilibrium which will locate each and every country, company and individual right where it, he or she belongs in the new world order. This may take time but, rest assured, 'interference' by governments in particular in these allegedly objective processes of restructuring will only muddle the process and postpone its beneficent outcomes.

The public and many of its representatives are now beginning to realize that virtually everything ordained by the neo-conservative agenda is either patently untrue, manifestly hypocritical, generative of severe contradictions, inconceivable as social, economic and political practice and/or dangerous in consequence *to the long term stability of capitalism itself*. This in addition to the threat this agenda poses to the public and social systems in which capitalism has been headquartered for the past century or more.[25] Everything depends on being able to act on the 'right' of capital mobility, using the sledgehammer of globalization as an allegedly objective and inexorable process beyond effective human control and direction to justify these policies. This is to occur while capital continues, and at the same time modifies in ways believed beneficial, established methods of value extraction and public capital co-optation using the traditional state-capital relationship as the fulcrum.[26] After all, it is on social

Press, 1999); Joel Nelson, *Post-industrial Capitalism: Exploring Economic Inequality in America* (Thousand Oaks, California: Sage Publications, 1995).

[24] See Richard McKenzie, *Quicksilver Capital: How the Rapid Movement of Capital has Changed the World* (New York: Free Press, 1991); and Storper, *op. cit.*

[25] Hicks, *op. cit.*

[26] Hay, *op. cit.*

stability and the continued, if not heightened, support of general publics through the electoral mechanism that capitalism appears to depend in its efforts to transform existing extractive and co-optative processes in the desired direction.

It is therefore to intermediary institutions and agencies that capitals and their supporters can be expected to (continue to) turn if they are to carry out the desired transformation successfully. Thus, capitals would rely on political parties, formal elections and the right to organize interest groups and lobby governments to sustain their leading position in the economies of capitalist democracies and, ideally, to improve it in the ways indicated. As Offe has argued, it is the opportunity (or 'right') to carry out precisely these activities that has made democracy 'safe' for capitalism.[27] The new or emerging situation in Western capitalist countries has modified this arrangement in a number of significant ways, however. First, there now exist not only parties of conservative restraint but liberal and social-democratic parties which support the neo-conservative agenda through their policies and programs. Second, capitals have been able to vastly extend, partly as a consequence of this and partly independent of it, their influence far beyond advertising and marketing to other elements of the mass media. This has been complemented by a more direct presence in all aspects of the educational process through privatization strategies and the parallel retreat of public authority.[28]

This means that while it continues to be necessary for capitals to make use of mediating structures and processes that possess both legal-rational and traditional legitimacy, the equation has been altered. This is partly a result of the heightened effort to persuade members of general publics that they are, after all, commonsense 'experts' in economics and finance. For this purpose, nothing will serve as well as mass media—particularly broadcasting—and the ongoing, if subtle, processes by which elementary and secondary public education, as well as community colleges and universities, are being privatized. Reaching people continuously, at an early age and intermittently

[27] Offe, 'Competitive Party Democracy and the Keynesian Welfare State: Factors of Stability and Disorganization', in Offe, *Contradictions of the Welfare State* and in *Policy Sciences*, Volume 15, No. 3 (April 1983).

[28] Wilson, *No Ivory Tower: the University under Siege* (Ottawa: Voyageur Publishing Co., 1999); Wilson, *Retreat from Governance: Canada and the Continental-International Challenge* (Hull: Voyageur Publishing Co., 1989).

thereafter long past retirement, creates and sustains the support of general publics who have internalized a set of ideas which now appear to be objectively 'correct', rather than gospel, doctrine, dogma or propaganda. To sincerely believe, as vast numbers in these countries now do, that neo-conservative policies and programs are the only solution is to acquiesce in the foreclosure, not only of the role of relevant past experience but of future possibilities for creative alternatives to the present.

If this seems inconsistent with earlier remarks about how capitals have retreated to the economy, narrowly defined, preparatory to (or as a springboard for) a concentrated effort to establish themselves globally, or supranationally and continentally, this is easily explained. Few matters are more important to the transformation that capitals in democratic countries wish to realize than the socialization of members of the general public on whom their ability to get the kinds of specific support they need depends. The general support that made those forms of extraction and co-optation possible in a less direct and intensive form under the earlier Keynesian consensus is no longer seen to be sufficient. *All* political parties, even those of a social-democratic persuasion, must acknowledge and support the neo-conservative agenda, and this result can only be realized by setting up and propagandizing members of general publics independent of their partisan political persuasion.[29] It has not been lost on capitals and their supporters that social-democratic parties are frequently *more* conservative than liberals on matters relating to collective morality and discipline, a point only too evident from the 'conversions' such parties and governments have undergone since the mid 1970's in many capitalist democracies.

It is the other side of Offe's argument concerning a reciprocal 'safety' arrangement between the institutions of capitalism and the institutions of democracy that is most instructive, however. For it is here that we realize how much the tacit arrangement, such as it was, has broken down almost completely—in spirit if not in reality. What makes capitalism safe for democracy, he argued, was mainly

[29] Hellinger and Judd, *op. cit.* David Croteau and William Hoynes, *The Business of Media: Corporate Media and the Public Interest* (Thousand Oaks, California: Pine Forge Press, 2001). Much of the support for a new left-wing party in Canada is a response by Federal NDP members to the enactment of neo-conservative policies by provincial NDP governments.

social welfare, social administration, regulation and an active public and social sector of services, benefits and programs generally.[30] The neo-conservative agenda has felt sufficiently emboldened to accelerate its efforts to make extraction and co-optation processes more direct and continuous. It has done this using capital sector institutions and agencies of government, while devastating or privatizing those functions specifically concerned with social welfare, regulation and public services. This indicates how free it feels from the kind of obligations and fears that motivated earlier generations of capitalists to accept as necessary, if not desirable, such activities and seek to make the best of them or turn them to their advantage.

In effect, capitals now feel sufficiently 'safe' for the reasons indicated that they are more than ready and willing to upend the real contract on which their relationship with the democratic nation-state has existed since at least 1945.[31] Having succeeded in bringing vast numbers of the general publics in many capitalist democracies 'on side', they can now use this agenda with its gospel of restraint in order to justify the collapse or devastation of the very agencies which once made capitalism safe for both democracy and society. Their command of, or substantial influence over, politicians, media figures and public and higher education boards has allowed capitals and their supporters to recast these agencies in the role of villains. Instead of making capitalism safe for democracy, publics are increasingly persuaded that it is precisely these agencies which make the Keynesian consensus unsafe not only for capitalism but for democracy and society as well![32] Implicit in this development is also the belief, carefully nurtured whenever it can serve the interests of capitals, that *representative democracy itself* is unsafe for capitalism to the extent that it favors parties who promise to spend on regulation and public and social services, benefits and programs!

Thus capitals will only support representative democracy where this (to them) unseemly competition to outspend one's opponents at

---

[30] Offe, *op. cit.*

[31] Wilson, *Bureaucratic Representation*, chapter 2, 5; Stephen Craig, *Broken Contract?: Changing relationships between Americans and Government* (Boulder, Colorado: Westview Press, 1996); Hicks, *op. cit.*; Kreml, *op. cit.*

[32] As, for example, in David Osborne and Ted Gaebler, *Reinventing Government: How the Entrepreneurial Spirit is Transforming America* (New York: Penguin/Plume, 1993, 1997). For a critical response, Wilson, 'The Downside of Downsizing', *op. cit.* and *Bureaucratic Representation* generally.

election time is suppressed in favor of a notion of social responsibility vastly different from the one that preceded it. A more direct and continuous extraction of value and co-optation of the public capital that it helps produce is thereby insured with this collapse and redefinition of what constitutes the proper relationship between capitalism, representative democracy and what is left of the Keynesian regulatory, public and social service state. Reliance on a fragmented system of representative democracy, organized on the basis of political parties converted to, if not originally espousing, the neo-conservative agenda, has been more than complemented by increased opportunities to co-opt state actors through active, agenda setting interest and lobby groups. Instead of a situation that constitutes little less than an economic and financial disaster on the verge of taking place, if not already in progress, we can now see a radically different scenario almost totally at variance with neo-conservative 'dire warnings' about the size and scope of government.

By sowing doubts in the public mind about the value of the public and social policies effected through the representative democratic process since World War II, they have cast public doubt on the process itself. The resulting public alienation and distrust now encompasses not just individual politicians, but political parties, campaigns and even the electoral process. No less important is the impact on public attitudes toward public and social *institutions*, particularly those agencies which capital now believes it can openly attack on grounds they are at the very least dispensable if not positively dangerous for the economic and financial health of the system.[33] Seen as a whole, this highly successful effort to upend and redefine capital-state-society relations constitutes nothing less than a direct take-over of the state apparatus, albeit with the acquiescence of consistent majorities and pluralities voting, however apathetic and however low their turnout. The purpose of this effort has been to guarantee a more direct and continuous relationship between value extraction and the co-optation of public capital. It has been carried out in such a way that only those government agencies which are thought to serve the interests and institutions of capital, rather than those of the public and society, will be left standing when the process is completed.

---

[33] Martin and Schumann, *op. cit.*; Paul Sniderman, *The Clash of Rights: Liberty, Equality and Legitimacy in Pluralist Democracies* (New Haven: Yale University Press, 1996); John Rohr, *To Run a Constitution: the Legitimacy of the Administrative State* (Lawrence, Kansas: University of Kansas Press, 1986).

Any attempt to account for this titanic sea change in the relationship between capitalism, democracy and society cannot ignore the longevity and continuity of those structures of government that serve capital's interests. They have been in existence at least as long as, and probably longer than, institutions of the public, including the regulatory system, and much longer than the social service infrastructure, most of which came into being only after 1930. Institutions representing the interests of capital came into being with the modern, secular state, and may well have been the raison d'etre justifying this state in its original form.[34] Add to this the fact that these structures have by now acquired increased legitimacy as a consequence of the impact of the neo-conservative agenda on public attitudes and governmental policy preferences. Popular sovereignty, expressed through party structures and electoral processes, has been turned against those who support policies which neo-conservatives and their supporters believe will increase deficits and the debt. These have now come to comprehend virtually all expenditures on regulation and on many public and social services, benefits and programs not perceived to be in their interests. They also include key sector interventions and (especially) initiatives in the areas of transportation, communications and energy, where the preferred response is one or another form of privatization strategy if not outright dismemberment.[35] It would appear from this recitation of events that capitalism's legitimacy could not possibly be more secure than it is today.

It is at this point that we come face to face with a matter of considerable importance to the question of capitalism's legitimacy in the context of popular sovereignty and the system of representative democracy that allegedly gives expression to it. While capitalism's legitimacy has no doubt increased in the public mind, at least for the moment, this legitimacy depends in a more direct and immediate way on public attitudes than has ever been the case before. Its hold on the public extends to political parties of all stripes who function as its agents in the running of governments under rules of representative democracy that are themselves being streamlined to speed up the passage of this agenda and to stifle opposition. While there

[34] See Wilson, *Bureaucratic Representation*, chapters 2, 5.

[35] Herschel Hardin, *Privatization Putsch* (Halifax: Institute for Research on Public Policy, 1989); Eliot Sclar, *You Don't Always Get What You Wanted: the Economics of Privatization* (New York: Cornell University Press, 2000).

is the promise of a full-fledged 'recovery' from our profligate and debt-ridden reality, capitalism's present legitimacy actually rests far less on proven 'performance' than it does on a fraudulent rendition of the present situation. In effect, capitalism's basis of legitimacy has shifted away from a combined traditional and legal-rational form toward one more directly dependent on the people, acting through their representative processes and elected officers, precisely because of the erosion of bureaucratic representation that its policies have brought about.[36]

On their own the people, in the absence of responsible mediating institutions, are a very unstable platform on which to base the institutional legitimacy of capitalism, particularly when its economic performance is so dependent on both the erosion of public and social institutions and continuing consumer spending. If chickens in fact do come home to roost, then the present effort to persuade publics that blame for economic and related difficulties lies elsewhere cannot go on forever. Indeed, the suspension of disbelief on which this entire process of deflecting blame has rested is already becoming shop-worn in a number of national state contexts. This justifies more skepticism on our part about capitalism's legitimacy under a neo-conservative agenda, if only because this agenda gives what is at best a false sense of stability and security to the process of social, economic and political transformation that we are witnessing today. It bears a striking similarity to what occurred with respect to public attitudes toward capitalism in North America and Western Europe in the 1920's. The longer-term consequences of this ongoing devastation of the regulatory, public and social service infrastructure have been seriously misunderstood and underestimated, in large part because of a refusal to attend to and learn from past history and experience.

This infrastructure and the functions it performs are not extraneous to the economies of capitalist democracies but elemental and essential to them. They are an integral part of the structure of these societies rather than a set of agencies tangential to them. Even if these agencies and bureaus appear to lack the institutional legitimacy that those elements of government and the public sector supportive of capitals possess, especially now, the basis of the latter's legitimacy

[36] Gough and Olofsson, *op. cit.*; Marquand, *op. cit.*; Hollingsworth and Boyer, *op. cit.*; Boswell and Peters, *op. cit.*; Nelson, *op. cit.*

is unstable, if not shaky in the extreme. This is in large part because of the de-stabilizing impact of neo-conservative policies themselves. The regulatory, public and social service infrastructure may lack institutional status relative to functions of government more supportive of capitalism like the legal system, but the range of functions it performs is just as essential to the success of capitalism as those agencies that promote and protect capitals directly.

Whatever the justification for this series of policy shifts and institutional transformations, neo-conservatives are making a serious mistake if they believe they can secure a more direct and continuous extraction of value and co-optation of public capital on a permanent basis by this combination of initiatives. There is no way that capitals can be allowed to revert to a narrow concept of the economy in this way, whether preparatory to going global, continental or supranational or for some other reason. The implicit contract that capitalism has made with democracy and society is not something that even majorities of the people themselves can terminate, as will be evident in the years to come. Public and social services, benefits and programs constitute essential functions for and in the total system, not extraneous activities that can come or go depending on ideology, dogma or gospel.[37] All that we know about functional interdependence in such systems tells us that one cannot devastate one set of activities in a given system without wreaking serious havoc on other parts of that system.

That capitalism's present claim to legitimacy, premised on its (and the public's) confidence in the neo-conservative agenda, is unstable at best is something that is even less apparent now that it has felt sufficiently confident to proclaim its preference for 'free trade' over 'industrial policy'. Yet this constitutes what only appears to be two extreme choices on the matter of the role of governments in the economy. This is because 'free trade' is itself an industrial policy, albeit one less explicit and less honest about the state-capital relationship than more active key sector, threshold firm approaches to

---

[37] This raises a theoretical question of what constitutes the appropriate 'unit of analysis' that is different from the concern for institutional embeddedness addressed by Hollingsworth and Boyer, *op. cit.* See especially Immanuel Wallerstein, *The Modern World System, Volume III* (New York: Academic Press, 1989); and most recently Terence Hopkins and Immanuel Wallerstein, with John Casparis, *The Age of Transition: Trajectory of the World System, 1945–2025* (London: Zed Books, 1997).

this relationship. It is the persistence of long established, even traditional, relationships and arrangements between the state and capital in all capitalist democracies which underscores the extent to which 'free trade' is no less a euphemism domestically than it is in international and global trade.[38] The only caveat to what is admittedly a skeptical view of free trade as an approach that favors *laissez (nous) faire* is the fact that the WTO, successor to the General Agreement on Tariffs and Trade (GATT), presently appears much more determined to enforce it. That it is attempting to do this in the face of mounting support for supranational trading blocs and multilateral trading arrangements suggests that these latter are as much defenses against free trade as anything else.

Having said this, it is nevertheless true that more explicit industrial policy approaches than 'free trade' itself have gone underground. No longer do capitals in Western countries assert publicly, as they did two decades ago, that the processes and mechanisms of representative democracy are an obstacle to efficient government and public and social administration that must be supplanted by speedier executive and technocratic systems of decision making.[39] In addition to this was the contention that in the absence of such institutional streamlining capitals would no longer be able to underwrite improvements in, or even the maintenance of, the social service system. This argument stressed the need to model the state and its apparatus of political and administrative decision making after the private sector firm since national states, following the lead of Japan in particular, were increasingly the relevant units competing in the new global economy. The clear anti-democratic overtones of such a proposal were only heightened in their impact by the fact that firms are not

[38] See Mark Rupert, *Ideologies of Globalization: Contending Visions of a New World Order* (London: Routledge, 2000); Colin Hines, *Localization: A Global Manifesto* (London: Earthscan, 2000); John Gray, *False Dawn: the Delusions of Global Capitalism* (New York: New Press, 1998); Douglas Irwin, *Against the Tide: an Intellectual History of Free Trade* (Princeton: Princeton University Press, 1996).

[39] See H.T. Wilson, 'The Quagmire of Industrial Policy', *The New World Economic Order*, edited by Tom Wesson (Toronto: Captus Press, 2001); Wilson, 'Industrial Strategy: Its Challenge to Social Policy in Canada', *Moral Expertise*, edited by C.D. MacNiven (London: Routledge, 1990); Wilson, 'Once Again: the Industrial Strategy Debate', *Atkinson Review of Canadian Studies*, Volume 2, No. 2 (1985), pp. 33–40; Wilson, 'Technocracy and Late Capitalist Society', *The State, Class and the Recession*, edited by Stewart Clegg, Paul Boreham and Geoff Dow (London: Croom Helm, 1983), pp. 152–238.

democracies, and do not purport to be. Publics and their leaders, it turns out, were being asked to choose between social and public services that allegedly required ever greater productivity and innovation to pay for them, and the processes and mechanisms of representative democracy, which allegedly impeded realization of these noble objectives.[40]

To be sure, the rudiments of the present preference for 'free trade', coupled with the determination to devastate the public and social sector, were plainly evident in the demand that the streamlined executive and technocratic processes that had been recommended function as *de facto* agents of capital. This in turn would allow the political and administrative apparatuses in question to function as vehicles of a more direct and continuous extraction and co-optation process than already existed. What made this apparatus cumbersome for capitals, however, was not just the pace at which it made and implemented decisions. It was rather *the decisions themselves*, and the bias which they continued to exhibit for public and social sector activities and functions which was the problem.[41] Even though capital was not yet sufficiently emboldened to embark upon the devastation that is now taking place, it was prepared to undertake a protracted propaganda war against deficits and the debt to this end. A process that is now well underway has taken less than three decades to get up and running to already significant results. Even in the face of the major and minor disasters which neo-conservatism has wrought, its doctrinal standing with the public and its representatives now appears to be virtually impregnable.

Again, however, this standing is as potentially unstable (if not more so) than legitimacy based on charismatic authority. Supporters of the neo-conservative agenda are running out of culprits, something that has already begun to test the public's patience, as noted. The fact that parties and governments supportive of this agenda have often failed to even stabilize the rate of growth of the deficit, forget decrease it, speaks volumes to the day of reckoning which can only be put off for so long. This is even true for the United States, the only country in the G8 to claim to have had a surplus. However, this claim consistently ignores consumer debt, trade deficits, serious infra-

[40] Wilson, 'Industrial Strategy: Its Challenge to Social Policy in Canada', *op. cit.*
[41] Wilson, 'Technocracy and Late Capitalist Society', *op. cit.*

structure problems in the key sectors of energy, transportation and communication and entitlement, health care and educational systems in grave need of upgrading and extension to vast segments of the American population.[42] This day will be a very different day to the one that neo-conservatives claim must be avoided at all costs. Their (alleged) concern for the warnings and threats of the WTO, IMF, key central banks and the bond rating companies has led them to engage in what amounts to largely *symbolic* action related to deficits and the debt, employing what is clearly an American technique for 'downsizing' and 'restructuring'. Blame public and social sector institutions instead of those agencies of government that are part of the capital sector. These latter agencies have been responsible for making and for backing up and securing bad loans made by financial and commercial institutions, while engaging in other activities which impugn the public interest in favor of private maximization, extraction and co-optation.

Institutional balance either already is, or soon will become, the major concern of general publics in Western capitalist democracies, and it is a concern that will not be put off much longer; neo-conservative policies have seen to that. This is why many capitals have already begun to distance themselves from the neo-conservative agenda, and why many more will soon begin to do so. The short term advantages they appear to have gained from streamlining state-capital relationships and arrangements so as to realize a more direct and continuous extraction of value and co-optation of public capital are already colliding with the bottom line they are always talking about. Capitalist democracies can only provide the illusion that they function as a household if a whole host of needs and interdependencies are taken into account and given pride of place in reality if not in theory. The problem here lies with the fact that the two dominant metaphors of the neo-conservative agenda, the nation-state as a household and the nation-state as a firm, are not only incompatible but irreconcilable. What has made it possible for the two to co-exist over the past twenty-five years of neo-conservative domination of the policy process is the largely unacknowledged reality and central role of

---

[42] See generally Gosta Esping-Andersen, *Social Foundations of Postindustrial Economies* (New York: Oxford University Press, 1999); Harry Shutt, *The Trouble with Capitalism: an Enquiry into the Causes of Global Economic Failure* (London: Zed Books, 1998); and Nelson, *op. cit.*

bureaucratic representation. Whether on purpose or by accident, the present devastation of public and social sector bureaucracies, alongside de-regulation, is making this representative function more and more difficult to carry out.[43] There are constructive ways to deal with debt and deficit problems which supporters of this agenda have consciously and unconsciously denied themselves because their real purpose has never been to reduce or eliminate deficits and the debt at all. The belief that maximization, extraction and co-optation processes can much longer be carried out under the present agenda without it becoming more than just an instance of wanton hypocrisy is one of the most necessary but consequential illusions of its supporters.

Their real goal, a state apparatus which is minimal to non-existent save in those areas which directly or indirectly serve the interests of capital, is not something that can or will be brought into being without evoking substantial resistance using the ballot box and related social and occupational means. More to the point, such a 'bare bones' state apparatus has never existed. Capitalism so defined and understood, is inconceivable, *more inconceivable than any other economic system*, in the absence of established state-capital relations of reciprocal dependence and interdependence and the public and social institutions that go with them. For better or worse the capitalist democratic societies we live in resemble (among other things) systems. The interdependence of functions which is the essence of such structures and processes includes public and social services, benefits and programs no less than it includes those agencies which serve capital as constituents of the present social system. They are an integral part of a total structure that is to be looked at and dealt with as a whole, as noted, not an intervening condition intruding on the structure from 'outside', as more scientistic models from the natural sciences presume.[44] The greater polarization of the class structure that is already evident will soon place bureaucratic representation and other non-electoral forms at the centre of the issue of capitalism's legitimacy in circumstances in which capitals will have no other choice but to turn against the neo-conservative agenda itself.

[43] See Wilson, 'The Downside of Downsizing', *op. cit.*; and *Bureaucratic Representation*.

[44] This tendency has been severely aggravated under neo conservatism, as is evident from Kingdom, *op. cit.* On wholes and intervening conditions in natural scientific thinking, see Quentin Gibson, *The Logic of Social Enquiry* (London: Routledge and Kegan Paul, 1960).

CHAPTER SIX

WHAT THE PEOPLE DO FOR CAPITALISM

In one sense, it may be appropriate to follow a chapter on the relationship between capitalism and democracy with one on what the people do for capitalism. In another, however, the intended focus of this chapter runs so contrary to neo-conservative conventional wisdom that it is almost bound to be misunderstood. Its concern to provide a more balanced assessment of the capital-state-society relationship must be clear, particularly in light of its intention to discuss state and societal structures which (allegedly) do and do not serve the interests of capitals, either directly or indirectly. Disentangling these structures, processes, mechanisms, instruments, arrangements and relationships in earlier chapters was intended to show how well they are embedded, to the point of providing institutional legitimacy and an indirect tie to principal legitimacy, or sovereignty.[1] An entirely different spin is put on popular sovereignty and the 'voice of the people' in putative democratic nation states that are also capitalist by the fact that so much has long been in place to support, promote and defend capitals and capitalism. Recent real and threatened abandonment of the implicit contract between capitalism and the people by adherents of the neo-conservative agenda only underscores the problem and the need to address the people's role constructively.[2]

Offe's analysis compels us to acknowledge the fact that capitalism in its emerging neo-conservative form is simply *no longer safe for either democracy or society*! Therefore, in a sense it is no longer safe *for itself*, given the extent to which capitalism and democracy have become intertwined over the past century or more.[3] An unmistakable threat to the legitimacy of capitalism itself arises out of precisely this imbalance between those state and societal institutions available to the people and those available to capitals. Yet it is supporters of the

[1] Hollingsworth and Boyer, *op. cit.*
[2] Lindblom, *op. cit.*; Craig, *op. cit.*; Dogan, *op. cit.*; Kittrie, *op. cit.*
[3] Offe, 'Competitive Party Democracy and the Welfare State', *op. cit.*; Offe, *Contradictions of the Welfare State.*

neo-conservative agenda both inside and outside governments and their capital sectors who are spearheading this process of institutional devastation. No matter how much money, power and status capital possessed, it would not be possible for it to succeed in this endeavor without the active assistance of political parties as well as general and special interest groups. These parties and groups are not only hostile to government and the public sector but to the people and the institutions that are supposed to represent them and express its will. That capitals are being seriously misled by those who support this agenda, whether inside or outside their ranks, is something which is becoming increasingly clear with every passing day.[4] By devastating the post-war public and social framework and representative processes in this way, neo-conservatism is threatening the stability of capitalism itself.

Supporters of this agenda argue that the return to a narrow conception of 'social responsibility' restricted to economic and financial 'rights' is necessary if capital is to compete effectively in the emerging global economy. This is perhaps the most self-serving and hypocritical neo-conservative claim of them all.[5] It simultaneously fails to acknowledge the dependence of capital on the people and *all* its institutions in a democracy while it participates in the fiction that the new economy will somehow supersede rather than continue to depend on the sovereign national state and its people. All of the talk about capital flows, instant transfers of assets, and continuous transactions and decisions, whatever its merits, cannot change this dependence and interdependence.[6] The need for constant attention to problems of headquartering, location analysis and the reality of different *cultures* of capital around the world is virtually given to capitalism by dint of its *greater* dependence on governments and the public sector than any

[4] Hicks, *op. cit.*; Boswell and Peters, *op. cit.* Compare Reisman's notion of 'social economy', *op. cit.* to Clark Everling, *Social Economy: the Logic of Capitalist Development* (London: Routledge, 1997), for a contrast between the containing role of traditional values as against the threat of unrealistic expectations in assessing the political legitimacy of neo-conservative governments.

[5] Harry Glasbeek, 'The Corporate Social Responsibility Movement: the Latest in Maginot Lines to Save Capitalism', *Dalhousie Law Journal* (1988), pp. 363–402; Glasbeek, 'Why Corporate Deviance is Not Treated as a Crime', *Osgoode Hall Law Journal*, Volume 22 (1984), pp. 393–439.

[6] David Smith, Dorothy Solinger and Stephen Topik (editors), *States and Sovereignty in the Global Economy* (New York: Routledge, 1999); Quack, Morgan and Whitley, *op. cit.*

other economic system before or since. By making itself unsafe for democracy and the people through adherence to neo-conservative dogma, capital and its supporters jeopardize its standing in these countries while helping to undermine the performance of its capitals.[7]

No matter how well socialized a democratic people is in the 'correct' methods of disputation and protest, there is another element which affirms the threat to capitals inherent in the emerging institutional imbalance sponsored by neo-conservatism. Devastation of employment opportunities that require an active state, coupled with the impending collapse of the social framework and capital flight to other nation-states with a better promise of value extraction (and future co-optation), creates the conditions for severe social instability and disorder in capitalist democracies themselves. This is no less consequential for the neo-conservative agenda than the problem of the heightened, and increasingly exponential, dependence of capitalism in these countries on massive, permanent consumer indebtedness.[8] Political and social scientists in the recent past may have presumed that social, political and legal controls, if not socialization itself, would be more than sufficient to contain, sublimate and redirect the frustrations arising out of 'temporary' economic downturns and other crises and emergencies in their societies. They could not, however, have predicted the *purposeful* creation of an institutional imbalance of such proportions, one that would thereafter be justified on the grounds of a narrowed public and social responsibility to the very people who have helped guarantee the success of capitalism.[9]

Suspension of support for even the most hard-headed, pragmatic justifications for sustaining the balance between various elements of the social, political, economic and financial infrastructure indicates how far away from the implicit contract between capitals and the people the neo-conservative agenda has moved. As an example, note the well-established view, now clearly in eclipse, which argued that

[7] *The World Competitiveness Reports* (Geneva: 1982–1996) consistently rank criteria of non-economic institutional stability (11 of 19) at least as highly as economic factors.

[8] See particularly Jurgen Habermas, *Legitimation Crisis* (Boston: Beacon Press, 1975), for his discussion of the definition of economic performance as 'delivering the goods' in a consumer driven economy.

[9] William Dierckxsens, *The Limits of Capitalism: An Approach to Globalization without Neo-Liberalism* (London: Zed Books, 2000); Douglas Dowd, *Capitalism and its Economics: A Critical History* (London: Pluto Press, 2000); Wilson, 'The Downside of Downsizing', *op. cit.*; Wilson, *Bureaucratic Representation*, chapter 2.

public participation, alongside compensatory public and social welfare institutions, was an organizational imperative for institutional balance in all capitalist societies. Even in the absence of any sense of extended social responsibility like one would expect to see in a nation-state that wished to call itself a 'household', a sustained defense of this balance was justified on grounds it was in capitalism's interest to provide a safety net for the negative social effects that go with the system's *proper* functioning.[10] Now that these systems are arguably *not* functioning well, with negative social effects outpacing positive ones, it would be reasonable to expect an *even greater concern* about the need for this safety net on capital's part. Instead we see a full-scale flight from this responsibility, punctuated by attempts to blame these very institutions for the present crisis of debt, deficits, *etc.* This flight is both literal and figurative, since capital mobility continues to occur alongside downsizing and other neo-conservative policies. It is capital's confidence that revolutionary or other disorder is unlikely, particularly in North America, which helps account for both forms of flight.[11]

Let us now shift from discussing what capitalism does and doesn't do for the people to what the people have done and continue to do, even under the present neo-conservative agenda, for capitalism. In what follows, a vast number of institutional, organizational, structural and process relationships, mainly, but not exclusively, of a formal nature, will be discussed. Many of these came into in existence with the origins of capitalism in the early modern period, while others have arisen in response to subsequent developments of the emerging and established capitalist system. Many elements of the putatively private sector have benefited, and continue to benefit, from arrangements and relationships that have been entered into by governments directly, with or without the active support of individual capitals. They are absolutely indispensable to the continued functioning of capitalism as a system within and between nation states. In representative democracies in particular, but in all national states where such arrangements and relationships exist, it is the people who not

---

[10] For an early study associating responsible citizenship, thus 'proper functioning', with political passivity, see Sidney Verba, *The Civic Culture* (Boston: Little, Brown, 1965) and the critique in H.T. Wilson, *Political Management: Redefining the Public Sphere* (Berlin and New York: Walter de Gruyter, 1984).

[11] Wilson, 'The Downside of Downsizing', *op. cit.*; Wilson, *Bureaucratic Representation.*

only are ultimately responsible for creating and sustaining them, but who directly and indirectly carry their costs. This constitutes the foundation of any claim that it is the extraction of value from labor by capital, and the subsequent co-optation of public capital through the successful or unsuccessful operation of these institutionalized arrangements and relationships, which defines the essential nature of this relationship between capitalism and the people.

Max Weber's analysis of capitalism using the technique of the ideal-typical construction, discussed earlier, provides what is perhaps the most effective way of comparing and contrasting capitalism as an ideal with capitalism in reality.[12] For it is only when we begin to disentangle what capitalism claims to be from what it actually is as a form of economic and social life that we are able to attend in a meaningful way to what it owes to the people. It is obligated to and responsible for the people of the nation-states where it is headquartered, influential, and variously effective because of the many ways in which the people, through state, governmental and public sector activities, as well as directly, support and sustain this system, now as before.[13] Having been delegated the function, *but also the responsibility*, for running much or most of the economy in representative democratic states, capitals cannot now view this one-sidedly as solely an opportunity to maximize their utilities, narrowly defined, using the cliches of the neo-conservative agenda to displace the blame to the people and away from the system's overall performance. The essence of the implicit contract between capitals and the people is its status as a reciprocal arrangement involving obligations in return for powers and rights of maximization, extraction and co-optation.[14]

The key elements of Weber's ideal-typical construct of 'capitalism' include the following: (1) open and unrestricted struggle between autonomous economic groups in the marketplace; (2) a money economy in which prices, capital costs and wages are dependent upon this struggle; (3) the total absence of all monopolies, whether established politically (mercantilism) or the result of voluntary concentrations;

[12] Weber, *Economy and Society*, Volume I, Part 1, chapters 1, 1A, chapters 2, 1–14, 22, 23, 24a, 25, 27, 30–36.

[13] Kreml, *op. cit.*; Glassman, *op. cit.*; Norris, *op. cit.*

[14] Compare Craig, *op. cit.* to Kittrie, *op. cit.* on their respective understandings of the 'contract', but see especially C.B. Macpherson, *The Rise and Fall of Economic Justice and Other Papers* (London: Oxford University Press, 1985).

(4) formally free labor and open contractual relations between entrepreneurs and laborers; (5) absolute expropriation of the workers from the means of production; (6) individual ownership of enterprises.[15] From this brief list one can simultaneously discern the major features that distinguish capitalism from all other forms of economic life while at the same time understanding how far away from this construct the actual system falls. To be sure, this is not only necessarily the case given the focus on central attributes in the ideal type, but also constitutes a contrast which indicates the emergence of a full-fledged system of mutual advantage for *both* capitals and the people. That the ideal type, however much a prescriptive ideal for many (but not Weber), probably never existed is more than balanced by the subsequent emergence of an implicit contract which only underscores mutuality and reciprocity.

The ideal type provides the key elements of a capitalism which would be incapable of functioning in any real world, now no less than in the past. This approach to analysis is not put forward as a one-sided indictment of capital, since the comparison and contrast between the construct and the highly embedded system of capitalism as a social, political and cultural, as well as an economic and financial, reality indicates progress for both sides.[16] Thus the people at different times and by different means were able to make gains through the emergence of public, regulatory and social institutions, unemployment, pension and social insurance guarantees and collective bargaining rights, powers and provisions. Similarly, capitals were able to use their economic influence and knowledge to leverage the process of governmental decision making, to mute much of the effectiveness of economic regulation and to deflect a consistent amount of public agitation and protest through the party system into relatively ineffective channels. Until recently we had what amounted to an implicit contract between capitals and the people, which Offe cites as evidence of a feeling of safety through the operation of mutually agreed upon and accepted institutional arrangements in a rough balance, if not an uneasy equipoise, with one another. These arrangements now comprehend three discrete, albeit overlapping, sets of

[15] This summary of Weber's ideal type of 'capitalism' is found in Edward Shils, 'Some Remarks on the Theory of Social and Economic Organization', *Economica* (February 1948), pp. 36–50.

[16] Hollingsworth and Boyer, *op. cit.*

institutions in the order of their longevity and status: the capital sector, the public sector and the social sector.[17]

Many things that the people do for capitalism have been done most recently in the expectation that this bargain or contract would be upheld and defended. It is not a question of a Hobbesian, or even a Lockeian, contract in which every signatory is a consciously rational individual agent who wills such an outcome, not just once but continuously. By bargain or contract is meant an implicit collective and historical arrangement and understanding over time in which capitals gradually come to acknowledge and accept the right of all three institutional systems to exist in the democratic nation states where they are headquartered, influential and effective.[18] This usage also addresses the fact of agency implicit in the operation of all successful capitalist democracies, that is, the capacity, and even the responsibility, to represent the people in concrete ways, including but not confined to the electoral, which bear directly and indirectly on their relationship with capitals.[19] Far from these three institutional systems being tangential to the reality of capitalist democracies today, they constitute central modes and processes of articulation between capitals and the people that are the very essence of this system and the key to its success or failure.

A useful way to begin the list of things that the people do for capitalism and individual capitals is to look at the relevant clauses and provisions of national state constitutions and founding acts. Such a starting point is supremely revealing inasmuch as it shows how fundamentally economic and financial in nature these documents, and the legislative authorizations coming out of them, were as a basis for the emerging (and in some cases already established) capital – nation state relationship. Whereas more recent interpretations of, and additions and deletions to, these documents have often been in support of the people, the original provisions clearly indicate the extent to which their *purpose*, and not simply their effect, was to establish

[17] Offe, 'Competitive Party Democracy and the Welfare State', *op. cit.* But see Wilson, 'Industrial Strategy: Its Implications for Social Policy in Canada', *op. cit.*; Wilson, 'The Downside of Downsizing', *op. cit.*; and Wilson, *Bureaucratic Representation*, chapters 2, 5–8 for discussion of the three key institutional sectors.

[18] See Jose Merquior, *Rousseau and Weber: Two Studies in the Theory of Legitimacy* (London: Routledge, 1980)

[19] Italo Pardo, *Morals of Legitimacy: Between Agency and System* (New York: Berghahn Books, 2000).

the capital – nation state relationship on a firm footing.[20] In the case of both Great Britain and the United States, two of the three states where modern capitalism originated, we are referring to documents which date from the Seventeenth and Eighteenth Centuries respectively. Having said this, the implicit contract already alluded to only came into being and realized formal acknowledgement in the period after 1929. The focus on an implicit contract is one way of making sense of the emergence over a 150–200 year period of capital, public and social institutions, as well as alterations in capital-state-society relationships brought about by these institutions. It also suggests that the people have been engaged, directly and through their agents, in a protracted effort to 'catch up' to capital by supporting the development of *complementary* institutions and modes of access to the nation-state apparatus since at least the early Nineteenth Century. This process of catch up, and its tie to institutional functions and sectors, becomes increasingly precarious given the relative ease with which funding can be, and is being, removed from those functions with less longevity and status, particularly in the social sector.[21]

The major vehicle in virtually all cases was the law, in whatever form its abstract principles could be utilized through the aegis of application, interpretation or review. Whether we are focusing on: constitutions and founding acts; legislative statutes at whatever jurisdictional level; metropolitan, municipal and local ordinances of urban governments; administrative, regulatory and bureaucratic rules, regulations and orders; or judicial interpretations of all of the above, it is the use of legal and judicial legitimacy, as Weber has argued, which led the way. Weber, however, went further (and correctly so), arguing that this particular basis of legitimacy, premised as it was on a unique mode of peculiarly Western rationality, required the extension, elaboration and intensification of this mode far beyond the legal and judicial system. In the event, it subsequently came to function as a justification for the emergence of bureaucracy and those other parts of the nation-state apparatus committed to or supportive of capitalism and capitals over the next century or more.[22] Indeed,

[20] One of the most prominent examples in scholarship of evidence for this is Charles Beard, *An Economic Interpretation of the Constitution of the United States* (New York: Free Press, 1965, 1935).

[21] Discussed in Wilson, *Bureaucratic Representation*, chapters 2, 5.

[22] See Vatro Murvar (editor), *The Theory of Liberty, Legitimacy and Power: New Directions*

Weber argued conclusively that this mode of rationality was one which capitalism, science and the nation-state's legal institutions shared, providing for many a ready-made explanation of why the resulting system had become so formidable.

It is this very formidability which serves to challenge all explanations based on power and force which fail to acknowledge, in the face of these prior arrangements, that the people and their agents were *nevertheless* able to make substantial inroads on the established capital-nation state relationship.[23] The only thing which can possibly explain this progress, such as it was, is mutual need and emerging dependence, in this case of capitals on the people as labor power and as a market for the consumption of goods and services. It has been a long journey toward the achievement of this tripartite institutional balance, alongside an acknowledgement of its central role in capitalist democracies, one that is on the verge of being dismantled by neo-conservatism with the conspicuous assistance of anti-public and anti-social sector political parties. The consequences of this regression to earlier, more traditional conceptions of capitalist practice must be obvious first from the fact that these formal arrangements were put in place in the period of early commercial, *pre-industrial* capitalism. The second and corollary point is that it is precisely the relative newness of the people's provisions, institutions, structures and processes, particularly in the social sector, which has made them so vulnerable to recent attacks by advocates and supporters of the neo-conservative agenda.

The major provisions of the United States *Constitution of 1787–88* and Canada's *British North America Act of 1867* which offer direct support and assistance to capital are those which guarantee the performance of the following functions by the national states in question: issue of currency and regulation of its value; determination of standards for weights and measures; regulation of commerce and trade with other nations, and between states or provinces; promotion of science and the useful arts, and provision for patents, copyrights and other proprietary rights therein; raising of money by any mode or system of taxation; incorporation of banks and issue of paper money;

in the Intellectual and Scientific Legacy of Max Weber (London: Routledge and Kegan Paul, 1985).

[23] See Robert Jackman, *Power Without Force: The Political Capacity of Nation States* (Ann Arbor: University of Michigan Press, 1993); Hicks, *op. cit.*

issue of bills of exchange and promissory notes; provision for bankruptcy and insolvency; and public works and undertakings. Complementing this are the civil and criminal law defenses of the right to private property and enforcement of contracts duly entered into. Note that these functions were split in different proportions between the states or provinces and the federal or confederal governments, reflecting the greater amount of power granted to central authority in Canada than in the United States eighty years earlier. Virtually all subsequent developments in support of capital are based on these original provisions.[24]

There is one set of functions which deserves to be cited on its own, even though it will be discussed in considerable detail in a subsequent chapter. I am referring to the provisions in both documents which relate to the public debt, the borrowing of money on the public credit and the 'full faith and credit' provisions guaranteeing the debts of earlier municipalities that had now become part of these new national states. It is important to note that these provisions took full account of borrowing requirements, often for purposes of war and military preparation, but for other reasons (e.g. 'key sector' public projects) as well, long before the 'public debt' became pejoratively associated with the public sector and social services.[25] Indeed, one of the most compelling conclusions any fair-minded person must reach from even the most casual perusal of these two founding documents is that a public debt was something that national states were expected to have from time to time. Far from being a curse, to be dealt with in the harsh ways that characterized the response to individual, household and company debt by capitals and the state acting on their behalf, the public debt was absolutely necessary, among other things, for infrastructure development and improvement. Since the arrangements and relationships sanctioned by provisions provid-

[24] *United States Constitution*, Article I, section 8; Article IV, section 1; Article VI; Amendment I, part 4 and all legislation, judicial decisions and administrative rules, regulations, decisions and orders in all jurisdictions pursuant. *The British North America Act*, a statute of the Westminster Parliament (1867) provides not dissimilar details and specifications. It was superseded in 1982 by the *Constitution Act of Canada*, which, however, includes all relevant economic and financial provisions of the original act, as well as subsequent legislation, judicial decisions, and administrative rules, regulations, decisions and orders pursuant.

[25] Donald Stabile and Jeffrey Cantor, *The Public Debt of the U.S.: An Historical Perspective, 1775–1990* (New York: Praeger, 1991).

ing for a public debt were directed almost uniformly to benefiting capital, there was rarely if ever anything like the present clamor over debts and deficits that we see today.[26]

National state assistance to capitals in and through such provisions reminds us once again of Aitken's point about the purposes of the national state in North America, as compared to Europe. Whereas in Europe its traditional purpose, in whatever form, had been to maintain and secure public order, in North America the state was also responsible for promoting economic development, however much the methods may have differed in each case cited.[27] By the late Nineteenth Century, if not sooner, this latter function became no less central to European (and Japanese) states than it already had become to the United States and Canada. By comparison to virtually every other case cited the United States is instructive in the way that it repudiated direct governmental initiatives following the defeat of the Federalists and the rise of Jefferson and his successors. Instead of this leading to limitations on capital's access to the state apparatus and the public purse, the Election of 1800 provided the basis for the most wide-ranging process of maximization, extraction and co-optation by capitals that the world had seen until the rise of the Japanese superstate after 1960.[28]

In the American case, it was only with the rise of manufacturing capitalism in the 1830's and 1840's, accompanied by urbanization and immigration, that overwhelming pressure to extend the franchise and provide for regulations and public services led to the emergence of public sector institutions. Alongside this was the equally important need to anticipate and quell any threat of social instability that might leave the North unprepared for the Civil War in the 1860's. American leaders were well aware, during their century of 'non entanglement' in the affairs of Europe between 1815 and 1914, that instability could and did generate disorder, even revolution. Northern

[26] See Kaushik Basu, *Capital, Investment and Development* (Oxford: Basil Blackwell, 1993); Kenneth Arrow and Michael Boskin (editors), *The Economics of Public Debt* (New York: St. Martins, 1988); Kaj Areskoug, *External Public Borrowing: Its Role in Economic Development* (New York: Praeger, 1969).

[27] Aitken, *op. cit.*

[28] Chandler, 'The U.S.: Idea of Enterprise', and other studies in *The Cambridge Economic History of Europe, Volume 7*, edited by Peter Mathias and Michael Postan (London: Cambridge University Press, 1978), pp. 70–133; Chandler, *The Visible Hand* (Cambridge, Mass.: Belknap Press, 1977).

cities in particular were susceptible to just such cataclysms because of the lack of public and social services and regulations.[29] Local and city governments and the states where they were located led the way in passing much of the needed legislation, whether by statute, ordinance, rule, regulation or order. Meantime this process of catching up was more than complemented in both the United States and Canada by state and provincial statutes legislating compulsory formal education, public works and libraries, and the tax provisions necessary to pay for them.

While economic interpretations of the reasons behind constitutions and founding acts have long been a light industry in both the United States and Canada, the intention here is not to imply any sort of conspiracy in either instance. The concern is rather to point out that emergent forces, in this case capital as the dominant factor of production over land and labor, be understood to have long relationships of dependence upon and interdependence with the national state almost from the very beginning. These relationships are improperly understood if they are reduced to mere conspiracy. What makes them formidable, today no less than 200 years ago, is the fact that they are the product of historical forces which render them appropriate to the form and level of economic and social development of the time, culture and circumstance.[30] It is only by reference to an assertion like this that one can argue that the subsequent emergence of public and social institutions constitutes a similarly historical process of development that the present regressive neo-conservative agenda ignores at its peril. Conspiracy theories imply an effort to interrupt the process of historical development with plans, designs *etc*., whereas the purpose here is to argue that *both* events confirm the existence and central role of such processes.

Refusing to endorse the notion of conspiracy when discussing the central role of economic and financial elites and their concerns in these two founding acts, as well as in others, is a way of resisting the tendency to reduce the reality of historical processes solely to conscious will and design. Weber's point about the concepts-in-practice of rationality that all modern Western institutions share in common

[29] This is discussed by Alexander de Tocqueville in *Democracy in America* (New York: Oxford University Press, 1947).

[30] Marx, as is often the case even today, put it best when he stated that 'men make history but not just as they like'.

would argue for precisely this focus on historical processes, however much it opposed his own analytical bias in favor of the reduction of collective activities to their individual action components. But Weber's methodological individualism, unlike that of Marx, is a research focus which, in clear contrast to psychological reductionism, treats collective and historical events as solely the result of individual actions.[31] The fact that psychological reductionism is so often favored by neo-conservatives and their supporters is directly related to their desire to disentangle capitalism as an institutional form of economic activity from individual capitals. This is done not only to highlight the personal, even heroic, aspect of (alleged) entrepreneurial and corporate activity, but in order to make a case for not confusing the beneficence of the system with the occasional appearance of the odd rotten apple in the barrel. Implicit in this bias toward reduction to the individual as a causal agent and hero is also the idea that capital is a factor of production completely autonomous and independent from labor, something which will be looked at critically and in greater detail in subsequent chapters.

For now it is necessary to argue against this technique of distinguishing individual capitals from the form of economic activity and development called capitalism. By so arguing, both the one-sidedly optimistic view of capitalism and the one-sidedly optimistic view of the price we must pay for its beneficence in the form of individuals who 'deviate' from the norm is set aside. In its place is put a deeper analysis of *rationality values* that find common cause across a vast range of political, legal, administrative, economic, financial and scientific-technological activities and institutions in the West after 1700. Seen in this light, the world-historical phenomenon of capitalism is incomprehensible in the absence of these other institutions and the legitimacy (or principal legitimacy) which they have since come to possess in the public mind.[32] At a superficial level, it may be sensible to distinguish individual capitals from capitalism using the arguments cited above, but at a deeper level it simply makes no sense. When it is seen from the historical and institutional perspective suggested, it

[31] See text and references to H.T. Wilson, 'The Sociology of Apocalypse', *Human Context*, Volume 8 (Fall 1975), pp. 274–294 for discussion of this and related issues in social research methods, concepts and frameworks.

[32] Wilson, *Tradition and Innovation*, chapters 4–6 on rationality as a supreme value in the West/North.

denies conspiratorial thinking and actions, and with it any 'cult of personality', and focuses instead on the mutual need, dependence and interdependence of these very institutions, including most prominently capitalism and the nation-state.

That the functions cited in the constitutional documents referred to are the basis for subsequent derived functions follows directly from the changing forms capitalism has taken in different nation-states over the past 200 years. It has been able to extend itself from one element in a largely pre-capitalist collective form concerned with the economy narrowly conceived to the perimeters of society, the new form of collective life created by capitalism in alliance with the state and its law.[33] This process of thoroughgoing legitimation has required it to become dependent on the very people (and their agents) whose needs it seeks variously to satisfy or influence while realizing system and individual goals over time and in competition or co-operation with other elements in given nation-state cultures. Capitalism, and the capitals who express its sense, focused on several overlapping yet distinct activities in their movement outward from a narrow conception of economy. Most prominent among these were: co-ordination with financial institutions, aided and abetted by the state; concentration and monopoly, thereby absorbing traditional notions of price competitiveness at the margin; vertical integration backwards and forwards, often absorbing primary producers in the first case and retailers and distributors in the second; conglomerate diversification, in order to move into other areas and reap tax benefits as a result; consumerism and advertising, creating what is in many respects the greatest challenge to its stability; and research and development, with serious long-term consequences for intellectual property rights, knowledge acquisition and its transmission and critical thought in these societies.[34]

To this list may be added the initial development and subsequent use of the influence system. It helped capital from the very beginning not only to secure special standing with and privileged access to the people's agents and the institutional apparatus of legal and representative democratic government. This access translated more

---

[33] Giovanni Arrighi, *The Long Twentieth Century: Money, Power and the Origins of Our Times* (London: Verso, 1994); Hollingsworth and Boyer, *op. cit.*

[34] See Wilson, *The American Ideology* (London: Routledge and Kegan Paul, 1977); and David Noble, *America by Design* (New York: Oxford University Press, 1977).

specifically into tax benefits, subsidies, contracts and subcontracts, and the opportunity to extend far beyond earlier practices the state's willingness to put its 'full faith and credit' on the line for its capitals, both domestically and internationally. To be sure, this was from the start understood to constitute part of a reciprocal bargain or understanding with capital, which could be expected to respond quickly and patriotically to the military, political and economic requirements of national state governments. This influence system might be direct or indirect in nature, or a combination of the two, allowing for direct elite occupancy of political or administrative positions, the capacity to influence those who did occupy these positions, or (more likely) both. Ironically, the most recent effort to directly influence *all phases* of the public education of children and teenagers, alongside a sustained attempt to penetrate post-secondary vocational, academic and professional education and training, is taking place while neo-conservatives withdraw from the post World War II implicit contract with the people.[35]

Looking at the original functions discovered in the U.S. constitution and in Canada's British North America Act, one can see how directly these documents were intended to serve the interests of capitals.[36] Issuance of money currency and regulation of its value is indispensable to profit maximization and labor extraction in any collective form based on the priority of exchange value to use value. A uniform system of weights and measures makes it possible for production, pricing and contracting to occur, first for the vehicles of subsequent production and only later for purposes of consumption. Regulation of commerce and trade within the nation-state and between it and others establishes the foundation for the defense and promotion of a nation's capitals so central to the state's permanent 'protectionist' function on their behalf, even (or rather especially) under conditions of alleged 'free trade'. Promotion of science and the useful arts is the basis for temporary individual and longer-term corporate 'property rights' in given inventions through the provision for

[35] Craig, *op. cit.*; Wilson, *No Ivory Tower*; Howard Buchbinder and Janice Newson, *The University Means Business* (Toronto: Garamond Press, 1988); Maude Barlow and Heather Robertson, *Class Warfare: the Assault on Canada's Schools* (Toronto: Key Porter Books, 1994); Heather Robertson, *No More Teachers, No More Books: the Commercialization of Canada's Schools* (Toronto: McClelland and Stewart, 1998).

[36] See reference # 24, this chapter.

patents, copyrights *etc.* The defense of these rights became subject to increasing pressure on legislatures by large corporations in many countries following the rise of monopoly capital in the United States and elsewhere in the mid to late Nineteenth Century.

The power to raise money by any mode or system of taxation whatsoever, while clearly a central indicator of nation-state sovereignty in the modern world, should not be seen solely, or even mainly, as a restriction on the maximizing, accumulating and investing opportunities of capitals. Direct and indirect influence over parties and leaders by capitals has almost always guaranteed that the tax burden would be carried disproportionately by the people. Even when this has not been as clearly the case as is normally true, there have been ways of either changing the balance back to a system more favorable to regressive forms of taxation or shifting the burden to other jurisdictions. Finally, even in the presence of a tax system that seems to favor progressive modes of taxation, there are numerous opportunities, from 'creative accounting' to tax abatements, breaks, and expenditures, to evade altogether or minimize taxation. The result is the present patchwork of exceptions, complemented by more positive opportunities for subsidies, contracts and subcontracts, all readily available, particularly for medium and large capitals, but for others as well.

Incorporation of banks and the issue of paper money, alongside the power to issue bills of exchange and promissory notes, is another major basis for the later-to-emerge structure of capitalism as an economic *cum* social system that Weber describes in such detail in *Economy and Society*. Weber's description and discussion of the key institutional elements of the capitalist system in Western nation-states, though written a century ago, still constitutes one of the best concentrated introductions to an understanding of capitalism in the Twentieth Century.[37] Weber attributes tremendous significance, like Marx before him, to the rise of a money economy, with all that this implies about the priority of exchange to use value and its institutional consequences for the public and social, as well as the private sector. Thus does specifically *economic* action as a form of rationality oriented to the maximization of utilities presuppose: media of exchange; provision for credit and debt; a potential and actual market in goods and

[37] Weber, *Economy and Society*, Volume I, *op. cit.*; Shils, *op. cit.*

services, first mainly for producers, later for consumers as well; formal capital accounting practices; the existence of protective and promotive regulation for banks, financial markets and other elements of this system, including the money supply; and competition between individual and corporate units under the guise of an autonomous price mechanism.

Fundamental and derived guarantees which fully or partially protect economic units (particularly corporations) against bankruptcy and insolvency are perhaps the least discussed elements of the national state system consciously intended to shift the burden away from capitals and their supporters and onto the backs of the people. The system of taxation in every capitalist nation-state reflects the permanent success of this transferral of responsibility, and is directly related to key elements of a country's 'public debt'. Either by dint of recoveries from national treasuries or through arrangements for credit, value is transferred first to private sector institutional debtors and only thereafter (if at all) to individual shareholders, investors, depositors and creditors. Businesses and industries are often encouraged to 'try again' on grounds that past misfortunes provide a constructive learning experience, however much this occurs mainly at the expense of individual (and only thereafter institutional) taxpayers. Banks, near banks, trust companies and savings and loans and related financial institutions shift the costs of their insolvency directly onto the people as taxpayers, albeit with repercussions for the cost and quality of products and services in allied markets.

Provisions supporting public works and related undertakings are central functions performed for capitals by the nation-state. Whether we are talking about strictly local and municipal services like water, sewage, garbage collection, maintenance of other public facilities for mainly private uses, police, public safety, traffic or public expenditures for the construction or generation of facilities which will provide more direct incentives to capital, these are correlated with what is clearly the most regressive tax found in any part of the tax system in capitalist countries—the real property tax. Even where this tax is supplemented by taxes to economic and large residential units, individual householders carry the major burden, given the success of residential capitals at avoiding market value assessments. At more-inclusive jurisdictional levels, the tax system may be less obviously regressive and discriminatory, but this fact is more than matched by the scope and scale of public works undertakings and incentives provided to capitals, whether domestic or international. The tax codes and schedules of the national and state/provincial governments in all capitalist democracies need to be continuously studied, particularly the form in which they are elaborated in subsequent legislation, judicial decisions and administrative rules, regulations, decisions and orders pursuant. These latter are key vehicles for the transfer and legitimation of additions to the so-called 'public debt'. Passage, interpretation and implementation of these instruments in the context of taxation is a dynamic process involving immense discretionary power, exercised mainly on behalf of large, corporate capitals by the capital sector of a country's civil service.[38] This clearly underscores the presence, and success, of continuous leverage provided to capitals as a consequence of their greater capacity to affect and make use of the influence system by addressing their needs, resources and capacities to the people's representatives and civil servants.

A fully institutionalized capitalist economic, and (more recently) political and social system possessing a taken-for-granted legitimacy in the eyes of the people for the reasons indicated may nevertheless appear relatively autonomous from political and public administrative bodies. This is precisely because of the successful socialization of mass populations through advertising, 'public relations', public education and mass media campaigns that publics have undergone. Most significant in this regard are shibboleths about 'the market', 'competitiveness', the 'private sector', 'free trade', 'protectionism', 'privatization' and the alleged *social* causes of the 'public debt'. One of the most important and necessary correctives to such shorthands for thought and reflection is the irrefutable fact that capitalism has institutionalized itself in ways that contradict its ground rules in almost every national state and international instance. Weber once again put the point most concisely, stating that 'the formation of cartel agreements, no matter how rational their basis in relation to the market system [they] may be, immediately diminishes the stimulus to accurate calculation on the basis of capital accounting, because calculation does not take place at all, or with a high degree of accuracy, in the absence of an objective need for it.'[39]

---

[38] See Wilson, *Bureaucratic Representation*, chapters 2, 5, 7, 8.

[39] Weber, *Economy and Society*, Volume I, Part 2, 12, 3 (3), p. 106. On successful socialization through mass media and the role of keywords, Gee, Hull and Lankshear, *op. cit.*; Clark and Dear, *op. cit.*

It would be disingenuous, however, to look at only the corporate side of the process of capitalist development, thereby ignoring the process of 'creative destruction' so central to Schumpeter's analysis, among others. Therefore, it will be necessary to also attend to the indispensable role that governments and the public sector perform on behalf of invention, entrepreneurship and small business.[40] Nothing has become clearer, given the *real* function of protecting private concentrations at the heart of most of the regulatory apparatus in capitalist countries, than the need for active and continuing *public* support for new business undertakings. These latter frequently utilize and rely upon capital and public sector institutions that are usually *not* particularly friendly to large corporate capitals, like agencies concerned about size, competitiveness and restraint of trade for instance. Thus is it necessary that the protective and promotive function of economic regulation on behalf of large established capitals be supplemented, and often complemented, by public support, incentives *etc.* for invention, entrepreneurship and small business. It is the threat that these latter undertakings pose to the technical core and economic sunk costs of large corporations which explains why they require unstinting public support through government. Only with this support can capitalism renew itself in the face of the desire of large corporations to buy these new and fledgling enterprises out, dismember them or drive them under.[41]

Having said this, it remains the case in all capitalist nation-states that the public bears the costs of these latter undertakings when they fail, while larger aggregates all-too-often reap the benefits when they succeed, usually through buy outs, mergers and other forms of partial or complete acquisition. In addition, it is necessary to note that the nation-state's support for invention, entrepreneurship and small business, with only a few exceptions, is mainly tied to *starting up* new

---

[40] Joseph Schumpeter, *Capitalism, Socialism and Democracy* (New York: Harper and Row, 1942); Schumpeter, *Business Cycles: A Theoretical, Historical and Statistical Analysis of the Capitalist Process* (New York: McGraw Hill, 1939); Wilson, *Tradition and Innovation*, chapters 2–5.

[41] For a theoretical treatment of the issue of size, market power and their relation to innovation, see Jane Jacobs, *The Economy of Cities* (New York: Random House, 1969). It is the alleged reality of all-embracing 'globalization', among other things, that has pushed this concern for the dynamics of entrepreneurship and small business creation off center stage for many economists, particularly in the United States.

undertakings, along with the practical knowledge needed to run the activity once started. Rarely are these individuals protected through the social system of benefits, services and programs like employees, managers and directors of large companies and members of craft and trade unions and occupational associations. This different level of treatment and protection is explained by the opportunities for access which allow established large capitals to influence and lobby, often successfully, legislative and governmental bodies. Nevertheless, it is important to cite those state functions supportive of entrepreneurs and small business persons because these individuals are publicly supported in direct and indirect ways, however meagre by comparison they are to what larger and more organized capitals receive. Citing these functions is also justified because they are essential to the renewal of capitalism as an activity made up of individual capitals, rather than solely a system comprised of firms and corporations in structural relationships to public authority.[42]

Capital and public sector assistance to entrepreneurs and small business persons can be distinguished by whether the offering or opportunity is financial or non-financial in nature. With the conspicuous exception of venture loans that provide equity financing alternatives for small and medium sized business, term loans or loan guarantees and loans to students to start up small businesses, virtually all assistance is of a non-financial nature. Examples in both federal and state or provincial jurisdictions include 'start up' or 'do it yourself' kits. These kits offer advice on how to: arrange financing, forecast and budget, analyze financial statements, assess the purchase of a small business, deal with problems of credit and collection, and cope with stress in business. There are also general management seminars that offer assistance with: business plans, social issues, government legislation, staff relations, marketing, financing, personnel and motivation. Other services available include help with strategic planning, including systematic analysis of the business and its markets and a fully documented action plan; and counselling services for entrepreneurs and small business persons, including training and individual counselling through one or another form of community business initiative. Calling these forms of support non-financial does

[42] See John Mueller, *Capitalism, Democracy and Ralph's Pretty Good Grocery* (Princeton: Princeton University Press, 1999).

not deny that there may be financial payoffs to these individuals for taking advantage of such non-financial forms of assistance. Nevertheless, virtually all their financing will have to be acquired from banks and allied institutions instead of the market at much higher rates of interest, security and chattel than that required of large and well-established capitals.

Although it is true that such undertakings are 'riskier' in each individual case than those entered into by established firms from business, industry, finance and commerce, they are far less risky when looked at on the basis of aggregate consequences. The *likelihood* of failure and the *number* of failures may be greater in the first case but *not the consequences of failure*, as the recent history of failed banks, multinational financial empires and mega projects and the U.S. savings and loan movement only underscores. Thus the implication that the public is being better protected by more stringent controls on financial assistance to inventors, entrepreneurs and small business persons needs to be taken with the proverbial grain of salt, to say the least.[43] The hidden costs of what is clearly a non-competitive, and frequently an anti-competitive, capitalist system within and between nation-states should give us pause. This is partly because compensatory, but also even promotional and protective, arrangements favoring established large aggregates with ties to the state system are responsible for costs that are either concealed internally or take the form of transfers. In addition, however, there are incalculable but nevertheless significant costs in the form of foregone opportunities to serve the public on the part of economic actors small enough and new enough to want to take the relationship between themselves and the people more seriously.

This suggests that it may be fallacious to base an analysis of risk on the number and likelihood of failures focusing on size, power and market share alone. Economic, financial and other forms of risk will usually be better distributed where inventors, entrepreneurs and small business persons are consciously preferred, other things being equal. Thus it should be solely to the business plan and related matters, alongside the area of enterprise contemplated (or already engaged

[43] See Peter Drucker, *Innovation and Entrepreneurship: Practice and Principles* (New York: Harper and Row, 1985); David Harvey, *The Urbanization of Capital* (Oxford: Blackwell, 1985).

in) that one should turn in assessing the value and potential value to society of a given venture. Low interest loans, combined with forgiveness whenever stated targets or goals are realized, would probably provide the people with a far better guarantee of the social responsibility of capitals because their differences would be accentuated and their power disaggregated. Distributing economic and financial risk would be more than matched by a parallel distribution and disaggregation of political power. It is only when economic and financial risk become too subject to decisions monopolized by large, corporate capitals that it is possible, and lucrative, to attempt to socialize the risk held by these enterprises. In the event, the risk will then be distributed to the people as taxpayers in a way that is less substantively fair either than was the case before or would be the case in a more disaggregated system of private sector activities.[44] The present concentration of institutional power and legitimacy that large, corporate capitals now believe justifies turning away from the implicit contract so central to the Keynesian consensus would be challenged by more capitals better distributed and more dependent on the people than at any time in recent memory.

Of course the last thing that established economic and financial aggregates in capitalist states want is a system which distributes risk to the public in a fairer way by disaggregating their power base and their tie to institutional status and legitimacy. As Weber, among many others, has pointed out, the effect, if not the purpose, of much economic activity is to mobilize non-economic means in order to restrict or crush competition, open markets and an independent price mechanism to the greatest extent possible. In the absence of an objective and performance based *need* for the highest formal rationality of capital accounting practices and allied capabilities, efficiency and effectiveness will be seriously compromised in the actual operation of firms and financial institutions.[45] Sharing in the institutional legit-

---

[44] See generally, Barbara Adam, Ulrich Beck and Joost van Loon (editors), *The Risk Society and Beyond: Critical Issues for Social Theory* (London: Sage Publications, 2000); Ulrich Beck, *Risk Society: Towards a New Modernity* (London: Sage Publications, 1992). On privatizations and their bias toward the acquisition of large public sector enterprises, Herschel Hardin, *Privatization Putsch* (Halifax: Institute for Research on Public Policy, 1989), chapters 8, 11, 13.

[45] See reference # 39, this chapter. For an analysis of the 'limits to rationality' literature in social, economic, political and administrative sciences, see H.T. Wilson, 'Rationality and Decision in Administrative Science', *Canadian Journal of Political Science*, Volume 6, No. 3 (June 1973), pp. 271–294.

imacy of the system in the way that large aggregates of concentrated capitals do simultaneously allows them to hide operating inefficiencies while carrying out significant internal transfers of cost to the people. In the U.S., 'Pentagon Capitalism' has made these observations more difficult to deny, but only because it constitutes the most blatant case in point available to the public.

Lobbying and pressure, coupled with internal ongoing linkages to the people's agents and civil servants, even in the absence of the present agenda, has permitted significant concentrated control not only of the legislature but of the enforcement or implementation processes of governments. This consultation and influence, frequently bought and paid for with one or another form of financial 'contribution', is more than complemented by specific benefits flowing from preferential subsidies, tax liens, forgiveness or expenditures and contracts and subcontracts (military or otherwise) with governments. No wonder that these concentrated economic and financial institutions have little incentive to do anything more than provide inventors, entrepreneurs and small business persons with just enough support to achieve initial success before being bought out. Incentives to engage in these activities are always conditioned, (and understandably) by the fear established capitals have always had of invention, innovation and product, process or service improvements which might threaten the sunk costs they already have in their businesses. Better to give these people just enough financing to put them in a position where their success will eventually lead them to 'see the light' and sell out to a larger and better financed company that can hedge or distribute the risk. The result is that elements of the new activity or idea that threaten the buyer's technical core or product mix are suppressed altogether while those that do not are appended to the existing structure in ways that compromise their long-term impact.[46]

Forms of business activity, particularly incorporation, are also major vehicles that allow economic actors to acquire institutional legitimacy in the eyes of the public. Their status as contracting parties is directly dependent on the legal existence that such instruments provide. These instruments have emerged and developed, and are now maintained and defended, at public expense. While it is true that associations, partnerships, and companies are instruments that are also available

[46] Jacobs, *op. cit.*

to organize economic activity on a legal basis, and do provide a form of protection to publics, the same cannot necessarily be said for incorporation as an instrument and the modern corporation as the result. The former arrangements are essential features of any capitalist system that supports inventors, entrepreneurs and small businesspersons, thus their reciprocal function. Incorporation, on the other hand, has been mainly responsible for the emergence of large economic and financial aggregates headquartered and highly influential in given national states, and often supremely forgetful about their implicit contract with the people in consequence of this power.

The legal status of an incorporated economic or financial entity is qualitatively different from all other forms of business activity in capitalist nation-states. Incorporation, among other things, provides the entity in question with the status of a 'person' in the law. Corporations, however, confirm this peculiar status by their access to guarantees that real people lack, namely existence in perpetuity based on the presumption of collective continuity and what amounts to only a very restricted and limited liability for debts and indebtedness.[47] Corporations are eligible for virtually all the benefits, services and perquisites that exist for inventors, entrepreneurs and small businesspersons while receiving a wide range of hidden and publicly acknowledged 'gifts' from the people. Many of these have already been noted in the recitation of key constitutional and founding act provisions, as well as in the discussion of powers which flow from the possession of institutional legitimacy and participation in principal legitimacy, or sovereignty. In the first case it is mainly protection from bankruptcy and insolvency that underscores the privileges which flow from incorporation. In the second, it is precisely the way that large corporate aggregates, thus protected, have used their power and status to *change the intention of* some of the provisions cited which is of particular significance.

These provisions include: regulation of commerce and trade with other nations, and between states or provinces; promotion of science and the useful arts and provision for patents, copyrights and other

---

[47] On the role of economic instruments like incorporation in the development of capitalist infrastructure, see Hernando de Soto, *The Mystery of Capital: Why Capitalism Triumphs in the West and Fails Everywhere Else* (New York: Basic Books, 2000).

proprietary rights therein; and raising of money by any mode or system of taxation. It is the way that these large aggregates have used their power and status to take control of the legislative definitions and administrative applications of these (and other) provisions in the ways indicated which is particularly important. Constitutions and founding acts did not, after all, formally acknowledge this power and status from the start. It had to be *won* through lobbying and other forms of sustained and long-term influence over the people's agents and civil servants. This can readily be seen from the way commerce and trade legislation has been tailored to the needs of large corporations, largely in response to these processes. As for promotion of science and the useful arts and provision for patents, copyrights and other proprietary rights therein, solitary inventors began to lose substantial proprietary and related protections to large corporations over a century ago. Since that time, science in its applied form has become an organized and complex corporate pursuit, one that requires employees to contract in advance that all discoveries, inventions and innovations are corporate rather than personal intellectual property. Corporate ability to minimize or evade altogether their tax responsibilities requires no further comment in light of the evidence readily to hand of what is often little less than institutionally legitimated criminal activity.[48]

Any attempt to discuss what the people do for capitalism must begin and end in the observation that this should not be considered as unique or peculiar a way of putting the matter as we might assume. That we do tend to think of the relationship between capitalism and the people in a way that focuses on what capitalism does for the people owes much to processes of secondary socialization and the media undergirded by long-standing dogma premised on the close tie between capitalism and democracy. In this case, it is the assumption that capitalism makes democracy possible rather than the reverse that has always tended to carry the day.[49] No doubt this bias has been given further aid and comfort by the collapse of the U.S.S.R. and the Warsaw Pact over a decade ago, on the assumption

[48] Glasbeek, 'Why Corporate Deviance is not Treated as a Crime', *op. cit.*; Linda McQuaig, *Behind Closed Doors* (Toronto: Viking, 1987).
[49] Lindblom, *op. cit.*, chapters 12–15.

that this was an economic collapse which 'proves' the superiority of capitalism to 'socialism'. Certainly this event has further emboldened capital, making it feel even more secure in its determination to undo the Keynesian consensus, with its concern for balance between capital, public and social institutions, in order to sunder the implicit contract between capital, the nation state and its people.

CHAPTER SEVEN

PROPERTY, CAPITAL AND SOCIETY

To the question: Is capital property? the tentative answer at this juncture is: Yes and no. What makes the question significant is the fact that we presume a basic power of disposition to go with the assertion that this or that is someone's property, that is, that they *own* it and therefore that it is *theirs*. One of the most important things that the people do for capitalism and capitalists in particular is to elevate to a *right*, and often even a basic right, the 'right' to property. The argument in what follows will not challenge this idea, but will rather underscore its conditional and contingent nature by addressing what it means to *need* the people and its governmental and political structures to assert, sustain and defend this 'right'. The point is that property is only a conditional and contingent right because it is a *privilege* first and foremost. Because it depends on the institutional structures, particularly legal and juridical institutions and processes, for its sense and meaning, it is a conditional and contingent right which emanates from a need which is acknowledged, but only once specific and general limits are similarly acknowledged. Because conditions, contingencies and limits attach to its expression as a need, it is a right that is ultimately based in privilege.[1]

Many defenders of capital have argued that it is one of the most basic of all rights and that its legitimate expression approaches an absolute right of disposition. They argue that it is essential and fundamental to the social and economic order that they prefer and they also assert that this is the best order possible, if not the best possible order or system. The response is that property cannot be anything more than a conditional, contingent and limited right and that, when it suits them, capitals readily acknowledge and accept this fact of collective life and living. Capitals know that our social order could not survive if *everyone* demanded an absolute right to property *and*

[1] G.W.F. Hegel, *Philosophy of Right* (London: Oxford University Press, 1967, 1825), nos. 44, 45; Lawrence Becker, *Property Rights: Philosophical Foundations* (London: Routledge and Kegan Paul, 1977).

acted on this demand.[2] They may even realize that no allegedly capitalist system could survive were more than ten or twelve percent of the citizenry active capitalists, in contrast to being either passive supporters of capital, neutrals or part of the 'peaceable opposition'. The right to property can never be more than conditional, contingent and limited because otherwise it could not possibly be available in the socially embedded form that it is to as many persons as it has been. Though called a right, it is a publicly acknowledged need which must be held in check by and through the very public and legal processes that make it private *because it is already social.*[3]

Though called a right, it is a socially embedded and defined need that must take the form of a privilege and be subjected to controls through the selfsame processes and mechanisms that give it meaning as such. The *form* which acknowledgement of this need takes is therefore a conditional, contingent and limited set of privileges to individuals, groups and corporate entities which is grounded in law and/or legislation.[4] A most important distinction arises out of the need to control, monitor and supervise the expression of this right—the distinction between its passive and its active expression. When it is argued that the sense of this right is to be discovered in what power of disposition is entailed in any given instance of its expression, we can immediately understand why it must be subjected to controls. Possession can then be seen to constitute the performance of a collective function to which a benefit in monetary or related form accrues. This can occur as a consequence of good and legal stewardship of a passive kind or by dint of acts of use and disposition which generate collective benefits alongside (or in place of) individual benefits.[5]

Property, and the issue of a possible right to it in whatever form, calls both the past and the future to mind, that is, ancestry and posterity. Alongside the reasons for its right of disposition being condi-

---

[2] Ernest Beaglehole, *Property: A Study in Social Psychology* (London: George Allen and Unwin, 1931).

[3] Emile Durkheim, *The Division of Labor in Society* (New York: Macmillan, 1952, 1902).

[4] David Levine, *Needs, Rights and the Market* (Boulder, Colorado: L. Rienner, 1988); John Commons, *The Legal Foundations of Capitalism* (Madison: University of Wisconsin Press, 1957).

[5] Virginia Held (editor), *Property, Profits and Economic Justice* (Belmont, California: Wadsworth Publishing, 1980).

tional, contingent and limited which arise out of our collective, now social, nature are those which emerge from recognition of our evolving, historical reality over time. In the latter case, we are compelled to take account not only of a limit on the social space available for the active expression of an alleged right to property, but this social space looked at in terms of where we came from and where we are headed. Social space and its limits seen in terms of the active expression of given rights at any given time addresses threats to social order and the need for its persistence whether as an unbridled good or as a necessary evil. Social space looked at vertically and historically, however, views the ties between past, present and future in terms of evolution and change as necessary features of human life.[6] In contrast to the law, we cannot bias present policies toward property solely or mainly toward the past. Instead, we must see possession as a tangible, substantial reality which confers limited *powers* as the expression of circumscribed rights, where by both powers and rights is understood a socially embedded, publicly legitimated privilege.

To ask what kind of right, power or privilege the so-called right to property entails is to ask for a definition of property. This in turn requires us to address the origins of the concept, however briefly. A property of anything is its substance, its substantiality in material terms. Since the property or substance of any thing is based in nature and only leaves nature in a conditional, contingent and limited sense because it has been abstracted by human beings through labor, property as a human, social institution, in whatever form, always retains this tie to and interdependence with nature.[7] The active expression of human animals showing their interdependence with nature even as they abstract substance from it for whatever purposes is labor. To the extent that they recognize this labor as necessary to themselves and to others it acquires value in consequence. Value in use is the originary basis of this recognition, even if it can only be known through a contrast with its opposite—value on/in exchange. We only recognize value in use as value when we see it abstracted and exchanged, either in kind or (far more likely) for money, yet in this

[6] See Charles Wilkinson, *American Indians, Time and the Law* (New Haven: Yale University Press, 1987) for an example of the cultural limits of the assumption that an ordered society requires private property.

[7] Aristotle, *Politics*, 1266a37–1267b9, in *Aristotle: Selections*, edited by W.D. Ross (New York: Charles Scribner's Sons, 1927). Compare to Hegel, *op. cit.* nos. 41–43.

realization lies the beginning of an understanding of where value really inheres and what it really means.[8]

Although property as substance always begins in nature and always retains this tie, its abstracted status has long been recognized to be 'private'. It is specifically private because it creates some value that must belong to the person who engaged in the labor. It is generally private by dint of the notion that there must be some institution of private property that is defended by other institutions in all cultures. Of course we know that the latter is not true because many cultures, now as before, either resist successfully or are wholly ignorant of the notion of property *per se*, as well as *private* property. The idea of property as a private possession in the specific sense is based upon the view that nature is a passive larder or storehouse which belongs to no one because it does not belong to anyone. Many claims to a right of private appropriation based on labor as the act of abstracting substance and material from nature so conceived, thereby creating value, rely on the notion of a primordial 'state of nature'. The dangers and/or inconveniences of this state or condition must be ordered and organized, thus subjected to human definitions and purposes.[9] The key issue, even accepting for the moment this lifeless conception of a nature that belongs to no one because it does not belong to anyone, is what this substance or property is *abstracted into*. Indeed, is it not already in what it is allegedly abstracted into as a consequence of having become the object of a human purpose?

Instead of addressing the fact that the state of nature is an historical fiction useful in the main for supporting one or another theory of society, politics, powers, rights or duties, let us focus on the collective nature of each human being engaged in this abstracting process. His or her 'human nature' is clearly the result of being both an animal and a human being, *thus a human animal*. One could presumably say the same thing about any other animal, that is, that it is both an animal and a particular type of animal in consequence. Two factors complicate this straightforward observation where human beings are concerned. First, it is one that is made by human beings about one another and (as far as we know) no other animal does

[8] Karl Marx, *Capital, Volume I* (New York: Modern Library, 1906), p. 227 and *supra*; Diane Elson, *Value: the Representation of Labor in Capitalism* (London: C.S.E. Books, 1979).

[9] John Locke, *Of Civil Government*, Book II, section 25.

this. Second, these are on the whole unpopular observations about human beings that most Westerners prefer to ignore or deny. Modern Western civilization is dominated intellectually and conceptually by assumptions about human beings that separate and distinguish us from an external nature the purposes of which are seen to be dependent on human definition. Only in this way is it possible to formulate (and justify) the idea of an autonomous human world (collectivity, society, culture) within which we live, act and function.

The collective, cultural, social and historical roots and wellsprings of human nature both in nature and among human animals in various types of collective formation requires us to predicate our history on an ongoing interaction with the rest of nature which thereby comes to include human social interaction as well. Nature is both a *primary* reference for human beings, thus the basis of the concepts in practice of labor and value looked at in terms of the history of the species as a *natural* history, and the key *secondary* reference given the collective, now social, nature of human beings. Their perceptions, observations and thoughts arise out of general and specific human circumstances that underscore our uniquely historical 'nature'.[10] Only under capitalism, which begins to take shape as a system in Sixteenth Century Europe, do we see that steady and continuous process of commodification of both external nature and human nature which expresses itself in the gradual supplanting of use values by exchange values. Land and labor, equivalent to nature and human nature in the above formulations, are gradually commodified as a consequence of the emergence of capitalism and capitals. This leads to, and fully justifies, the process whereby the relationship between land, labor and capital is reduced to 'factors of production', where one of these factors—capital—is definitive and controlling precisely because of its commitment to the priority of exchange over use values.[11]

The idea that a property right or power, however conditional, contingent and limited, inheres in the ownership and possession of capital becomes even more problematic than the claim to property *per se* because of capital's greater fluidity, convertibility and mobility.[12]

[10] H.T. Wilson, *Marx's Critical/Dialectical Procedure* (London: Routledge, 1991).

[11] Marx, *op. cit.* pp. 41–96; Wilson, 'Time, Space and Value', *Time and Society*, Volume 8, No. 1 (March 1999), pp. 161–181.

[12] E.K. Hunt, *Property and Prophets: the Evolution of Economic Institutions and Ideologies*, 6th edition (New York: Harper Collins, 1990).

Human beings of many or most religions and cultural backgrounds have distinguished themselves from the rest of nature, and may even, in the case of the Western religions, believed they were outside 'nature' altogether. Yet it is only with the emergence of the world capitalist system beginning in Sixteenth Century Europe that nature came to be seen as an entity external to human being and as the basis of a specifically human project of continuous transformation. This project was justified initially by religious auspices, and thereafter by secular ones.[13] From a residual vision of land as a key element in human life that *might* be conceived of in terms of what it could be if subjected to transformation comes a religiously, then secularly, legitimated commitment to commodification which justifies the very existence of such land by reference to its potential viewed as raw material awaiting human intervention. The extension to human beings of this belief that potentiality is more important than actuality adds labor to land as the two factors of production which can only succeed in this project of transformation if subjected to, and directed by, the third—capital.[14]

It is as a result of this largely successful effort to redefine the meaning and proper purpose of nature and human being between 1600 and 1850 that capitalism realized its earliest legitimacy. Alongside support for one or another transformation from the newly organized national states where capitals found themselves went the central role of religious and moral teaching. From the very beginning this proved indispensable to organizing the labor power needed to carry out the projects jointly or individually contemplated by capitals and the secular authority. Because property was *already* recognized by the secular authority as a right or power which derived automatically from the recognition and acceptance of all forms of authority by the people, it became available to capital as a basis for its legitimation and a justification of its rights and powers.[15] At the same time, it now became *necessary* for capitals to attempt to extend this property right from land, humanly produced artefacts and wealth in money to the object of the commodification process itself—capital as the product of commerce, trade and production for exchange. Money, long impor-

[13] Max Weber, *The Protestant Ethic and the Spirit of Capitalism* (New York: Charles Scribner's Sons, 1952).

[14] Herbert Marcuse, *One Dimensional Man* (Boston: Beacon Press, 1964).

[15] Marx, *op. cit.* Part VIII.

tant as an intermediary between objects and their uses, became the key element in this effort. If money was part of a person's property and if a right or power of whatever kind inhered in its possession, then the result of its augmentation by any and all legal or customary means would also belong to this person.[16]

It is of the greatest significance that capitals successfully secured the legitimation of capital and its accumulation and investment prior to the emergence of representative democracy and subsequent efforts at 'catch up' which ultimately led to the emergence of public and social institutions alongside those belonging (or loyal) to capital. The fact that capital institutions have been in place for so long underscores the importance of later efforts to subject them, and the process of accumulation and investment which they legitimize, to controls at the same time that it explains why this process has rarely been very successful.[17] For both the secular authority, and later on the people, believed that they *needed* capitals and capitalism for a whole host of reasons which served to deflect criticism from the human and natural consequences of even the *proper* functioning of this emergent system. This belief was clearly more difficult to sustain during periods of contraction of the economy, particularly once the system's growth had necessitated interventions in more and more areas of collective life. Nevertheless, the combination of national state authorities dependent upon or interdependent with capitals, religious and moral teaching and the occasional foreign war was always sufficient to keep these societies committed to the project.[18]

An important, yet rarely acknowledged, point was the fact that over time and generations people gradually *forgot* that any other way of collective life and living had existed or could be viable. Though vestigial elements and remnants of past collective forms could be found even in those societies with economies and states most committed to capitalism, these forms could not compete with the doctrines of religious, moral and (more recently) civic teaching. The combined impact of these teachings has since come to constitute the most sustained process of 'socialization' the world has ever seen.

---

[16] *Ibid.*, Part II and *supra.*

[17] C.B. Macpherson, *Democratic Theory: Essays in Retrieval* (London: Oxford University Press, 1973); Wilson, 'The Downside of Downsizing', *op. cit.*; and *Bureaucratic Representation*, chapter 2.

[18] Weber, *op. cit.*; Hunt, *op. cit.*

Instead, vestigial forms and practices became quaint reminders of a time and circumstance we had (mercifully) progressed beyond. The accumulating total impact of capitalism's influence on the state, and thereafter on the unique collective form called 'society' which both it and the state had no choice but to bring into being, annihilated in the most effective possible way the people's capacity to envision the sense and viability of past collective forms, and with it the ability to conceive of realistic and desirable alternatives to the capitalist nation-state and its emerging world system.[19]

But there is another basis for justifying the inclusion of capital and the results of its accumulation and investment in a definition of one's property and the rights which accompany it, besides historical and temporal priority. It is the fact that capitals continue to be dependent on land, human artefacts and wealth in money in order to generate and sustain this allegedly self-augmenting entity. Thus, for example, real property in land, whether for the purpose of extracting some mineral resource or for its future 'development' after 'clearance' (or both), alongside the artefacts and facilities ('capital stock') to carry this out and the money to pay laborers to do the work required, all constitute property and require protection as well as legitimation. This becomes even more significant once technological discoveries like steam power make industrialization, with its massive capital stock requirements, feasible as a basis for the subsequent emergence of the manufacturing firm in the late Eighteenth Century. The emergence of firms redefines fundamentally what was understood to constitute 'the market' under conditions of simple (or relatively simple) exchange.[20] In the event, capital finds itself, if anything, *more* in need of ongoing legitimation, complemented by state and legal-juridical protection, than ever before.

A third basis for justifying the view that capital is private property is more complicated, because it depends on the claim to self-sufficiency on the part of the end product of capitalism's massive transformation project. By end product is meant the urban, secular, industrial-capitalistic, technological-scientific and highly organized

[19] Storper, *op. cit.*; Wallerstein, *The Modern World System, Volume II* (New York: Academic Press, 1980).

[20] Chandler, *Strategy and Structure: Chapters in the History of the Industrial Enterprise*; Chandler, 'The U.S.: Idea of Enterprise', *op. cit.*; R.H. Coase, 'The Nature of the Firm', *Economica*, Volume 4 (1937), pp. 386–405.

human world of the past century. In one sense, it is clear that the inclusive reality of this world has encouraged in us a supreme forgetfulness about relationships with and ties to nature that borders on, when it is not the active expression of, a thoroughgoing alienation. This in turn has inspired an even greater tendency to treat our relationships *within* this human world as essentially self-contained and independent of nature than was the case during earlier periods of capitalist development within and between nation-states in the West. It is this forgetfulness and subsequent alienation which sustains a view of human social and economic relations as autonomous transactions within this human world which can be captured both temporally and spatially through contracts and other legal instruments.[21] Contracts in particular are central elements in redefining the relationship between human beings because they establish relationships based on the expectation or requirement that a particular task will be performed, process honored or objective realized under given conditions and circumstances.

This aspect of contracts is highly significant not only for the notion of a right of property in the general or specific senses cited, but for the idea of capital as the private property of its owner or user. By severing the human world from external nature in the ways suggested, the capitalist process of world transformation establishes a basis for the view that contractual and related forms of legal transaction can be begun, carried out and concluded in a way that is similarly independent and autonomous. Because these relationships are alleged to be bound both spatially and temporally, and are the ongoing product of beginnings and endings with mutual obligations entered into and carried out in between, they are understood to establish and sustain property rights. These property rights are assumed to be self-contained in the sense that they are independent both of the rest of society and of the human being-external nature relationship.[22] Capital benefits immensely from this two phase (yet ongoing) process of severing off humanity from the rest of nature preparatory to establishing discrete human relations, expectations and obligations which are temporally and spatially bound and allegedly independent

[21] See Wilson, *Marx's Critical/Dialectical Procedure*, pp. 35–37; and Carol Gould, *Marx's Social Ontology* (Cambridge, Mass.: MIT Press, 1978), chapters 2, 3.

[22] Henri Lefebvre, *The Survival of Capitalism: Reproduction and the Relations of Production* (London: Alison and Busby, 1976).

of both the rest of society and nature as a consequence.[23] This is even more true in an age of virtually instantaneous transactions than it was in the past, or recent past.

A property right in capital is thus tied to presumptions involving (and legally defended on the basis of) not only the autonomy and independence of these allegedly discrete and distinct transactions, seen from both a spatial and a temporal perspective, but *finality* as well. Finality is the essential ingredient of what is in truth a metaphysical process of justification for the private appropriation of and subsequent control of capital as property. Finality is treated as a natural process which is automatic and indiscriminate, in nature no less than in society, when it is actually the basis of a tremendous power of discretion on the part of anyone able to both will such finality and enforce it. The idea of the human world as an ongoing process of interactions punctuated, and effectively dominated, by such artificially isolated beginnings and endings is what underwrites the idea of property as private and capital as property. No back referencing to the rest of society, and certainly none back to external nature, are seen to be required in the circumstances.[24] Human institutions determining what in any time and circumstance constitute legitimate possession and the powers or rights that go with it are *defined* as independent and autonomous, and that is (at least for the moment) the end of the matter.

The line of argument pursued thus far may appear to be defending a backward reference to external nature as a way to assert some modified version of the social contract as a real historical (or prehistorical) event that allegedly took us out of nature and into society. Nothing could be further from the truth. Its concern is rather to attend to the *present and emerging reality* by focusing on our unavoidable and continuing connection to nature, holistically conceived, and to collectivity, understood historically as the essence of our nature as human animals within nature. We could not even begin to abstract ourselves out of nature in our thinking until we possessed the concept of nature, defined as something that exists independently of and apart from us. We could not even predicate an autonomous or semi-

[23] See J.R. Hicks, *Capital and Time* (Oxford: Clarendon Press, 1973).

[24] Marx, *Grundrisse* (Harmondsworth, U.K.: Penguin/Pelican, 1973), Introduction (3), 'The Method of Political Economy', pp. 100–108; and Wilson, *Marx's Critical/Dialectical Procedure*, chapters 1–3, 5.

autonomous sphere of private rights until we had separated individuals out from the collectivity and made the human being that resulted from this notion a 'person'. In both cases, the first immediate and the second derived, we had to presume that nature, so understood, could be looked at as a residual entity which, as noted, belonged to no one because it did not belong to anyone.[25] It is this assumption which is the basis for the most vociferous assertions of a natural right to private property in all its guises, including the form of capital.[26]

The best way to address the sense of such an assumption is to focus on the second part of the premise as the presupposition for rather than the consequence of the first part. Thus, it is the idea that there must be a 'someone' with an individual possibility (if not right) of private appropriation of all of nature, and that this is the *only* sensible understanding of ownership, possession and control. It is this assumption which then becomes the basis for the conclusion that, since there is not, then the only alternative is that nature belongs to no one. Private, individual appropriation becomes not just the baseline standard for appropriation *per se*; it becomes the only option to the ownership of no one as a consequence. From a collective, now societal, perspective, this clearly presents difficulties, not because the 'correct' answer is that everyone really 'owns' nature after all, but because the notion of ownership, possession and control *per se* is thoroughly inappropriate in the circumstances. This is because particular powers and rights, *without any corresponding duties and responsibilities*, are seen to follow from such ownership.[27] From a societal perspective, it may appear obvious that collective ownership follows logically from an attack on a private right of appropriation of each individual. But this really only tells us that the thought process employed in this exercise is incomplete because these are not the only alternatives.

In the event, it is collectivity and historicity themselves which justify the claim that human beings have responsibilities as part of nature for the use that they put nature to as a species specific animal

[25] Hegel, *op. cit.*, discussion of 'personality' and 'individuality' for example, but particularly his view of nature as, among other things, a 'mere thought determination'.

[26] See C.B. Macpherson (editor), *Property: Mainstream and Critical Positions* (Toronto: University of Toronto Press, 1982).

[27] Compare to Wilkinson, *op. cit.*

with needs, desires, powers and the capacity to think, reason and reflect. The only way that labor can be employed as a defense of the right of private appropriation is as a basis for a responsible stewardship as a member of the human collectivity and the natural whole.[28] But this does not mean, or even imply, 'collective' ownership. Here, once again, we see the difficulties inherent in reasoning using allegedly self-contained premises, however logical it may seem to engage in such a process. For it turns out to be the premise which allegedly follows from one that is assumed to be prior which is really *substantively* determinative. Individual appropriation *of necessity* presupposes stewardship on behalf of and as a member of the collectivity, which in turn presupposes a prior and more concrete (rather than abstract) membership in the natural whole. This means first that individual appropriation cannot be 'private' and second that the 'social responsibility' which is entailed is derived from a prior membership in nature. Contrasting individual with private appropriation in this way effectively underscores the opposition between collectivity as a concrete whole prior in all ways to its individuals and collectivity as an aggregation of (allegedly) concrete individuals who are prior to this whole.[29]

Recognition of the existence of individual human beings, far from constituting a justification for private appropriation, opposes this precisely on the basis of the social and historical reference of individuality and 'personhood' itself. This in turn compels us to move 'backwards' toward the most concrete reference of all, the reference of nature and our membership therein. It is the basis for any claim we may wish (or need) to make within nature which addresses the secondary priority and concreteness of collectivity, not to the individual but to an all-inclusive nature. It is thus the reality of the most concrete form of membership—membership in nature—that makes it possible for us to see the derived sense of priority and concreteness within nature of collectivity and society as a basis for the only sense that individuality and 'personhood' can make.[30] Instead of being

[28] Clarence Glacken, 'Man against Nature: an Outmoded Concept', *The Environmental Crisis*, edited by Harold Helfrich (New Haven: Yale University Press, 1970), pp. 127–142.

[29] Marx, *Capital, Volume I*, pp. 197–206 and Part VIII.

[30] This only appears to be at variance with Marx's observation in *Grundrisse* that society is the supposition, the point of departure for inquiry, since it is precisely reflection as an active function given this supposition that sees the centrality of our

elided into the private as a basis for a defense of the private appropriation of either nature or human nature, individualism can be used to justify the extraction of value *from both* only if it presupposes a responsible stewardship as a member of both nature and society.[31] This requires us to look more carefully at abstraction and concretion as they are presently understood.

The belief in concrete particulars (parts) and of 'abstract' generalities is the basis for the notion that human collectivities, as well as nature itself, is an abstraction. Since collectivities and nature are more abstract than particular concrete objects, subjects *etc.*, it is assumed that the only claim to being wholes which these abstractions can make requires us to see them as aggregates of these allegedly concrete parts. Sociology since Durkheim has made it possible for us to go further, so that we are now able to acknowledge that the resulting aggregations of particulars may be 'more than the sum of their parts'. Even here, however, one is required to acknowledge that the 'more than' is abstract while the parts remain concrete, however incompletely they allow us to describe collective, now social, institutions and processes. One can readily see in this set of assumptions and beliefs the basis of a notion of individualism that equates it with the private, and in particular with the private appropriation of property and capital. That it constitutes the metaphysical and epistemological foundation of the modern and contemporary capitalist world-view is something that should not go unnoticed either.[32]

Here it is less the distinction between idealism and materialism than the distinction between atomism and essentialism that has proven definitive. Virtually the entire foundation of modern Western thought as the basis, justification and legitimation of subsequent (and ongoing) practices in capitalist nation-states (Japan and the East excepted) lies in acquiescence to an atomistic, and only collaterally to an idealist, world view.[33] Thus individuals, far from being first and foremost members of the human collectivity with its originary membership in nature, conceived as holistically prior in both a historical and a phenomenological sense, are assumed to constitute self-contained units

membership in nature as something not restricted to a passive 'looking backward'. See Wilson, *Marx's Critical/Dialectical Procedure*, chapters 1–3.

[31] Marx, *Capital, Volume I*, Parts I–III; Elson, *op. cit.*

[32] Wilson, *Marx's Critical/Dialectical Procedure*, chapters 4, 5, 7.

[33] *Ibid.* pp. 93–107.

in physical space without ties to anyone or anything, even their families. Feminism, understandably, has for the most part accepted such individualism with few modifications, because its social and political platform requires it to bring women into an equal partnership with men *in the present system* before attempting anything else. Think, for example, of what it means for a man and woman to say that they have decided to 'have a family', when each is largely what they are because they are already gendered and familied.[34]

What is there in this ahistorical and often asocial (or anti-social) conception which permits it to have the kind of power and influence over our common sense which it does. In large part, it expresses a bias toward futuristic thinking, combined with an understandable tendency to take both nature and society completely for granted because of an apparent (but unreal and false) isolation and insulation from both. Labor, work and action, in consequence, are seen as activities carried out by individuals or persons who understand themselves to be socially embedded only in the most immediate (e.g. abstract) sense, that is, as a member of some work or task group and/or some organized hierarchical or collegial structure. Even when social, political and environmental problems confront us, we do not see them in ways that fundamentally affect our sense of self in a late capitalist culture. They are too 'remote', too diffuse and unfocussed, to be taken seriously given the massive economic, political and social infrastructure which *predefines* our sense of individuality and personhood, while shunting our continuing membership in nature and humanity into what is at best a residual recognition.

An atomistic conception of human beings in nature and in humanity is thoroughly grounded in a view of cause and effect which gives it pride of place to what are claimed to constitute non-causal, therefore inferior, forms of explanation and understanding. 'Cause' is solely or mainly the product of atoms in collision, and the event-sequences which these collisions create are understood to be the temporary resultants of this activity. This supports a view of structural and process wholes as unstable, shifting and evanescent relative to the more concrete atomic particulars. At the same time, this view of the particulars resists any focus that would see them either as

[34] H.T. Wilson, *Sex and Gender: Making Cultural Sense of Civilization* (Leiden: Brill, 1989), pp. 46–71.

wholes of smaller particulars or as entities which have internal elements and structures that may explain both *how* they collide with others and what the result of such collisions so understood *means*. As it turns out, atomism privileges a conception of cause and effect which focuses on immediate and proximate event-sequences, thereby bounding the field of 'correct' explanation both spatially and temporally, while depicting other allegedly non-causal forms of explanation as 'deviations' from the correct, because more allegedly concrete, form.[35]

What does this conception more clearly resemble than the bias toward immediacy, proximity, spatial and temporal bounding and finality so central to the concept (and practice) of contracts as prescribed and ongoing transactions already discussed? Explanatory modes which since Aristotle have been understood to be causal in nature are relegated to an inferior position precisely because (and to the extent that) they assume that *more* must be included *inside* operative notions of what constitutes a coherent structure than atomism can or will permit. A major reason for favoring reduction to what are alleged to be the basic atomic constituents in both nature and society is to be discovered in the implications a wider and more comprehensive notion of structure has for finality, termination, completion. For if it can be argued that reduction to what are claimed to be the basic elements of a given whole is arbitrary, even ideological, then the focus on transactions, so central to the atomistic and economistic view of society and nature, can be revealed for what it is.[36] But how does this tie in with earlier remarks regarding the more recent impact of the firm and of sociology?

One answer is that while the firm has required a reassessment of the relationship between parts and wholes, individuals and groups by its impact on the market and consequent transformation of simple exchange, the economistic paradigm of cause and effect, it has not altered the atomistic conception of the concrete and the abstract.[37] As an example, note the world-historically significant development

[35] Max Weber, *Economy and Society*, Volume I, Part 1, chapter 1, I A, 3, p. 6. Aristotle discusses his four types of cause in Ross, *op. cit.* pp. 49–52, 56–63. On atomism and cause and effect, Wilson, *Marx's Critical/Dialectical Procedure*, chapter 5.

[36] Marx, *Grundrisse*, pp. 100–108.

[37] Wilson, *Marx's Critical/Dialectical Procedure*, index references to abstraction and concretion.

in the late Eighteenth and early-to-mid Nineteenth Centuries whereby corporations, already the most powerful collective economic aggregations of all time, came to be regarded as 'persons' in the law. In addition to everything else that this signified, it underscored the continuing view that only 'individuals' act, and that nothing that seeks to concretize large aggregations and structures can be permitted to succeed without the assistance of such conceptual legerdemain and terminological acrobatics.[38] The 'vested interest' of capital in atomism of all types as the basis of its economizing, maximizing *etc.* myths was now extended to incorporating personhood by personalizing the corporation.

In addition, there was the need to rationalize and legitimize these large aggregations, given their tremendous impact on exchange, markets, prices, people and collective life as a whole. They were, after all, the organizational basis of capitalism's movement backward, forward and outward from commerce to industry, production and manufacture, thus to producing, as well as trading, commodities for exchange. These products had heretofore been fabricated mainly by non-capitalistic guild methods and mainly for use rather than for exchange, and therefore were not yet, in a strict sense, really commodities at all.[39] Even if the external transactions resulting from this production took the form of exchange transactions based upon contracts that legislated discrete beginnings, endings and spatial and temporal boundaries, the firm needed to legitimize itself by obeisance to the reigning myths and folklore of capitalism's metaphysics and epistemology.[40] It is the failure of public and social bureaucracy, in contrast to their 'private sector' cousins, to acquire such legitimation that has made it so vulnerable to attack by capital, even though capital is, as Weber pointed out, no less dependent on bureaucracy than the public and social sector.[41]

---

[38] *Santa Clara County v. Southern Pacific Rail Road Co.*, 118 U.S. 394, 6 Supreme Court 1132, 30 L. Ed 118 (1886) is the American Supreme Court case of record on the matter of corporations being protected as 'persons' by the Fourteenth Amendment to the U.S. Constitution (1868).

[39] Fernand Braudel, *Civilization and Capitalism, 15th to 18th Century* (London: Collins, 1981–1984); Braudel, *Capitalism and Material Life* (New York: Harper and Row, 1975).

[40] Thurman Arnold, *The Folklore of Capitalism* (New Haven: Yale University Press, 1937).

[41] Weber, *Economy and Society*, Volume I, Part 1, chapter III, ii, 4, pp. 221–223; Wilson, *Bureaucratic Representation*, chapter 2.

As for sociology and other 'social' sciences, their increased influence pointed in part to the impact on early capitalism of capital's move to the firm and to bureaucracy as a basis for greater leverage over people as well as markets than could be had individually through simple(r) exchange. In addition, however, their ascendancy underscored the consequences of urbanization, secularization and heightened social organization for 'simple' relationships of all types. These disciplines became a light infantry whose task was to legitimize giantism by harmonizing the new social requirements with liberal-capitalist ideology. While one might reasonably have expected these new realities to have a significant impact on the atomistic metaphysics and epistemology of an earlier period, nothing of the sort transpired. The reason for this was that sociology and the other social sciences were no more inclined to challenge these foundations than political economy had been generations earlier. As it turned out, they were no less acquiescent in the idea that parts were concrete and wholes abstract than their predecessors, and differed only in their preference for studying such alleged abstractions as key factors explaining the conduct of the individuals in question.[42]

Thus greater emphasis on these aggregations and concatenations of individuals in no way challenges the abstract nature of the wholes studied, no matter what form they take. While there is a preference for 'collective representations' and 'social facts' in sociology, even Durkheim never intended this topical focus to imply that the whole was more than and (consequently) different from the sum of its parts in a way that displaced individuals as behaving and acting constituent units. Durkheim's major concern was with *forms of explanation* in sociology and the social sciences. As far as the concept of individualism is concerned, it is true that he attacked prevailing theories that saw it to be in a zero sum relation to society. But he only did this in order to substitute an alternate theory that was more in harmony than its predecessor had been with society as the newly emergent form of collective life.[43] Since society is an historically and culturally *specific form* of collective life and living created and sustained by capitalism and the nation-state, rather than a synonym for collectivity *per se*, this on its own presented no difficulties for anyone. This was

[42] H.T. Wilson, 'The Sociology of Apocalypse', *Human Context*, Volume 8 (Fall 1975), pp. 274–294.
[43] Durkheim, *op. cit.*

especially true given the emphasis in these disciplines on 'deviance', 'roles', 'anomie' and the need for recognition of and adjustment to societal requirements.[44]

In the event, sociology in particular aided the emerging and established capital-nation state institutional arrangements by equating society with collectivity, implying that society was not simply the only form of collective life available, but the best one as well. The ideology of progress which equates progress with economic and/or technological development rather than the emergence of institutional infrastructure, including the institutions of the public and society as well as those of capital, found significant aid and comfort from this discipline and its near-relatives.[45] This was to a considerable extent the result of their preoccupation with political and economic status and the legitimation of their disciplines as professions, if not 'sciences'. Their subsequent acceptance into these statuses spelled the end of a brief period during which their practitioners had sought the reform of governments and the increased social responsibility of capitals in the large cities. Once ensconced in the universities, their ties to politics and the economy ceased to be anything more than accommodative and facilitative.[46] Its concerns to this day have been dominated by a preoccupation with upper middle class respectability, expressed through secular preachments either from higher education organizations or from safe moorings in public sector institutions that often only belong to the people because they belong simultaneously to capital as well.

A final point about the illusory nature of sociology and the social sciences as disciplines of the people is in order. It refers to the 'status' of the forms of explanation these disciplines have no choice but to employ, and their attitude toward them relative to other, putatively more 'individualistic' forms and disciplines. The modern and contemporary understanding of what is meant by the term 'causal explanation', as noted, tends to favor immediacy, proximity, strict spatial and temporal boundaries and finality in line with capital's

---

[44] Adorno, 'Society', *op. cit.*; Frankfurt Institute, *Aspects of Sociology* (Boston: Beacon Press, 1972), I (Sociology), II (Society), III (the Individual), IV (the Group), VIII (Sociology and Empirical Social Research).

[45] Weber, *Methodology of the Social Sciences* (Glencoe: Free Press, 1949), pp. 33–37 on the different meanings of 'progress'.

[46] C. Wright Mills, *The Sociological Imagination* (New York: Grove Press, 1959).

preference for contracts and transactions. Though sociology and the social sciences often allude to 'social causation', they know that this latter claim is unlikely to be taken seriously as a form of causal explanation precisely because it lacks the attributes cited above that are thought to constitute the essence of such an explanation. They must thus rest satisfied with what is called 'functional' explanation, and must accept its present designation as a non-causal form, however central to these disciplines it might be.[47] Sociology and the social sciences rest relatively content with this form and the status which goes with it, taking heart from the description of it as 'reverse causality', explaining causes by effects rather than the reverse, offered up by many of its practitioners and their supporters for generations now.

It is important to state explicitly what has only been implied thus far. If capitals and their supporters could have avoided giving any legitimation to sociology and the other social sciences in favor of political economy, economics, a psychology of adjustment and a horse and buggy descriptive political science focused solely on government structures it would have. As it turned out, however, they had to make few if any compromises beyond the most superficial level of disciplinary activity, but these compromises were nevertheless absolutely necessary for capital. It was the very success of capitalism that required it to intervene in more and more sectors of collective life once it had acquired wide-ranging legitimacy in Nineteenth Century Europe and America. As this occurred, and a capitalist economy embedded in a largely pre-capitalist collective form began to give way to a capitalist society and culture, it became clear that political economy, economics, psychology and political science would be insufficient to defend the legitimacy of this process of extension, elaboration and intensification. In order to legitimize the emerging capital nation-state relationship discussed in earlier chapters, the new collective form being created through this activity—society—would have to be legitimized as well.[48]

[47] Robert MacIver, *Social Causation* (New York: Oxford University Press, 1942). Compare Harold Fallding, *The Sociological Task* (Englewood Cliffs, N.J.: Prentice Hall, 1968) with W.W. Isajiw, *Causation and Functionalism in Sociology* (London: Routledge and Kegan Paul, 1968) on the matter of the status of causal vs. functional explanations in sociology.

[48] See especially Karl Mannheim, *Man and Society in an Age of Reconstruction* (London: Routledge and Kegan Paul, 1940).

Today, ironically enough, it is *capitals* rather than the people who are attempting to undo and retreat from the institutional arrangements and infrastructure that resulted from this tremendous (and eminently successful) effort at legitimation. The hegemonic power of capitals, buttressed by their supporters in the national state, the public sector, political parties, interest groups, agencies of secondary socialization and the mass media, has been turned to this task. This is in large part because they believe that these societal disciplines are thoroughly in hand and can be counted on to continue doing what they have done at least since the end of World War Two. Meantime, capital feels sufficiently emboldened as a partial result of this confidence to return openly to the disciplines and world view which have always been, and still remain, its first love—political economy and 'economic science', the true science of capitalism.[49] The fact that capital's assessment of these disciplines has proven to be correct, even in the presence of recent propaganda around 'free trade' and 'privatization' and recent scare tactics focused on the alleged 'public debt', not only explains this emboldenment but underscores the need to reflect critically on the social function these disciplines perform for capitals rather than for the people.

The key vehicle which links this hierarchical status order of variously more and less productive forms of reasoning and explanation to the capitalist world-view and its defense of capital as private property is *logic*. Logic, frequently (and incorrectly) treated as a neutral tool or instrument central to sound reasoning and argumentation, embodies clear biases, preferences and more enduring values regarding what constitutes correct and incorrect reasoning. Not surprisingly, these notions favor atomism and an individuated and subjective view of the person as a causal agent even in the face of the socializational and structural realities of capitalist hegemony in and between national states. Most significantly, logic justifies reliance on a particular protocol that clearly contradicts what is known to be substantively real regarding human social relations and interdependencies.[50] This is the belief in and practice of a logic of reasoning and argumentation which asserts (or assumes) it to be independent of the very objects of knowledge and truth which have made it a cornerstone

[49] Marx, *Grundrisse*, pp. 100–108 and *supra*, 'The Method of Political Economy'.
[50] Wilson, *Marx's Critical/Dialectical Procedure*, pp. 35–37.

of modern and contemporary Western thinking on relations between thought and reality.

The central element in this process whereby a procedural protocol becomes the basis for constructing an imaginary realm absent of relations of dependence and interdependence is the concept of a *fact* and its sense in logic. Facts are *known* to be interdependent with one another in ways that validate a focus on wholes as the real structures, but are assumed for purposes of such protocols to be independent of one another. It is this latter assumption which allows sociology and the other social sciences, as well as psychology and allied disciplines more focused on individual behavior and cognition than structure and process, to get their work done and maintain their status, while providing deep legitimation for the capitalist worldview.[51] In effect, it is this willingness to support the intellectual *and commonsense* fiction that facts can, for all professional purposes, be treated as independent from one another when they are known to be interdependent which is so consequential. It is mainly what justifies the belief that reducing statements to their allegedly most basic constituent elements and thereafter reconstituting and reassembling them is the best way to understand their meaning. In the social, behavioral and administrative-managerial disciplines, the arbitrariness inherent in determining what constitutes the 'independent' and 'dependent' variables is too well-known to require extended comment.

What has been said about these disciplines makes it plain that they have functioned, now as before, in both purposeful and unwitting ways as legitimating agents increasingly central to capital's agenda. In this sense they are clearly part of the hegemonic structure which simultaneously reaffirms and undergirds capital's extension, elaboration and intensification to the outer and inner perimeters of society, the form of collective life it had no choice but to build in concert with the nation-state and allied institutions. The fact that capital is presently attempting to undo the societal arrangements and understandings that produced the Keynesian consensus, however incomplete and unsatisfactory they may be from the standpoint of some public and social values, now requires these disciplines to assist them in what only appears to be a contradiction. This process of withdrawal

[51] Wilson, *Tradition and Innovation* (London: Routledge, 1984) on our 'form of life' being a preoccupation with appropriating 'facts of life'.

and abandonment from prior public and social responsibilities to the very people who continue to constitute its markets, audiences and employees must receive sociological and social-scientific legitimation. While this is happening, it is particularly important to the neo-conservative agenda that property and contractual rights be shored up and that capital be thoroughly accepted by the people as the private property of capitals, using the mechanisms and protocols already discussed.[52]

There is one notion that has always been central to capitals in their effort to justify a view of themselves as free from any interdependence with, and dependence upon, other factors of production. It is the view that capital is essentially 'self augmenting' in nature and that, as such, it can have no other 'extraneous' obligations implicit in the process of its accumulation and disposition that capitals themselves do not acknowledge, recognize and accept voluntarily. While this notion of independence and dissociation from other factors of production, particularly labor, has always been a central element of capitalist ideology, the success of the neo-conservative agenda has vastly increased its determination to acquire formal recognition of this claim. Neo-conservatism now wants sociology and the other social sciences to validate this patent fiction as one that is not only true but necessary for the good health of all capitalist societies as well as their respective economies. What is perhaps most interesting about this is its attempt to claim for capital something similar to what technological determinists like Ellul claimed for technique and technology forty years ago. The argument he put forth then was that technical progress had become unhinged from and independent of capital rather than intimately tied (among other things) to capital allocation decisions.[53]

Capital now asserts that it is self-augmenting, thus independent of land and (especially) labor because it increases itself by its own capacities both incrementally and exponentially and has unopposed power to substitute technology for labor. The initial problem with this rendition is that the *failure* of this alleged self-augmentation to occur is

[52] Arnold, *op. cit.*; Fred Block, *The Mean Season: the Attack on the Welfare State* (New York: Pantheon Books, 1987); Block, *Revising State Theory: Essays in Politics and Post-industrialism* (Philadelphia: Temple University Press, 1987).

[53] Jacques Ellul, *The Technological Society* (New York: Alfred Knopf, 1964); Wilson, 'The Sociology of Apocalypse', *op. cit.*

precisely what shows us that the claim itself is fraudulent. Capital cannot be free of labor, humanity and nature when it can only succeed by being severely dependent upon them and the institutional infrastructure of which they, and capital itself, are an inescapable part. In this sense the maximization of utilities is indistinguishable from the process whereby value is extracted from labor, either directly or through land, and co-opted from public and social institutions in the form of public capital. It is the failure of these maximizing efforts that reminds us of the *real substantive* dependence and interdependence of capitals on labor, humanity and nature, no matter what the models of economists and the propaganda of the political economists would have us believe. The way we come to this realization is not dissimilar to the way we come to an understanding of the idea of value-in-use, that is, by realizing that it is the other, more basic, side of value-on-exchange.[54] It is what brings to consciousness and reflection our awareness of commodification as the essence of capitalism.

If we want to provide further support for the critique of any argument for the self-augmenting nature of capital, we can note as well the more specific dependence of capital and its augmentation processes on public and social institutions. This includes the provision for facilities either at public expense or maintained and protected at public expense, alongside the comprehensive range of public functions, laws and customs which make it possible for maximization and profit-taking to occur and be publicly accepted. In addition, of course, is the fact that capital is only property in the sense that property itself is ultimately a privilege grounded in collective needs and in the performance of social as well as (or in place of) individual functions. Since property can never be private in the sense that it permits a one-sided exclusive right of disposition absent of duties and responsibilities, capital is bound to a similar requirement precisely because, if it is property, then it can only be property in this limited, conditional and contingent sense. These necessary restrictions on, and re-definitions of, so-called 'property rights' address directly issues presently (and for the foreseeable future) at the forefront of concerns about land uses, renewable and non-renewable resources, and the relationships between earth, air, fire and water as the essence of responsible environmental and ecological stewardship.

[54] Marx, *Capital, Volume I*, pp. 52–56.

A final point relates to labor as that alleged 'factor of production' which can never legally become anyone else's property but does so in reality all the time, particularly in the form of 'wage slavery' and 'shadow work'.[55] Capitalism's greatest claim to fame, namely, that it outlawed and rendered impossible and illegitimate slavery in all its forms, can be seen in retrospect to be of only conditional validity. The only basis on which one can make such a claim where wage labor is concerned would argue that *in theory* individuals are free to take up and leave a given employment at will. Not only was this simply not true of historical capitalism for manifold reasons, including its early and continuing dependence on carceral and related forms of labor. Even today it is not true because the forms that wage slavery has taken may not look like a property right or power in a person, and certainly is not normally regarded as such under the law, but in reality often constitutes an equivalent form of restraint. This is because in place of a property right or power has gone *the commodification of labor power*, its thoroughgoing subordination to value on exchange. Paralleling this, and no less significant, has been capitalism's dependence on unpaid shadow work, (e.g. housework, food preparation, child-care and supervision), carried out mainly by women, but by children, the elderly, the handicapped and the mentally ill as well.

The implications of what has been said here require us to rethink the notion of what property means, what right or power of disposition it can or should entail, and what relation it bears to land, labor and capital as the three factors of production set out by political economy. It also calls to mind the tie to both humanity and nature *as progressively more concrete, because progressively more inclusive*, realities of present day life in capitalist nation-states no less than elsewhere in the world. The illusion that we have escaped nature through the construction of an artificial realm embodied in cities, factories, machines and computers has come back to haunt us once more. This is also true for the idea that our humanity and collectivity is optional, or at best an inconvenience, rather than elemental and essential to our progressive self-understanding as a species whose particular forms of collectivity and historicity cannot overcome our real-

[55] Michel Foucault, *Discipline and Punish: the Birth of the Prison* (New York: Vintage, 1979); Ivan Illich, *Shadow Work* (London: Marion Boyars, 1981); Illich, *Gender* (New York: Pantheon, 1982); Wilson, *Sex and Gender* (Leiden: Brill, 1989).

ity as human animals. Finally, there is the reality of hegemony extending far beyond the normally understood structures co-operating with capital, and with or without the people's knowledge and consent. This chapter has argued that these structures include not only agencies of secondary socialization and mass media, but also modes of reasoning and argumentation and academic and professional disciplines dependent on these modes as well.

CHAPTER EIGHT

PUBLIC CAPITAL AND ITS CO-OPTATION

The objective thus far has been to underscore the direct and continuing linkages that necessarily tie capitals and capitalism to the secular authority, governments and the public sector in Western capitalist democracies. The idea of *laissez (nous) faire* as anything more than ideology holds only for the most fledgling enterprises and undertakings, and then for relatively brief periods of their life history. Such folklore constitutes perhaps the most significant indication of the embeddedness of capitalism as an institution and its interdependence with the many socializing agencies that provide ongoing legitimation for it.[1] It is only the fact that we (understandably) take this process almost totally for granted which helps explain both its success and our overall lack of awareness of what is going on while we are experiencing its effects. The legitimation of capitalism and capitals is something that may seem so secure and uncontroversial as to make us wonder why this process is necessary even when the system prescribed appears to be working well. It is the very interdependence with and dependence of capitals on wide-ranging social, political and cultural values, structures and processes which both necessitates such efforts and makes them of central importance as objects of knowledge.[2]

The concept of public capital and the ongoing practice of its co-optation is central to the survival, as well as the legitimation, of capitalism in all capitalist democracies, something that its basis in the extraction of surplus value from labor only underscores.[3] Efforts no less Herculean than those that legitimized property as private and capital as property must be put in the service of securing support for these practices and the institutions and values which sustain and defend them. However, a major difference presents itself here, one that can be (and has been) argued to include capitals themselves, as

---

[1] Arnold, *op. cit.*, pp. 75–77, 96–97, 11–112, 187 190, 342–344. More recently, see Gee, Hull and Lankshear, *op. cit.*; and Engler, *op. cit.*

[2] Quack, Morgan and Whitley, *op. cit.*; Hopkins, Wallerstein and Casparis, *op. cit.*; Hollingsworth and Boyer, *op. cit.*

[3] See chapter 1, 'Introduction', this study.

well as students of capitalism, amongst those unaware of these practices. Thus, a case can be made that capitals are unaware that their social obligations to the people are part of, rather than extraneous to, the ongoing exercise of the rights, powers and opportunities delegated to them. This lack of awareness could be explained by the fact that public capital and its co-optation, like the extraction of surplus value from labor on which it depends, is so hidden, however essential it is to the survival of capitalism, that few are aware of its central, indispensable function.

The sovereign national state is the key repository of public capital and the original and sustaining basis for its generation, accumulation, husbanding and investment, as noted in earlier chapters. Even if Locke and Smith were respectively concerned with how property could be justified as a private possession and how capital could become property, neither lost sight of the central role of labor as the foundation of any theory of value in political economy. Smith in particular was far less influenced by the laissez (nous) faire doctrine of the French Physiocrats, with its predictible effect on the status of labor as more than a mere 'factor of production', than was Ricardo.[4] The national state unit is the central vehicle through which capitals not only legitimize themselves domestically, regionally and internationally but grow and prosper as well. This, in turn, depends on the state in question being recognized and acknowledged as the repository of public capital by other states and by national banks, bonding companies and international organizations.[5] Recognition in general and specific ratings and rankings in particular are predicated on a given state's endowment of all three factors of production, *including land and labor.* What is most significant in this regard is less the emphasis placed on natural resources and geographic and climatic endowments, important as these are, than the central role played by those attributes of a nation's people derived from, and expressed in

[4] John Locke, *Of Civil Government*, Book II, section 25, on the relation between labor 'mixed with the objects of nature' and a conditional right to private property in the form of subsistence only. Adam Smith's *An Inquiry into the Nature and Causes of the Wealth of Nations* (New York: Oxford University Press, 1998, 1776), however important, needs to be read in the light of his earlier *Theory of Moral Sentiments* (New York: Augustus Kelley, 1966, 1759). Also see David Ricardo, *Principles of Political Economy and Taxation* (Amherst, New York: Prometheus Books, 1996, 1911, 1817).

[5] Smith, Solinger and Topik, *op. cit.*; Kurt Burch, *'Property' and the Making of the International System* (Boulder, Colorado: Lynne Rienner Publishers, 1997); Thomas Franck, *The Power of Legitimacy among Nations* (New York: Oxford University Press, 1990).

the form of, labor. It is these attributes, habits and values, and the activity of labor that results from them, that create, sustain and develop the unique institutions, and sets of institutions, on which the past, present and future generation of public capital depends.[6]

One of the best examples of how globalization has gone beyond multinational corporations to formally recognize national-states themselves as central units in the world economy is the annual *World Competitiveness Reports*.[7] The increasing significance which attaches to a country's position in this particular schema of ratings and rankings (and ones like it) only underscores the fact that the state's role with regard to the generation, accumulation, husbanding and investment of public capital is more important than that of any other institution. Many might view a particular country's position and attributes in this schema as most useful for deciding whether and where to invest or participate in its economy. Here, however, the objective is also to suggest that it is mainly the properties and characteristics of a people that relate directly or indirectly to their values and the labor resulting from these values that should be of the greatest interest to capitals. Indeed, a mutually correct fit between capitals and these values in action can often make the best use not only of a country's labor but other features of its public capital endowment. However diligently political economy attempts to collapse unique characteristics into general categories like 'capital stock', 'natural resources' or 'human resources', the fact remains that the value to capitals of seeking a balanced approach to extraction and co-optation demands attention to unique institutions and attributes of a people and its country. The significance of studies like the *World Competitiveness Reports* is not so much that they rate and rank states on the basis of their ability to generate capital, but rather that they do so based on the presence of particular stocks and country characteristics conducive to its generation and accumulation. National characteristics of a non-economic and non-financial kind affect directly, as well as indirectly, the bond rating of a given country and that of its sub-units, as well

[6] On Canada, see Herschel Hardin, *A Nation Unaware: the Canadian Economic Culture* (Vancouver: J.J. Douglas, 1974); and H.T. Wilson, 'Institutional Complementarity and Canadian Identity', *Canadian Review of American Studies*, Volume 27, No. 3 (1997), pp. 175–190.

[7] *World Competitiveness Reports*, 10 Volumes (Cologny/Geneva: Foundation for the European Management Forum, 1986–1995). Also see the Foundation's *Reports on International Competitiveness* and *World Competitiveness Yearbooks* (1986–1995).

as the interest rate set by its national bank or reserve system. This is often evident in the fact that different ratings and rankings prevail in countries where the amount and nature of debts and deficits and economic and financial capacities are substantially the same.[8]

It is an understatement to note that the accepted understanding of competitiveness is now much more *concrete*, because broader and more comprehensive and integrative, than it was in the past.[9] This has much to do with the fact that nation-states, for so long the responsible parties in this process of generating public capital, are now coming to be recognized and acknowledged for their role in this activity. This is because the generation and accumulation of public capital is (rightly) seen to be of decisive importance for the good health, growth and prosperity of capitals, as well as the states where they operate or are headquartered. Whereas traditional, narrow conceptions of competitiveness are focused on industrial efficiency and examine short term labor costs, productivity, profitability, taxation and inflation in a given state, newer, broader understandings look at non-traditional measures like the 'dynamism' of the economy overall as well as its international 'outward' and 'future' orientations. Most important for putting these latter measures in context are those factors which address labor, the people and their states and governments, alongside natural endowments in land, renewable and non-renewable resources and geographic and climatic advantages and disadvantages.[10]

In effect, what this revised conception of competitiveness is recommending is a return to a more institutionally customized version of Smith's focus on the national wealth, in contrast to the narrow focus on GNP or GDP.[11] National states and groups of states in supranational systems remain the dominant organizational and institutional players and points of reference for the exercise of competitiveness, even in the face of the globalization of production, marketing, trade and finance. The need for a more balanced approach to the status and role of other factors of production in these systems, and labor in particular, is evident from the emphasis on developing and

---

[8] Quack, Morgan and Whitley, *op. cit.*

[9] See Hendryk Spruyt, *The Sovereign State and its Competitors: an Analysis of Systems* (Princeton: Princeton University Press, 1994).

[10] See generally the *World Competitiveness Reports* under each factor cited. Pages vary depending on volume, but order of treatment of the series of factors is consistent.

[11] Smith, *Theory of Moral Sentiments*; Smith, *An Inquiry into the Nature and Causes of the Wealth of Nations.*

enhancing public and social, as well as capital institutions throughout this study. Attempts to collapse land, and particularly labor, into terminology which is 'metaphorically correct' (capital stock, natural resources, human resources) are themselves based on the assumption that labor is nothing more than a commodity, thus at best a subsidiary factor in determining a nation's wealth. But this ignores the costs to capital of treating labor and its institutions as a mere means in its haste to realize short and medium-term objectives which they wrongly believe do not include it.[12] Studies like the *World Competitiveness Reports* challenge both the traditional ideology of competition and markets, while they force us to reassess the sense of capital's obsession with the increasingly more direct and continuous conversion of use values into exchange values.[13]

Looking first at natural resources, the criterion of 'natural endowment utilization' in the *Report* focuses not only on the quantity of renewable and non-renewable natural resources but the effectiveness (incorrectly called 'efficiency') with which a country uses them. The point here follows directly from the *Report's* emphasis on 'managing' resources, since it concentrates mainly on the degree to which given countries are concerned about 'long term needs' and ecological and environmental sensitivity and balance (e.g. recycling, substitute materials), as opposed to immediate political and private disposition. Efficiency is a concept that relates exclusively to the utilization of 'means' on the assumption that ends are given or unproblematic. Effectiveness, in contrast, is far more appropriate to the *Report's* concerns and objectives because it addresses Smith's (and pre-Ricardian political economy's) commitment to the priority of rank-ordering the ends or goals of human activity on the assumption that it is the means, not the ends, that are scarce.[14] Effectiveness, far from presuming the given and unproblematic nature of ends, thus makes their rank-ordering the central public and social function of states.

Whatever anyone might wish to say of Smith and political economy regarding their *invention* (rather than 'discovery') of 'scarcity', and

[12] Gosta Esping-Andersen, *Social Foundations of Postindustrial Economies* (New York: Oxford University Press, 1999); Harry Shutt, *The Trouble with Capitalism: An Enquiry into the Causes of Global Economic Failure* (London: Zed Books, 1998).

[13] Wilson, 'Time, Space and Value', *op. cit.*

[14] The confusion between economic and technical rationality is addressed constructively in Paul Diesing, *Reason in Society* (Urbana, Illinois: University of Illinois Press, 1962), particularly chapters 1 and 2.

their allied claim that scarcity is inherent in nature rather than a property of human beings under a capitalist order, one cannot deny the following point. Smith in particular provides a far more balanced analysis than Ricardo does of the role of land and labor in an integrated assessment of a nation's wealth.[15] In addition, there is implicit in Smith's political economy-for him a division of moral philosophy-a commitment to the central role of rank-ordering or prioritizing ends given scarce means. This activity is the key to improving representative democratic and other public and social processes in capitalist countries, because it underscores the delegated nature of capital's role *vis à vis* the people.[16] Smith's emphasis on *wealth* rather than (exchange) value in *An Inquiry Concerning the Nature and Causes of the Wealth of Nations* implies a view of the nation's abundance that is far more sensible. As such, it is far less influenced by the belief that capital is the dominant factor of production than would be discovered a generation later in the writings of Ricardo and the political economists. This bias also indicates Smith's commitment to a more balanced relationship between use and exchange values because the object of improvement was the national wealth, not the GNP or GDP.[17]

Focusing on criteria in the *Report* based on labor, broadly (therefore *more* rather than less concretely) conceived, one discovers the category of 'human resources'. Here the *Report* examines 'competitive advantage based on people's skills, motivation, flexibility, age structure and health'.[18] Countries which rank high overall here are clearly ones that have a strong and sustained commitment to public and social values, processes and institutions, particularly in the West, but elsewhere as well. Indeed, this criterion underscores the organizing role of the state and its public and social sectors as the indispensable elements without which a nation's competitiveness, thus its wealth, will be irretrievably compromised.[19] To be sure, one could

---

[15] Compare Smith, *An Inquiry into the Nature and Causes of the Wealth of Nations* to Ricardo, *op. cit.* in particular.

[16] Lindblom, *op. cit.*, pp. 161–188.

[17] On the consequences of our shift under capitalism from dearth to scarcity as the prevailing assumption of economics, coupled with a parallel conceptual movement from wealth to the productivity of 'factors of production', see Ivan Illich, *Gender* (New York: Pantheon, 1962), pp. 3–4, 10–12, 18–19, 28, 45, 61–62, 81, 84, 144, 169, 178, text and titled and untitled footnotes.

[18] *World Competitiveness Reports.*

[19] A theory of institutional balance between capital, public and social sectors as the key to the successful movement of all capitalist democracies into the 21st century

argue that the very emphasis on human beings as 'resources' indicates the supremacy of both capital as the mediating factor of production and the creation of exchange value as its first priority. Nevertheless, there is in this set of concerns an acknowledgement of the joint significance of human beings and of state, public and social institutional sectors. Along with land (resources, ecology, environment *etc.*) it points to the revival of a more concrete understanding of the relationship between the three factors of production.

The remaining criteria include 'the impact of the state', 'international' and 'future' orientations and 'socio-political stability'. In the first case there is the typical two-faced disclaimer about 'less being more' where the governmental 'contribution' is concerned. Thus 'taxes, regulation and defence spending are all negatives', particularly 'high taxes on capital, property and income' (which allegedly discourage 'the will to work'), yet countries are typically ranked more highly if they have strong social security systems. The bias here is neo-conservative because it takes completely for granted the institutions of state, people and society which serve the interests of capitals while attacking those which point to the social responsibilities that go with the rights, powers and influence that capitals have in capitalist democracies.[20] With the happy exception of defence spending, the *Report's* view of the state and public sector 'contribution' reaffirms the neo-conservative commitment to theoretical *laissez (nous) faire* in the form of privatization, deregulation and allied forms of public and social sector downsizing and withdrawal. In the process, it ignores what the state and its people do for capitalism in and through democratic, public and social institutions.[21]

'International' and 'future' orientations are criteria which belie the role that the state and public and social sector infrastructures play in inculcating, supporting and legitimizing values and states of mind conducive to and supportive of a capitalist society and economy. In the first instance, the *Report* looks at 'government policies aimed at protecting domestic enterprises . . . with disdain', as if such protectionist policies bore no relationship to the power and influence of

is initially developed in H.T. Wilson, 'The Downside of Downsizing', *The New Public Management: International Developments*, edited by D. Barrows and H.I. Macdonald (Toronto: Captus Press, 2000); and Wilson, *Bureaucratic Representation* (Leiden: Brill, 2001).

[20] Lindblom, *op. cit.*; Craig, *op. cit.*; Kreml, *op. cit.*; Alexander Hicks, *op. cit.*

[21] But see Ronald Glassman, *Caring Capitalism: A New Middle Class Base for the Welfare State* (New York: St. Martin's Press, 2000).

capitalism and the desires of specific capitals in a given nation-state.[22] Instead, it views such policies as the result of unwarranted state and public sector 'interventions', while conveniently ignoring the well-established, ongoing dependencies and interdependencies between capital and the nation-state that frequently make such interventions a continuing objective of capital. Indeed, most studies criticize, even vilify, the (alleged) intervention and interference of governments in domestic, supranational and international economic activities, then turn around and recommend that these same governments do this or that to rectify the situation prior to returning these activities to the private sector of 'free markets'. As a rule, it is only in the public and social institutional sectors that capital wishes to see less or no government 'intervention', unless it transfers profit-taking opportunities with less or no risk to them. Not surprisingly, it is in the capital institutional sector of state activity that one sees a massive expansion and intensification of functions, contradicting neo-conservatism's vaunted attack on bureaucracy and government.[23] While the *Report* attaches great significance to 'high value added' exports, it says virtually nothing about the public and social costs of start ups, subsidies, protection and promotion of these products and services.[24]

The factor of 'future orientation' goes far beyond a focus on investment in research and development, itself totally dependent on prior secondary socialization, education and training from four to twenty four and beyond. It addresses, even if it does not give pride of place to, the individual and collective mind-set of peoples and cultures that (allegedly) makes them more competitive.[25] Ancillary emphasis on certain specific results which should ideally issue from an increased future orientation like research and development, commercialization of technology and number of patents and copyrights cannot hide the dependence of these outcomes on more concrete publicly and socially grounded institutions which ultimately determine their presence and

[22] Harry Dahms (editor), *Transformations of Capitalism: Economy, Society and the State in Modern Times* (New York: New York University Press, 2000) for discussion of American 'industrial policy' as a hedge on 'the market'.

[23] See Wilson, *Bureaucratic Representation*, chapters 2, 5.

[24] David Coates, *Models of Capitalism: Growth and Stagnation in the Modern Era* (Malden, Mass.: Polity Press, 2000); David Korten, *The Post-Corporate World: Life after Capitalism* (San Francisco: Kumarian Press, 1999); David Marquand, *The New Reckoning: Capitalism, States and Citizens* (Malden, Mass.: Polity Press, 1997).

[25] *World Competitiveness Reports.*

incidence. Once again, we see the consequences for thinking about and assessing competitiveness (among many other things) of the inversion of the concrete and the abstract discussed in the last chapter. Particular outcomes are 'concrete', thus far more real, than the more 'abstract' activities that ground them and make them possible. The causal chain, as noted, does not go back (and out) far enough to include these activities in what is clearly an atomist-individualist narrative, and for good ideological reasons. For it would show these activities and institutions to be the real concrete from which more narrow and specific notions of outcome are 'abstracted'.[26]

The final criterion cited—socio-political stability—has in common with the rest of the *Report* its preference for addressing specific outcomes rather than the institutional practices and values that variously ground, legitimize and make sense of them. Thus socio-political stability is reduced to 'such things as industrial relations, judicial impartiality and income distribution', alongside 'the administration of justice, economic literacy, high levels of leisure spending . . . general purchasing power and labor relations record'. Apart from the usual bias against unions as well as the protective and promotive functions of governments, one cannot ignore the heterogeneous nature of the outcomes and indicators addressed as part of an operational definition of socio-political stability.[27] The fact that they could have been placed (along with others throughout the *Report*) under many different criteria underscores the element of false concreteness and abstraction, while privileging the *Report's* terminology, conceptual structures and contents toward atomism, the individual and the private.[28]

In spite of these and other limitations, the *World Competitiveness Report* does draw the careful reader's attention to the role of institutions, legitimacy and the collective, cultural and political grounding of capitalism in public, social and historical activities and processes, even though it clearly has no intention of doing so. The reality of centuries of dependence and interdependence manifests itself even (or especially) in the midst of efforts to employ shop-worn ideology and rhetoric to claim otherwise.[29] What makes this all the more interesting is the fact that it goes on without most advocates of capital

[26] Wilson, *Marx's Critical/Dialectical Procedure*, pp. 35–37, 98–113.
[27] See especially Hollingsworth and Boyer, *op. cit.*
[28] Wilson, *Marx's Critical/Dialectical Procedure*, pp. 89–92.
[29] Arnold, *op. cit.*; Gee, Hull and Lankshear, *op. cit.*

and most of the people being aware of it. To be sure, these reports are usually carried out under the direct or indirect auspices of supporters of the neo-conservative agenda whose purpose is to make a case for less, and occasionally no, government, or so they think. But close inspection of the deeper meaning and significance of the criteria, as well as the epistemological basis on which they are constructed, reveal a very different reality, one that could not be acknowledged even if those who support the agenda in question were aware of it.

The *World Competitiveness Report* and allied studies, reports and documents claim to compare between 24 and 34 industrialized and industrializing countries using questionnaires and documentary research based on 292 criteria aggregated into the nine or ten categories that have been discussed. A careful perusal of the methodology employed, while both important and rewarding, is significant because of what it reveals about the larger inconsistencies, confusions, omissions and portrayals of what has (allegedly) been 'discovered'. As an example of the self-serving nature of the 'internal audit' which it provides once all limitations have been acknowledged in a protocol fashion, note this excerpt from the *Report's* 'Final Remarks on Methodology'.

> International competitiveness is a vast, multidimensional subject. Part of it being a perception, no study on it can claim to be fully scientific. Nevertheless, if comprehensiveness is impossible to achieve, the *World Competitiveness Report* aims at least at giving a sharper image of competitiveness. The quality improvement obtained by raising the number of criteria from the few used in the past to . . . 292 . . . can be compared to the change from traditional to high definition TV.[30]

For the significantly different (and clearly opposed) reasons that have been spelled out in the foregoing, this study is in complete agreement with this assessment and conclusion.

Turning now to an examination of the phenomenon of co-optation, an attempt will be made to explain why the process or activity that this term depicts helps us to make sense of the way in which capitals, individually and in the aggregate, make use of or depend upon public capital. This, however, will require us first to reiterate what is meant by public capital, in order to underscore how it relates and gives dynamic expression to the notion of a nation's wealth. Public capital is the past, present and future stock of embedded,

---

[30] *World Competitiveness Reports.*

existing and potential value that comprises a people's history, culture, experience, knowledge, habits and institutions. It is this stock, more than anything else, on which capitals, other nations, central banks, bonding companies and international organizations, *should, and still frequently do*, base their decisions and assessments.[31] Whether it is decisions by capitals as to whether to participate, or continue to participate, in a country's economy, or assessments by governmental and central financial actors that pertain to risk and debt capacity, this stock of value, considered in the aggregate, is and always ought to be decisive.[32]

The fact that this stock of value, so conceived, has been designated by the term public *capital* could perhaps be cited as evidence of my own capture by political economy's agenda of metaphorical correctness. To this I would respond by noting that there is a great deal of difference between formulating this term on purpose in order to make a point and being oblivious to how inclusion of the word 'capital' might be construed. This is all the more true in light of the intention to use the term in order to *challenge* the idea of capital as property and property as private, save in the very restricted senses cited in the last chapter. Thus the term 'public capital' is posed in order to compel us to acknowledge and attend to what many might otherwise consider little more than an oxymoron.[33] It is also anxious to challenge the sense of what is concrete and what is abstract in this term by bringing together two concepts (public; capital) that are understood by many to be in a contradictory relation to one another. In the final analysis, it is the *phenomenon* of public capital itself that invalidates the view that it must be less, rather than more, concrete than capital.[34]

Some would argue that resort to this tactic simply demonstrates the extent to which economic theory has penetrated political theory, something that is difficult to refute, particularly given the time and circumstances in which we live. Macpherson is correct in this regard to note the significance of this penetration because it forces us to

---

[31] For an early statement on the central role of geographic, climatic and environmental factors as determinants, see Baron C.L. de Secondat Montesquieu, *The Spirit of the Laws* (New York: Hafner Publishing Co., 1959, 1748).

[32] *World Competitiveness Reports.*

[33] As already noted in chapter 1, and elsewhere throughout the text, reference to 'public' capital means social, as well as public, resources, institutions and values.

[34] On its superior concreteness as capital, relative to the greater abstractness of 'private' capital, see generally Wilson, *Marx's Critical/Dialectical Procedure.*

reflect on the key value assumptions we make as members of capitalist society and as the products of its institutions, as well as those of the people.[35] The determination here to make use of this fact of life by drawing attention to the reality and central role of public capital points to the way that concepts and terminology can be (and are) used to legitimize as well as criticize established practices and values. They do this by excluding or ignoring efforts to generate alternate structures of thinking through recourse to the use of contrary, opposed or even contradictory words in the composition of a term or concept. Public capital draws on what I have already argued that capital itself really is, along with property. Public capital is not only more concrete, but as a result both conceptually and historically prior to capital, however much it appears (wrongly) to be a modified form or special case of it. In a parallel vein Marx noted that even if use values could only be known through the observation of value on exchange, they are prior to them in every sense *for this reason.* Durkheim's argument against both the Utilitarians and Spencer and the Social Darwinists pointed out that, far from exchange relations creating solidarity, it was a prior and continuing solidarity that grounded exchange relations and made them possible.[36] In addition, it expresses that aspect of collective reality in capitalist societies that comprehends the significance of *both* the institutions of capital and those public and social institutions of the people.

Public capital, by fixing on a more balanced assessment of the role and significance of 'factors of production', alone and in combination, promotes a focus on a nation's wealth, concretely and holistically conceived, rather than on either GNP or GDP, as noted. By doing so, it intentionally takes us away from a concept of value which favors the priority, and often exclusivity, of value on exchange to value in use toward an alternate vision which embeds exchange in what makes it possible and sanctionable as a practice.[37] The concept-in-practice of public capital can make no real difference if its sense does not force us to rethink the biases we have (and express) in favor of exchange value. It is precisely because exchange value is

[35] Macpherson, *Democratic Theory: Essays in Retrieval* (London: Oxford University Press, 1973); Macpherson, *The Rise and Fall of Economic Justice, and Other Papers* (London: Oxford University Press, 1985).
[36] Marx, *op. cit.*; Durkheim, *op. cit.*
[37] See Elson, *op. cit.*

so totally disembodied that it constitutes the sort of impersonal basis for rating and ranking the three factors of production that always leads us to give capital pride of place, as if it were the only real contestant in the field. This study has argued that it is the tie to labor and to public and social, as well as capital, institutions that confers direct or indirect legitimacy on capital's values and practices, particularly those in the state, public and social sectors. That capital depends on this labor and these institutions for its survival and legitimation much more than many once thought has most recently (September, 11, 2001) been brought home by the terrorist attacks on New York and Washington and their aftermath.

A preference for the term *public* capital over either social or collective capital may perhaps be more difficult to understand, save for the fact that 'social capital' has itself recently been co-opted by a movement that has close ties to neo-conservatism. After all, one could argue that it is the collectivity that constitutes the repository of this stock of past, present and future value and institutions, thus that the notion of the public makes reference to one of the many roles which members of the collectivity play.[38] An earlier publication titled *Political Management: Redefining the Public Sphere* took explicit exception to the reduction of citizenship and the public sphere exclusively to one of a number of potentially available *roles*. This text was less concerned with the economic than with the social or sociological penetration of political theory. It did not seem then, and does not seem now, that a focus on roles does anything more than extend and legitimize forms of thought and practice supportive of capital. Furthermore, it does this in ways that undermine our ability to see the reality and persistence of the political or public dimension, thus that of public capital, as well.[39]

Public capital is nothing less than the wealth of a given nation looked at dynamically rather than statically. But it is even more than this, because it also implies the existence of a *process or activity* by which this wealth is taken in hand by capitals, with or without the consent of the people.[40] Although it is true that public capital can

[38] Alan Thomas, 'Audience, Market, Public: An Evaluation of Canadian Broadcasting', *Occasional Paper No. 7* (Vancouver: UBC, Department of University Extension, 1960).

[39] Wilson, *Political Management: Redefining the Public Sphere* (Berlin and New York: Walter de Gruyter, 1984), especially chapters 5, 7, 8, 10.

[40] Lindblom, *op. cit.*, chapters 12–15, 22.

be found in all collective structures, its sense is clearest when we talk of industrial societies that are also representatively democratic, therefore based, at least in theory, on the consent of the people in and through their elected leaders, parties *etc.* For it is here that the reciprocal bargain between capitals and the people, embodied in three discrete yet overlapping sets of institutions, along with Lindblom's observation that the people have delegated to the 'private sector' the responsibility for running the economy in these states, rings most true.[41] Public capital is only collectively and socially embodied and embedded because it is *already* a property of institutions in the capital, public and social sectors which confer direct or indirect legitimacy on capitals by defending, promoting and valuing their activities.[42]

Most significantly, it is the tie to sovereignty or principal legitimacy which is the basis, both internally and externally, for simultaneously providing legitimacy for capitals and capitalism and (as a consequence) making the co-optation of public capital possible, while facilitating this very process. In fact, this absolute dependence of capitals on a continuous supply of public capital in a myriad of forms is better looked after in countries with representative democratic and rule of law political and legal systems than it is anywhere else. This runs absolutely contrary to what many or most might think, given the seemingly disorganized and disorderly nature of these societies relative to their undemocratic challengers. Its sense is also well captured, from the other side, in the deeper meaning of Pope's observation that societies that are best administered are best, where the operative words are found in his two references to 'best'.[43] Having said this, however, it is necessary to enter an extremely important caveat. While capitals would seem to prefer such systems because of the freedom to purchase, consume and spectate that they support far more than authoritarian systems do for their denizens, there is a clear limit to the disorganization and disorderliness that can be

[41] *Ibid.*, chapter 6 on the limited competence of markets, and chapter 8 on 'market socialism'. Compare Lindblom, *op. cit.*, chapters 2, 9–12, 20 on political values and democracy to Wilson, *Bureaucratic Representation*, chapter 3 'The Limits of the Electoral Mode' as a basis for and form of popular representation.

[42] Hollingsworth and Boyer, *op. cit.* This focus completes, rather than challenges, the logic implicit, and often explicit, in Lindblom, *op. cit.*

[43] Compare Claus Offe, *Disorganized Capitalism* (Cambridge, Mass: MIT Press, 1985) to Scott Lash and John Urry, *The End of Organized Capitalism* (Cambridge: Polity Press, 1987), and Lash and Urry's reconsideration of their earlier argument in *Economies of Signs and Space* (London: Sage Publications, 1994).

tolerated. Reference was made in an earlier chapter to the amount of stability and predictability that capitals require, and the *World Competitiveness Reports* were just cited to demonstrate the significance of their support for 'protestant ethic' work values and discipline.

There is more at stake than this, however, particularly today in an age of increasingly technocratic decision structures and processes in these countries. In addition to the general (and understandable) preference for stability and order that privileges processes and mechanisms over unprogrammed and spontaneous acts of political or public display in these systems must be added the ongoing, and largely successful, effort to further stabilize these putative democracies by bureaucratizing and technocratizing politics. Here the goal is to seek to persuade publics (wrongly) that their problems are really administrative rather than 'political' in nature. This in contrast to the thoroughly sensible, but decidedly anti-conservative, observation that bureaucratic representation, *in concert with electoral and other forms*, can be one of the most effective and responsible kinds.[44] In the case of the technocratic reduction of politics to administration, there is the presence of two (or more) 'teams', ready, willing and able to 'take charge' should the present one lose the public or legislative confidence. In parliamentary systems in particular, but elsewhere as well, there is the all-too-well-publicized and determined effort, also thoroughly successful, by cabinet and executive bodies to control the parliamentary agenda far more than was the case even thirty or forty years ago. This has led to frequent complaints that elected representatives, now required to follow the 'party line' over ninety percent of the time, are often unable to honor the instructions of a majority of their constituents on any given issue.[45]

Yet another development, already alluded to here and in earlier chapters, points to the nation-state as a 'firm' organizing its factors of production for the increasingly important global and international competition all about us which can no longer (if it ever could) be ignored. Clearly, this further qualification to the statement that capitals

[44] H.T. Wilson, 'Technocracy in Late Capitalist Societies', *The State, Class and the Recession*, edited by S. Clegg, P. Boreham and G. Dow (London: Croom Helm, 1983), pp. 152–238. Compare to the arguments made in Wilson, 'The Downside of Downsizing', *op. cit.*; and Wilson, *Bureaucratic Representation.*

[45] See Wilson, *Bureaucratic Representation*, chapters 3–5 for analysis and discussion of alternate forms given the limitations of the electoral mode of representation, however indispensable it remains.

prefer representative democracies over undemocratic political systems holds most strongly where the country in question is committed to one or another form of industrial policy approach. As already pointed out, it contrasts strikingly with the quintessentially neo-conservative attempt to portray the nation-state as a household, as part of a thoroughly contradictory effort to impress upon citizens the danger of 'public', in contrast to consumer, debt.[46] But it is characteristic in a general way of all representative systems under neo-conservative dominance where capitals and capitalism have an established, accepted and legitimate presence at the centre of the economy, if not in other sectors of the society and culture as well. This is especially the case where there is, alongside it, support for technocratic forms of governance and leadership determined to reduce politics as much as possible to non-substantive issues and (ideally) non-conflictual problems of administration and management. This raises the matter of why, given movement toward an ever-greater control of this putatively democratic apparatus by capitals, anyone should wish to persist with the term public capital.

It is imperative that the public, rather than only the collective or social, nature of capital be defended. This defense is directly tied to the revival of representative democratic practice in the form of a better balance between the use of institutional mechanisms and processes on the one hand and spontaneous acts of individual and aggregated display on the other. Having said this, this better balance must include recognition of non-electoral processes and institutions like bureaucratic representation precisely because it is always tempting to expect too much from citizen participation in political life in capitalist democracies.[47] This constructive tension between polity and politics is even less supported by capitals today than it was thirty years ago by the authors of the *Civic Culture*, whose major concern was to keep politics and the political under control, lest stability and order be challenged or disturbed.[48] The openness of the kind of representative democracy that capitals prefer, it turns out, is one which favors the openness and pluralism of individuals in the

[46] Lindblom, *op. cit.*, especially chapters 15, 16; Wilson, 'Industrial Strategy: its Challenge to Social Policy in Canada', *op. cit.*

[47] Discussed in Wilson, *Political Management*, chapter 5 and *supra*; and in Wilson, *Bureaucratic Representation*.

[48] Sidney Verba, *The Civic Culture* (Boston: Little Brown, 1965).

marketplace and as consumers and audiences to media, but *not* as either workers and laborers or as citizens and members of the public. Capitals used their historical leverage over legal and restricted democratic machinery to forge and underwrite an early system of dependence and interdependence with the state as the dominant secular authority.[49] This allowed them to realize a consequential lead over the later-to-develop public, but especially social, institutions that now seems harder to overcome than at any time in recent memory for the reasons indicated.

It is its use of the processes and mechanisms of representative democracy to open out market, consumer and audience-spectator roles, while seeking to constrict and control workplace participation, the exercise of citizenship and public and social institutions, that most clearly and unambiguously defines the contemporary capitalist nation-state today. Capital's preference for polity over politics follows naturally from this, and is consistent with the fact that it is the institutional reference points, embodied in and expressed through laws, values, habits and ongoing socialization processes, that are the defining characteristics of capital's control over the political system. This control, whether capitals are aware of it or not, is absolutely necessary. Its major purpose is to obscure the reality of public capital and the indispensability of its continuous co-optation as the central process through which capitalism alternately seeks legitimacy and survival as a system. In the absence of this realization, particularly today, the result has been the emergence of what can only be called a 'surplus legitimacy' for capital and its institutions, however superficial and ephemeral it is, and however contrary to a deeper legitimacy based on reciprocity it may be.[50] The boldness of contemporary capitals and their supporters in governments that is an essential feature of the neo-conservative agenda generates the conviction that a more direct and continuous process of co-optation is both possible and necessary. Ironically, it is this boldness that threatens to expose capital's ever-greater dependence on this very process precisely because of its two-faced retreat from the Keynesian consensus. This retreat requires the hypocritical embrace of capital's right of mobility, coupled with

---

[49] Wilson, 'The Downside of Downsizing', *op. cit.*

[50] See Robert Kuttner, *The Economic Illusion: False Choices between Prosperity and Social Justice* (Boston: Houghton Mifflin, 1984); and Kuttner, *Everything for Sale: the Virtues and Limits of Markets* (New York: Alfred Knopf, 1997).

trans-national political efforts to control it, and the hypocritical embrace of the nation-state as a fiscally responsible household, coupled with capital's increased dependence on excessive consumption and resulting consumer debt.

At this point, let us turn to the process by which the public capital that is the lifeblood of capitals and capitalism is continuously secured. Use of the term co-optation is intended to draw attention to the decisiveness and continuity of these recurrent acts, and also to their process character over a long period of time as vehicles of legitimation, even as they provide indispensable aid and support to the survival of capitals.[51] Participation in, or at least direct access to, the institutions of nation-state sovereignty (principal legitimacy) and allied institutions in the government and public sphere is the *sine qua non* without which public capital in any or all of its forms cannot be co-opted. These institutions possess legitimacy in the eyes of the public, a legitimacy directly or indirectly sustained by elections and related democratic and representative practices in virtually all capitalist societies. The key to the success of co-optation as a process is that most publics and capitals are unaware of it, any more than they are aware of how its very indispensability to capital explains why this process is consistently ignored by those who are aware in favor of a focus on what capitalism does for the people.[52]

The mass media, alongside agencies of secondary socialization, and increasingly the family itself, are absolutely essential, if unwitting, agents in this ongoing reconstruction of social, economic and political reality. More significant by far than this, however, is the fact that most capitals are totally oblivious to the existence and central role of the process. When one thinks about it, one realizes that capitals would indeed *have to believe* their version of reality in order to be capitals. This is not a conspiratorial claim, if only because capitals for the most part believe their propaganda. Thus conspiratorial theories miss the mark by ignoring the fact that virtually everyone (including capitals) believes that capitals are entitled to rights, powers and privileges far in excess of the duties and responsibilities which

---

[51] See chapter 1, this study, for an introductory discussion of 'public capital' and its 'co-optation'.

[52] See Gee, Hull and Lankshear, *op. cit.*; Hellinger and Judd, *op. cit.*; and especially Gordon Clark and Michael Dear, *State Apparatus: Structures and Language of Legitimacy* (Boston: Allen and Unwin, 1984).

they owe to the people.[53] On what other basis could the present legitimacy of capitalism be premised? The objective of offering this different and conflicting picture of past, present and emerging future reality is to support the urgent need for a reassessment of the capital-state-people bargain in capitalist societies. This concern is only heightened by the consequences of the neo-conservative agenda over the past twenty–five years in these countries.

While co-optation, as defined in the literature of social science and organization theory, helps us see some important characteristics of the capital-nation state relationship over the past two to three centuries, it can only take us so far. The intention of using this term is to dynamize its present meaning by beginning with this understanding, then concretizing it by addressing features like mutuality and reciprocity as the essence of its continuous and process nature, now as before. Co-optation is defined as the election or appointment of an outsider to a group by a vote or decision of its membership. The issue of who is and who is not an outsider and what constitutes election or appointment in this definition are, of course, the key questions. On the other hand, co-optation has also been understood to mean 'the process of absorbing new elements into the leadership or policy-determining structure . . . as a means of averting threats to its stability or existence', a definition that reverses the power relationship cited in the first two understandings.[54]

The point of contrasting these differing points of focus and emphasis is to argue that in a sense both are correct, but only if taken together. Each is incomplete without the other because neither taken alone adequately stresses the mutuality and reciprocity which is unavoidable in such a long-term continuous activity with so many formal process aspects to it. Another point that necessitates such 'dynamization' of the concept goes beyond the incompleteness of static models to underscore the unwitting as well as the witting characteristics of co-optation. The most useful way of addressing the fact that in co-optation we have a continuous set of activities and formal processes at the very heart of our political, economic and social

[53] Lindblom, *op. cit.* chapters 6, 15, 16, 22.

[54] *Chambers 20th Century Dictionary, New Edition* Cambridge: Cambridge University Press, 1983), p. 276; J. Thompson and W. McEwen, 'Organizational Goals and Environment: Goal Setting as an Interaction Process', *American Sociological* Review, Volume 23 (February 1958), pp. 23–31. Also see Philip Selznick, *TVA and the Grass Roots* (New York: Harper Torchbooks, 1966, 1947) for his discussion of co-optation.

order is to treat it as the essence of secondary socialization in and through a country's legitimacy-conferring institutions.[55] These institutions would constitute the central elements and properties of a country's political and economic *culture*. Support for them below as well as at the level of conscious awareness would therefore be the most desired (and needed) outcomes of its attempt to continuously socialize people in their appropriateness, correctness and indispensability.

As already noted, it is of the greatest significance that capitals and capitalism got involved in these mutual and reciprocal processes with the state and public authorities long before the people did. A major reason why the neo-conservative agenda has been able to upend the Keynesian consensus with such relative ease has been alluded to several times already. The processes whereby individuals are schooled or socialized in a capitalist country's public, but especially its social institutions and framework are usually newer and less secure than the older, more established processes that school or socialize people in the legitimacy of the institutions of capital. While this is especially true in the United States and Canada, this imbalance is a dominant characteristic of the capital-nation state relationship in all capitalist countries.[56] For the reasons already given, this is the central factor that explains why capitalist countries are almost always representative democracies of one type or another. Only in representative democracies can capital develop and expand the idea that individual rights and freedoms are best realized through market, consumer, audience and spectator activities rather than citizenly and occupational ones.[57]

But there is another feature of co-optation that needs to be brought to light as a consequence of the contrast between witting and unwitting aspects of this continuous activity and process. It bears directly on the issue of legitimacy, and capital's use of and dependence upon key institutions of the state and public sector to secure and maintain it. I am referring to Robert Merton's distinction between manifest and latent functions as the essence of collective, now social, life and its need for institutions conferring legitimacy. Since legitimacy can only be conferred where the institutions carrying out this central task are *accepted by* the people, the *perpetuation* in reality of the

[55] Clark and Dear, *op. cit.*: Gee, Hull and Lankshear, *op. cit.*; Hellinger and Judd, *op. cit.*

[56] Wilson, *Bureaucratic Representation*, chapter 2; 6, section II.

[57] Lindblom, *op. cit.* chapters 12–16, 21.

distinction between an institution's manifest functions and its latent functions is of the utmost importance.[58] Murray Edelman, writing in a more cynical vein almost forty years ago, noted that the only reason people were satisfied with what he called 'symbolic reassurance' from these institutions, while organized interest groups representing capital received their tangible benefits, is that they were unaware that this was the case.[59]

It is hardly surprising that capitals themselves are usually oblivious to these functions because they too have internalized the values that are so central to secondary socialization in capitalist countries. 'We win, you lose' is not only directly relevant to discussions about the 'public debt' that is the topic of the next chapter. It also explains why the privileged position of capitals is so taken-for-granted throughout capitalist societies by individuals schooled and continually socialized in what capitals and capitalism do for the people and its institutions, but not in what the people do for capitalism. Nothing is better calculated to reverse this situation than a concerted effort to see capitalist societies as organized political-economic units engaged in a continuous process whereby public capital is co-opted to private uses employing the institutions of sovereignty and legitimacy backed up by agencies of secondary socialization to this end. That almost no one is aware of this process is of the essence of Merton's distinction between manifest and latent functions.

Thus capitalist societies are defended and promoted as places where individualism is honored in and through constitutional and legislative provisions and agencies of secondary socialization that declare it to be indispensable to our social order—the manifest function of this concept and these provisions and agencies. But the deeper function they secure on a continuous basis is support for individualism only if it is expressed either through capitalist maximization or through market and consumer or audience and spectator roles. Too much citizenly or occupational individualism is seen to be destabilizing, even if only a few do it. The manifest function of property emphasizes its availability in the form of *private* property (including capital), to every individual, while its latent function is to maintain social

[58] Robert Merton, 'Manifest and Latent Functions', *Social Theory and Social Structure* (New York: Macmillan, 1957), pp. 19–87.

[59] Murray Edelman, *The Symbolic Uses of Politics* (Urbana, Illinois: University of Illinois Press, 1964), especially chapters 1–3, 9.

order while protecting the one-sided rights without responsibilities of owners—including their right to extract labor power. So-called communist systems were once pointed to as the only alternative to capitalist societies in ways intended to obscure the fact that it was representative democracy and the rule of law, not capitalism, that mainly distinguished us from what in truth were *pre-capitalist* (and by implication pre-democratic) collective forms.

The manifest function of an institution is what it is alleged to do *and what it may actually even do*, while the latent function is what it does that is more fundamental and more important than what it says it does, or actually does.[60] Comparing capitalist societies to communist societies underscores the extent to which this distinction between manifest and latent functions so central to functionalist thinking is usually premised on the assumption that *it is the manifest rather than the latent functions that are indispensable.* The argument here makes precisely the opposite claim. Viewing institutional processes and activities in capitalist nation-states as a continuous, long-term co-optation of public capital upends the functionalist argument. It does this by exposing the fraudulence of its assumption that the indispensability of certain functions necessary for social order and cohesion can be equated with activities and processes carried out by given structures at given times and places. It shifts the spotlight from what we have been socialized and trained to believe are the central institutional realities to activities and processes which have either been ignored or interpreted in ways that see them as secondary, derivative or altogether insignificant.

A preference for focussing on the distinction between manifest and latent functions is a way of underscoring the difference between two realities, not illusion and reality. One adopts (or adapts) the official version of what the real functions of political, economic and social institutions in capitalist societies are, while the other focusses on the co-optation of public capital. This difference is well-captured in Merton's point that latent functions are ones that occur 'below the threshold of superficial observation'.[61] Because there is no conspiracy, the truth of the distinction and the greater importance of latent

[60] The conceptual approaches of both Merton, *op. cit.* and Edelman, *op. cit.* thus provide the basis for a very useful matrix for analyzing the functions of institutions, and the nature of their (alleged) indispensability.

[61] Merton, *op. cit.*, pp. 64–65.

rather than manifest functions *may be totally unintended* by those in positions of power and influence over co-optative processes. The point is rather that below the surface there is a completely different set of processes and activities at work alongside different ways of understanding and making deep sense of these processes and activities. The point of departure is always someone's inability to reconcile the official or approved version of reality with what they have observed. In the case of the co-optation of public capital, it is the conflict between the apparent role of capital *vis à vis* other factors of production and the secular national state and the real significance of labor, land and the public realm relative to capital which is at issue.[62]

The co-optation of public capital is a long term, continuous, unending process in all capitalist societies because it is absolutely indispensable to the success of individual capitals and the persistence of capitalism. The official or approved version of what is happening is simply incapable of providing an explanation adequate to the complexity and sophistication of its subject-capitalist society and the capitalist nation-state. By dynamizing co-optation as a process which allows both aspects to survive through an emphasis on mutuality and reciprocity, it is only being faithful to the essence of this process as real, human activity, however long-term, continuous and often formalized it must be. It is the very dynamic and reciprocal nature of this process that makes public capital, defined as a people's stock of past, present and potential values and embodied in their labor, habits and institutions, so eminently subject to co-optation for private uses. The continuous requirement of public capital thus arises out of the very necessity of creating and recreating it anew, while it attests to the people's central and indispensable role in doing this, occasionally in conscious, but usually in unconscious ways.

Public capital needs to be created and recreated anew by the people because capitals are continually using up public capital by converting it to value on exchange either in place of or alongside use values.[63] When capitals create use values, whether accidentally as a

[62] Marx discusses the difference between perceiving and thinking and comprehending in *Grundrisse*, *Capital, Volume I* and elsewhere. See Wilson, *Marx's Critical/Dialectical Procedure*, chapters 2–6 for discussion of the procedure employed, especially the role of 'retroduction' in Marx's thinking in chapter 6.

[63] This is one way of addressing the 'transformation problem' discussed in Anwar Shaikh, 'Marx's Theory of Value and the Transformation Problem', Jesse Schwartz (editor), *The Subtle Anatomy of Capitalism* (New York: Goodyear Publishing Co., 1977), pp. 106–139.

by-product of creating exchange values or by miscalculation, they assist in the creation of public capital stock. Nevertheless, the key ingredient of, and agent in, this creating and recreating of public capital stock is the people, who confer legitimacy on capitals and capitalism by acquiescing, usually unconsciously, in the view that co-optation, while certainly not an unmitigated evil, is often a necessary one. The creation and recreation of public capital is partly the result of the activity of capitals who create use values in the process of creating exchange values, to be sure. But their role, and that of capital as a factor of production, is nowhere near so central to the persistence and development of these societies as we have been led to believe. In particular, it is the denigration of public and social sector institutions as agents of the people in representative democracies that has been most severely distorted by the official and approved versions of capitalist ideology in its neo-conservative variant.[64]

This analysis suggests that the husbanding of public capital by and through public and social, as well as capital sector institutions constitutes the key vehicle through which capitals are often compelled to put the creation of use values ahead of the creation of exchange values. Indeed, the only process that equals it in the creation and recreation of use values is the very one that has made the subsequent development of public and social institutions themselves possible-the representative process of democratic elections. The present neo-conservative agenda has sought to seriously subvert this balance between the creation of exchange and use values by capitals, putting a far heavier burden on the people to create and recreate the stock of public capital than was true under the Keynesian consensus. To be sure, this has occurred with the complicity, if not duplicity, of anti-government political parties hostile to public and social institutions and highly supportive of those of capital in the state and government system. The point is that more and more pressure is being placed on the people to create and recreate the stock of public capital directly through their labor, while the very public and social institutions on which the creation of use value depends are being eliminated, downsized, contracted out and privatized. This is creating a crisis of representation as well as a crisis in use value, and

[64] Boswell and Peters, *op. cit.*; Clark and Dear, *op. cit.* See Wilson, *Bureaucratic Representation*, for the many ways that public and social bureaucratic institutions are being given capital functions, if not being taken over and colonized completely by them.

thus public capital, creation. It is occurring because capitals are using up the stock of public capital faster than they are helping to create it by co-opting it at an excessive rate in their unbalanced determination to privilege the creation of exchange values over use values. This imbalance is evident in the demand for (and attainment of) more direct, intensive and extensive methods of continuous co-optation than capitals have dared to use since before the Depression.[65]

The process whereby the stock of public capital is co-opted to private uses must be balanced by the social obligations and responsibilities of capitals to honor the other side of the bargain. Capital must assist the people in the creation and recreation of the use values that are the key to generating public capital stock for reasons bearing on its own legitimacy as well as for more immediate instrumental reasons having to do with the need to create exchange values. On the one hand, capitals are understandably preoccupied with co-opting public capital because of its central role in the creation of exchange values. On the other, however, so much of this occurs without anyone being aware of what is happening that the imbalance and lack of mutuality and reciprocity cannot be seen and understood for what it signifies and foreshadows. The present situation demands reflection and careful analysis inspired by the lack of fit between a deeper comprehension of reality and the official or approved version of events. This, in turn, underscores the importance of focussing on latent functions like the co-optation of public capital and the extraction of surplus value from labor, and the potential and actual conflict between the creation of use values and the creation of exchange values. It is their understanding that allows us to appreciate the reciprocal interdependence on which capitalism's legitimacy, as well as that of public and social institutions, depends.

The urgency of restoring this balance, and even improving what briefly existed under the rapidly disappearing Keynesian consensus, rather than jettisoning it in a fit of ideological pique or pecuniary greed, should be evident for the following reasons. Along with what has already been said, there is an inability on the part of capitals to realize how seriously the present imbalance between co-optation for the purpose of generating exchange values and the responsibility for creating public capital stock jeopardizes and threatens the

[65] Kreml, *op. cit.*; A. Hicks, *op. cit.*; Block, *op. cit.*; Marquand, *op. cit.*

legitimacy of capitalism itself. This is yet another way of saying that markets, far from being self-correcting, absolutely require the continuous intervention of 'extra-market' institutions.[66] Capitals and their supporters have always been dependent on this balance in one form or another, whether capitalism was restricted to commerce and trade prior to industrialization, or confined to relatively limited producer roles in the economy once industrialization had expanded the opportunities for value on exchange. The fact that capitals are using up the stock of public capital at a significantly faster rate than they are assisting in its creation is a matter that should concern them and the people and their leaders in all capitalist countries, where the 'victory' over communism is generating an unseemly and dangerous new system of justifications for accelerating this imbalance and exacerbating its effects.

[66] Kuttner, *Everything for Sale*, p. 362 and *supra*.

CHAPTER NINE

THE PUBLIC DEBT: WE WIN, YOU LOSE

Debate and discussion about the so-called 'public debt' has polarized around two sets of discourses. There is first the solemn rhetoric of economists whose use of the term is intended to address something that actually exists and to which the term is intended to refer. Largely (but not completely) derived from this is a second, more pejorative, usage which has now, more than ever before, become part of a common, social discourse bemoaning the public debt and its consequences, now and (especially) in the future (allegedly) for generations to come. The belief that 'globalization' has supplanted the public debt in the neo-conservative lexicon because it is a more neutral, even positive term, while superficially correct, ignores the way that the public debt functions in the background to justify the social and economic choices governments supportive of this agenda make.[1] Along with this, of course, goes an emerging consensus on how the public debt has come about and who is to blame for it. The second and first usages all-too-often have in common their support for a neo-conservative rendition of the (alleged) problem which implies, when it does not state outright, what the ideal solution to this problem might be.

The observation that the terms and concepts used to define an apparent (or real) problem are central signifiers, and that the way this problem is formulated is a key factor in the way it is comprehended by citizens and publics, is certainly not new. Yet no attempt to address present discourses around the concept of the public debt can ignore the impact that the very use of the term has. This is particularly true when one considers how public perceptions and discourses might be altered by reliance upon other terms and concepts like those alluded to in earlier chapters. Having said this, however, it is still necessary to acknowledge the fact that there is an element of truth in the term public debt, but not in what it is allowed to imply under the present neo-conservative domination and management of political, economic and administrative discourse. Ultimately,

[1] See Hay, *op. cit.*, pp. 234–235.

it is correct to state that it is the public that is 'responsible' for dealing with this debt, but this does not mean that the public is responsible for causing it or bringing it about.[2]

The point of distinguishing these two understandings of 'responsibility' returns us once more to the central themes of legitimacy and the co-optation of public capital. For it must be clear from what has already been said that private capitals *must* co-opt public capital as it is defined here in order to survive and prosper. For this, capitals and their institutions need a consistent and continuing assumption (and supply) of legitimacy on the part of most of the people, even if the form this takes is passive or the result of a preoccupation with other matters.[3] Those who resist and dispute this legitimacy, particularly if they are seen to be potentially or actually influential, must be marginalized, sidelined or even 'one dimensionalized' in the ways cited thirty years ago by Herbert Marcuse in *One Dimensional Man*.[4] Management and manipulation of the key terms of these discourses is especially important now, with the emergence of more direct and continuous methods of co-opting public capital than we have seen since before the Depression. This falls largely to those anti-public and anti-social political parties that have cleared the way for the neo-conservative agenda to become law and practice over the past twenty-five years in so many capitalist democracies.

It is the way these parties directly manipulate the institutions, practices and discourses of the people and of capital, or employ one or another form of *laissez nous faire* to abandon, withdraw from or vacate areas of responsible public action, that has served to define the scope and nature of neo-conservatism in these societies.[5] Nothing is more central to persuading citizens and publics of the superiority, and even the objective necessity, of this agenda than management of three key terms that will be addressed critically in the chapters that follow—the 'public debt', 'privatization' and 'free trade'. To have captured the conventionally accepted understanding of these terms and what

[2] Peter Warburton, *Debt and Delusion: Central Bank Follies that Threaten Disaster* (Harmondsworth: Allen Lane/Penguin, 1999); James Harless, *The Indebted Society: Anatomy of an Ongoing Disaster* (Boston: Little, Brown and Co., 1996); Jukka Kilpi, *The Ethics of Bankruptcy* (London: Routledge, 1998).

[3] MacIver, *op. cit.*; Clark and Dear, *op. cit.*; Nathanson, *op. cit.*

[4] Boston, Beacon Press, 1964.

[5] Teeple, *op. cit.*; Walter Stewart, *Dismantling the State* (Toronto: Stoddart, 1998); John Shields and B.M. Evans, *Shrinking the State* (Hallifax: Fernwood, 1998).

is assumed to follow from them is no mean feat. It has required nothing less than the collapse of the liberal, Keynesian and neo-Keynesian consensus for which both the right and the left, as well as its own practitioners, are largely responsible. This has been accompanied by an even more serious parallel collapse of the liberal, neo-Keynesian discourses that once accompanied this more sensible and balanced approach to relations between the institutions of the public and society and those of capital.[6]

Successful management of discourses addressed to the public debt relies on what is nothing less than a complicated morality play. It involves everything from the desire to participate in the illusion of shared expertise, through protocols and tactics of inclusion and exclusion, to rituals of expiation, guilt and rectitude based on being 'born again' with a new (and correct) vision. While some of this is a process that is knowingly engaged in, most of it goes on without conscious understanding of precisely what is taking place.[7] It was noted earlier in discussing the co-optation of public capital as the essence of capitalist societies that the reason this process can occur at all is a function of the commonsense capacities and cultural pre-understandings that we all share. This is true even as we seek to distinguish ourselves from one another through the various activities (citizenship, occupation) we perform and roles (consumption, spectating) we occupy, and indeed constitutes the platform that makes such efforts at distinction possible.[8] An analysis of discourses around the public debt, it turns out, is an indispensable element in any effort to address the present legitimacy of capitalism.

Murray Edelman observed, almost forty years ago, that special interests mainly received tangible benefits as a consequence of their (successful) utilization of the law-making and implementing processes of democratic governments. The people, in contrast, almost always got what he called 'symbolic reassurance' intended to make them more passive, compliant and 'quiescent'.[9] While the argument to

---

[6] Robert Kuttner, *Everything for Sale*, introduction and chapters 1–3. On the crucial difference between established notions of the 'politically responsible' and the more stringent demand for the 'responsibly political' in democratic politics and society, see Wilson, *Political Management*, chapter 8.

[7] Hellinger and Judd, *op. cit.*; Gee, Hull and Lankshear, *op. cit.*

[8] Wilson, *Political Management*, chapters 2–5, 10.

[9] Murray Edelman, *The Symbolic Uses of Politics* (Urbana, Illinois: University of Illinois Press, 1964), chapters 1–3, 7, 9.

follow largely concurs with this observation where analysis of the public debt (and privatization and free trade) is concerned, it remains incomplete because of its failure to distinguish between the earlier institutions of capital in these nation-states and the later-to-emerge institutions of the public and society. It is the success that special economic interests, and the political parties supporting their more direct co-optation of public capital, have had in persuading the people that their institutions are inferior to those of capital and that these latter institutions can better 'represent' them and serve the public interest that must be addressed critically.[10]

Any dispute with Edelman on these matters must acknowledge that his study was part of a larger 'realist' agenda in political science research which focused, often somewhat cynically, on the political system as a virtual conspiracy of private interests aided by politicians (particularly legislators) effectively in their pockets. It is important to note that relations between the three sets of institutions so central to the line of argument pursued in this text was, if anything, more balanced at the time Edelman wrote than it is now for the reasons already indicated. Edelman, among many other scholars and intellectuals of the period between 1945 and 1975, was part of an attack on interest group liberalism as it manifested itself politically during this period in United States history.[11] This attack was based in large part on the view that the political system was a creature of the past, and consequently, lagged behind the social and economic accomplishments embodied in the neo-Keynesian agenda in practice.

What Edelman failed to notice, however, was the fact that along with consistent symbolic reassurance went a modicum of tangible benefits to many members of the general public. The idea that we are (or were) involved in a zero-sum game between special interests and the public on the matter of tangible benefits ignores not only the *material* benefits which flowed to members of the general public, *for whatever reason*. It also fails to acknowledge the many special interests that have been unsuccessful in their search for these benefits and the leverage that confers them. Nevertheless, many capitals and their sympathizers amongst the special interests were seeking at the

---

[10] Lindblom, *op. cit.*, chapters 12–17, 22; Wilson, *Bureaucratic Representation*, chapter 5.

[11] Compare to Theodore Lowi, *The End of Liberalism: Ideology, Policy and the Crisis of Authority* (New York: W.W. Norton, 1969, and subsequent editions).

time to supplant parties that supported a better balance between the institutions of the people and those of capital with elected, appointed and scheduled officials whose values and interests would support a more direct and continuous co-optation of public capital. It is to the triumph of an old set of discourses in new guise rather than to a change in 'objective conditions', even in the face of exponentially increasing debts and deficits in the 1970's, that we must turn in order to understand how and why this happened.[12]

Discussing the components of the morality play cited earlier should provide a more helpful approach to addressing the sense, meaning and present significance of the way that the idea of the public debt is presently being manipulated and understood by publics and capitals alike. Its function in these discourses must be carefully distinguished from both privatization and free trade. It is the major conceptual vehicle around which the alleged problem is being formulated and discussed, whereas privatization and free trade are two of the apparent solutions to the problem which a neo-conservative focus on the public debt allegedly requires.[13] In one sense this makes public debt discourse even more central to the agenda and practice of neo-conservatism than privatization and free trade discourses. On the other hand, however, these discourses are often inverted in both commonsense and professional usage, such that one's visceral (or other) support for privatization and free trade compels him/her to return to public debt discourses in order to defend and make sense of these purported 'solutions'.

Looking first at the illusion of shared expertise allows us to address those aspects of the public debt discourse in which professional and commonsense conceptions and understandings are most securely joined. As a term or concept which functions as both a referential and a condensation symbol in *both* sets of usages, the idea of the public debt as concept and reality is both more and less than it seems.[14] It seems larger than life when its utilization is combined

[12] Patrick Brantlinger, *Fictions of State: Culture and Credit in Britain, 1694–1994* (Ithaca, New York: Cornell University Press, 1996); John Kingdom, *No Such Thing as Society* (Buckingham, U.K.: Open University Press, 1992); J. Agell, M. Persson and B. Friedman, *Does Debt Management Matter?* (Oxford: Clarendon Press, 1992).

[13] H. Chorney, J. Hotson and M. Seccareccia, *The Deficit Made Me Do It* (Ottawa: Canadian Centre for Policy Alternatives, 1992).

[14] Edelman, *op. cit.* borrows this distinction from Edward Sapir, 'Symbolism', *Encyclopedia of the Social Sciences* (New York: Macmillan/Free Press, 1934).

with and related in one way or another to: the deficit, inflation, interest rates, employment and unemployment figures by jobs, sectors, regions, countries, seasons, classes, age groups and genders. This point is only underscored by looking at its linkages to savings, investment, taxation, public sector growth, budgets, fiscal and monetary policy, economic development, the so-called Third World, and socialism and communism. A final set of indicators locates public debt discourses within case studies, historical panoramas, theoretical and conceptual controversies and various strategies and techniques of management and administration in and around one or more academic or professional disciplines.[15]

By contrast, the public debt seems significantly smaller than life when one demands a definition of this term, something that amounts to a description of what it was, is or could be in the so-called 'real world'. It is at this point that problems arise with its largely metaphorical status *vis à vis* 'real' debts owed to individuals. Suddenly the idea that a real debt can be somehow public in nature temporarily overwhelms the common senses, until the mantle of trained incapacity in its guise as professionalism and objective expertise comes to their rescue and resolves the matter. This is an essential element in the illusion of shared expertise, or, indeed, of objective expertise on its own.[16] For careful scrutiny of professional and academic discourses around the concept of the public debt shows that a wide range of variation in opinion exists regarding its relationship to the other concepts outlined. Not only can it be bad, good, necessary or unnecessary. It can even be neutral, so economists—particularly theoretical economists—tell us, in its impact on other economic and financial phenomena.

The illusion of shared expertise is a fundamental feature of the morality play not only because of the identification it permits non-professional and non-academic members of the citizenry to delude

[15] For example, Kenneth Arrow and Michael Boskin (editors), *The Economics of Public Debt* (New York: St. Martin's Press, 1988); Janet Ford, *The Indebted Society: Credit and Default in the 1980's* (London: Routledge, 1988); J. Frenkel, M. Dooley and P. Wickham (editors), *Analytical Issues in Debt* (Washington: International Monetary Fund, 2000); James Clayton, *The Global Debt Bomb* (Armonk, New York: M.E. Sharpe, 2000); Michael Rowbotham, *Goodbye America: Globalization, Debt and the Dollar Empire* (Charlbury, U.K.: J. Carpenter, 2000).

[16] The notion of 'trained incapacity' is from Thorstein Veblen. Also see Karl Mannheim, *Man and Society in an Age of Reconstruction* (London: Routledge, 1940), pp. 49–60 and *supra*, where expertise is equated with 'functional' rather than 'substantial' rationality.

themselves with. It is fundamental because at a deeper level the very reliance today on a term like the public debt, in whatever discursive form, cannot help but influence public discussion away from questions of legitimacy based on the co-optation of public capital. While at a more superficial level of unreflective disciplined observation, the modern approach of objective expertise, it does seem possible to treat a focus on the public debt as neutral and 'value-free', reflection shows that this is an illusion. The public debt is no more neutral than any other concept, and the Weberian commitment to the use of concepts as 'heuristic' devices cannot cover over the fact that today it *must* function pejoratively, almost without regard to what is said, concluded or valued and alleged by those employing the term.[17]

The fact that this is often not understood or taken seriously by virtually all competent critics of the neo-conservative agenda makes them an unwitting party to the illusion of shared expertise as individuals unaware of the symbiotic relationship between the idea of a public debt and this very agenda. The person, group or institution who controls the use and meaning of concepts and terminology controls the points of view and opinions of the people who read, listen or otherwise participate in these efforts at shared understanding. These critics, in effect, become the leading edge of an unregenerate or heretical element that is party to an effort to use the concept of public debt in order to deny that it really is a debt at all. As such, it is their exclusion from the illusion of shared expertise participated in by members of the now-reborn citizenry which makes this participation seem all the more real and authentic.[18] Apart from everything else that is involved in the difference between professional and commonsense understandings, how much more difficult is it for non-professional members to see through rather than embrace the public debt as a 'real' debt?

Another matter that cannot be ignored in discussions about participation in the illusion of shared expertise was brought up in the last chapter. It discussed the practice of causal reasoning and the

---

[17] Even Weber admitted that the protocol of 'value neutrality' presupposed a prior commitment to 'value relevance' in the selection of topics 'most worthy of being known' in *Methodology of the Social Sciences*, pp. 76–79. His discussion of the ideal type as a 'heuristic device' is in *Ibid.*, pp. 89–111 and in *Economy and Society*, Volume I, Part 1, 1, pp. 6–7, 21–22 and *supra*.

[18] Mannheim, *op. cit.*; Russell Jacoby, *Dialectic of Defeat* (New York: Cambridge University Press, 1981).

false concreteness of the real as necessarily discrete, logically unconnected and individuated in line with the preference for focusing on events based on a linear and sequential notion of time rather than on wholes as both structures and processes.[19] A key element in false concreteness is the presumption that the designation of a more empirically concrete phenomenon makes it more real than one that is (within this world-view) more vague and abstract. By inverting the abstract and the concrete in this way, citizens are persuaded that they have a more secure grasp of reality than can be realized through reliance on concepts like public capital, co-optation and legitimacy, or even the original factors of production themselves—land, labor and capital. To be sure, at the same time that they gain this feeling of greater security by participating in this false concreteness they are able to identify with elite and learned opinion.[20]

In a certain sense this is correct and understandable, because it appeals to the public's limited attention horizon and perceived need for quick fixes and problem-solution matrices that are clear and unambiguous. Even if theoretical, conceptual and methodological controversies leave the public cold and fail to engage its interest, professional endorsements of straightforward empirically concrete and individuated actions strung together in event-centered sequences of cause and effect do provide a strong basis for its willingness to identify with such 'commonsense' solutions. On the other hand, while this may work because the link between commonsense and professional rationalities is to be found in their common embrace of traditional theory and empirical method, for many the added stimulus of fear and anxiety generated by dire pronouncements and media terrorism may be required, both initially and intermittently.[21] Fortunately for the neo-conservative agenda, the fact that the first priority of mass media is all-too-often sensationalism leads it to opt for increasing circulation or audiences by adopting or participating in this attempt to generate the (allegedly) needed new morality in exactly this way.

---

[19] On causality, see especially Mario Bunge, *Causality and Modern Science*. Third Revised Edition (New York: Dover Publications Inc., 1979, 1959); G.H. Von Wright, *Explanation and Understanding* (Ithaca: Cornell University Press, 1971); Von Wright, *Causality and Determinism* (New York: Columbia University Press, 1974); J.L. Mackie, *The Cement of the Universe: A Study in Causation* (Oxford: Clarendon Press, 1974); and Wilson, 'Time, Space and Value', *op. cit.*

[20] Wilson, *Marx's Critical/Dialectical Procedure*, chapters 3–5.

[21] Wilson, 'Critical Theory's Critique of Social Science, I and II, *History of European Ideas*, Volume 7, No. 2 (1986), pp. 127–147 and Volume 7, No. 3 (1986), pp. 287–302.

Being in a position to participate in the illusion of shared expertise, with or without this stimulus, the public, which is really being passive, compliant and quiescent, is persuaded that it is engaged in the activity of self-government and meaningful citizenship. To this end, it is electing leaders and parties that will carry out their will by taking control of a profligate political, bureaucratic and social-occupational apparatus that has run completely off the rails.[22] Meantime, the process by which public capital is co-opted to private uses, and use values to exchange values, not only carries on unabated but extends itself and intensifies by becoming both more direct and more continuous than it has been since before the Depression. Participation in the illusion of shared expertise is as much a problem for professionals and experts as it is for citizens and members, but only in an abstract sense. Their class, occupational and status position, with all that this confers, is the essence of the difference, but it also underscores the consequences for commonsense publics of the aid and comfort professional elements provide for those presently co-opting public capital in the ways indicated.

Being thus imprisoned in an interlocking set of language games, neither professionals nor non-professionals can escape the abstract consequences of conceptual reliance on the idea of a public debt. This is even true when the concrete consequences, as understood through traditional theory and these language games, impact in very different ways on one group than on the other.[23] The identity that citizens and members achieve with professional opinion in one or another form is more than complemented by the sense of security they realize through the manipulation and management of the concepts, terminology and sequences of causal and proto-causal reasoning. These serve to convert identification and the illusion of shared expertise into a perception of actual, ongoing participation. With this the first phase (or second, if preceded by media terrorism) is completed, faith in the professional and academic experts having been converted into 'works' characterized by consistent or occasional participation. This is accompanied by a perception of one's membership on the virtuous or technically correct 'side' of what may seem

[22] Clark and Dear, *op. cit.*; John Rohr, *To Run a Constitution: the Legitimacy of the Administrative State* (Lawrence, Kansas: University Press of Kansas, 1986).

[23] On 'language games', Ludwig Wittgenstein, *Philosophical Investigations* (New York: Macmillan, 1953). Also see Brian Torode, *The Material Word* (London: Routledge, 1979).

to be little less than a battle between good (us) and evil (them).

It is the alliance between neo-conservatism's essential simple-mindedness and the public's perception of its rhetoric as more concrete, thus more empirically real and credible as a formulation and resolution of the problem, which permits its morality play the overwhelming influence it presently possesses. For as Arthur Laffer once pointed out, as well as David Stockman after he 'recanted', the message is religious, even evangelical in nature, however many 'facts' can be marshalled by tying the public debt to other key concepts in the neo-conservative lexicon of 'economically correct' concepts. Indeed, what makes these 'facts' so attractive is precisely the way they provide the basis for a clarion call to the multitudes allegedly oppressed by irresponsible politicians, bureaucrats and regulators and by a profligate welfare state, with its service-soddened citizenry in need of discipline and self-reliance. The result is a problem-solution matrix bringing together concepts, terminology and facts in a way that makes it obvious that it is only fallen nature that makes those responsible for the public debt unable or unwilling to overcome their condition by acknowledging the truth and doing the right thing.

While protocols and tactics of inclusion and exclusion are clearly vital to participation in the illusion of shared expertise, the different consequences of this commitment for professional experts and for citizens can never be overstated. In the abstract, it is shared expertise which is the illusion, but looking at the matter concretely, it is the very different effects experienced by citizens supportive of this agenda that is of most enduring significance. For it is the fact that they get most of the symbolic reassurance, in contrast to experts and special interests, who get most of the tangible benefits, that makes even the short term effects of this agenda in practice such a zero sum game.[24] 'We win, you lose' is the essence of this morality play converted into public, social and economic policies which the illusion of participation in shared expertise only serves to mask. Any agenda that shifts the burden of taxation so clearly in a regressive direction, usually toward those less or least able to pay, while simultaneously curtailing, cutting back or privatizing services needed by these people and others depends heavily on being able to sustain this gap between illusion and reality. This does not even address the advantages that

[24] Edelman, *op. cit.*, chapter 2.

capital continues to receive through 'full faith and credit' and related provisions of constitutions, organic acts, basic laws, and legislation, judicial decisions, rules, regulations and orders pursuant, particularly on matters related to bankruptcy, administration and receivership.[25]

The technique or strategy of addressing the citizenry employing a neo-conservative vision allegedly beyond the 'us' and 'them' rhetoric of more critical approaches addresses the sense of this in a most pragmatic way. In place of a contrast between middle, lower middle and working class majorities on the one hand and those capitals and their allies in the upper reaches of the class structure on the other, we are provided with a rather different view of society. In this view everyone was actually dis-benefiting from neo-Keynesian policies, even if they were unaware of it, until a few saw the light and emerged to enlighten (or convert) the majority in the interest of virtually everyone.[26] No class-focused approach can possibly prevail, particularly in North America, once the citizenry believes that *it* is responsible, either directly through the franchise or indirectly through the behavior of its politicians and its appointed and scheduled 'servants', for the public debt and deficit. At the same time that this strategic redefinition of society upends class as a basis for political and economic sense-making, it characterizes many or most of those who believe they are benefiting from public and social services, benefits or functions as unaware of their real interests.[27]

In contrast to the alleged 'rigidity' of class as a basis for locating individuals and groups, the neo-conservative redefinition of the 'us' 'them' rhetoric, with all its religious and evangelical refrains and motifs, still seems more 'open'. This is because the people whom it depicts are understood to be misinformed and/or unaware of what their real interests are. As such, they are always (so it is argued) free to see the light, accept conversion and join the righteous. On the other hand, there are unacknowledged limits to this apparent openness which neo-conservatism has been ready, willing and able to

---

[25] See especially Kilpi, *op. cit.*; and John Hamer, *Troubled Debt Restructuring: An Alternative to Bankruptcy?* (Ann Arbor: UMI Research Press, 1985).

[26] Compare to A. Hicks, *op. cit.*; and Kreml, *op. cit.*

[27] H.T. Wilson, 'Notes on the Achievement of Communicative Behavior and Related Difficulties', *Dialectical Anthropology*, Volume 12, no. 3 (1988), pp. 285–305 addresses critically the notion of talking out rather than acting out for both domestic and Third World 'others'. On abstract versus concrete policy and practical interests, Wilson, *Bureaucratic Representation*, chapters 3–6 and 9.

trade on and take advantage of. Moral majority, xenophobic and 'know-nothing' elements in these countries have often taken advantage of the present situation, and have been encouraged by neo-conservatives in doing so. To this end, they have castigated and excluded racial, ethnic, linguistic, cultural and religious minorities as well as the mainline poor, infirm and aged as unworthy (if not worthless) recipients of public largesse and the national wealth for a variety of thoroughly invalid reasons.[28] The relationship between public and mob attacks on these people, especially if immigrants or refugees, and the neo-conservative agenda should not go unnoticed.

While it is easier to carry out tactics and protocols of inclusion and exclusion on minorities than on possible or actual majorities in any particular jurisdiction, this is especially true if they cannot vote or speak the dominant language. Nevertheless, neo-conservatives have been more recently emboldened in their attacks, or support for attacks, on mainline elements by both primaries and their equivalent and low voter turnout in general coupled with the sheer impact of the morality play being discussed. What matters most is that significant (and increasing) numbers of the citizenry have either taken responsibility directly for the alleged state of affairs depicted by neo-conservative attacks on the public debt, acknowledged their indirect responsibility by blaming their elected, appointed and scheduled officials, or treated the matter as a conspiracy. This conspiracy may involve officials on their own, or it may include those elements of the citizenry who can be counted on to support universal public and social services, the so called welfare state and regulation of business, finance, commerce and industry out of complicity, confusion or fallen nature.[29]

The catalogue of complicit, confused or unregenerate members of the citizenry who have supported or encouraged such (allegedly) profligate policies would include the following. Welfare recipients, state, public and social sector employees, intellectuals, graduate students in non-scientific, non-technological and non-professional disciplines,

---

[28] See John Miller, *The Unmaking of Americans: How Multiculturalism Has Undermined America's Assimilationist Ethic* (New York: Free Press, 1998); and Ian Gough and Gunnar Olofsson (editors), *Capitalism and Social Cohesion: Essays on Exclusion and Integration* (New York: St. Martin's Press, 1999).

[29] David Reisman, *Conservative Capitalism: the Social Economy* (New York: St. Martin's Press, 1999); Stephen Nathanson, *Should We Consent to be Governed?* (Belmont, California: Wadsworth Publishing Co., 1992); Mattei Dogan (editor), *Comparing Pluralist Democracies: Strains on Legitimacy* (Boulder, Colorado: Westview Press, 1988).

members of left-of-center political parties, labor unions and significant elements among immigrant and refugee groups, especially those who have recently arrived in a given country, would constitute prominent groups on this list. These groups have consistently been targeted, explicitly or by implication, by proponents and supporters of the neo-conservative agenda as those principally responsible for the public debt and the deficit that increases it with every passing year.[30] In place of a focus on the co-optation of public capital and the reality of fundamental class and related antagonisms, we have a wide-open indictment of the values and needs of a vast number of people who must be isolated and defined as intentionally evil or unintentionally misinformed or deluded.

Instead of economic theory and public policies being inspired by or dependent upon religious tenets like the 'protestant ethic', economics of a certain type itself becomes a religion, or something barely distinguishable from a religion. Out-group members ('them') must either see the light, confess their sins and acknowledge their guilt and thereafter seek absolution through a commitment to 'economic correctness', or confirm their unregenerate and profligate nature by refusing to embrace the faith. It is its redefinition of economics as a religion in its own right that makes neo-conservatism's view of who is 'really' responsible for the public debt so religious and moralistic, as well as hypocritical, in its day to day and overall impact. It is no coincidence that President George W. Bush's major concerns and the public discourses he uses to address them, both before and since the terrorist attack of September 11, 2001, often combine the values and general interests of fundamentalist religion and neo-conservative economic morality.[31] Ironically, but not surprisingly, this approach, and the illusions, tactics and protocols so central to its success and persuasive power, are precisely what conservatives in the 1940's and 1950's condemned the 'world communist conspiracy' for perpetrating on American, European and Asian peoples. Though communism was only acknowledged to be a 'religion' in the worst possible sense, its ideological and dogmatic nature was often assumed

[30] Stephen Craig (editor), *Broken Contract?: Changing Relationships between Americans and their Governments* (Boulder, Colorado: Westview Press, 1996); David Marquand, *The New Reckoning: Capitalism, States and Citizens* (Malden, Mass.: Polity Press, 1997); Stanley Aronowitz, *False Promises* (Durham: Duke University Press, 1992), Introduction, chapters 1, 2 and Epilogue.

[31] See Wilson, *Bureaucratic Representation*, preface, introduction, chapter 5 and *supra*.

to be indistinguishable from religion, so understood. That the self-same observation could be made for neo-conservative discourses on the 'public debt' today is a telling indictment of this agenda.

Interaction back and forth between religious and secular motifs is really what gives neo-conservatism its effective cutting edge in discussions of the public debt, but elsewhere in allied discourses as well. Its reliance on rituals of expiation, sin, guilt, conversion and rectitude quite purposely mix and mingle condensation symbols from both religious and secular discourses. They are then able to intersect persuasively with discussions of the 'hard facts' of economic and social life and the (alleged) 'proper' role of governments that can be extracted from these facts. But this strategy works only if the nature and causes of the public debt as neo-conservatism depicts it is assumed to be both true and objectively correct! Thus it is the implicit, when not explicit, ability to mobilize these divergent, but similarly inspired, religious and secular discourses which accounts for the overpowering 'condensation concentration' found in neo-conservative propaganda. Indeed, it is the impending collapse of the distinction between referential and condensation symbols altogether in these discourses which often allows the resulting pronouncements to appear at one and the same time morally and religiously inspired and objectively and concretely factual and 'correct'. If society was the new secular religion a century ago, reflected to some extent in the subsequent rise of both nationalism and post-war Keynesian and neo-Keynesian policies, economy is the new secular religion for neo-conservatives. Indeed, it is their endorsement of 'globalization' as an objective process beyond effective public and social control that encourages an almost-religious passivity precisely because it makes people feel so powerless.[32]

Thus there is not only a secular 'crisis', but one which can also be characterized to be of 'apocalyptic' proportions. Not unlike Frederick Taylor's claim at the turn of the century that the worker was not over-worked but rather underpaid because of his lack of efficiency, the present crisis/apocalypse is translated into commonsense terms. In this form, it becomes a crisis of confidence of the people in their constitutional, representative and collective bargaining institutions in contemporary capitalist democratic societies.[33] The assertion that

[32] Durkheim, *op. cit.*; and Linda McQuaig, *The Cult of Impotence: Selling the Myth of Powerlessness in the Global Economy* (Toronto: Viking, 1998).

[33] Jorge Valadez, *Deliberative Democracy, Political Legitimacy and Self-Determination in Multicultural Societies* (Boulder, Colorado: Westview Press, 2001); D. Archibugi, D. Held

constitutional democracies are comprised of three sets of institutions, those representing capital, the public and society, pointed out that the former precede the latter two in historical time by a significant margin. Its purpose was to underscore how consequential for the people it is when they are persuaded to follow the advice of particular elites and their supporters and give priority to the institutions of capital in determining the nature, scope, meaning and limits of public and social policies. Apart from this 'capital preference', of course, there is also the serious impact of such collective decisions and choices on the progress of fundamental democratization itself.[34]

The clear bias of neo-conservative elites in contemporary constitutional democracies is toward controls on representative democracy and public and social legislation. Not only is a plebiscitary conception of and approach to politics preferred. Reliance upon a Burkeian 'discretionary' model of constituency representation over a Rousseauian 'instructed delegate' model is also in evidence. While this may appear compatible with industrial policy or industrial strategy models which view the nation-state as a 'firm' competing with other nation-states in the international, global arena, their reason for controls is quite different when looked at from the standpoint of economic policy. The purpose of the neo-conservative agenda is not nationalistic in this sense, but rather favors one or another approach based on 'free trade' to the extent that it assists in the more direct and more continuous private co-optation of public capital in whatever form and in whatever jurisdiction. The state and governmental-bureaucratic apparatus exists for this agenda mainly to facilitate co-optation and related processes, not to organize the factors of production, or employ fiscal or macro-economic policies in a given nation state to benefit its people. Indeed, the operative, and clearly self-serving, assumption is that 'the market' continues to do this almost automatically.[35]

---

and M. Kohler (editors), *Re-Imagining Political Community: Studies in Cosmopolitan Democracy* (Stanford: Stanford University Press, 1998); Paul Sniderman, *The Clash of Rights: Liberty, Equality and Legitimacy in Pluralist Democracy* (New Haven: Yale University Press, 1996); Nicholas Kittrie, *The War against Authority: From the Crisis of Legitimacy to a New Social Contract* (Baltimore: Johns Hopkins University Press, 1995).

[34] Hans-Peter Martin and Harald Schumann, *The Global Trap: Globalization and the Assault on Prosperity and Democracy* (Montreal: Black Rose Books, 1998); John Dryzek, *Democracy in Capitalist Times: Ideals, Limits and Struggles* (New York: Oxford University Press, 1996); Ellen Wood, *Democracy against Capitalism: Renewing Historical Materialism* (Cambridge: Cambridge University Press, 1995).

[35] See Harry Dahms (editor), *Transformations of Capitalism: Economy, Society and the State in Modern Times* (New York: New York University Press, 2000); Hendryk Spruyt,

A focus on the morality play described here that emphasizes 'hard economic realities' is indispensable to the success of the neo-conservative agenda to the extent that its goals include a preference for the institutions of capital and a distrust of the later-to-emerge institutions of the public and (especially) society. From the perception of the present situation in these societies as one of crisis or apocalyptic proportions must emerge support for an almost completely free hand for these parties and their supporters to take initiatives and employ discretion to repair it. After all, the people themselves, along with or operating through public and social sector institutions, have been responsible, either directly or indirectly, for the present morass haven't they? This clearly implies that it is their demand through the franchise for public and social institutions, alongside rights to bargain collectively (but never market or consumer roles), that are responsible for the public debt and deficits. What institutions more clearly belong to the people, and are more clearly resisted (or at best tolerated) by capital than these? Neo-conservatives have even encouraged citizens to view public policy preferences in terms of zero-sum options that require them to choose between representative democracy and good public and social programs. The implications of this are that the first is a liability for the efficient and effective delivery of the second and should be replaced by more executive 'streamlining' and less legislative deliberation and discussion.[36]

On the way to conversion and rebirth, there are secular (and often directly religious) motifs which appeal to a religious or moral sense of what is right and what is wrong (sin; guilt). The process of expiation is quite literally an atonement in the sense that those responsible must seek a state of grace which can only be conferred on them when they own up to what they have done or permitted to be done and stop acting like irresponsible or wayward children. The appeal today to acting like an adult rather than 'being a man', its politically incorrect predecessor, is tied directly to the notion that it is our contemporary secular profligacy (since the 1950's) which encourages

---

The Sovereign State and its Competitors (Princeton: Princeton University Press, 1994); Robert Kuttner, *The Economic Illusion: False Choices between Prosperity and Social Justice* (Boston: Houghton Mifflin, 1984).

[36] An early neo-conservative example is A.J.R. Smith, 'Equality and Efficiency: the Big Trade Off', *The Canadian Business Review* (Autumn 1976), pp. 4–7. For commentary, Wilson, 'Industrial Strategy: its Challenge to Social Policy in Canada', *op. cit.*, pp. 86–89.

adults to act like children, postponing the real decisions and avoiding the hard realities. Giving up the ways of children is a biblical injunction that has an impact, not only on the allegedly loose and unregenerate morality of the 1960's, but the loose and unregenerate economics practised from the end of World War Two (if not before) to 1979–80.[37] It is the combined nature and interdependent structure of religious and secular discourses around the public debt that has made the neo-conservative message so powerful and so persuasive.

It is now time to address one of the most important developments arising out of the neo-conservative focus on expiation, in this case of guilt. It is more than appropriate that it be the secular rather than the religious (e.g. sin) focus for atonement that is at center stage here. This is because this particular modification of the biblical requirement that children's things be put away and grown-ups become adults borrows heavily from the Enlightenment tradition and the liberalism and socialism it gave rise to. And it does so just in case the religious and secular motifs and discourses already cited are not enough to bring the unregenerate and profligate to full recognition of the evil or confusion of their ways to the desired result. More recently, it is to environmental movements that we must turn in order to see the most full-fledged, and thoroughly justified, development of this modification of the obligations of the responsible adult. Here, however, the appeal to posterity, to future generations of human beings, our own and others, becomes a basis for the neo-conservative attack on the public debt and deficits that is far less justified, if it is justified at all.[38]

That this invocation of Enlightenment rhetoric and cant addressed to posterity is not consistent with Burke's statement to the effect that society is a partnership of the dead, the living and the yet-to-be-born is evident from his very different (and opposed) reasons for such a description of society. Burke was a contemporary of the

[37] *1 Corinthians*, chapter 13, verse 11.

[38] Carl Becker, *The Heavenly City of the Eighteenth Century Philosophers* (New Haven: Yale University Press, 1932) on the relation between progress and posterity. On capitalism, globalization and the environmental movement see Tim Luke, *Capitalism, Democracy and Ecology: Departing from Marx* (Urbana, Illinois: University of Illinois Press, 1999); and Ted Schrecker, *Surviving Globalism: Social and Environmental Challenges* (New York: St. Martin's Press, 1997). More generally, and in light of recent decisions by the George W. Bush administration, see Abraham and Antonia Chayes, *The New Sovereignty: Compliance with International Regulatory Agreements* (Cambridge, Mass.: Harvard University Press, 1995).

Enlightenment who consistently inveighed against its rationalism, concern for history and future orientation. In its place he supported a view of human nature as something which acquires its moral sense principally (if not exclusively) as a consequence of its dependence upon (and subordination to) custom, convention, tradition and local, parochial sentiments. Alongside this went an abhorrence of individualism as the highest achievement of civilization in favor of the view that whatever is good in civilization is a function of communities and one's membership in them. Burke's view of 'eternal society' as a 'great primeval contract . . . linking the lower with the higher natures, connecting the visible and invisible world' makes him at the very least a social evolutionist, one who treated the institutions of both state and society as part of a divinely inspired moral order.[39]

Far from providing support for a confidence in Enlightenment values and hopes around individualism, reason, posterity and progress, Burke saw these as naive paeans fraught with serious potential and actual consequences. His support for 'eternal society', characterized by the dominance of custom, convention, tradition and local, parochial sentiments, reaches a crescendo in his attack on the French Revolution because it endorses precisely the Enlightenment values and hopes cited. This only underscores how far from a real interest in posterity, progress and the idea of human perfectibility through history and reason Burke was.[40] Contemporary invocations and dire warnings about the public debt, the deficit and other alleged profligacies that trade on posterity and future generations do so by co-opting a concept and value from the Enlightenment tradition. This is then discussed employing forms of discourse and rhetoric not dissimilar to those used by the environmental movement. This should hardly come as a surprise, given the fact that what is today called neo-conservatism is far more the stepchild of a combination of nineteenth century economic liberalism and evangelist fundamentalism than it is of Burkeian conservatism. Europeans correctly refer to what Americans call neo-conservatism as neo-liberalism. American preference for the misnomer of neo-conservatism allows them to refer to policies that have been clearly social-democratic or even socialist, at least since the Franklin

[39] Edmund Burke, *Reflections on the Revolution in France* (1790), in *Works*, Volume II (London: Oxford University Press, 1906–1907) pp. 347–370.

[40] See Burke, *Thoughts on the Causes of the Present Discontents* (1770) in *Ibid.*, Volume I (London: Oxford University Press, 1906–1907), at p. 372 and *supra.*

Roosevelt administration, as 'liberal', or 'more liberal', thereby avoiding what for them has always been 'politically incorrect' labelling.[41]

It is now necessary to attend to some of the factual claims made by neo-conservatives and their fellow travellers about the nature and consequences of the public debt as well as who is responsible for it. An initial observation is that public debts are quite normal and standard features in the emergence and development of national states. It is not how much the debt is but rather what causes it and what can be counted on to diminish, and in some cases, eliminate it altogether that is significant. Treating it as a 'real' debt is part of the 'discipline and responsibility' ploy already alluded to because this metaphorical reliance on the idea of debt is itself not only rhetorical and propagandist, but terroristic. Its purpose is to hide what capitals really achieve through heightened co-optation of public capital once significant pluralities and majorities have been persuaded that the debt is real in the sense of being avoidable, finite and owed to specific individuals, groups and institutions. These parties, it is implied, are simply not going to continue to support a given country unless something decisive is done about it. However, it must be noted that most of this 'public debt' is comprised almost completely of corporate debt, bank debt, consumer debt, inflated charges for printing and borrowing money, the result of bankruptcies, administrations and receiverships, international and other obligations of governments and the resulting interest compounded at the 'normal' rate.[42] International organizations, national state central banks and bonding companies are central agencies in this effort to make the public debt look like a real debt.

While various techniques of measuring (or mismeasuring) the public debt can be used to make the point unambiguously, one of the most effective approaches is to employ an absolutely false analogy to the household. The irony here is that even if this analogy were valid, capitals and their supporters have become almost totally dependent on the 'real' household running consistent debts and deficits in order to maintain continuously high rates of commodity and service consumption even (or especially) in tight economic times. This, above

[41] See Roger Scruton, *A Dictionary of Political Thought* (New York: Harper and Row, 1982), pp. 90–92 and 268–270, entries under 'conservatism' and 'liberalism' respectively.

[42] Warburton, *op. cit.*; Harless, *op. cit.*; Kilpi, *op. cit.*; and Morris Miller, *Debt and the Environment* (New York: United Nations Publications, 1991).

all else, constitutes the governing hypocrisy inherent in neo-conservative discourse about the public debt.[43] It is precisely the fact that the so-called public debt is *not* like this kind of debt that requires us to turn our perspective on it upside down. Steps can be (and regularly are) taken to deal with real debts in *any* society. Steps taken to deal with the public debt that are compatible with the neo-conservative agenda have virtually no impact even on the rate of its real growth, forget its diminishment. In addition, they depend on real household debt and deficits to assist them in their more direct and continuous co-optation of public capital while deflecting attention away from this fact and one's 'real' debts. A recent example of neo-conservative bankruptcy is the George W. Bush 'tax refund', which clearly promotes spending rather than saving, with American citizens encouraged to consume as an expression of patriotism. Its disappointing results have only been compounded, not created, by the terrorist attacks of September 11, 2001 and their economic aftermath.[44]

The idea is to persuade significant pluralities or majorities to forego the deployment of public capital for the extension and improvement of key public and social institutions like health care, education and training and retraining, social welfare, public services, economic regulation, pensions, unemployment and sickness and accident benefits. In its place the pursuit of a manifestly transparent claim that foregoing this deployment will allow it to control and diminish its 'public debt' is encouraged. This is the standard technique whereby this store of value is made more directly and continuously available to capital through its state and administrative institutions.[45] The importance of the fundamental shift that occurs following on the success of this persuasive effort, centered in the morality play around the public debt already discussed, is that it can only occur if capital and its supporters are emboldened, and see a clear opportunity, for whatever reason. It is this key shift by nation-states supporting the neo-conservative agenda that has not only brought about the collapse of these and other public and social institutions, but has led to the

[43] On personal savings and its favorable impact on the need and amount to borrow, especially 'offshore', see Michael Boskin, *Private Saving and Public Debt* (Oxford: Basil Blackwell, 1987).

[44] See especially Agell, Persson and Friedman, *op. cit.*; Brantlinger, *op. cit.*; and Fred Block, *Postindustrial Possibilities: A Critique of Economic Discourse* (Berkeley: University of California Press, 1990).

[45] Hellinger and Judd, *op. cit.*; Craig, *op. cit.*; Kreml, *op. cit.*

displacement, habitation or supercession of these institutions by those of capital. This, in turn, has generated increased support for mobility rights and total or partial relief from taxation and contributions to public and social benefit schemes, alongside harebrained investments and resulting losses leading to bankruptcy and receivership and many other irresponsible and profligate excesses at public expense.[46]

One would be hard pressed to deny that this constitutes a most useful way to make sense of what is at stake today in what capitals and their henchmen call the process of 'global restructuring'. This allegedly objective and irresistible process clearly requires this shift away from public and social institutions toward those of capital because *it is public capital (thus the people) as I have defined it that is really paying for this so-called restructuring*. This process is nothing more than the shibboleth used by propagandists of capital to objectify and neutralize a fundamental shift in the way that public capital is co-opted to private uses (and abuses), while the public is left to pay the bill.[47] The public debt, for which the people, through public capital as the real source and essence of the wealth of nations is *always responsible*, is therefore caused not by the people themselves. It is caused by private sector capitals, either directly or backed up by parties and governments supportive of their agenda at any given time. The price the people pay for such a shift has already been noted. Not only are the institutions of the public and society ransacked in alleged commission of this false errand of reducing or eliminating the public debt. They are left with its costs and consequences, which are thereafter justified by neo-conservatives as (among other things) the 'wages of sin' for past and present indiscretions on their part.[48]

The real facts about what the public debt is and how it is presently tied to the devastation of public and social institutions and the heightened extraction of surplus value and co-optation of public capital

[46] Kilpi, *op. cit.*; and Fred Block, *The Mean Season: the Attack on the Welfare State* (New York: Pantheon Books, 1987).

[47] Thereby once again raising the question of the legitimacy of neo-conservative governments. See Jonathan Boswell and James Peters, *Capitalism in Contention* (New York: Cambridge University Press, 1997); Linda McQuaig, *Shooting the Hippo: Death by Deficit* (Toronto: Viking, 1995); and Nathanson, *op. cit.*

[48] Kreml, *op. cit.*; Dryzek, *op. cit.*; Marquand, *op. cit.* But see Ronald Glassman's pacan to the possibility of a new capitalist ethic compatible with both maximization and 'the welfare state' in *Caring Capitalism: A New Middle Class Base for the Welfare State* (New York: St. Martin's Press, 2000) and compare to Glassman, *The New Middle Class and Democracy in Global Perspective* (New York: St. Martin's Press, 1997).

must never be divorced from the short-sightedness of capitals and the hypocrisy of neo-conservatism. Capitals are short-sighted because these tactics may not assist them even in the short run, while they always eventually threaten their legitimacy rather than assisting in shoring it up. Capitals are hypocritical because the entire morality play around the gravity of runaway public debts and deficits is intended to both deflect from and justify the more direct and continuous co-optation of public capital that necessitates ransacking public and social institutions in favor of those of capital. Short-sightedness and hypocrisy come together when it is realized that these acts, no matter what labels and terminology are employed to make them seem inevitable, irresistible or objective, generate a serious imbalance within and among capitalist nation-states between the public capital institutional values being used up and those being created. It is only a matter of time before 'objective conditions' of a very different kind begin to come into play in response to this allegedly objective process of 'global restructuring'.[49]

The public debt at any given time is caused not only by private sector, corporate greed, miscalculation and incompetence, however directly or indirectly tied to states and governments it may be. It is also caused by extortionate interest charges on the debt and deficit. To the question: Why are these interest rates and charges so high, the answer is that they just are, because bonding agencies, backed up by central banks and international organizations, have deemed that the risk being taken warrants such rates and charges. But what is the risk—*the real risk*—in this case, and on what possibilities and exigencies are assessments really based? The manifest lack of objectivity in determining these rates and charges, *which is often the key growth factor in much or most of any 'public debt'*, suggests that the determining criteria for rating national state borrowers are at base ideological. This is true both in terms of the ideological proclivities of those agencies who determine these rates and charges, and their opinion of the institutions, habits and values of the governments and peoples allegedly accumulating these debts and deficits.[50] It is interest rates as a whole, but particularly interest charges on public debts

[49] Richard Robbins, *Global Problems and the Culture of Capitalism* (Boston: Allyn and Bacon, 1999); Shutt, *op. cit.*; Martin and Schumann, *op. cit.*

[50] Chorney, Hotson and Seccarecchia, *op. cit.*; Block, *Postindustrial Possibilities: A Critique of Economic Discourse*, and Block, *Revising State Theory: Essays in Politics and Postindustrialism* (Philadelphia: Temple University Press, 1987).

in nation-states around the world, which helps us realize what the deeper purpose of this morality play is.

The bias of the neo-conservative agenda, both domestically through government policies in given nation-states and internationally through the decisions and actions of bodies like the WTO, IMF, central banks in capitalist nation-states and bond rating companies in major world cities, could not be clearer. It favors deep concern about interest rates, inflation and 'punitive' taxation rates on business and industry, but almost completely ignores unemployment and vocational and occupational training and retraining. Why are these latter 'indicators' not priorities? Why are we allowed to endorse 'tolerable unemployment' but not tolerable inflation? *The World Competitiveness Reports*, though for the most part a concoction of conflicting values and priorities, do lay far greater stress on these latter factors, by implication if not directly, than the agencies and organizations cited above.[51] For this reason their discussion and emphasis is clearly more compatible with a realistic sense of what the national wealth actually consists in. This is because of their subtle emphasis on the costs and consequences for capitals of playing fast and loose with it, therefore with the people themselves, even if they appear to lack any appreciation of the central role played by public capital in shoring up and increasing this wealth.

Allied to this one-sided approach to analysis of given domestic economies is rampant hypocrisy by capitals and their supporters about the relationship between alleged globalization and the reality of the private co-optation of public capital. We are encouraged to believe that as a consequence of this process, economic activity will become essentially 'international' and 'global' in nature, with national states becoming less and less significant reference points for capital. To be sure, this assumes that neo-conservatism's thoroughgoing support for the uncontested freedom and mobility of capital continues. The point here is that there is a great deal of difference between a preponderance of international transactions by given corporations in given areas of production and services and independence from key capitalist nation-states, indeed, any and all nation-states.[52] Today capitals, if anything, rely even more than they have in the past on state

[51] Cologny/Geneva: Foundation for the European Management Forum, 1986–1995. See the discussion of factors relevant to 'competitiveness' in chapter 8, this study.
[52] Susan Strange, *Rival States, Rival Firms* (Cambridge: Cambridge University Press, 1991); Strange, *States and Markets* (London: Pinter, 1988).

and governmental support for their private co-optation of public capital and the value on which it is based. Indeed, their conduct over the past twenty-five years in these countries indicates that their reliance has reached a fever pitch, leading them to seek more direct and continuous ways to extract and co-opt substantially more than was true prior to the early 1980's.

One way of making sense of this preoccupation with and demand for ever-greater capital mobility would tie the realization of this goal, synonymous with 'globalization' but lacking the co-optative aspect so central to 'restructuring', to the ever-increasing requirement of public capital and the value on which it is based. For it is precisely the imbalance between the rate at which capitals are creating use values and using them up through a one-sided obsession with value on exchange which, ironically enough, makes them continue with this ultimately futile course of action, one which depends on ever-greater capital mobility.[53] As long as they and their henchmen in governments, political parties and academia are able to persuade significant pluralities and majorities in capitalist nation-states that the secular and religious discourses comprising the contemporary morality play around the public debt make good sense and are 'correct', or at least are more plausible than any competing definition of the situation, their parties and supporters will stay in power.[54] The question which remains is how long it will take the public to realize that no significant reduction of the public debt can ever come about in this fashion because this, after all, is not the real purpose (or latent function) of this morality play at all.[55]

The history of virtually every capitalist nation-state shows a national (or 'public') debt to be a persistent element in its development, *particularly at key points of take off and growth.* While the question of how the public debt is diminished or retired at any given time and place is a fair one, taken in isolation, the issue we must raise is why present-day public debts, such as they are, appear not only beyond retirement but beyond diminishment as well. The answer, now as before, is that countries normally grow past or out of debt through

[53] Michael Storper, *The Capitalist Imperative: Territory, Technology and Industrial Growth* (Oxford: Basil Blackwell, 1989).
[54] Hellinger and Judd, *op. cit.*; Chorney, Hotson and Seccarecchia, *op. cit.*; Gee, Hull and Lankshear, *op. cit.*
[55] Merton, *op. cit.* pp. 19–84, at pp. 68–82.

development and new activity, including most centrally the private, *but balanced*, co-optation of public capital. This growth process is normally characterized by intelligent, innovative and often unique combinations of factors of production in pursuit of national economic, public and social goals. Public debts are *never* diminished or retired by treating the country in question as if it were a household, especially now that actual households cannot realistically be permitted to function with balanced budgets and free of debt.[56]

The truth is that capitals and their henchmen can *never* get the debt down (or out) as long as all this *private debt*, accompanied by high interest charges on it and the public debt, continue. Yet capital really has no alternative to encouraging consumer and related forms of private debt because it is using up value in the form of labor and public capital faster than it is helping create it in concert with other factors of production. This drive toward a more one-sided creation of exchange values over use values, leaving the latter to be increasingly created by accident rather than design, is one thing that gives the apparent element of anarchy to 'globalization'.[57] The same can be said of 'restructuring' as Susan Strange, among others, interprets it when she indicts this activity as little more than 'casino capitalism' because of its preoccupation with mobility and what amounts to *increasing capital flight*.[58] This is why the present historical conjuncture differs so fundamentally from past experience on the matter of what to do about the public debt. Ironically, virtually all of this apparent concern about the public debt by neo-conservatives turns out to be an illusion that they themselves are participants in, largely in consequence of their total ignorance of what is really happening.

Were it not for the fact that public debts can be dealt with effectively by *not* trying to treat the nation-state as an alleged household, we would be in serious trouble. This is because, truth to tell, private capitals *cannot really afford* to have the debt even diminish significantly, forget be retired, in the ways that they and their supporters say are absolutely necessary. As evidence of this false errand,

[56] Kreml, *op. cit.*; A. Hicks, *op. cit.*

[57] See, for example, Claus Offe, *Disorganized Capitalism* (Cambridge, Mass.: MIT Press, 1985); Scott Lash and John Urry, *The End of Organized Capitalism* (Cambridge: Polity Press, 1987). The relation between time and space and exchange values (value) and use values is addressed in Wilson, 'Time, Space and Value', *op. cit.*

[58] Susan Strange, *Casino Capitalism*, revised and updated (Oxford: Basil Blackwell, 1989).

consider what states do when they decide they must fight a war, or respond to international and domestic emergencies of a natural or humanly caused kind. The conduct of the United States government following the terrorist attacks of September 11, 2001 is a case in point. Do they suddenly opt out saying that nothing can be done because the cost of the fiscal and macroeconomic initiatives needed is too high? They most certainly do not.[59] The neo-conservative claim that 'The deficit (or debt) made me do it' is thoroughly unpersuasive when seen against the backdrop of historical and institutional realities and a focus on the co-optation of public capital and its relation to the wealth of nations. The only way we can make sense of the clearly contradictory policies on the public debt and related matters practiced by neo-conservatives is in terms of a morality play of the sort cited. The effectiveness of this morality play lies in its use of mixed religious and secular symbols, metaphors and motifs, combined with sheer ignorance on the part of the cast of this production as to what is really happening and how much is at stake.

On one matter related to the public debt, however, we do have an important option bearing on how we create money, in particular, *which institutions* create a given country's money supply and how the rate of interest for institutional and individual borrowers is determined. Monetarists, in alliance with neo-conservative governments, have, since the late 1970's, decreased significantly the percentage of the money supply created by central banks, while radically increasing the percentage created by private banks.[60] This would be uneventful were it not for the fact that private banks are not only permitted, but encouraged, to lend money at far higher rates of interest than the central banks traditionally have done. Indeed, it is usually neo-conservative governors and directors of central banks in given nation-states, strongly imbued with monetarist doctrine, who have been responsible for supporting this shift of money creation to private banks. Even present day interest rates, low only by comparison to those ordained by earlier monetarist-inspired governments, are significantly higher than rates set by central banks from 1945 to 1970.

---

[59] Donald Stabile and Jeffrey Cantor, *The Public Debt of the U.S.: An Historical Perspective, 1775–1990* (New York: Praeger, 1991) provides an excellent example, along with Jeffrey Cantor and Donald Stabile, *A History of the Bureau of the Public Debt: 1940–1990, with historical highlights from 1789–1939* (Washington: Bureau of the Public Debt, 1990).

[60] Chorney, Hotson and Seccarecchia, *op. cit.*

This fact may help us to understand *why* interest rates and charges really are central factors not only inhibiting, but intended to inhibit, our ability to diminish or eliminate the public debt.

Forty years ago Leon Festinger completed the research that would lead to publication of *When Prophecy Fails*, a persuasive empirical analysis, then and now, of how a group predicting the end of the world responded to the failure of their prediction to come about.[61] Neo-conservatives have a distinct advantage over this fundamentalist group not only because they have successfully employed secular as well as religious symbols, metaphors and motifs in their public discourses. They also have never been pinned down to an exact time when the problem will be solved under their leadership. In addition, they are a political as well as a social (and residually religious) movement, so they can always blame their inability to make progress toward the (allegedly) desired result on past governments, bureaucrats, other political parties, international events and generally on unanticipated occurences.[62] This they have done very well, in large part because it is in the nature of representative democracies under the rule of law to be pluralistic rather than monolithic in the way that partisan and other power is distributed. This, far from being counted a curse, or even a mixed blessing, is rather a 'godsend' for neo-conservatism.

It is the resistance to broad-based democratic developments on the part of neo-conservatives that helps us to understand their thinking and practice at both manifest and latent functional levels. At the manifest level, their view of too much democracy as something that is disruptive fits in with their more fundamentalist preference for monolithic approaches and top-down power systems once the 'truth' is known. At the latent level, this very pattern of conduct helps us understand why it is that almost none of this morality play in its day to day manifestations is carried out consciously and with conspiratorial intent.[63] Many or most of these people, both inside and outside governments and economic organizations, are what Eric Hoffer called 'true believers', and this is all-too-often what makes them both persuasive and dangerous.[64] While it is true that implementation of

[61] Leon Festinger, Henry Riecken and Stanley Schachter, *When Prophecy Fails* (New York: Harpers, 1964).

[62] Merton, *op. cit.*, pp. 51 and *supra.*

[63] Hellinger and Judd, *op. cit.*; Gee, Hull and Lankshear, *op. cit.*; Clark and Dear, *op. cit.*

[64] Eric Hoffer, *The True Believer* (New York: Harper and Row, 1951).

the policies called for by the neo-conservative agenda does require a more direct and continuous co-optation of public capital than has been the case since before World War Two, its deeper consequences are rarely understood by either the perpetrators or their supporters.

This is perhaps most evident in the fact that international bond holders still have what amounts to a vested interest in achieving zero (or near zero) inflation through high (or higher) interest rates. This is true even (or rather especially) if the effects of such a policy are virtually guaranteed to dampen or negate altogether a nation's economic recovery and the growth in its productive assets which normally accompanies such recovery. It almost goes without saying that this vested interest extends especially to job creation and to any movement away from what neo-conservatives consider to be 'tolerable unemployment'. Even a 'jobless recovery' can be severely problematic if it compromises the desired or expected return on investment for these bond holders because it too will be inflationary, if not now then some time soon. The attitude that these international debt holders have toward a 'sick' economy is nicely summarized in their demand that it be kept in a stable condition rather than be given what it needs to recover full health.[65]

Otherwise, the inflation that economic recovery inevitably brings with it will erode the value of the debt they hold, an amount that constitutes a steadily increasing percentage of that country's total indebtedness. Central banks and bond rating agencies, supported by the IMF and the WTO, actively aid and abet neo-conservative governments in their determination to purposely eschew all forms of fiscal, macroeconomic and industrial policy in favor of monetarism and the manipulation of interest rates. Confinement to these economic policies, policies conducted on behalf of international debt holders with little or no public or social stake in the indebted country, virtually guarantees that a nation's 'public debt' will never be significantly diminished, forget retired. After all, why would anyone want to give up the guarantee of extortionate interest charges from an entity that cannot go bankrupt, when all that is required to maintain this situation in perpetuity is a sizeable to massive 'public debt' that it cannot significantly affect with the tools available to it?

This chapter has addressed a central set of discourses around the 'public debt' in order to show the nature and impact of the resulting

[65] McQuaig, *Shooting the Hippo: Death by Deficit.*

morality play, while arguing in favor of a non-conspiratorial approach to the analysis of the neo-conservative phenomenon. Its reference to 'we win, you lose' is much less a way of depicting a zero-sum game, although it is often this too. It is instead a way of pointing to the dangers for capitalism and capitals implicit in their one-sided pre-occupation with using up public capital in their quest for exchange values at a faster rate than they are creating the use values on which the generation of public capital depends. Public debt discourses are central elements of this morality play because this concept is the central point of reference, even by comparison to interest rates, inflation and (certainly) unemployment, for framing what the real problem is supposed to be. The next two chapters extend and develop further aspects of this morality play by looking at two of the most important 'solutions' to the public debt and related problems which neo-conservatives have proposed—'privatization' and 'free trade'.

CHAPTER TEN

PRIVATIZATION: HYPOCRISY TRIUMPHANT

If the public debt is a (or the) key concept for defining the problem with mature capitalist economies for neo-conservatives, then privatization is certainly one of the major vehicles for resolving it. Because privatization refers to a process or strategy rather than to a phenomenon which is the source of a problem, its use as a condensation symbol with at best residual referential content is even more a fact of present day discourse than is the case for the public debt.[1] Indeed, things have gone to such extremes over the past two decades that many now believe privatization to be *the* 'quick fix' needed to turn the values, priorities and behaviors of given government and public sector organizations around so that they are headed in the right direction.[2] To be sure, privatization as a strategy and process presupposes that movement from one state or condition to another is both necessary and beneficent. In this case, it is movement out of the 'public sector' (and occasionally the 'social sector') into the 'private sector' which is touted as one key to turning our economies around, by realizing (or restoring) the correct balance between these sectors.[3]

It is not too much to argue that use of the term privatization in the ways indicated is on the verge of crowding out completely the more fundamental relationship between the public, private and social on which the entire fabric of Western societies has rested for over

---

[1] Edelman, *op. cit.*, especially chapters 1–3, 8; Hay, *op. cit.*

[2] Osborne and Gaebler, *op. cit.* But see Dexter Whitfield, *Public Services or Corporate Welfare: Rethinking the Nation State in the Global Economy* (Sterling, Virginia: Pluto Press, 2001); and Joel Handler, *Down with Bureaucracy: the Ambiguity of Privatization and Empowerment* (Princeton: Princeton University Press, 1996).

[3] For a sample of some of the issues involved and positions taken, see Stuart Nagel (editor), *Critical Issues in Cross-National Public Administration: Privatization, Democratization, Decentralization* (Westport, Conn.: Quorum, 2000); Terry Anderson and Peter Hill (editors), *The Privatization Process: A Worldwide Perspective* (Lanham, Maryland: Rowman and Littlefield, 1996); Jacek Tittenbrun, *Private versus Public Enterprise: In Search of the Economic Rationale for Privatization* (London: Janus, 1996); Brendan Martin, *In the Public Interest? Privatization and Public Sector Reform* (London: Zed Books, 1993); Donald Kettl, *Sharing Power: Public Governance and Private Markets* (Washington: The Brookings Institution, 1993); John Donahue, *The Privatization Decision: Public Ends, Private Means* (New York: Basic Books, 1989).

a century.[4] To the extent that concepts and symbols are indispensable elements in making sense of our reality in and through discourse, these three concepts and their relationship are in dire need of recovery, not just in academic and professional discourses but in commonsense modes as well.[5] As a key element on the 'solution' side of the morality play discussed in the last chapter, it is hardly surprising that we have the imbalance that we do between condensational and referential uses in neo-conservative (and often citizen) discourse. After all, a basic characteristic of a morality play is the reduction of the referential aspect of key concepts in its discourse to summary statements of either the problem or its solution. Such shorthands are, if anything, even more necessary when the play in question claims to be a problem-solution matrix addressed to secular problems of economy, society and polity rather than solely or mainly to religion and salvation.

Discourses supportive of a given group, in whatever form, can lull that group into relaxing its critical and analytical edge in its approach to problem definition. Even if given practitioners of an activity or function deeply know that what they do is heavily dependent upon or interdependent with the very groups being pilloried or otherwise criticized in a given discourse, they may tend to acquiescence in the praise and confidence being bestowed upon them. This may be less because they are lulled, even relieved, to have 'good press' after a long drought than because they sincerely believe that the result will simply be a better balance between the institutions of capital and those of the people.[6] Whatever the explanation or rationale, a special dilemma manifests itself in reliance upon privatization as a quick fix solution for our economic woes. First, the public may be too much in need of such a fix to consider the more total system and long-term consequences of its adoption. Second, it is extremely difficult to recover what has been lost once a privatizing decision has been taken, implemented, and is thereafter found wanting.[7]

---

[4] Compare Wilson, *Bureaucratic Representation*, especially chapters 1, 2 and 5 to Stephen Edgell, Sandra Walklate and Gareth Williams, *Debating the Future of the Public Sphere: Transforming the Public and Private Domains in Free Market Societies* (Aldershot, U.K.: Dartmouth Publishing Co., 1995).

[5] Gee, Hull and Lankshear, *op. cit.*; Sniderman, *op. cit.*

[6] Wilson, *Bureaucratic Representation*, chapter 2.

[7] Wilson, *No Ivory Tower*; Kenneth Saltman, *Collateral Damage: Corporatizing Public Schools—A Threat to Democracy* (Lanham, Maryland: Rowman and Littlefield, 2000);

A key factor to be considered is the institutional point of origin of a given nation-state economy which is alleged to be sick or ailing and in urgent need of treatment. It is at this point that another set of discourses kicks in, in order to offer aid and comfort to the morality play already discussed. In each case the appeal is to those who can or will see the situation in terms of professional medicine or psychological therapy. This vastly increases the audience beyond those taken in directly and immediately by the religious-secular morality play cited, with its evangelistic and fundamentalist overtones. It now includes a vast number of persons outside the private sector in professional or semi-professional occupations, as well as other citizens knowledgeable of or respectful toward these occupations and functions.[8] But the idea that a particular institutional arrangement is not just a problem, but an illness or disease, both ignores the deeper social functions it serves, while it encourages people to adopt the cure on the assumption that the end-state derived is both realizable and problem-free once realized.[9] Capitals and their neo-conservative supporters delude themselves by believing that the journey recommended by privatization either results in such a state of affairs, or can be reversed once governments are (allegedly) 'out'.[10]

Apart from addressing an apparent gap between ideal and reality, this suggests that privatization strategies are potential or actual 'one way trips' precisely because the public is frustrated, wants solutions, especially in the form of quick fixes, and may not care about institutional balance—at least not for the moment. Not only is it likely to be persuaded that privatization makes a given public debt disappear or diminish rather than simply becoming private debt *for which it remains responsible.*[11] It fails to realize that precipitous action requiring governments to vacate their established, even traditional,

---

Sunita Kikeri, *Privatization and Labor: What Happens to Workers When Governments Disinvest?* (Washington: World Bank, 1997); Philip Morgan, (editor) *Privatization and the Welfare State: Implications for Consumers and the Workforce* (Aldershot, U.K.: Dartmouth Publishing Co., 1995).

[8] Arnold, *op. cit.*; Craig, *op. cit.*; and Allan Engler, *Apostles of Greed: Capitalism and the Myth of the Individual in the Market* (London: Pluto Press, 1995).

[9] Ronald Burke and Cary Cooper (editors), *The Organization in Crisis: Downsizing, Restructuring and Privatization* (Oxford: Blackwell, 2000); Christopher Foster and Francis Plowden, *The State under Stress: Can the Hollow State be Good Government?* (Buckingham, U.K.: Open University Press, 1996).

[10] Sclar, *op. cit.*; Alan Shipman, *The Market Revolution and its Limits: A Price for Everything* (London: Routledge, 1999).

[11] Whitfield, *op. cit.*; Simon Jenkins, *Accountable to None: the Tory Nationalization of Britain* (London: Penguin Books, 1995).

responsibilities for economic activity, with the aid and encouragement of neo-conservative parties, is much easier to effect than restoring these activities and functions once the institutional destruction of the public sector is well under way or has been completed. Even without the dominance of neo-conservative parties and governments, it is much more difficult to argue for restoring public institutions (thus expenditures) which have been devastated than it is to argue for their dismemberment, particularly given the power of the religious and secular discourses supporting dismemberment and privatization.

Thus a major concern is less with whether forced evacuation of public sector institutions responsible for a given country's political economy can be accomplished than with whether its realization can be *reversed* once citizens and capitals alike realize the consequences of what has transpired. This is an undertaking with grave consequences for citizens (and many or most capitals) in all capitalist nation-states. But it is especially problematic for the large majority of states who not only depend on substantial and direct public sector spending to maintain their society and economy, but *admit* to such dependence rather than attempting to hide it in the private sector. This latter occurs through transfers of value, tax abatements, tax liens, 'tax expenditures', and a legal double standard generally where large corporations are concerned.[12] Neo-conservative governments may have increased significantly the temptation to hide this dependence by making it appear that the private sector is mainly responsible for wealth creation and its beneficent effects for society. But no one has been in a position to fully institutionalize such behavior like the United States, which stands virtually alone in this regard.[13]

Chapter Seven argued that two central assumptions of our political economic discourse in the West are that property is private and that capital is property. It went on to try to reconstruct what is really being said about property in these assumptions, en route to asserting that privacy presupposes limit, that is, responsibilities as well as rights. Thus, the idea of private property, so understood, is justified as a privilege rather than a right because it addresses culturally and socially constituted needs.[14] Concurrently, it sought to argue against

---

[12] Glasbeek, *op. cit.*; Tittenbrun, *op. cit.*

[13] See Kuttner, *op. cit.*; Christopher Hood, *Explaining Economic Policy Reversals* (Buckingham, U.K.: Open University Press, 1994).

[14] G.W.F. Hegel, *The Philosophy of Right*, nos. 41–81, 188–194.

the inclusion of capital as property unless these limits to its right of disposition were not only recognized, but *extended* to comprehend the role of public capital as the ongoing fount of and basis for private capital. As such, 'public capital' as a seminal concept is an essential vehicle for updating the labor theory of value by reconciling it with Smith's conception of the wealth of nations. Chapter Eight focussed on the ongoing process of co-optation, a process built on top of and always presupposing the extraction of surplus value from labor, in order to explain how capitals transfer and transmute, rather than create, use value. It then argued that ignorance and confusion about the real role of capitals, and private capital, was based largely on the fact that the legal and juridical institutions of capital appeared prior to those of the public, and thereafter society. This in turn presupposed a balance between exchange and use values reflected in the activity of these three sets of institutions, a balance that is not presently being honored by neo-conservative parties and governments.[15]

An important consequence of failing to maintain a balance between exchange and use values is that the process of co-optation of public capital to private uses becomes too direct and continuous. The result is that public and social institutions are deprived of the support they require to maintain the needed balance relative to what is being accumulated by the institutions of capital. But since capitals depend on an ongoing supply of public capital, organized in and through the modern territorial state in the form of a given country's national wealth, this imbalance can only be carried so far without damaging the interests of capitals themselves. This may happen either directly through the operation of the economy or indirectly by threatening their privileged position as those collectively delegated, in large part, the job of running this economy in capitalist nation-states.[16] The present 'flight' of capital, presently formulated brazenly as capital's 'natural right' to a mobility denied other factors of production, is pointed to not only to argue that the 'invisible hand' must now be permitted to operate globally. It also requires that capital detach itself from the nation-state so that it can float freely over the earth, deciding for itself what the proper institutional balance should be between the extraction of use values and co-optation of public capital and their creation and generation.

[15] Wilson, 'The Downside of Downsizing', *op. cit.*; 'Time, Space and Value', *op. cit.*
[16] Lindblom, *op. cit.*, chapter 13.

The idea of an ongoing pool of public capital organized as the national wealth of a given country on which capitals are dependent rings true because private capitals are key vehicles in its creation, even if this fact clashes with neo-conservative economic, social and political doctrine. Political economy quickly converted from its early support for labor as the ultimate source of all value to the view that capital, thus the so-called 'private sector', created all value. Government in this reckoning did little more, apart from using value up, than enforce a framework conducive to value creation by private capitals, and then only when it was working at its best.[17] When it was not it, and the institutions of government and society it otherwise represented, did nothing but imperil the institutions of capital and the private sector they supported by using up value while making it difficult or impossible for private capitals to do their job and create it. Recourse to the unseen hand was implicit in the assumption that private capitals possessing private property automatically served the public and social interest in the very act of attempting to maximize their private utilities, rather than as an indirect by-product of these maximizing efforts.[18]

The entire edifice of privatization as an ideology-cum-strategy relies on public support for political economy's revised rendition of the role of capital *vis à vis* other factors of production in the creation of value. Privatization as a proper goal relative to its present (alleged) alternative hitchhikes on the greater utility and superior record that political economy in its neo-conservative variant is supposed to have accumulated according to the revised, and now updated, sequence.[19] It is as if public and social institutions and public capital count for nothing in what has been achieved in capitalist nation-states, including in particular representative democracy and an extended conception of legal rights encompassing non-capitals, the poor, aged, infirm and marginal, victims of discrimination, and immigrants and

[17] David Ricardo, *On the Principles of Political Economy and Taxation* (Amherst, New York: Prometheus Books, 1996, 1911, 1817); J.R. McCulloch, *Principles of Political Economy* (New York: Augustus Kelley Reprints, 1965); and Marx's critique in *Theories of Surplus Value, Part II* (Volume IV of *Capital*), p. 164 and *supra*.

[18] Bernard Mandeville, *The Fable of the Bees; Or Private Vices, Publick Benefits* (Oxford: Clarendon Press, 1924). On Adam Smith, compare his earlier *Theory of Moral Sentiments* (New York: Augustus Kelley, 1966, 1759) to Smith, *An Inquiry into the Nature and Causes of the Wealth of Nations* (New York: Oxford University Press, 1998, 1776).

[19] Arnold, *op. cit.*; Hood, *op. cit.* Compare to Herschel Hardin, *Privatization Putsch* (Halifax: Institute for Research on Public Policy, 1989).

refugees. Apart from failing to comprehend or take seriously their ongoing dependence on public and social institutions and the interdependence between these institutions and those of capital, there is a deeper inability to see, or unwillingness to acknowledge, the difference between institutions *per se* and mere organizations and groups. This can be laid for the most part at the doorstep of the social, behavioral and administrative-managerial sciences, committed as they always have been to the view that collective life is best understood as a rational social organization synonymous with what we today call society.[20]

That society as such is a culturally and historically specific *form* of collective life rather than a synonym for such life and living arises directly out of the recognition that Western civilization is a general culture rather than constituting an alternative to culture. The social, behavioral and administrative-managerial disciplines are 'sciences' of society because their goal is the full realization of this form of collective life over all others, alongside an implicit defense of civilization as a human formation which is beyond (and by implication superior to) culture.[21] Having said this, it is necessary to underscore the ties that bind society and its disciplines to capitalism and political economy. Society is that collective form that is most conducive to the full-fledged emergence of the consumption and spectating functions and activities on which capitals depend. This has temporarily been lost sight of during the imposition of one or another version of the neo-conservative agenda on capitalist societies over the past twenty-five years. That it is capitalism's very dependence on these activities which will invariably compel it (and citizens) to recognize what is problematic about the present unbalanced process of cooptation is becoming clearer with every passing day.

Property and capital are tied irrevocably to society so defined and understood in ways that always argue against anything remotely

[20] Adorno, 'Society', *op. cit.*; Wilson, *The American Ideology*, especially chapter 8.

[21] See Wilson, 'Rationality and Decision in Administrative Science', *Canadian Journal of Political Science*, Volume 6, No. 3 (June 1973), pp. 271–294; 'Anti-Method as a Counterstructure in Social Research Practice', *Beyond Method*, edited by Gareth Morgan (London: Sage Publications, 1983), pp. 247–259; *Political Management*, chapter 8; 'Critical Theory's Critique of Social Science, I and II', *History of European Ideas*, Volume 7, No. 2 (1986), pp. 127–147 and Volume 7, No. 3 (1986), pp. 287–302; 'Essential Process of Modernity', *International University of Japan Annual Review*, Volume 5 (1988), pp. 1–42; 'Culture versus Civilization in the Theory and Practice of International Understanding', *Maydan: Japanese Journal of Middle Eastern Studies* (September 1988), pp. 10–13.

approaching an absolute power of disposition, the moreso when property is argued to be private so that capital can be included in its definition. Political economy, and now the neo-conservative agenda, have always argued that capital should be freer than other forms of property from social and political constraints. But the present claim, bordering on a 'natural right' of mobility, only underscores the need to make it no less free of such limits and constraints than other forms, and perhaps even more subject to them precisely because of its central role.[22] To be sure, none of this is meant to imply acquiescence in the notion that capital, uniquely among the factors of production, augments itself without the others and (in particular) without the support and assistance of governments and public and social institutions and sectors. Nor does it deny or ignore the ties that bind society and its disciplines to what is often limited to substantial support for a better, neo-Keynesian balance between the functions of public and social institutions and those of capital.

Nevertheless, it is precisely the dependence of this balance on the relationship between the production of use *vis à vis* exchange values that tells the tale. For capitals have been consistently delegated a dominant role in running the economy of capitalist nation-states even though they perform nowhere near this dominant role in creating real use value that their ideology, now updated in accordance with neo-conservatism, says they do as a by-product of creating exchange values. Coupled with this is the capacity of their supporters and henchmen to persuade publics that the latter are themselves to blame for the present economic and social state of affairs. One established 'local' version of this has already been referred to as the 'Chamber of Commerce' model, where citizens are told they can have good social programs with executive dominance or strong democracy, but not both.[23] They have relied overmuch, and for too long a time, it is said, on the view that their institutions, rather than those of capital, know what is best for them. Only through this new understanding, both caused and accompanied by the advent of anti-public and anti-social political parties, can society be brought back to what neo-conservatives believe to be the correct institutional balance between

[22] This 'right', as noted, is what justifies both flight itself and efforts to subject it to supranational and international controls beneficial to U.S. interests under *NAFTA*, the emerging *Free Trade Agreement of the Americas* (*FTAA*) and the WTO.

[23] See A.J.R. Smith, 'Equality and Efficiency: the Big Trade Off', *Canadian Business Review* (Autumn 1976), pp. 4–7.

the three sectors.[24] On matters like this, most practitioners of the sciences of society fall silent, or vote with their feet, thereby acknowledging their genealogical relationship to political economy in its revised version, while at the same time using society's division of labor to justify leaving such matters to the economists.[25]

The relationship between public and private in contemporary capitalist nation-states is incomprehensible in the absence of recognition of the mediating role of society and the social. This holds no less for the discourses which resist the idea of a relationship between them than it does for the institutions which perpetuate, and in consequence only serve to underscore it.[26] Only in society is it possible for this contradiction between concepts and symbols and the institutional reality of dependence and interdependence to exist in a continuous, if occasionally precarious, equipoise.[27] The problem here is that the citizenry all-too-frequently allows that which is public to be elided into the social or societal in their discourses. The result is that the difference between public and social institutions is lost, with serious consequences for a proper understanding of privacy and the private.[28] After all, is it not the very ubiquity of society and the social that leads the denizens of Western capitalist states to be so preoccupied with and protective of their 'privacy'? This in turn has generated resentment toward what is somewhat euphemistically called the 'public sphere' precisely because public and social or societal life have been elided, with serious consequences for all that is (or should be) public.[29]

Hannah Arendt was the first to point out the fundamental hypocrisy implicit in our societal discourse on the relation between public and private spheres. Capitals and their supporters defend, almost religiously,

[24] Jeffrey Gates, *Democracy at Risk: Rescuing Main Street from Wall Street* (Cambridge, Mass.: Perseus Publishing Co., 2000); Gough and Olofsson, *op. cit.*; Dryzek, *op. cit.*; Marquand, *op. cit.*; Craig, *op. cit.*; Foster and Plowden, *op. cit.*

[25] Wilson, 'The Counter Revolutionary Function of the Social Sciences in Advanced Industrial Societies: A Post Revolutionary Analysis and a Revolutionary Alternative', *History of European Ideas*, Volume 11 (1989), pp. 167–177; *Marx's Critical/Dialectical Procedure* (London: Routledge, 1991), chapter 5 and appendix.

[26] Hannah Arendt, *The Human Condition* (Chicago: University of Chicago Press, 1958).

[27] Adorno, 'Society', *op. cit.*; Wilson, 'Reading Max Weber: the Limits of Sociology', *Sociology*, Volume 10, No. 2 (May 1976), pp. 297–315; Wilson, 'The Poverty of Sociology: "Society" as Concept and Object in Sociological Theory', *Philosophy of the Social Sciences*, Volume 8, No. 1 (March 1978), pp. 187–204.

[28] An excellent example in this regard is Richard Sennett, *The Fall of Public Man* (New York: Vintage Books, 1978).

[29] Wilson, *Political Management*, chapter 3.

the absolute right of their citizens to privacy at the same time that they subject this alleged right to incessant invasion by using every available weapon at their disposal to encourage consumption (and spectating) beyond one's financial (and often physical) capacity. At the present time, two thirds of U.S. economic activity is comprised of consumer spending. President George W. Bush defended his 'tax refund' not just because it would stimulate consumer spending, but because he believed that the surplus should be held by taxpaying families and individuals, not the federal government.[30] It has already been suggested that the fatal flaw of capitals lies precisely in this dependence on accelerating patterns of consumption, and how it leads to private (thus public) indebtedness and consequent hypocrisy on virtually all matters related to the public debt. The kernel of truth implicit in encouraging people to identify their personhood and status with their ability to consume (and display) commodities and services is that consumption is the essence of what was originally understood to constitute privacy as it expressed itself in and through family life.[31] Needless to say, this conception of privacy was not intended to allow consumption in particular to become as central a feature of collective life as it has become under the dominance of capitalism, and its stepchild society, underwritten more recently by neo-conservative discourses and policies.

The shift away from a familial conception of privacy and the private toward a collective, now societal, one, far from being at loggerheads with modern and contemporary notions of individualism, is therefore thoroughly compatible with them.[32] Indeed, the idea of the individual and individualism *per se* is able to protect one's 'privacy' in society only to the extent that one expresses (consumption; spectating) or embodies (status; possession) it in societally approved ways. The private is therefore social not just generally but in a very specific sense, something which can readily be demonstrated by the ease with which discourses on privacy and one's 'private life' or

---

[30] Discussed on *Newshour*, first story 'The Disappearing Surplus' (Washington: Public Broadcasting Co., August 28, 2001).

[31] Arendt, *op. cit.*, chapter 2.

[32] It is the flip side of Durkheim's concept of 'positive' individualism first promulgated in *The Division of Labor in Society* (New York: Macmillan, 1952, 1893). Compare to C.D. Macpherson, *The Political Theory of Possessive Individualism* (London: Oxford University Press, 1962). Also see Wilson, *Sex and Gender: Making Cultural Sense of Civilization* (Leiden: E.J. Brill, 1989), chapters 2, 3.

'lifestyle' fit into discussions about what makes society itself so culturally and historically unique.[33] When supporters of society, and the capitalism which makes its conception (and practice) of individualism possible, wax euphemistic about privacy as a 'right', they are doing nothing more than underscoring the way, as well as the fact, that society and these conceptions of individualism and the private 'belong together'. Meantime, we are led to believe that society is superior to all other forms of collective life because without it these conceptions of the individual and the private could not have taken root and flourished.

Since a major vehicle for expressing capital's priority to the institutions of the public and especially those of society has been the legal and constitutional defence of 'property rights', one can never escape the following realization. The right of every citizen as consumer and spectator to privacy in the expression of this right is subject not only to legally (e.g. societally) defined limits but presupposes that property itself is private and that capital is property. It is the *relationship* between these two notions of the private, one from political economy and the legal framework which gives rise to capitalism, and the other (later on) from the social, behavioral and administrative-managerial disciplines (including marketing) and constitutional law, that is crucial. It shows how and why these two value systems were able to come together in defense of consumption and spectating as the essence of 'responsible', that is, private thus social, individualism.[34] The ability of these two sets of discourses, superficially different yet thoroughly complementary, to come together in this way is no chance occurrence. Instead, it expresses what Macpherson has called capitalism's unending quest to persuade us that our needs are synonymous with infinite desire, and that this can best be guaranteed by allowing private capitals extensive rights to extract and co-opt labor and value from human beings, their institutions and external nature.[35] A recent public issue that provides a clear contrast between an economistic approach to resources and one more concerned with social and environmental matters is the present

[33] This was anticipated fully by Hegel in *op. cit.*, Third Part (i) and (ii) a.

[34] Wilson, *The American Ideology*, chapters 8, 10; 'The Counter Revolutionary Function of the Social Sciences in Advanced Industrial Societies', *op. cit.*

[35] C.D. Macpherson, *Democratic Theory* (London: Oxford University Press, 1973), especially pp. 28–52, 87–94; Macpherson, *The Rise and Fall of Economic Justice, and Other Papers* (London: Oxford University Press, 1985).

(alleged) 'energy crisis' (2001) in the United States. Should this crisis be addressed by a heightened search for new sources of petroleum in the Arctic and elsewhere and support for building more power stations, as President Bush wishes, or by concerted (and government supported) efforts to control and limit petroleum consumption and preserve wilderness areas?

By attacking the root assumptions that property is private, save in a very limited sense, and that capital is property which must be permitted virtually unlimited mobility (including 'flight'), one challenges the continued validity of these two notions of the private on which the entire edifice of consumer capitalism rests. While it may seem 'accidental' or 'coincidental' that the term 'private' has come to be used in what only appears to be such divergent ways by capitals and by marketers, social scientists and constitutional lawyers, this fact reflects their common allegiance to society and its values. The effects of this common allegiance do not necessarily redound to the advantage of either representative democracy or more 'social' institutions of the people.[36] Apart from this, 'private' carries with it in consequence of this tie a positive, affirmative connotation as something which can be presumed on the whole to be beneficent, and subject to criticism or limit only when it is used to excuse or justify conduct not in the societal interest. These alliances, first between the private and capitals, and now with society and its preferred form of individualism (consumption; spectating), make it even harder to defend the indispensability of public and social institutions and a focus on public capital than was the case prior to the advent of neo-conservatism.

The idea that the private is good rather than simply necessary, albeit in a limited form, supports the elision of the discourses defending property and capital rights with those defending the rights of individuals in a mass society. In one sense, it is clearly ironic that this has happened, since it is the mass society favouring consumption and spectating that has necessitated this very defense.[37] At a deeper level, however, the idea that the private *really is* the societal rather than an escape from it reminds us once again that the relationship between the two is necessary rather than accidental, and thus determined in its essence and nature rather than the product

[36] Lindblom, *op. cit.*; Wilson, *Political Management*, chapters 4, 10.

[37] See C.D. Macpherson (editor), *Property: Mainstream and Critical Positions* (Toronto: University of Toronto Press, 1978); and Macpherson, *Democratic Theory*.

of contingencies.[38] The discursive resonances of the private as a beneficent state or condition cover *both* the rights of capitals to property as a power of disposition and use *and* the rights of the people to express their individuality by consuming the commodities and services capitals produce through the extraction of their surplus value and the co-optation of public capital. The dependence of capitals on society and its legitimizing disciplines, having now become total, becomes severely problematic because of the priorities and conduct recommended (and enforced) by the neo-conservative agenda. Today, even mainstream social science disciplines are regularly ignored when their practitioners insist on a more public and social focus against those who believe that only the economy, the market and technology are legitimate initiating factors in the production of wealth. Not surprisingly, the latter position supports a more direct, intensive and continuous co-optation of public capital than the former.[39]

One must go even farther in analyzing the relationship between these two notions of the private, however, since the apparent right to privacy for those whose real job is to consume and spectate is defined in terms that make privacy little more than time off from work, rather than 'leisure'. This implies that the stress associated with responsible job holding and employee status, even at the best of times, is something that consumption and display is supposed to compensate for. Privacy as the societal right to individuate oneself through commodities and services is intended to compensate for the fact that one is him/her self a commodity in the job and occupational setting, and perhaps elsewhere as well. By the time all of this takes place or is carried out, there (ideally) should be little if any time to take citizen and public activities seriously.[40] While capitals take advantage of their status as 'private' parties, the rest of us are expected to do the same thing in ways that are societally approved,

[38] For an interpretation of Marx's distinction between the necessary and accidental and the inevitable, determined and contingent see Wilson, *Marx's Critical/Dialectical Procedure*, index references.

[39] Anticipated by both Macpherson, *Democratic Theory*, and Lindblom, *op. cit.* On the relation between privatization and the social sciences, see Derek Braddon and Deborah Foster (editors), *Privatization: Social Science Themes and Perspectives* (Brookfield, Vermont: Dartsmouth, 1996).

[40] See Sebastian DeGrazia, *Of Work, Time and Leisure* (New York: Twentieth Century Fund, 1962); Juliet Schor, *The Overworked American: the Unexpected Decline of Leisure* (New York: Basic Books, 1991); Schor, *The Overspent American: Upscaling, Downshifting and the New Consumer* (New York: Basic Books, 1998).

and this does *not* include either occupational activism or citizenly initiative and display unconnected to society's socializing agenda.[41]

The dilemma of capitalism is that it has no international enemy that anyone believes exists any more, so must figure out ways to cover over the fact that it is its own internal illogic, expressed in terms of this unseemly dependence on a consumer society, that has backfired. To keep the show going it must hide its need for private (therefore public) debt, alongside its inability, or rather congenital lack of desire, to significantly diminish or eliminate it given this abject dependence.[42] Privatization as a discursive remedy, if little else, can still be counted on to denote a responsible process moving in what is alleged to be the right direction. Nevertheless, much or most that is supposed to be so central to privacy and the private is morally and even economically bankrupt because of what privacy really means (consumption; spectating) and what it seeks to realize (unbalanced creation of exchange over use values). Like every other support in the neo-conservative house of cards, the worst nightmare for advocates of privatization is the certain knowledge that at its end this process will reveal nothing so much as the reality of human greed and our infinite capacity for delusion. This is particularly true when put in the form of a morality play which intersperses religious, secular and professional discourses, symbols and motifs.

The best antidote to the threat of such an eventuality is to argue that privatization has not really happened very much if at all, no matter what anyone, including neo-conservative pundits, think. This has become an increasingly popular 'strategy' for avoiding recognition of just how empty and meaningless this alleged 'quick fix' really is, while it unintentionally, but nevertheless effectively, keeps the discursive terrain far away from discussions of public capital, its co-optation and the real national wealth.[43] As ideology and discourse, privatization talk makes reference to an idealized process which can never really come to fruition, no matter how many anti-public and anti-social parties come to power and sing its praises as a desirable,

[41] Hellinger and Judd *op. cit.*; Wilson, *Political Management*, chapters 2–5, 10.

[42] Warburton, *op. cit.*; Harless, *op. cit.*; Ford, *op. cit.*; Nathanson, *op. cit.*

[43] Gee, Hull and Lankshear, *op. cit.*; Whitfield, *op. cit.*; Paul Leduc Browne, *Unsafe Practices: Restructuring and Privatization in Ontario Health Care* (Ottawa: Canadian Centre for Policy Alternatives, 2000); Tittenbrun, *op. cit.*; Kikeri, *op. cit.*; Saltman, *op. cit.*; Philip Morgan, *op. cit.*; Robert Suggs, *Minorities and Privatization: Economic Mobility at Risk* (Washington: University Press of America, 1989).

realizable goal. At the same time, such talk legitimizes a far more direct and substantial co-optation of public capital than is good for either 'private' capitals or the capitalist system as a whole in Western nation-states. Yet the resulting institutional imbalance is both increasingly necessary in the form of dependence on increasing rates of consumption, and increasingly problematic. This is because it is using up public capital at a faster rate than it is creating it as a consequence of a one-sided preoccupation with value on exchange, one that is less restrained by public and social obligations to create use values than was formerly the case.

While looked at along one dimension it is certainly true that definitions of privatization run the gamut from a 'quick fix' to a full blown interventionist strategy, at least in theory, along another one can plot various degrees of change in a 'private' direction from strong to relatively weak formulations. If in the first case we are concerned with the relative proportion of condensational to referential content in the concept, in the second we are interested in how substantial the change from one state or condition to another will be.[44] As noted, these uses of privatization can be variously mixed and mingled to the desired result in government, 'private sector' and interest group statements and pronouncements. The one thing that is consistent, however, is the technique or 'strategy' of pointing to strong senses of the concept in order to argue that privatization has not 'really' been tried. Thus, allegations that it is empty rhetoric masking a more direct and continuous form of institutionalized avarice are therefore thoroughly wrongheaded and unfair.[45]

Stanbury, like many others, employs this device in discussing privatization in the Canadian setting. For him the concept is mainly referential and, in addition, is not only a possible but a desirable state of affairs, particularly for countries with political-economic systems which he believes are 'government-centred' rather than 'market-centred'.

> The broadest concept of privatization consists of any effort designed to strengthen the role of the market at the expense of the state. This concept, therefore, includes: selling off Crown corporations to private

[44] Joel Handler, *Down from Bureaucracy: the Ambiguity of Privatization and Empowerment* (Princeton: Princeton University Press, 1996); Nagel, *op. cit.*

[45] Whitfield, *op. cit.*; Hood, *op. cit.*; Jenkins, *op. cit.*; J.D. Kay and D.J. Thompson, 'Privatization: A Policy in Search of a Rationale', *The Economic Journal*, Volume 96 (March 1986).

> investors; deregulation in total or in part (particularly the removal of direct or economic regulation); and shifting from compulsory taxation to a voluntary, user-pay approach to public services.[46]

He goes on to describe various ways that public enterprises may be sold off, including a shift from 100% (or controlling) government ownership to 100% (or controlling) private ownership, and notes that it is even possible for governments to maintain 'legal control' with a minority interest. Privatization can also mean taking away a public enterprise's monopoly or quasi-monopolistic status, forcing them to borrow in the marketplace, requiring them to pay income taxes and property taxes 'like their private sector counterparts', or 'contracting out' their production and service functions while retaining a system of public financing.[47]

Stanbury goes on to look at the history of federal and provincial efforts to privatize in what he acknowledges is a 'public enterprise' country, focusing on the nature and type of privatization which the Canadian federal government has generally preferred—'outright sales to a single buyer'. He also notes that several privatizations have involved firms that were formerly in the private sector before becoming public enterprises.[48] There follows a discussion of 'candidates' for privatization, standard rhetoric (and occasionally practice) for all governments of a neo-conservative persuasion. In the concluding sections of his article, Stanbury concentrates on three hypotheses about privatization that are particularly interesting from the perspective on the issues discussed here. First, he argues that privatization is the partial result of changes 'in the ideology of the federal and some provincial governments' or 'electoral decisions' favoring parties philosophically [sic] committed to 'downsizing the state'. Second, it is a

---

[46] William Stanbury, 'Privatization in Canada: Ideology, Symbolism or Substance?', in *Privatization and State Owned Enterprises: Lessons from the United States, Great Britain and Canada*, edited by Paul MacAvoy, W. Stanbury, G. Yarrow and R. Zeckhauser (Boston: Kluwer Academic Publishers, 1989).

[47] *Ibid.* See also Hardin, *Privatization Putsch*; Wilson, *No Ivory Tower: the University under Siege*, pp. 11–14 and supra; and Wilson, *Bureaucratic Representation: Civil Servants and the Future of Capitalist Democracies*, index references and especially p. 26 for the many and (increasingly) varied forms that privatization has taken.

[48] On Canada as a 'public enterprise' country and the consequences of this fact for the development of capitalism and public and social institutions in Canada, see Herschel Hardin, *A Nation Unaware: the Canadian Economic Culture* (Vancouver: J.J. Douglas, 1974); and Wilson, *Retreat from Governance: Canada and the Continental-International Challenge* (Hull: Voyageur, 1989).

'political' (and bureaucratic) response to the failure of public enterprises to serve (or serve well) the public policy purposes for which they were designed. Third, and most relevant for the purposes of this study, privatization is a form of 'symbolic politics designed to appease the critics of government while doing little or nothing to divest the largest public enterprises'.[49]

Stanbury concludes that even though there are serious problems with respect to the operation of Canadian public enterprises centred around accountability and control, management, financing and competition, 'it is too early to say whether privatization will solve the widely-perceived problems with Crown corporations'. This conclusion was premised on the fact that privatization had not occurred either as extensively or intensively as had been the case in Britain, 'the leader in the field', thus that we really cannot either endorse or dismiss it as a public policy option. He elaborates on this in his discussions of 'privatization as political symbolism', pointing out that 'not all public policies are designed to produce a substantive result', but rather 'to alter the perceptions of voters without making a substantive change'.[50] This observation, correct as far as it goes, is intended to make just the opposite point to that offered in this text. Stanbury laments that Canada, and by extension other 'mixed' capitalist systems, has not really bitten the bullet, on the assumption that privatization 'works' whenever it is undertaken in earnest.

Another way of seeing this empty symbolism and rhetoric is as a discursive vehicle permitting a more direct and substantial co-optation of public capital to private uses than can otherwise be justified in a mixed economy with a full-fledged (or even residual) neo-Keynesian agenda. Instead, Stanbury treats privatization as a best practice ideal which has not really been converted into practice because of confusion with regard to implementation, a lack of political will, or a desire to delude the public about how, when or where it has taken (or will take) place. Thus, while he is correct to point out that 'Governments act from multiple motives', the fact that 'large scale privatizations' have not taken place cannot be explained away by observing that the public supports more rather than less government

[49] Stanbury, *op. cit.*

[50] *Ibid.* On 'symbolic reassurance' to publics, Murray Edelman, *The Symbolic Uses of Politics* (Urbana, Illinois: University of Illinois Press, 1964); Gordon Clark and Michael Dear, *State Apparatus: Structures and Language of Legitimacy* (Boston: Allen and Unwin, 1984).

'intervention'. The implication here is that this policy choice on the public's part is politically and/or economically irrational, something that cannot be presumed but rather constitutes a point of departure for research and study. Indeed, one could argue from the other side that it is the unique positive and affirmative *representative* functions performed by public and social, as well as capital, bureaucracies that makes them indispensable and should preclude the privatization or contracting out of their functions.[51] Privatization *per se* can be a largely discursive exercise mixing a little real with a great deal of symbolic action in a concoction that appears more substantial than it really is because of the quick fix rhetoric often invoked. On the other hand, it can also take the form of a socio-economic and political *process* in given nation-states, something Stanbury plays down in his focus on individual cases and forms rather than on an overall society-wide development.[52]

It is on the meaning and use of the term 'intervention' that the analysis and discussion offered here would wish to make one of its strongest points. This study has been at pains to show how closely (and necessarily) intertwined capitals have been with political and governmental authority, in particular the sovereign national state. It is this national state entity more than any other that has guaranteed the priority of the institutions of capital to those of the people for virtually the entire period of modern development in the West. The idea that there has been a 'free market' and a 'competitive' economy with an independent price mechanism functioning free of government and public authority, or that such a notion is a realizable and/or noble ideal, is perhaps the greatest illusion of all. On the other hand, exonerating anti-public and anti-social political parties whose public policies favor 'privatization' on the grounds that citizens are fearful, confused or intransigent, and that this results in their refusal (or inability) to really bite the bullet and privatize, ignores this interdependence from the other side, as it were. Most significantly, it allows us to ignore what has really happened when acts of privatization have occurred in Western capitalist countries, and how this is related to an ongoing societal (and global) process.

---

[51] Stanbury, *op. cit.* On the effectiveness and indispensability of bureaucratic representation see Wilson, 'The Downside of Downsizing', *op. cit.* and *Bureaucratic Representation*, relevant index references.

[52] See Vincent Wright (editor), *Privatization in Western Europe: Pressures, Problems and Paradoxes* (New York: St. Martin's Press, 1994).

There is much more to privatization in the context of recent Western social, political and economic development than is revealed by professional and commonsense economic (and 'economistic') analysis of the problem. This is evident in the fraudulent claims to objective status made by those economists, interest group spokespersons and leading figures in governments and political parties who are the major supporters and advocates of the neo-conservative agenda.[53] Attempts to obscure the fact that this is *an agenda* that can readily be inferred by careful study of its styles of argument, its symbolism and rhetoric, and the metaphors it trades on and mixes, is part and parcel of the technique to deal with what is in truth a failed (or failing) effort. The three step argument goes like this: (1) it never happened, folks; (2) it happened, but it was sabotaged by you know who; (3) it requires (much) more time for it to happen because the full-scale commitment to privatization is simply not there, for whatever reason. When it is convenient for its supporters to argue that privatization is a simple and straightforward process, it is claimed that it really is easy to install and implement. When it isn't convenient, for whatever reason, the argument shifts to its inherent complexity.

The point, of course, is that it is *both* an act and a process, looked at in microcosmic and macrocosmic terms. This becomes apparent when we examine individual acts of privatization, while viewing them as part of the ongoing process of privatization, however disjointed and apparently uncoordinated it may appear to be. It is at this point that we can contemplate the possibility, even likelihood, of landing somewhere near the middle of the matrix cited earlier. In this instance, the mid-point between condensational and referential uses of the concept intersects almost perfectly with the mid-point between strong and weak notions of what constitutes the appropriate definition of privatization. A corollary observation relating to both the latter and the former mid-points is the extent to which privatization is defined as an act addressed to an individual enterprise or bureau or a process which is society-wide (either ideally or in reality) in its ambit. Use of these options in discussions about the meaning of privatization is the key element that allows incessant shifts in the mix of referential and condensation symbols. These shifts are central factors promoting the idea that the process to which the concept refers is an elusive

[53] Sclar, *op. cit.*; Shipman, *op. cit.*; Robert Kuttner, *Everything for Sale: the Virtues and Limits of Markets* (New York: Alfred Knopf, 1997).

phenomenon, all the moreso when the purpose of such discourses is increasingly to obfuscate what is really happening (or not happening).

Herschel Hardin, in two important studies, has exposed the actual pattern of privatization behavior in North America and the United Kingdom since 1975, in order to show the real functions that such activity performs, in contrast to the hypocritical claims of neo-conservatives and their spin doctors. Far from it being the case that unsuccessful public enterprises are privatized in order to make them healthy and well, it is usually viable public enterprises that are auctioned off, often at fire sale prices, to 'privateers'. In this event, it is neo-conservative governments that can almost always be counted on to stand behind these transactions as guarantors in direct and indirect financial ways. Frequently this will necessitate not only an initial transfusion of public money, but intermittent, when not continuous, infusions. 'Hospitalization' refers to the process by which former public enterprises, robust and healthy prior to privatization, often find it necessary to *return* to the public sector for intermittent resuscitation and sustenance once privatized.[54] This follows a pattern long ago inaugurated by so-called private enterprises who responded in similar ways when they could not cope with organized labor, domestic and international competition or unanticipated events generally. The most recent example of the impact of an unexpected event is the request for government 'bail outs' in the U.S., Canada and numerous other countries following the terrorist attacks of September 11, 2001 on New York and Washington, with their predictable effect on air travel sales.

What makes this contrast between the alleged and the real sequence of privatization as a process so significant is the doubt it casts on privatization as either a quick or a slow fix in the absence of mountains of public monies initially and continuously infused in ways that obscure the real costs. Privatization, from the standpoint of both functional performance and economic efficiency, is a problem far more than it is a solution for the public. Indeed, it turns out to be a solution only for the myriad 'new bureaucracies' that Hardin observes springing up everywhere in the so called 'private sector' in

[54] Hardin, *Privatization Putsch*, particularly chapters 3, 4 and *supra* on 'hospitalization' and the fact that privateers quite naturally prefer to buy profitable to very profitable public enterprises unless thoroughly subsidized against losses, and even profit levels that are too low.

response to the privatizing opportunities that have come on the scene in Western capitalist democracies since 1975. Besides 'traditional' corporate, advertising and marketing and stock market bureaucracies, we now have 'branches' devoted to 'paper-entrepreneurialism', 'derivative-paper', 'money-management', 'culture and sports' and (last but not least) 'dogma'. The real function of these bodies is directly related to the most wasteful and irresponsible method of co-opting public capital of all, the multiplication of transactions through the often-exponential creation of 'middle persons'.[55] The result is the creation and legitimation of a long-term structural and systemic imbalance in which use values are increasingly sacrificed to the one-sided creation of exchange values.

Hardin's new bureaucracies are the latest (and most extensive) version of the process of multiplying transactions that has always been central to capitalist waste-making and inefficiency in the unbalanced creation of exchange values at the expense of use values. While it can be argued that this is the essence of the one-sided co-optation of public capital and the labor and value embedded therein, it is an extreme case which has only come into prominence with the ascendancy of neo-conservatism as the basis of governmental practice. What makes it particularly significant is the fact that such practices are no longer restricted in the main to peripheral or marginal and suspect economic and financial activities. Instead, they have acquired a legitimacy that allows them to increasingly constitute the norm, if not the ideal form of economic practice in Western capitalist societies imbued with neo-conservative dogma. 'Privatization' is clearly a central rallying cry because of the cultural bias in capitalist societies favoring the private and disparaging the public and social, as noted. The process that emerges defends a thoroughly bankrupt notion of 'shareholder democracy', which is really debt-holder democracy, while underwriting the ever-greater concentrations of economic power needed for the one-sided extraction and co-optation that 'globalization' is seen to require.[56] Yet what the act or process amounts to is a gigantic transfer of wealth from the people to capitals and their supporters and well-wishers in the old and new private bureaucracies, as well as in the capital sectors of neo-conservative governments.

---

[55] *Ibid.*, chapter 7; and Hardin, *The New Bureaucracy: Waste and Folly in the Private Sector* (Toronto: McClelland and Stewart, 1991).

[56] Hardin, *Privatization Putsch*, chapters 1, 2, 5, 6, 12, 15, 16.

Healthy and vital public enterprises are normally turned over to privateers by neo-conservative governments not because they are not economically or financially viable but because of a dogmatic obsession with 'downsizing' government and the public and social sectors generally, *regardless of performance*.[57] The height of irrationality in decision-making manifests itself in such transfers of value and wealth to privateers. It is they who attempt to impose the new techniques of accounting, management, finance *etc.* that Stanbury cited on a body that is often fulfilling its economic, financial and other responsibilities admirably and at a high level of competence. There may even be a desire on the part of such parties and governments to destroy the public enterprise *precisely because it is (or has been) successful*. Auction, sale or transfer to the 'private sector', and the economic and financial collapse that often results, can then be explained away as evidence that the enterprise was not really a viable entity after all. The epitome of hypocrisy occurs when it is then argued that it only appeared to be in good shape because it was protected by its public status from the 'real world' of corporate and global competition.[58] Nothing better captures this hypocrisy than the realization that neo-conservatism is now far more ideologically driven in its policy decisions, particularly on privatizations, than is the case with the left-of-center parties that were often legitimately accused of being excessively ideological in the past.

Let us not forget that privatization is an act or process that can only occur if someone in the private sector can be persuaded to invest the time, energy and (often residual) capital in an existing institutional activity presently in the public, and occasionally social, sector. The very fact that capitals by definition cannot be required to undertake such activities indicates that one or another incentive must be present and available to motivate them. This may (and often does) include an infusion of cash, the guarantee of continuous subsidies and preferential access to banking and financial institutions. The result is the generation of a 'fail safe' atmosphere that is particularly dysfunctional for the competitive and market values that privateers and their supporters are always extolling. Indeed, few things are better calculated to sabotage and undermine economic and

[57] *Ibid.*, chapters 6, 16.
[58] *Ibid.*, chapters 8–13, 15.

financial effectiveness than these kinds of special conditions.[59] Since privateers quite naturally prefer to buy and run healthy enterprises rather than those that are 'ill', and even then only when the perquisites and advantages cited are forthcoming, one needs to ask what happens to other enterprises according to those supporting the neo-conservative agenda.

Borins has referred to these cases as 'experiments in failure' which 'cost the taxpayer billions'. His conception of the functions of enterprise and economic activity is inspired, not surprisingly, by a private sector, thus a relatively narrow, notion of what the 'bottom line' means.[60] Without disputing the possibility that public sector managers and executives will make mistakes just as readily as their 'private' sector counterparts, such a narrow conception of function, arguably inappropriate even for the private sector, completely ignores the *raison d'etre* for public enterprises wherever we find them. Public enterprises are a response to: a public or social need that cannot (or will not) be met by private enterprise; a manifestly political function incompatible with narrow economic and financial criteria of performance; a belief that the requirement of secure supply warrants monopoly; or a matter of national security. In these cases, we are talking about the non-economic functions of economic activity, functions that are frequently used to justify Western capitalism and the democratic, public and social forms that until recently invariably accompanied it. Hardin makes it clear not only that public enterprise performs a number of necessary, even indispensable, non-economic functions, but that the way people do things economic and political is a central element of their national culture, not something separate and distinct from it.[61]

Instead of focusing on the ways in which a public enterprise committed to the performance of key non-economic functions like those cited might perform them more effectively, narrow bottom line criteria which private corporations can themselves rarely meet are held up as the standard. All of this transpires as if those who set up and operate these public enterprises were unaware that narrow profitability

---

[59] The classic observation on this tendency is in Max Weber, *Economy and Society*, Volume I, Part 1, chapters 2, 12, 3 (3), pp. 106–107.

[60] Sandford Borins, with Lee Brown, *Investments in Failure: Five Government Corporations that Cost the Canadian Taxpayer Billions* (Toronto: Methuen, 1986).

[61] Lindblom, *op. cit.*; Wilson, *Bureaucratic Representation*; and particularly Hardin, *A Nation Unaware: the Canadian Economic Culture.*

and even market share criteria bearing on growth must to some extent be sacrificed by the very nature of what their mission is. Even in the extreme case in which a public enterprise is continuously subsidized in order to maintain social stability in a region characterized by dangerously high levels of unemployment, there is a realization that the undertaking is an attempt to buy time while alternate solutions are sought. All neo-conservatives can do when faced with these examples is to endorse, or threaten to endorse, the depopulation of given regions, citing narrow economic and financial criteria which require the government to stop subsidizing the employment of people who wish to remain in a region in which they were born and grew up.[62] What neo-conservatives are really doing when they endorse the privatization of public enterprises, it turns out, is opting for one form of subsidization, one manifestly abusive of democratic, public and social values, over another.

Alternatively, governments of a neo-conservative persuasion may either decide that a given function, service or benefit is totally or partially unviable as it stands, or discover that they are unable to secure a buyer for an existing public undertaking. Privatization, however abusive of democratic, public and social function values it may be, is, after all, not the only alternative for such governments. As an act, and as part of a process, there has to be a series of transactions to move the enterprise from one alleged state or condition to the other. While on the surface it may have been true that movement from private to public status and back again was characterized symbolically by either signing a form or tearing it up, there is much more, for better or worse, to privatization than this. Even apart from what has been said in criticism of this act and process, the alternatives may be even worse. If a neo-conservative government feels a given function to be incompatible with its mandate, it may disband a given agency or enterprise in the absence of a buyer or, in the case of benefits and services, so drastically cut them back that little remains that can be defended at the next assessment.[63]

Even when a public enterprise is meeting all conceivable criteria of economic and financial effectiveness, the advent of a neo-conservative government may lead to an irrational decision to privatize,

---

[62] Whitfield, *op. cit.*; Kikeri, *op. cit.*; Philip Morgan, *op. cit.*; Suggs, *op. cit.*

[63] See reference no. 47, for some sources on the panoply of techniques and 'strategies' available to privateers and governments supportive of privatization.

downsize or eliminate it on the grounds that government has no business being in (this) business. Here the claim is made that the very presence of this public or social sector activity is skewing or threatening 'market forces' by excluding a field of potential economic activity from the private sector.[64] At this point, performance criteria are in fact suspended in favor of dogma, but this is masked by the claim that the activity at issue should really be one where market forces and the private sector operate. Consequently, it is often argued that governments have an obligation to support privatization in all capitalist democracies for this reason. This is the flip side of Lindblom's observation that private enterprise is delegated the responsibility for running the economy in capitalist societies. It must be provided with what amounts to a monopolistic, or oligopolistic, access, one that is protected, promoted, subsidized and publicly backed up by governments and laws. At the same time, they are not only allowed, but encouraged, to honor the narrowest and most self-serving notions of 'responsibility' to the public whose capital they are co-opting and to the society where they are located.

The conclusion that many have reached following study of privatization as an act, process or phenomenon is that no one should be surprised that such quick (or even slow) fixes really don't work, after all. The fact that we allow ourselves to accept short-hands in the form of dogma, ideology and rhetoric mainly saves us the trouble of looking critically at what is really happening, because we lack either the time, energy or (apparent) expertise to do so. However, the fact that something is happening but not what the public has been led to think need not and should not mire us in a preoccupation with conspiracy thinking. This is because most participants to and beneficiaries of extraction and co-optation sincerely believe the rhetoric they have internalized, however superficially. It fits comfortably and snugly into the morality play already discussed, one that focuses on the public debt as the problem and privatization and free trade as solutions to this problem. Once public debt discourses are allowed to control and dictate problem formulation in the way that they do, it is almost inevitable that privatization, with its bias toward the private in all its guises, will come to the fore as a major basis for problem resolution.

---

[64] Hardin, *Privatization Putsch*, chapters 1, 2, 12, 15, 16.

Defining the privatizations that have occurred as at best pale imitations of the real thing, however elusive and impracticable this latter ideal may be, is the now-classic way that subsequent revelations of what the real sequence is can be side-stepped or ignored. After all, these examples can now be cited as (or implied to be) perversions rather than versions of privatization.[65] More problematic still is the lumber-headed determination to ignore the necessary, even indispensable, public and social functions of public enterprise and the fact that, in common with so much public sector activity, the needs these undertakings are meeting are usually ones that the private sector either cannot or will not meet. The claim of marginal utility theory, to the effect that if the public has a real need this need can *always* be met, or met better, by private enterprise, has never been viable save as dogma. This is now even more transparent from the recent practices of successive neo-conservative regimes in the West than was the case during the Depression and its aftermath in the 1930's. Beyond this, however, is the question of the empirical validity of the public-private distinction itself.

For it is by no means clear that we should restrict our critique of the concept and practice of private enterprise solely to an analysis of the gap between illusion and reality in privatization activities. This study has been at pains throughout to challenge the idea that the critique of privatization should be considered unique, as if 'real' private and corporate enterprises could ever stand on their own given their continuing dependence on public capital and public and social institutions.[66] Private capital's narrow economic function is to co-opt public capital in the ways indicated, while their social function is to do so in ways that maintain a balance between assisting in the creation of use values and generating value on exchange. Too much of an imbalance, for too long a time, is not only devastating to the large majority of people who live in 'mixed economy' capitalist societies. It is also bad for capitals, particularly entrepreneurs, inventors and small businesspersons, who are effectively left in the lurch when the one-sided generation of exchange values and the consequent waste of use values favors an exponential production of transactions and middle persons. These latter contribute little or nothing (save by accident) to real wealth, except their propensity to consume, something

[65] Hood, *op. cit.*; Gee, Hull and Lankshear, *op. cit.*; Tittenbrun, *op. cit.*

[66] Wilson, *Bureaucratic Representation.*

which in and of itself is turning out to be a mixed blessing for the reasons suggested.

Privatization is a symbol for an activity or process that will take us from a sick (or sinful) state or condition into one of health (or grace). It has been able to trade on a vast structure of rhetoric and discourse to which Veblen and Arnold, among many other students of (American) political economy, drew early attention.[67] Whether private refers to property rights or the space (and time) of consumption that capitals make possible through the exercise of these rights, it is alleged to be part and parcel of how to diagnose and resolve the public debt 'crisis'. This crisis is one that neo-conservatives have not only manufactured but have even contributed to in fundamental ways. Privatization is alleged to get government out of business and economic activity, where it is presumed to be behaving badly, inefficiently, ineffectively or irresponsibly, while at the same time attacking elements of the debt and deficit which such activity has created. The public is unaware that the effect of privatization has often been to downsize or eliminate necessary public and social functions while hiding their accelerating costs under private management devices and techniques. The debt being carried, far from going off the books, or even decreasing, continues to be *its* responsibility as part of the *private* debt of a nation now even more irresponsibly out of control because of the one-sided system of extraction and co-optation that is occurring.

Borins' major criticism of the five public enterprises he studied was that managers sought to maximize political (e.g. vote maximization) criteria, even though he readily admits that government decisions were not simplistic in the sense that they ignored either financial prospects or budgetary realities in the process. This seems to be the nub of the problem that neo-conservative attacks on the performance of public and social functions in and through public enterprise and other forms of economic activity only serve to highlight. For while there are ways that one can discern the appropriate mix of economic and non-economic values in the decision processes

[67] Thorstein Veblen, *Theory of Business Enterprise* (Boston: Heubsch, 1904); Veblen, *The Higher learning in America* (Boston: Heubsch, 1918); Veblen, *The Vested Interests and the Common Man* (Boston: Heubsch, 1919); Veblen, *Absentee Ownership and Business Enterprise in Recent Times: The Case of America* (Boston: Heubsch, 1923); Arnold, *op. cit.*, and Thurman Arnold, *The Symbols of Government* (New York: Harcourt, Brace and World, 1962, 1935), chapters 4, 10.

of public enterprises with clear public and social, as well as economic functions, these can only be worked out *in situ* on a case by case basis. But is this really such a remarkable observation, or is the point rather that *all* enterprises, private and corporate no less than public and governmental, are obliged to carry out and/or find unavoidable this mixing and mingling of the strictly economic and the non-economic?[68] The essence of hypocrisy is the view that this is an issue that should be of concern to public enterprise alone in the 'mixed' economies of Western capitalist societies.

If we look carefully at who the most fervent supporters of privatization are, not only in the United States but elsewhere, we discover, alongside and overlapping with the members of what Hardin has called the 'new bureaucracy', the following elements. There are first investment groups and individual corporations anxious to pick up a good business, preferably a monopoly, at fire sale or auction prices. Second are senior executives of public enterprises anxious to evade control for their day-to-day decisions and desirous of the superior salary and benefits packages that privatization can bring. Third are advocates and supporters of privatization within neo-conservative parties, governments and think tanks, whose major motivation often combines ideological satisfaction with illegal pay offs. Fourth are pro-business, financial, industrial and commercial interest and lobby groups and trade associations, particularly those favoring closer institutional ties of an economic kind to the U.S. economy.[69] The long and the short of how and why pro-privatization elements have been so successful in Western capitalist countries reduces, not surprisingly, to the following. First, effective manipulation of the morality play discussed; second, reliance on symbols and discourses trading on the public's respect for the private; and third, their ability to combine the financial and economic resources with political access in order to influence the public through the mass media.

Notice that none of these lists of supporters of privatization includes entrepreneurs, inventors and small business persons, nor is it likely to. Not only is there little for these people in privatization, for the

[68] Wilson, 'Values: On the Possibility of a Convergence between Economic and Non Economic Decision Making', *Management under Differing Value Systems*, edited by G. Dlugos and K. Weiermair (Berlin: Walter de Gruyter, 1981), pp. 37–71.

[69] See the chapter by chapter list, and a justification for their inclusion, provided by Hardin in *The New Bureaucracy*.

obvious reason that it mainly functions to generate transactions and the middle persons they require for their one-sided appropriation of exchange values and waste of use values. The entire neo-conservative agenda in practice has been almost uniformly hostile to individuals who see a need in society and its publics and try to meet that need economically, and for understandable reasons. The old and new private bureaucrats who are either the supporters or the products of privatization have diametrically opposed economic concerns, the essential consequences of which are waste-making and the profligate and irresponsible generation of exchange values. The very different concern of entrepreneurs, inventors and small businesspersons with a more balanced production of use and exchange values is directly contrary to such privateering approaches to the co-optation of public capital. These approaches are characterized by reliance on every religious and secular by-line that will serve to cover over the dangerous institutional imbalance that is being created by this particular 'solution' (and others) to the alleged problem of the public debt.[70]

The claim that hypocrisy is the essential feature of privatization as a key element of the neo-conservative morality play does not mean that there is a conspiracy of elites to upend the political, administrative and economic institutions of Western capitalist democracies. What makes hypocrisy triumphant is what supporters of privatization need to do to turn aside, or so they think, criticisms that show what is really happening. The real danger, noted earlier, is that most of these individuals *really believe* that all economic activity, whether carried out in the putative private or public sector of these societies (but particularly in the latter) is, can be or should be made amenable to strict economic maxims and requirements. It is not so much that public enterprise performs key public and social functions at the same time that it carries out economic activities, though it clearly does both. The point is rather that 'private' enterprises of all types and descriptions do the same thing, often less efficiently and almost always less effectively. That is why the protection and promotion they receive by and through governments cannot be divorced from the performances, however good or bad, of these very different public and social functions. The only real 'competition', in terms of symbolic and rhetorical appeal, that privatization has in the neo-conservative arsenal is the dogma of 'free trade', to which we now turn.

---

[70] Warburton, *op. cit.*; Harless, *op. cit.*; Ford, *op. cit.*

CHAPTER ELEVEN

FREE TRADE: THE SUPREME ILLUSION

No concept functions more definitively as a rallying cry for neo-conservatives than 'free trade'. All manner of authority has been invoked to justify it as *the* answer to economic and financial problems in all capitalist democracies, but particularly the United States and the United Kingdom. Sometimes this 'solution' is touted as one which has already proven itself, but more often than not free trade is put forward as the best or only solution for the future, given globalization and international competitiveness as firm (and nation-state) realities which cannot be ignored or side-stepped.[1] Of the two major solutions to the alleged problem of the 'public debt' it, even more than privatization, is mainly a condensation rather than a referential symbol. This is for the most part because free trade is even harder to pin down than privatization and the private in the public mind. While residual referential content may be seen to inhere in privatization because of its apparent (and real) empirical reference to privacy and the private, the best that can be done with free trade is to conjure up the idea (and ideal) of an unfettered two-person relationship.[2]

It is, however, also the case that publics, like capitals, often believe that it was once an actual state of affairs, one which has since been fettered by government interference or intervention, monopoly, oligopoly and economic concentration generally. Forget that the banner of free trade as a doctrine allegedly opposed to all forms of state intervention—therefore favoring *laissez (nous) faire*—has as its first premise Mandeville's maxim that 'private vices do public virtues make'.[3] The idea that profit-maximizing activities carried on under a loose (and anti-interventionist) interpretation of legality and morality *automatically*

---

[1] Compare for example Robert Gilpin, *Global Political Economy: Understanding the International Economic Order* (Princeton: Princeton University Press, 2001) to John Gray, *False Dawn: the Delusions of Global Capitalism* (New York: New Press/Norton, 1998).

[2] See Arendt, *op. cit.* and other references to the debate regarding the relation between the public, private and social in chapter 10, this text.

[3] Mandeville, *op. cit.*

serves the public interest, and that such conduct should therefore be granted a wider scope and latitude than is permitted other activities, is, after all, a mainstay of free trade litany. Similarly with the problem of 'conspicuous consumption' prefigured in early Protestantism and its ethic. The abject dependence of capitals on consumerism and consequent private (thus public) debt has required it to expand infinitely the operative notion of 'need' so that it becomes virtually indistinguishable from desire, as Hegel fully anticipated in 1821.[4]

This text takes serious issue with the view that governments are 'interventionist' whenever they pass beyond their allegedly appointed role as referees of private market forces because the assumption that their only job is to facilitate such relations and nothing more is only true in a very limited sense. Advocates of free trade initially argued that the essence of non-intervention was the restriction of governments to the performance of three functions: protecting private property; enforcing contracts; and providing for a nation's 'common defense' against foreign invasion. Looked at in terms of the apparent number of functions involved—three—this would seem to imply a collective form in which most relations and arrangements were subject either to custom and tradition, the market, or (more likely) a combination of the two. It is only when these three generic functions are broken down into the vast number of more specific activities that government performs for business, however, that we realize the scale and scope of the capital sector of the state apparatus in capitalist democracies. This sector, in effect, provides ongoing justification and legitimation through these activities for a massive cooptation of public capital and, therefore, of the governments that organize, collect and pool it for private uses.[5]

Further to the point is the way that the so-called 'refereeing' function has been interpreted. The idea that governments simply set the 'rules of the game' and restrict themselves to the performance of what are alleged to be three simple and straightforward functions completely ignores the role of lobbying by pressure groups and trade associations as *part of the structure of governments in capitalist democracies.* While this is certainly not the only way that public capital is coopted for private uses, or even the most efficient method of doing

[4] Hegel, *The Philosophy of Right*, Third Part, (ii) (a), especially Nos. 190–198.
[5] Lindblom, *op. cit.*, chapters 6, 8, 13.

it, it is absolutely central to the emergence, development and extension of capitalism in these societies. The fact that it is so central speaks once again to the long-term implications of the fact that the institutions of capital coincide with those of early modern legalism and constitutionalism and precede those of the public and society.[6] Indeed, a major purpose of legality and constitutionalism was to provide secure (and 'legitimate') foundations for the emerging economic order, while supplanting any and all pre (or anti) capitalist customs and traditions standing it its way.

As an example of how comprehensive and unending the extension and expansion of the three 'simple' functions cited has become, think first of the implications of protecting property rights once property has been seen to include capital and all that it allegedly generates through the process of 'self-augmentation'.[7] On the matter of enforcing contracts think of the relative power position, both historically and today, of capital in comparison to labor, and the continuing effort to escape unions and/or higher wages which still functions as a major justification for 'capital flight'. It is this latter threat of 'flight' that is presently being used to keep the people and their institutions in line, however often their acquiescence and that of sympathetic governments fails to do the job.[8] As for providing for the 'common defense', so-called 'Pentagon capitalism' and the international armaments industry on which virtually all industrialized countries continue to depend, has simultaneously made a 'business' and a hypocrisy out of the original reasons for military preparedness 'in the common defense'.[9] In all three instances, these once simple

[6] John Commons, *Legal Foundations of Capitalism* (Madison: University of Wisconsin Press, 1957); Wilson, 'The Downside of Downsizing', *op. cit.*; *Bureaucratic Representation*, chapters 1, 2, 5.

[7] See David Harvey, *The Urbanization of Capital* (Oxford: Basil Blackwell, 1985); E.K. Hunt, *Property and Prophets: the Evolution of Economic Institutions and Ideologies* (New York: Harper Collins, 1990); C.B. Macpherson (editor), *Property: Mainstream and Critical Positions* (Toronto: University of Toronto Press, 1978).

[8] Lieberman, *Unfit to Manage* (New York: McGraw Hill, 1988); Aronowitz, *False Promises* (Durham, N.C.: Duke University Press, 1992); Cuddington, *Capital Flight: Estimates, Issues and Explanations* (Princeton: Department of Economics, 1986); Lessard, *Capital Flight: the Problem and Policy Responses* (Washington: Institute for International Economics, 1987); Storper, *The Capitalist Imperative: Territory*, Technology and Industrial Growth (Oxford: Basil Blackwell, 1989).

[9] Melman, *op. cit.* The speed and comprehensiveness with which the American military responded to President George W. Bush's call for a 'war' against the Taliban is a recent case in point.

functions have become incredibly complex and have led to massive and continuous supports to capitals by governments.

Another point worth addressing in this initial section is the issue of monopoly, oligopoly and economic concentration, and its relation to alleged government 'intervention'. Free trade, anti-interventionist rhetoric has always claimed that governments skew, compromise and/or destroy 'market forces', on the assumption that left to themselves capitals maintain an equilibrium, based on Mandeville's maxim, which benefits the consumer by guaranteeing the lowest possible price for commodities and services 'at the margin'. In contrast to this is our oligopolistic and economically concentrated reality, particularly in light of more recent supranational and global developments. In many cases where competition was alleged to be *the* beneficent effect flowing from free trade and free markets, it was government 'intervention' through the regulation of business, commerce, industry and finance that responded to economic concentration, often by breaking up combinations alleged to be 'in restraint of trade'. Left to their own devices, populist, and even centrist, governments often saw no other way to restore the very competitive equilibrium that capitalism usually found it impossible or undesirable to sustain in the absence of such 'intervention'.[10]

This gap between the apparent ideal and historical and contemporary reality goes to the very heart of capitalism's dependence on a set of institutions found in all capitalist democracies and enforced by governments on capital's behalf. It is thus the need for access to governments and legislatures which helps explain why it is rarely in the interests of successful capitals to defend an equilibrium of small sellers, at whatever level of market size and complexity, if they can realize a concentrated rather than a competitive position. Even oligopoly and the 'new' competition which came forward to justify its upending of the rules of free trade in free markets is preferable because of what such concentration is able to do to the fiction of an 'independent price mechanism'.[11] Utilization of governments is

[10] Hardin, *Privatization Putsch*, chapters 9, 10, 11 and 13; and Hardin, *A Nation Unaware*, where he also argues that recent privatizations have contributed significantly to economic concentration and are usually less effective, and even less efficient, than public enterprise in performing the same private, as well as public and social, functions.

[11] Weber, *Economy and Society*, Volume I, Part 1, chapter 2, 11, 12, 24a, 25, 27, 31; and R.H. Coase, 'The Nature of the Firm', *Economica*, Volume 4 (1937), pp.

consistently complemented by collusion and pooling where domestic, and occasionally supranational, international and global markets are concerned, and this continues to constitute the basis for distinguishing long-term success from early or eventual failure among capitals.[12]

Looked at from the standpoint of both motivation and organizational intelligence, the present congeries of industrial, business, commercial and financial systems of capital, at whatever level of scope and complexity, are supremely remindful of the truth of Max Weber's astute observation just after the turn of the century. Weber noted that 'the formation of cartel agreements, no matter how rational their basis in relation to the market situation . . ., immediately diminishes the stimulus to accurate calculation on the basis of capital accounting, because calculation does not take place, at all or with a high degree of accuracy, in the absence of an objective need for it'.[13] Weber's point was that any process of what he called 'rational capital accounting' presupposed the existence of competition. The more extensive the competition in a given market sector, the more necessary was this formally rational system of accounting. By the same token, the less extensive the competition the less scope for and need to rely on this formally rational system. Since it is all-too-often competition, free markets and an independent price mechanism that capitals consistently seek to put an end to by every means available *in their own interests*, the function of government intervention cannot help but challenge the conventional wisdom found in free trade litany.[14]

While it is true that generally only governments supporting the institutions of the people rather than those of capital have supported such justifications for alleged government intervention, it is of signal importance that powerful capitals have often opposed practical efforts to re-instate competitive and free market policies.[15] This gap between

386–405, for Coase's analysis of the most basic economic distinction from which all the others derive—the distinction between the market and the firm.

[12] See Jane Jacobs, *The Economy of Cities* (New York: Random House, 1969), particularly her discussion on how new work begins, and her comparison of Birmingham and Manchester as urban sites for capitalist development.

[13] Weber, *Economy and Society*, Volume I, Part 1, chapter 2, 12, 3 (3), pp. 106–107.

[14] Hardin, *Privatization Putsch*, chapter 7; and Hardin, *The New Bureaucracy*, on the wastefulness and inefficiency of the 'new' and 'emerging' private, corporate sector.

[15] See Government of Canada, *Royal Commission on Corporate Concentration* (Ottawa: Queens Printer, 1978), for an early Canadian statement about the tensions between increasing domestic size of firms and decreasing aggregate and industrial concentration

ideal and reality is thus nothing less than a contrast between theory and experience, with the allegedly rough and ready free traders the theorists rather than those basing their analyses and critiques on practical experience. This in turn compels us to address every other aspect of free trade and allied doctrines in order to discover whether or not it is anything other than the proverbial 'tip of the iceberg' of privately proffered litany on the subject. Apart from any claim that this fraud could be perpetrated on publics as a consequence of the control of mass media by private capitals lies the realization that neo-conservative governments in capitalist democracies have what Veblen called a 'vested interest' in promoting private values at public expense.[16]

Along another dimension lies one of the most essential features of a system of justification and legitimation based on extensive use of condensation rather than referential symbols. In this case it is the technique of trading on an apparent prescriptive ideal as if it were a formerly realized and/or a presently possible and desirable state of affairs. The litany already cited serves no one save for the odd inventor, entrepreneur or small business person, and then only until the 'community' finds out so that it can bring its individual or collective leverage to bear. Not only is it not descriptive of the past or present, but not prescriptive for any future possible state of affairs which virtually any capital could possibly desire.[17] Thus, it should come as no surprise to discover that the prescriptive belongs with theory rather than with practice, and that this realization necessitates matrix thinking on our part. It is not simply that the described is really prescribed or 'normative', but also that the prescriptive is unreal in the sense of being *both impossible and undesirable of realization for capitals themselves*, save in the most extreme and temporary circumstances.

Even in these marginal instances, however, a question arises as to whether we should continue to allow the inventor, entrepreneur or

---

ratios in a continental and global context, an issue also of great moment for Canadian banks in this period.

[16] Thorstein Veblen, *The Vested Interests and the Common Man* (Boston: Heubsch, 1919); John Galbraith, *The Affluent Society* (Boston: Houghton Mifflin, 1958).

[17] On the impact of successful corporate lobbying of Congress and resulting changes to patent and copyright protection and exclusivity rights in the 19th and 20th centuries, see David Noble, *America by Design* (New York: Oxford University Press, 1977).

small business person of capitalist lore (as well as reality) to masquerade as both the prescribed and actual 'capital' of thought, discourse and research. It has already been pointed out that such individuals, while once the majority, are less and less so, with more and more of the machinery of *all* capitalist democracies stacked against them, if not from the outset then certainly from the onset of their first success in the marketplace. The fact that there has been a significant shift in the nature of capitalism which is directly reflected in the declining empirical accuracy and truth value of capitalist ideology becomes harder and harder to dispute.[18] Alongside whether a claim is descriptive or prescriptive, or based in theory or experience, is what makes it three-dimensional for analytical and practical purposes, namely, whether it is a truly desirable state of affairs for capital if so, when (and when not).

One way of addressing this gap between theory and experience, illusion and reality, is to focus on the hortatory way in which the term 'free' is allowed to function in discussions about or appeals to 'free trade' and 'free markets'. Though reference to free trade clearly originated at a time prior to the full-fledged emergence of representative democratic and legal democratic institutions of the people, use of this word nevertheless trades on an ideal of freedom, liberty and individualism with manifestly, and often intendedly, political overtones. Today this is even truer than it was between 1900 and 1960. Indeed, one could make a strong case for the claim that reliance on this conception of freedom has actually increased at precisely the time when anything but the illusion of free trade has been harder and harder to sustain.[19] As the 'competing' units, organized systems and 'playing fields' have become progressively more comprehensive in scope and complex in structure and function, there has been increased recourse to a notion which reflection would now indicate is at best quaint and at worst delusional.

The historical circumstances which initially justified reliance on this reference to free trade were utilized by apologists for capitalism,

---

[18] See John Mueller, *Capitalism, Democracy and Ralph's Pretty Good Grocery* (Princeton: Princeton University Press, 1999); and Joel Blau, *Illusions of Prosperity: America's Working Families in an Age of Economic Insecurity* (New York: Oxford University Press, 1999).

[19] John MacArthur, *The Selling of 'Free Trade': NAFTA, Washington, and the Subversion of American Democracy* (New York: Hill and Wang, 2000); Susan Aaronson, *Taking Trade to the Streets: the Lost History of Public Efforts to Shape Globalization* (Ann Arbor: University of Michigan Press, 2001).

and particularly capitalist industrialization, in order to legitimize the new doctrine of political economy as a beneficent change agent. The ascendancy of capital, in consequence, was linked to liberation from pre-capitalist feudal and mercantile fetters prejudicial to the values, relationships and social and economic arrangements essential to the development of this new approach to economic activity.[20] While the result was a steady attrition and collapse of pre-capitalist institutions unfriendly or indifferent to capital, this did not mean that the emerging order and its apologists did not from the very start seek to supplant these social, political and economic institutions with new relations and arrangements. Particularly in the case of legal, political and governmental systems, the emerging secular, modern national state functioned almost from the beginning as the central vehicle for pooling and organizing (and often even disbursing) the public capital on which capitalism in all its forms has always depended.[21]

Recourse to 'freedom' thus has a historically and conceptually circumscribed sense that has long since ceased to be relevant, if it ever was, to the defense of this prescriptive, theoretical and thoroughly fraudulent doctrine. In the period between 1870 and 1920, the large majority of capitals in Western nation-states clearly became the dominant class in the political and economic systems of their respective countries. To the extent that the doctrine of free trade continued to function symbolically, and mainly condensationally, for capitals and their apologists, they relied more and more on representative democratic rather than pre-capitalist images and motifs.[22] Not only had the institutions of the people made significant progress in Great Britain and the Empire, France and the United States. They had done so as a result of pressure on the state exerted by newly franchised elements of the population, as well as those seeking this status and recognition. Capital traded on the status and recognition of *citizenly* freedom and liberty in order to gain subsequent acquiescence

[20] See the early discussion of the tension between pre-capitalist and early capitalist values in Adam Smith, *Theory of Moral Sentiments* (1759) and how his views alter in *An Inquiry into the Nature and Causes of the Wealth of Nations* (1776).

[21] See chapter 6, this text, for discussion of the central role played by constitutional, organic and other founding documents in the development of these institutions.

[22] Candidate Steve Forbes, multi-millionaire son of the late Malcolm Forbes, subtitled his information package to supporters 'a new birth of freedom', extolling the flat tax and allied anti-government proposals, in his unsuccessful bid to represent the Republican Party in the U.S. Federal Election of 2000.

and support from the people for a concept *and practice* of freedom which was far more exclusive in kind, however dependent on states and governments it might be.[23]

This is only underscored when we turn to what is, if anything, an even more central prescriptive and hortatory notion than freedom in the arsenal of political economy—individualism and the conception of every human being as an individual.[24] While this concept also has democratic political resonances, its major institutional reference point is the legal and constitutional systems which began to be extended and expanded in support of the people only after capital had helped fashion them for its own purposes. Admittedly, this expansion occurred in large measure in response to the inclusion of formerly disenfranchised elements of the population in the opportunities and responsibilities of citizenship. Nevertheless, it was the way that the people *used* their rights and powers that made it necessary for governments, parties and other supporters of capital to significantly modify their methods. No longer as able to rely on a more direct utilization of the mechanisms of state power, capital and its supporters embraced persuasion, rhetoric and ideology, long since supplemented, and now increasingly complemented, by advertising, marketing and sustained recourse to public relations in and through mass media.[25]

Reliance on the goal and value of individualism allows capital to trade on both an operative political understanding of the essence of citizenship in a representative democracy and an accepted legal and constitutional view of the human being. In the event, virtually every adult human being of continuous residence in a given state becomes a legitimate 'person' in the law or in society.[26] This quite apart from

[23] Anthony Howe, *Free Trade and Liberal England, 1846–1946* (Oxford: Clarendon Press, 1997); Wilson, *Bureaucratic Representation*, chapters 2–5.

[24] Allan Engler, *Apostles of Greed: Capitalism and the Myth of the Individual* (London: Pluto Press, 1995).

[25] David Croteau and William Hoynes, *The Business of Media: Corporate Media and the Public Interest* (Thousand Oaks, California: Pine Forge Press, 2001); Paul Sniderman, *The Clash of Rights: Liberty, Equality, and Legitimacy in Pluralist Democracies* (New Haven: Yale University Press, 1996); Giovanni Arrighi, *The Long Twentieth Century: Money, Power, and the Origins of Our Times* (London: Verso, 1994).

[26] In *Santa Clara County versus Southern Pacific Railroad Co.*, 118 U.S. 394, 6 Sup. Ct. 1132, 30 L.Ed. 118 (1886), the United States Supreme Court, speaking through its Chief Justice, stated that corporations were protected as 'persons' under the 14th Amendment of the U.S. Constitution. This was not the original intention of the amendment, which was to protect newly freed former slaves by extending due

whether these two references are themselves valid or invalid as realistic ways of conceptualizing the human being thus reduced to his or her solitariness for purposes of voting, consuming, spectating or otherwise legitimizing economic practices. Reliance upon these images, theoretically available, or soon to be available, to all in the categories cited, underwrote and consequently served to justify the exercise of that more available notion of individualism expressed through buying and selling, producing and consuming, investing and divesting and moving and removing by capitals.[27]

Tied inseparably to this expression of free individualism as the essence of the free society of capitals promoted by political economy was utilization of the simple trading relationship between two individuals as both indicative of the goodness of the emerging and established system and prototypical of it at its core. This image, needless to say, becomes progressively more inappropriate and ludicrous as it becomes ever more necessary, either directly or in the indirect sense that is captured by reliance upon and recourse to the term 'free' and allied words and concepts.[28] Thus, as we gradually cease to have any empirical reference point in reality which would make sense of our (and capital's) use of these concepts and terminology, residual symbolic and condensation symbols continue to persist, and not only because of some alleged gap between reality and its popular understanding. They persist because their invocation is absolutely necessary if there is to be continued support for a neo-conservative agenda which has persuaded the people, at least for now, that the institutions of capital can look after their interests better than their own can.

The mythology of the two-person relationship as the essence of the free society of capitals utilizes both freedom and individualism in order to foster the illusion that institutions, like culture, are regressive and restrictive properties of past collective forms. They are, it is alleged, to be found today only in 'primitive' or evil societies which

process protection to states as well as the federal jurisdiction when it was ratified in 1868.

[27] See Douglas Irwin, *Against the Tide: an Intellectual History of Free Trade* (Princeton: Princeton University Press, 1996).

[28] Marx, in *Capital Volume I*, pointed out the insufficiency and inappropriateness of the two person exchange model often used to justify the complex transactional reality of capitalism.

have no place in our own developmental paradigm. Institutions are equated with feudalism, mercantilism and pre-modern or repressive values, as if mercantilism, or merchant capitalism, were not itself a form of capitalism.[29] Think of the increasing correspondence between mercantilism and contemporary capitalist systems exhibiting state interdependence, a preference for monopoly and concentration, powerful organized corporate bureaucratic structures and a bias toward status rather than contract in privatization strategies. This may go a long way toward explaining why this carefully crafted and sustained illusion is absolutely necessary, the moreso in what is alleged to be the heyday of 'globalization' and 'international competitiveness'.[30]

Durkheim understood well the sociological assumptions underlying Adam Smith's preference for free individualism and contractual relations in *An Inquiry into the Nature and Causes of the Wealth of Nations*. He thus argued forcefully in *The Division of Labor in Society* and elsewhere that exchange relations between 'free individuals' presupposed the existence (and force) of prior collective understandings. In effect, a pre-existent basis for interaction and the consequent presence of shared values at or near the core of this society made capitalism a *cultural* as well as an economic phenomenon.[31] Durkheim went on to argue that 'individualism' itself was at base a social category, not only in the generic sense of being anchored in collective cultural understandings but more specifically because its emergence and development coincided with the rise of society. By society he meant a culturally and historically specific *form* of collective life rather than a synonym for such life and living.[32] As the stepchild of capitalism, understood to be the basis of a *social* as well as an economic system, society bears the same relation to it that its disciplines, the

[29] Both Durkheim and Weber tended in this direction. Durkheim contrasted 'organic' to an earlier 'mechanical' solidarity in *The Division of Labor in Society* (New York: Macmillan, 1952, 1893/1902). Also see his discussion of the 3 types of dyadic relation at *ibid.* pp. 54–56. Weber, on the other hand, contrasted rationalization and the routinization of charisma as modes of change in *Economy and Society*, Volume I, Part 1, chapter 3, i–v (Berkeley: University of California Press, 1968, 1900–1914).

[30] See Corinne Gilb, *Hidden Hierarchies* (New York: Harper and Row, 1966).

[31] Durkheim, *op. cit.*, especially the criticism of Spencer in Book I, Chapters 6 (4) and 7 (1); and the discussion of individualism in: Book I, Chapter 3 (4); Book II, Chapters 3–5; and Book III, Conclusion. On forms of capitalism and ways of doing things economic and financial as a *cultural* phenomenon, see Herschel Hardin, *A Nation Unaware*.

[32] See Adorno, 'Society', *op. cit.*; Wilson, *The American Ideology*, especially chapter 8.

social, behavioral and administrative-managerial 'sciences', do to political economy—the science of capitalism.[33]

The reference of individualism and the individual as collective and social concepts and categories took shape in Durkheim's thinking in response to Herbert Spencer's claim that exchange relations constituted the basis of the system of social relations underlying capitalism and the emerging society. Durkheim's point was that there already had to be a pre-existent solidarity present in order for any possibility of exchange relations to occur. He argued further that these pre-understandings could not help but challenge the operative shibboleths of Social Darwinist litany and rhetoric, committed as they were to the idea that individuals established contractual relations in a collective and institutional void.[34] Collectivity was viewed as a constraint on these free individuals, and was equated with pre-capitalist institutions rooted in feudalism and mercantilism. The idea that capitalism required (and strove for) an alternate collectivity and institutional system, using already existent forms and structures only as long as they served its purposes, was anathema to the emerging system of justifications.[35]

Not only was it the case, Durkheim argued, that freedom and individualism were collective and societal concepts and categories whose institutional source undergirded exchange and contract as superstructural relationships which presupposed already existing understandings. The basis of these pre-understandings, while elemental to the emergence, development and persistence of capitalism as an economic and social system and a culture, continued to be pre-capitalist in essence.[36] Durkheim even claimed to see in this continuing recourse to individualism and freedom a collectively unconscious attempt to create an alternate order to that left behind as the legacy of feudalism and mercantilism. It was his view that this emergent economic order in the Europe (particularly the France) of a century ago was dangerously incomplete. This was because it had failed to

[33] Anticipated by Durkheim, *op. cit.*, Preface to the Second Edition (1902) and Conclusion.

[34] *Ibid.* Book II, Chapter 2 (4); Chapter 5 (3).

[35] See Weber's claim that his focus on rationality and endorsement of methodological individualism as an analytical strategy did not imply a bias toward either instrumental rationality or individualism in *Economy and Society*, Volume I, Part One, chapters 1 and 2, 1–13.

[36] Wilson, 'Time, Space and Value', *op. cit.*

acknowledge its social and cultural nature as a collective form that urgently needed a new and revised understanding of both freedom and individualism *precisely because of the decline of pre-capitalist sentiments and institutional forms.*[37]

The new system of solidarity that Durkheim wished to see is significant today because of its realization as a largely finished state of affairs in Western capitalist democracies after 1965. Large-scale public and private sector organizations, extended secondary socialization and the central role of a more positive *occupational* individualism are the cornerstones of his theory in practice. This was certainly not the purpose of Durkheim's plea for a solidary societal organism which would support a more positive (and available) notion of individualism and freedom a century ago but it was to a great extent its result.[38] Durkheim had claimed that the desired system, premised as it was on a societally based respect for individuals as legal and occupational 'persons', was necessary if social stability was to be restored and maintained. In harking back to the guilds of the medieval and early modern West for his inspiration, he provided support for the very social and cultural institutions which neo-conservatives presently cite as indicators of the decline of capitalism and its civilization. Ironically, the role that he prescribed for the modern professions, alongside sociologists and other social scientists, receives neo-conservative support today only if it is reformulated in terms of exchange and contractual relations.[39]

Capitalism, as a system of commercial relations, and thereafter as an industrial system, an economy, a social system and (finally) a full-fledged culture, initially in the West and now to some extent globally (but with the qualifications noted), has intermittently sought direct ideological legitimation employing the litany and rhetoric cited. When not a central part of an explicit discourse, it has functioned residually, but still consciously, as a basis for 'member-shipping' oneself in

---

[37] Durkheim, *op. cit.*, Book II, Chapters 3, 5; Book III, Conclusion; Preface to the Second Edition.

[38] On Durkheim's more 'available' form of individualism, see H.T. Wilson, *Tradition and Innovation: the Idea of Civilization as Culture and its Significance* (London: Routledge, 1984), chapter 2.

[39] Durkheim, *op. cit.* Preface to the Second Edition; Gilb, *op. cit.* For an example of professional territorialism from the discipline of Sociology itself, see William Goode, writing in the *American Sociological Review's* 'The Profession: Reports and Opinions' section for 1966.

the culture and checking on the credentials of others. The question of the accuracy of the empirical referent of key concepts like freedom and individualism, while mainly condensational in nature, has rarely if ever been as close to the surface of this process of member-shipping since before World War Two.[40] The idea of free individuals, however much the conscious, and intended, product of secondary and primary socialization by capital through its influence over communities, schools and mass media—remains simultaneously a set of condensational symbols and an ideal, occasionally of the past but often of the future as well.

Neo-conservative resistance to Durkheim's commitment to a societal conception of freedom and individualism only makes sense when its more positive and institutional aspects are seen to favor the sort of society in which a commitment to full employment and social welfare grounds what is essentially a neo-Keynesian agenda. Even though Durkheim did not necessarily support such an agenda, particularly given his view of and attitude toward government, his prescribed system of solidarity, positive conception of individualism and institutional conception of society is far more compatible with neo-Keynesianism than with neo-conservatism.[41] This is only underscored by his view of the required system of solidarity as a cure for the generalized malaise of *anomie* or 'normlessness' which capitalist industrialization had brought in its wake. Responding to Comte in particular, Durkheim had argued that the problem was not that an essentially pre-industrial system of values and norms had collapsed, but rather that no alternative form of solidarity had come forward to replace it.[42]

The reason why his proposal in *The Division of Labor in Society* is so compatible with a neo-Keynesian agenda relates to his view of the proper *functions* which society as the new collective form should ideally carry out. However much Durkheim resisted an expanded role for government, and sought the intermediation of professional and intellectual guilds and associations as an alternative to it, he saw society and the social as a system of overarching norms and values.

[40] Engler, *op. cit.*; Gee, Hull and Lankshear, *op. cit.*

[41] Durkheim, *op. cit.*, Preface to the Second Edition. Also see the work of one of Durkheim's foremost (and best known) disciples Elton Mayo, *The Human Problems of an Industrial Civilization* (Cambridge, Mass.: Harvard Business School, 1933).

[42] Durkheim, *op. cit.*, pp. 364–365, in criticism of Comte.

In this scheme, it was Adam Smith's notion of sympathy rather than the egoism and self-interest of political economy and Social Darwinism that came to the fore.[43] Indeed, Durkheim castigated Social Darwinism's zero-sum conception of individualism and its anti-social conception of freedom precisely because each refused to acknowledge the pre-contractual basis of any collective form where contracts and exchange relations were prominent or pre-eminent. It is probably true that his consistent invocation of or reference to medieval institutions and values led many to the thoroughly mistaken view that he was nostalgic for a return to the past. Nevertheless, the society within which Western capitalism found itself prior to the advent of neo-conservatism probably met many or most of his functional and solidaristic requirements.[44]

It is on the matter of the role of governments and the legal system that capitals have always been most evasive and ideological, however. The relative ignorance and/or lack of currency amongst publics with intellectual and academic theories has always been something which capitals could count on, particularly if these theories made no pretence to, or seemed to have no bearing upon, economic matters and the economy generally. One of the strongest points in favor of economics, and before it of political economy, was its claim to be less theoretical and more practical from the standpoint of real, everyday-life problems than the other, more 'social' sciences. Even someone as supportive of the discipline as a whole as Peter Wiles has pointed this out.[45] Reference in an earlier chapter to political economy's inversion of the concrete and abstract and its illusion of a simple and straightforward connection between cause and effect sought to draw attention not only to the greater popularity and sense of relevance and practicality that economics has in the public mind. It also suggests how and why the more social sciences are so often sorely tempted to either move in a more 'economistic' direction, or claim to be doing so when they clearly are not.[46]

---

[43] The 'early' Smith expounded this notion of 'sympathy' in *Theory of Moral Sentiments*.

[44] Also see Mayo, *op. cit.* and his subsequent analyses in *The Social Problems of an Industrial Civilization, with an appendix on the Political Problem* (London: Routledge, 1975).

[45] Peter Wiles, 'The Necessity and Impossibility of Political Economy', *History and Theory*, Volume 11 (1972), pp. 3–14; and a response in H.T. Wilson, 'Capitalism, Science and the Possibility of Political Economy', in *Marx's Critical/Dialectical Procedure*, 'Appendix', pp. 180–200.

[46] See chapter 7, this study, 'Property, Capital and Society'.

It is of more than passing interest to note that the neo-conservative attack on the social sciences, based on social-scientific support for the more balanced approach to the creation of use and exchange values found in neo-Keynesianism, often equates 'social' with 'socialist'. Neo-conservatism's clutch of illusions includes ongoing criticism of this latter agenda because it seeks (like Durkheim) to use economic activity to serve non-economic values, and grounds this commitment (also like Durkheim) in the prior and determining reality of the social or societal. It is the neo-Keynesian insistence on treating capitalism (correctly) as part of a full-fledged social and institutional system and culture that upsets neo-conservatism. Neo-conservatism, in contrast, views society, perhaps hypocritically, as little more than egoistic individuals seeking comparative advantage in the face of institutions which (allegedly) misappropriate the product of their efforts while doing nothing but using up the value which these efforts create.[47] Once again, this serves to completely obscure (among other things) the functions that government and law perform for capitals while confirming neo-conservatism's debt to economic liberalism *rather than to conservatism.*

This illusion of an institutional void, particularly where explicit and implicit support for capitals by the state is concerned, continues to ground the rhetoric and litany of free trade discourse long after one would have thought it possible for either publics or capitals to take such talk seriously. As an example, consider the number of studies and reports that simultaneously attack the activity of governments in the 'marketplace', then follow their analyses with recommendations to repair this situation which invariably begin with 'The government should do this. The government should do that'.[48] This is yet one more indication that the real issue, whether capitals and their supporters are aware of it or not, is what the government does for capitals versus what it does for the people. The last thing capitals really want is for governments to go 'out of business', particularly given the fact that the system is clearly set up to serve the interests of large, corporate capitals rather than inventors,

[47] John Kingdom, *No Such Thing as Society* (Buckingham, U.K.: Open University Press, 1992).

[48] Apart from numerous Royal Commissions and Green and White Papers issuing from Federal and Provincial governments in Canada, excellent examples of this practice included reports of the *Economic Council of Canada*, terminated in 1992.

entrepreneurs and small business persons, save in the highly restricted ways already cited.

One way of addressing the fallacious nature of free trade discourse builds upon the clear differences between Durkheim's and Smith's thinking and that of political economy and Social Darwinism. It would require us to consider the claim that all collectivities (including society) have key functional requisites that must be carried out if they are to persist and survive.[49] The neo-conservative focus on 'globalization' and consequent need for 'restructuring' seeks to obscure such claims, by arguing that the objective imperatives of 'change' have made such concerns irrelevant, if not obsolete, particularly since they (allegedly) relate to the individual nation-state as the collective and societal unit. But this ignores the reality of capitalism as part of a *trans-national culture* that is unavoidably tied to a set of political, legal, economic, financial and social institutions which supporters of capital point to hypocritically in order to speak to this alleged irrelevance and obsolescence. Instead of taking issue with this fact, the point is rather to show how the situation it correctly depicts continues to depend, now as before, on capital's continuing dependence on the individual nation-state as the major entity for organizing, pooling and co-opting public capital for private uses.

A major problem with the focus on functional requisites is less the idea that they exist and can be enumerated than that they are so often confused with the structures performing them at any given time, place and circumstance.[50] Thus, even if we accept the claim that any collective form must have institutions of one kind or another which: support some type of 'family' around mothers, children and other adults; prepare the young for entry into the collective as young adults; meet basic physiological, psychological and other human 'needs'; provide arrangements for making binding decisions for the collective; and defend the collective from attack, this is not to assume that the structures presently performing these functions are similarly indispensable. Indeed, in the case of at least two (if not more) of the requisites cited above, the structures of mature capitalist democracies would appear to be doing a mediocre to bad job at perform-

[49] Durkheim, *op. cit.*; Smith, *Theory of Moral Sentiments*; Merton, *op. cit.*

[50] Irving Louis Horowitz, *Professing Sociology* (Chicago: Aldine Press, 1968), chapter on the 'myth' of functionalism and functional analysis in sociology.

ing these functions for a significant number of their citizens.[51] Without in any way exonerating supporters of the neo-Keynesian and allied agendas from this mediocre to poor performance, neo-conservatism has clearly aggravated, in some cases seriously, many problems of this sort that existed prior to 1975–80.

The functions enumerated above suggest that Durkheim was correct when he (and others) argued that they are *pre-societal* in nature and type, however much tied to the survival and persistence of all collective forms they may be. If society is a culturally and historically specific form of life found only in mature capitalist democracies, and if this characteristic holds whether we are looking at the system domestically or in its trans-national aspects, then calling these functional requisites pre-societal is virtually synonymous with calling them pre-capitalistic. This is evident not only from considering their central role in the pre-capitalist (and pre-societal) West, but by comparing them to collectives that are alleged to be not only technologically and economically 'underdeveloped' but culturally and institutionally different and distinct. One of the most significant realizations that comes out of this focus on functional requisites, it turns out, is the doubt it casts on the theory and practice of development itself, defined and understood to mean economic and technical 'progress'.[52]

In addition to institutional and collective-structural 'denial' by neo-conservatives we can also note that the structures presently performing (or attempting to perform) functional requisites in these societies may be manifestly inferior to those that have emerged in other cultures, past or present, to do essentially the same thing.[53] Indeed, neo-conservatism in practice has exacerbated already existing prob-

---

[51] Discussed in Wilson, *Sex and Gender: Making Cultural Sense of Civilization* (Leiden: E.J. Brill, 1989).

[52] See Weber's discussion of 3 types of 'progress' in *Methodology of the Social Sciences* (Glencoe, Illinois: Free Press, 1949), pp. 34–39, where he distinguishes: '(1) merely 'progressive' differentiation, (2) progress of *technical* rationality in the utilization of means and, finally (3) increase in value'. It is by reference to (3) that one can dispute the association of progress with both societal complexity and progress in technique together or on their own in favor of more political and administrative conceptions more compatible with institutions and functions.

[53] Horowitz, *op. cit.*; H.T. Wilson, 'Functional Rationality and "Sense of Function": the Case of an Ideological Distortion', *International Yearbook of Organization Studies, 1980*, edited by G. Salaman and D. Dunkerly (London: Routledge, 1981), pp. 72–98.

lems of 'fit' between function and structure while bringing (or bringing back) others into prominence that were being dealt with relatively adequately before its emergence. We need to distinguish carefully not only between capitals and the people and different types of capitals but between different *functions* and the way that neo-conservatism differentially rank orders them in its hierarchy of value on the basis of their relative importance. This is particularly evident in the cavalier way that neo-conservatives seek, often successfully, to withdraw financial and other support for the first two requisites cited, while seeking to redefine the third and fourth and make a seven course meal out of the fifth, especially (and again) since September 11, 2001.

In part this is facilitated by their view of cultural and institutional realities as essentially pre (or anti) capitalist in nature, alongside their already-noted propensity to reduce institutions to organizations and culture to 'civilization'.[54] Even the invocation of apparently social institutions like the family (and 'family values') serves an anti-institutional agenda to the extent that it is paired with privacy and the private, individualism and the individual, and freedom and independence from societal demands voiced through governments. There is also, of course, the illusion of the autonomous family in its nuclear form which capitalism itself produced so it would have mobile and compliant laborers no longer tied to the kin network and the community, and now needs for the accumulation of crippling consumer debt.[55] None of this justifies capitalism's claim that it can really survive without pre-capitalist institutions and the functional requisites they perform. The point is rather that even within the present institutional system neo-conservatives have skewed societal and political priorities in ways which have generated a consequential imbalance in the creation of use versus exchange values, with serious consequences for infrastructure development and renewal.[56] This quite

[54] Wilson, *Bureaucratic Representation*, introduction and chapter 1; Durkheim, *op. cit.* references to 'civilization' itself having no 'intrinsic value', pp. 52–54 and *supra*; Wilson, 'Culture versus Civilization in the Theory and Practice of International Understanding', *op. cit.; Tradition and Innovation*, preface, chapters 1, 5 and reprise.

[55] E.P. Thompson, *The Making of the English Working Class* (Harmondsworth, U.K.: Penguin, 1968); 'Time, Work Discipline and Industrial Capitalism', *Past and Present*, Volume 38 (December 1967), pp. 56–96; J. Goody, J. Thirsk and E.P. Thompson (editors), *Family and Inheritance: Rural Society in Western Europe, 1200–1800* (Cambridge: Cambridge University Press, 1976); Ivan Illich, *Gender* (New York: Pantheon, 1982); Wilson, *Sex and Gender*, chapters 1–3.

[56] See Wilson, 'Time, Space and Value', *op. cit.*

apart from the no less significant question of whether other cultures perform these functions better than 'ours' does.

This section has tried to make a case for an analysis of our present collective form-society-that is based on key functional requisites that all collectives require. At the same time, it has used the tension between functions and structures to challenge the idea that the indispensability of functions can be reduced to a defense of the structures presently performing them in a given country or culture. This does not mean, however, that the resulting priorities can be assessed solely in institutional terms, no matter how central to their understanding institutions remain. This would be to fall into the self-same tendency to reduce institutions to organizations and effectiveness to efficiency that is the hallmark of neo-conservatism.[57] Such a 'bare bones' approach, however problematic, is rarely put forward in an attempt to hide or deny reality, except by some neo-conservative supporters among the academic and professional strata who really know better. Yet this is precisely what makes neo-conservatism so dangerous, alongside its continuing ties to political economy and Social Darwinism. What is at issue here is the fact that functional requisites possess a symbolic as well as an instrumental component, with the symbolic aspect at least as significant for the persistence of collective forms, albeit not necessarily standing apart from the instrumental function of institutions.

It is just as foolish to ignore symbolic functions as it is to ignore latent functions, since both must be taken into account in assessing the *effectiveness* (as opposed to efficiency) of an institution. Confining oneself to efficiency and to instrumental functions while ignoring symbolic and latent functions, however dependent one is upon them, only makes sense for people who are preoccupied with disembedding structures from their historical origins and ongoing cultural realities as part of their own system of justifications and legitimations.[58]

[57] In *Methodology of the Social Sciences*, p. 37, Weber addresses a significant change in 'economic science' when he notes its consequential shift from the task of rank ordering ends on the assumption that means are scarce to one of determining the most efficient means to the realization of ends that are either given or unproblematic. Illich, in *Gender*, stresses the historical origins of the 'invention' of scarcity, in contrast to dearth. On the difference between economic and technical rationality see Paul Diesing, *Reason and Society* (Urbana, Illinois: University of Illinois Press, 1962), chapters 1, 2.

[58] Diesing, *op. cit.*; Edelman, *op. cit.*; Merton, *op. cit.*; Wilson, 'Values: On the

It is the policy consequences of these values and beliefs in practical operation that so completely upend the appropriate balance and demand immediate attention and concern for the reasons already cited. Even Durkheim failed to realize that his three types of association based on similarities, differences which repel and differences which attract were not, after all, dominant types appearing serially in historically successive collective forms, but rather necessary or unavoidable features of *all* collective forms, now as before.[59] This expressed his own resistance to the idea of basic collective functions required by all peoples, past, present and to come, functions that could never be superseded because of the presence of a bedrock 'human nature' possessed by everyone solely by dint of their being human.

Let us now turn to the contemporary discussion of 'free trade' and 'free markets' in the light of these observations and reflections. The purpose of this digression has been to show how considerations of a collective and (cross) cultural kind may be of value to us in situating the discourses, rhetoric and litany of neo-conservatism as they relate not only to free trade, but to 'privatization' and the 'public debt' as well. Symbolic and latent functions, after all, must be included in an intelligent assessment of institutions not only in their active or practical dimension but in their discursive and linguistic aspects as well. Indeed, an apparent functional analysis along the lines suggested here is seriously incomplete (at best) if it fails to take account of the fact that language and discourse are no less central to the performance of various functions than practical action allegedly distended from them. As it turns out, functional analysis, working at its best, and within its limits, must ultimately acknowledge that its notion of function comprehends thought and language no less than a practicality allegedly free from them at the level of action in any minimally adequate discussion of institutions.[60]

The most important, even startling, feature of contemporary discussions and debates around free trade has been the extent to which they have become almost totally detached from the historical and

---

Possibility of a Convergence between Economic and Non Economic Decision Making', *op. cit.*

[59] Durkheim, *op. cit.*, especially pp. 54–63.

[60] See Jurgen Habermas, *Between Facts and Norms: Contributions to a Discourse Theory of Law and Democracy* (Cambridge, Mass.: MIT Press, 1996).

ideological claims that have been put forward to defend free trade as the essence of capitalism. This becomes evident when we consider the level of size and complexity of the collective and institutional units being looked at. Free trade advocates, for example, talk about multinational corporations and nation-states, tied in various ways to supranational and international organizations, in the same breath as free enterprise, unfettered rights to accumulate, invest and consume and a domestic and global market system ideally free of the heavy hand of governments.[61] This anomalous, even contradictory, tendency on their part indicates the magnitude of the gap between ideology and reality in their thinking. It presents itself most starkly when these individuals dispute their views with supporters of one or another form of 'industrial policy' approach that sanctions a more direct and continuous role for governments.

The debates between advocates of free trade and those committed to industrial policy, particularly in the United States, exhibit nothing so much as the fact that free traders don't really mean what they say. Their rhetoric is that any consumer ought to be able to purchase any commodity made anywhere on earth at an open and independent market price absent of all fees, tariffs and other forms of protection. In addition to serving the comfort and/or profit of the consumer, this policy is supposed to stimulate producers and other capitals to ever-greater efforts, even if this includes capital flight to low wage countries with poor to non-existent social, labor, safety and environmental standards. The economic dislocations that ensue in the country of origin as a consequence of its being 'more developed' than those which are the recipients of capital flight are taken as a sign that its economy is not working at its best, at least in the relevant industry or sector. Little or no account is taken of the fact that other factors of production—in this case labor—possess little or no such mobility.[62] In effect, it is the very fact of capital mobility itself which demands incessant attention to the infrastructure costs of this and related forms of dislocation brought about by 'global-

---

[61] Graham Dunkley, *The Free Trade Adventure: WTO, the Uruguay Round and Globalism: A Critique* (London: Zed Books, 2000); Mark Rupert, *Ideologies of Globalization: Contending Visions of a New World Order* (London: Routledge, 2000); John Gray, *False Dawn: the Delusions of Global Capitalism* (New York: New Press/Norton, 1998).

[62] Kikeri, *op. cit.*; Suggs, *op. cit.*; Ian Gough and Gunnar Olofsson (editors), *Capitalism and Social Cohesion: Essays on Exclusion and Integration* (New York: St. Martin's Press, 1999).

ization' and consequent 'restructuring', whether it pertains to the people of donor or recipient countries.

It is the nation-state system at different levels of economic and technological development in a world allegedly undergoing 'global restructuring' and the emergence of new forms of competitiveness that is therefore responsible for both the constraints upon and the opportunities for capital's superior mobility to manifest itself. Free trade advocates accept the vast discrepancy between donor and recipient countries, arguing that this will lead eventually to wage improvements and resulting infrastructure in these latter countries in due course.[63] The fact that this process is occurring more and more rapidly only underscores their concerns about restrictive and protectionist trade practices for both consumers in the country of origin and the multinational corporations who have relocated production to developing countries, while still being headquartered in their countries of origin. Free traders not only object to country of origin restraints on trade, whether with foreign producers or relocated multinationals. They appear to be convinced that even when other countries discriminate against foreign goods while expecting free access to the markets of the country of origin, this should be permitted within limits.[64]

A major stumbling block for 'free traders' in the U.S. emerged in relations with Japan and the leading countries of the EU in the 1990's. Most free trade advocates support not only the North American Free Trade Agreement (NAFTA), but also 'political' (allegedly non-market) retaliation to countries who refuse to trade under similar rules of engagement. This indicated their assent to the idea that supranational trading blocs were inevitable, but only as a means to achieving global free trade rather than in place of it. They believed

[63] Maxwell Cameron and Brian Tomlin, *The Making of NAFTA: How the Deal was Done* (Ithaca: Cornell university press, 2000); Michael Lusztig, *Risking Free Trade: the Politics of Trade in Britain, Canada, Mexico and the United States* (Pittsburgh: University of Pittsburgh Press, 1996). Far from being a leader in wages for similar labor being carried out elsewhere in Mexico, wages in the 'macquiladores', a 'free trade showplace' on the border with the U.S., are now among the lowest in the country.

[64] Delia Conti, *Reconciling Free Trade, Fair Trade and Interdependence: the Rhetoric of Presidential Economic Leadership* (Westport, Conn.: Praeger, 1998). One difficulty for American companies that have taken over formerly Canadian owned enterprises is the fact that they themselves have become the targets of 'unfair trading' charges before Congress, the state legislatures and NAFTA's Dispute Settlement Panel. An excellent example is Weyerhauser's treatment by U.S. companies and governments since its take over of Macmillan Blodel of British Columbia, Canada.

that over a decade of setbacks to the General Agreement on Tariffs and Trade (GATT) since 1979, now superseded by the World Trade Organization (WTO), made NAFTA an absolute necessity, given Japan's and the EEC's 'restrictive' trade practices. However, this does not mean that free traders endorse the 'fair trade' views of industrial policy advocates in the U.S. (and elsewhere). Advocates of fair trade wish to redress unfair advantages and the absence of the proverbial 'level playing field' by penalizing, surcharging and/or restricting trade *to and from* any country adjudged to warrant the imposition of sanctions. The manifest hypocrisy of the free trade position is nowhere more evident than in its desire to 'protect' American business and industry, *albeit in non-traditional 'political' ways*, while yet permitting its 'right of flight' to developing countries in Latin America and elsewhere, in clear contrast to industrial policy advocates.[65]

Free traders thus compromise their position not only by being committed to government activity, and even initiatives, in the three traditional areas cited earlier, now vastly extended and expanded in their scope, ambit and comprehensiveness. They have also stated that at a certain point the behavior of a 'competitor', like Japan, the EU, or one of its leading countries, ceases to be a strictly economic matter and becomes essentially 'political' in nature. It is at this point that state action is both warranted and justified, but not before. They espouse a not-dissimilar position on the matter of trade relations with communist or former communist (but not rightist authoritarian) states. In this case, they do not claim that human rights violations make dealings with such countries a problem but instead state that the rights and freedoms of capitals, along with those of local consumers in these countries, are being violated or compromised. One recent example of how quickly human rights considerations can disappear from the screen was the 'done deal' for the 2008 Summer Olympics. In this case, some of the strongest lobbying for Beijing (besides American networks) came from U.S. multinational corporations whose contracts with the Chinese government depended upon the success of its bid. The rationale for such 'about faces' then becomes the claim that 'free trade' is the best way to effect the future development of legal and democratic institutions.

[65] See Jagdish Bhagwati and Robert Hudec (editors), *Fair Trade and Harmonization: Prerequisites for Free Trade?* (Cambridge, Mass.: MIT Press, 1996); Hood, op. cit.

To be sure, this is perfectly consistent with their attitude toward political corruption, labor exploitation and the near-total absence of *enforced* social, labor, safety and environmental standards in developing countries that are the recipients of capitals in flight, always with the support of host governments and leaders.

Industrial policy advocates define the 'refereeing' function which governments must perform in ways that sanction immediate responses of a wide-ranging nature, but do so not only to protect country-of-origin economies from sectoral and regional economic dislocations caused by capital flight to developing countries. They see these powers as a necessary response to the restrictive and protectionist practices of Japan, other Pacific Rim countries and the EU, who they call two-faced because they have been granted relatively open access to the U.S. market, yet continue to support trade barriers to American products. Even though the U.S. supported such uneven trade relations in the past for political and military reasons, based on the view that post-war economic development and resulting stability would be a bulwark against the further expansion of communism in Europe and Asia, this situation no longer exists. Not only are these countries now well developed economic powers but the threat of communism has vanished.[66]

Industrial policy advocates also point out that Japan, other Pacific Rim countries and the EU all have affirmative and interventionist economic policies backed up by either the national state or supranational authority. All they wish to do is legislate and enforce a 'level playing field' that will make free trade a reality rather than a hypocrisy for all countries dealing with the United States. Free traders have had a mixed response to the propensity of the U.S. Congress and the President to apply countervail and retaliation as vehicles for selectively enforcing one or another version of 'fair trade' as a basis for 'free trade', now that traditional tariffs and quotas have been set aside. Industrial policy advocates would rather legislate new rules of the game in advance and for the future instead of limiting the enforcement of fair trade practices to selective and essentially *ad hoc* responses

[66] Conti, *op. cit.* But see Patrice Franco, *Toward a New Security Architecture for the Americas: the Strategic Implications of the FTAA* (Washington: Center for Strategic and International Studies, 2000). Greater recent U.S. interest in South American countries on the Pacific Ocean is a way of simultaneously bounding the Western Hemisphere on that side while negotiating with Japan and other Asian 'Pacific Rim' countries through the Asia Pacific Economic Community organization (APEC).

to individual situations by Congress and the President. While none of this would limit the right of the government to take independent action, it would, it is argued, provide capitals from the U.S. and other countries with greater predictability.

It is increasingly clear that 'free trade' itself, no less than 'fair trade', really constitutes a form of industrial policy intended to benefit capitals, almost without regard to country of origin. This observation is only compromised within the present set of discourses on the matter, and in particular with regard to the dispute with admitted industrial policy advocates, by the fact that its supporters not only desire, but expect, 'trading partners' to adhere to *virtually the same rules*. The country of origin of these rules, not surprisingly is the United States, the only remaining hegemonic power.[67] Since developing country governments quite reasonably believe they have much to gain from hosting capitals in flight from their country of origin, it is these countries that can be counted on to provide the same sort of assistance that country of origin governments did at in an earlier time. These rules ideally protect capitals by permitting them surcease from the kinds of 'impediments' that they discover in social, labor, safety and environmental legislation like that which their country of origin may be imposing upon them. Even the passage of such statutes in developing countries, often by unilateral decree, usually means nothing because there is no will, and/or few resources, to enforce them. They turn out to be little more than 'window dressing' on closer examination.

As for competitors like Japan and leading powers in the EU, free traders may balk at legislation that lays out the rules of 'fair trade' so that a 'level playing field' may be created which will permit what industrial policy advocates call 'free trade' to take place. But they certainly support *ad hoc*, case by case, countervailing or retaliatory responses by Congress and the President respectively where the trading situation has become so 'unbalanced' because of poor to non-existent market access that what they call a 'political' (as opposed to an economic) response is called for. Free trade may thus be a less formally structured and managed approach to trade than advocates of industrial policy wish to see. However, the main point remains that *free trade is itself a form of industrial policy* intended to benefit cap-

[67] MacArthur, *op. cit.*

itals everywhere and anywhere, particularly those from the country of origin. The only limitation on this is that these capitals not be the beneficiaries of a system which has its own industrial policy approach based on a consistent commitment to highly restricted or non-existent market access by capitals from other countries.[68]

A major feature of the free trade platform, however hidden or ignored, is its support for unrestricted access to markets outside the country of origin *and vice versa*. The purpose here is to protect trade and related arrangements between the home and host divisions of multinational firms based in the country of origin. This is a (perhaps *the*) central feature of its open-ended support for free trade with no protectionism of any kind short of the point where they believe economic matters become clearly political in nature and demand a governmental response. Not surprisingly, this latter provision is addressed to the most prominent exception or anomaly of all, Japan, since this is the major instance where U.S. multinationals have not been able to establish a substantial foothold that would allow them to benefit from 'free trade' between divisions.[69] On the other hand, supporters of free trade must grit their teeth and continue to support the position that all other countries, including Japan, have free and open access to the U.S. market. This continues to be subject, of course, to eventual resolution of any and all 'political' issues that may arise, even if this means the exponential growth of Japanese intra (and inter) firm trade between divisions located world-wide.

Reconciling contemporary free trade discourses with the origins of free trade in simple relations and early commercial, then industrial, economies is no easy task.[70] General publics are not normally aware of the contradictions between these discourses and the size, complexity, structure and relational, functional and geographic comprehensiveness of the aggregates to whom they are addressed. Alongside this is the exponentially *greater* dependence of capitals on nation-state governments and the supranational and international political organizations that such trade possibilities require. Even though defenders of free trade quite purposely focus on the rights of the disaggregated

[68] Bhagwati and Hudec, *op. cit.*; Nicholas Gianaris, *The North American Free Trade Agreement and the European Union* (Westport: Praeger, 1998); Kreml, *op. cit.*

[69] See reference no. 64, and Joyce Hoebing, Sidney Weintraub and M.D. Baer (editors), *NAFTA and Sovereignty: Trade Offs for Canada and the United States* (Washington: Center for Strategic and International Studies, 1996).

[70] Howe, *op. cit.*; Irwin, *op. cit.*

individual consumer, not only in the country of origin but around the world, this turns out to be far less central to their platform and concerns. Their first loyalty is to the rights and freedoms of capital and capitals to move freely, unimpeded by any legislation in any jurisdiction that would inhibit profit maximization, growth, or some other (but related) form of comparative advantage. The scope and power of these economic aggregates, backed up and supported by home and host nation-state governments, gives the ultimate lie to free trade by showing it to be the supreme illusion, given the central role of state and/or supranational political authorities.[71]

Standing behind all of this, for free traders no less than for industrial policy advocates, and even more important for the former than the latter, is the home country's willingness to continue to take an expansive view of the three traditional functions of government, particularly provision for the 'common defense'. In a period when the property and contractual rights of capital are under attack and regularly subject to social limitations and new responsibilities, the role of the military acts as a bulwark and a guarantor, even (or especially) in the post-Soviet international and global economic and political setting.[72] It is in this context that the ultimate paradox of free trade, particularly if it involves U.S. capitals but even if it does not, comes to the fore. Any of the notions which justified free trade in earlier times, places and circumstances like freedom, liberty and individualism cease to be relevant to contemporary issues and controversies, not the least of the reasons for this being that a government presence and support is even more necessary to its success than it was in the past.

A final point concerns legality and representative democracy as requirements for becoming a full-fledged trading partner with the U.S. Industrial policy advocates fear not just the absence, or lack of enforceability, of social, labor, safety and environmental standards in countries that are the recipients of U.S. capital flight. They are also concerned about the huge gaps in standard of living and quality of life and the absence of legal and democratic institutions. To this free

[71] Jeffrey Schott, *The World Trading System: Challenges Ahead* (Washington: Institute for International Economics, 1996); Aaronson, *op. cit.*; Dorinda Dallmeyer, *Joining Together, Standing Apart: National Identities after NAFTA* (Boston: Kluwer Law International, 1997); Colin Hines, *Localization: A Global Manifesto* (London: Earthscan, 2000).

[72] Franco, *op. cit.*

traders respond that they have no business legislating values and morality for other countries and cultures. As long as these countries do not permit serious market access imbalances to occur, and do not transgress or challenge the U.S. as a political and military power, trade can proceed. Indeed, they claim that free trade and free markets are the best, and really the only, way to guarantee that legal and democratic institutions will eventually come into being without being imposed from the outside. In fact this cavalier and dismissive attitude toward the large majority of the people in these countries is consistent with their attitude toward the majority in their country of origin.[73] It indicates their willingness, indeed commitment, to see to it that 'free trade' occurs in a context in which access to capital, as well as its goods and services, is unimpeded by the presence of any political and legal standards, save those which might require or justify a military presence.

The key concepts of free trade discourse have credence in the contemporary world of superstates, mega-corporations and international and supranational authorities only because they address the rights and powers of capital, and the many middle persons who support and defend their interests before sympathetic governments all over the globe. Freedom and individualism are really only meaningful in a thoroughgoing way for capitals in these circumstances, since they presuppose legal, political and civil rights and liberties available to them in their country of origin but virtually no place else which can be enforced, or even called upon. Capitals from these countries depend at least as much on these latter rights of free individualism enforced in their respective countries of origin as they do on those that permit and legitimize the accumulation, investment and movement of capital. Perhaps this more than anything else underscores how the people's struggles for civil and political rights and liberties helps capitals even as they seek to escape the responsibilities for protecting these rights elsewhere in the world, and often even in their countries of origin as well.

[73] This is the clearest indication of the very different priorities of NAFTA and the European Union. See Gianaris, *op. cit.*

CHAPTER TWELVE

LEGITIMATION CRISIS?

Thirty years ago Jurgen Habermas published the original edition of *Legitimation Crisis*, addressing himself to a social-scientific concept of crisis and its role in discerning 'crisis tendencies' in advanced industrial societies during the late 1960's and early 1970's. His initial problematic is well-captured by the first sentence in this text: 'The application of the Marxian theory of crisis to the altered reality of "advanced capitalism" leads to difficulties.'[1] Habermas was at this time to a great extent convinced that the 'advanced' nature of Western mixed-system capitalist societies meant that they had now superseded Marx's analysis and predictions about systemic crises resulting from the concentration of capital in fewer and fewer hands and the resulting emisserization of an ever-burgeoning proletariat. At the same time, however, the concept of crisis continued to be relevant to these societies inasmuch as the occurrences which give rise to crises 'owe their objectivity to the fact that they issue from unresolved steering problems.'[2] These in turn call our attention, he argued, to the relationship between system integration and social integration.

Habermas went on to delineate what he considered to be the key elements for a responsible social-scientific analysis of crisis tendencies—power, status, culture, risk, money and politics. This to the end of claiming that there were four areas that the notion of crisis requires us to focus upon if we are to understand its sense: economy, rationality, legitimation and motivation.[3] Throughout the study, Max Weber's thinking looms large, particularly in Habermas' own view of what makes improved 'communicative competence' in advanced capitalist societies so imperative. Here he contrasts the tension between the systemically-focused demands of work settings governed by norms of instrumental rationality, and the commonsense public requirement of and need for symbolically mediated interaction through language,

[1] Jurgen Habermas, *Legitimation Crisis?* (Boston: Beacon press, 1975), Preface, xxv.
[2] *Ibid.*, p. 4.
[3] *Ibid.*, chapters 3–8.

discussion and discourse.[4] Habermas' problematic, so configured, is more indebted to Weber than Marx here. Marx's contrast between substructure and superstructure is less directly relevant for Habermas' own analysis of what the deep crisis of advanced capitalist societies is than Weber's contrast between rationalization as an inexorable process coming from the substructure and de-enchantment as its superstructural effect.[5]

While it may be true that the substructure-superstructure distinction continues to be a dominant way of conceptualizing such problematics, it is Weber who puts the flesh on its bones by dynamizing it. Weber sees an inexorable process at work wherein rationalization, understood as the subordination of all areas of life to formal and instrumental rationality, is gradually *taking over* activities heretofore subject to other norms and values. Focusing on language, discussion and discourse as central modes of symbolically mediated interaction, Habermas sees interaction not only as the form of life ('life-world') most directly threatened by work, systemic thinking and instrumental rationality, but the key to reversing this process and subordinating rationalization to a responsible politics.[6] In the act of resuscitating discussion and discursive interaction, thus the life world relative to the systems world, Habermas intends (and expects) to overcome the very tendencies to alienation and de-enchantment that Weber found so threatening. Habermas' purpose is not to revive spheres and realms of irrationality and magic, but rather to bring rationalization and the system world under public control.

Habermas' concept of 'communicative competence' is therefore both a normative standard and a practical need and desire for him.

[4] *Ibid.*, especially Part III, introduction and chapter 1. Also see Habermas, 'Toward a Theory of Communicative Competence', *Recent Sociology, No. 2*, edited by H.P. Dreitzel (New York: Macmillan, 1970), pp. 115–148; Habermas, 'Aspects of the Rationality of Action', *Rationality Today*, edited by Theodore Geraets (Ottawa: University Press, 1979); Habermas, *Communication and the Evolution of Society* (Boston: Beacon Press, 1979); Habermas, *Theory of Communicative Action*, 2 vols. (Boston: Beacon press, 1984–1989); Habermas, *The Philosophical Discourse of Modernity: Twelve Lectures* (Cambridge, Mass.: MIT Press, 1990); Habermas, *On the Pragmatics of Social Interaction: Preliminary Studies in the Theory of Communicative Action* (Cambridge, Mass.: MIT Press, 2001).

[5] Weber, *Economy and Society*, Volume I, Part 1, chapters 1–3, on the relation between reason, rationality and rationalization and de-enchantment in the economy, science and technology, bureaucracy and legal and other forms of authority.

[6] Habermas, 'Technology and Science as Ideology', *Toward a Rational Society* (London: Heinemann, 1971), pp. 81–122; 125–127.

It is his realization over thirty years ago, in common with many others, that this process of rationalization was not occurring independently of the life world of language, discussion and discourse but was taking place *with its conscious and unwitting assistance.* This in turn led him to focus on this sphere of essential, and collectively self-defining, human activity as both the key to understanding the crisis and the key to its overcoming. Even without pointing to the way in which capitals and their supporters and henchmen in governments and elsewhere *use* language and symbols to create and justify their commodities as real human needs through advertising, marketing and the mass media, it is clear that a more subtle process is at work. This process undermines literacy and the ability to conceptualize the world in ways which foreground the possibility of real alternatives to what already exists and possesses legitimacy in consequence.[7] Habermas' preoccupation with the preservation and extension of the life-world *vis à vis* the system world is expressed in the view that improved communicative competence is the key to recapturing a responsible language as the precondition for recapturing the public sphere.[8]

One aspect of Habermas' analysis addressed in an earlier chapter relates to his claim that in capitalism we have a system that for the first time seeks to legitimize itself from below rather than above.[9] While there is clearly an element of truth in this idea, it is seriously incomplete to the extent that it over-concretizes the empirical split between 'above' and 'below'. Although capitalism's ability to 'deliver the goods' does constitute a basis on which 'the people' *might* decide abstractly either in favor of or against such a system, they rarely if ever can be expected to have an alternative or be sufficiently mobilized to bring it into being even if they did. None of this is to argue that this should not indeed be the case, even if it presents conceptual,

[7] *Ibid.*; Habermas, 'Toward a Theory of Communicative Competence', *op. cit.* See also Claus Mueller, 'Notes on the Repression of Communicative Behavior', *Recent Sociology, No. 2* (New York: Macmillan, 1970), pp. 101–113; and Wilson, 'Notes on the Achievement of Communicative Behavior and Related Difficulties', *Dialectical Anthropology*, Volume 12, No. 3 (1988)), pp. 285–305.

[8] Initially formulated in Habermas, *The Structural Transformation of the Public Sphere* (Cambridge: Polity Press, 1989, 1963). This theme once again became dominant after his discussion of the consequences of the student protest movements in West Germany and the rest of Western Europe after 1968. See *Toward a Rational Society*, chapters 1–3, especially, chapter 3, p. 49.

[9] Habermas, 'Technology and Science as Ideology', *op. cit.*, pp. 96–98 and *supra.*

logistical and practical problems once it is accepted.[10] The issue instead is the absence of the proverbial experimental group, plus the tendency of the life-world to incorporate values, views and assumptions into its ongoing reality that are hostile to the imperative need for interaction and for the persistence and integrity of a public sphere and public control.

The fact that this has occurred with the greatest force and consistency in representative democracies only serves to underscore the tie between capitalism and democracy. However, it also draws our attention to the modern secular nation-state itself as a (if not the) key vehicle whereby capitalism established its legitimacy through state legal and constitutional institutions, structures and processes in advance of those of the people.[11] Apart from anything else, this gradually eliminated the likelihood of the missing experimental group emerging, while it strongly suggested that there was something approaching an objective historical process of development at work here. Neither Smith, Marx, Durkheim nor Weber were fundamentally in doubt about what the nature of this process was, even if each assessed it differently and accentuated and emphasized different starting points, key events and points along the way in their respective analyses. What is of lasting significance is the distinctly modern view that the substructure is important, indeed central for the superstructure, and that this means that it cannot be left to its own devices based on continued confidence in the persistence of once-stable traditional systems of deference to authority.

It is the ability of private interests to utilize the institutions of the public sphere by eliding public and private interests, while persuading the people that confidence in their own institutions is inimical to their real economic interests, that necessitates concern about these apparently 'rational' and 'objective' processes. Without addressing the rhetorical function 'rationality' performs in defending and justifying present neo-conservative policies and practices, it is important

[10] Habermas' may be the most sensible theory of 'rational' (mass) participation for representative democratic and legal-constitutional societies that we have, but it cannot help but presuppose already existing bureaucratic, judicial and direct democratic institutional supports and possibilities for general publics and general interests in society. See Wilson, *Bureaucratic Representation* (Leiden: Brill, 2001), chapters 3, 4.

[11] Charles Lindblom, *Politics and Markets* (New York: Basic Books, 1977). See chapter 5, this study.

not to lose the concept and reality of *class* in an effort to defend the idea that this is an inexorable and irresistible objective process at work.[12] What most clearly underscores the difference between the 'legitimacy crisis' to which Habermas and others drew attention between 1965 and 1975, and the question of the legitimacy of capitalism today, is the intervening period of neo-conservative dominance. This dominance included victories in and through the electoral process in capitalist democracies that have led to significant changes in the way that publics now conceive and understand politics, the public sphere and society.[13]

As significant as anything in this regard is the way that the unfolding of events since 1978 has demonstrated to citizens not only that both *the problems and solutions* proffered by neo-conservative parties and governments are ultimately unrealistic and unworkable. It is increasingly clear that these anti-public and anti-social political parties themselves function, consciously or unwittingly, in an unbalanced way on behalf of capitals and their institutions, constitutional rights and powers and laws rather than those of the people. In effect, the once-alleged objectivity of some inexorable process of 'rationality' is no longer even credible as a way of making sense of present developments and problems in these societies, economies and polities, in contrast to the period before 1970.[14] The realities of class-based powers, privileges and prerogatives, reflected in greater access, influence and resulting impacts and effects, both tangible and intangible, cannot be denied, no matter what the media, interested groups, parties and governments and the 'private sector' tell us. We are not all in this together![15] The Marxian concept of crisis, as Habermas has argued, may indeed raise more difficulties than it resolves, but the concept of class (and its more abstract derivatives) still remains the

---

[12] Weber, *Economy and Society*, Volume I, Part 1, chapter 4; and Wilson, Notes on the Achievement of Communicative Behavior and Related Difficulties', *op. cit.* on Weber's attempt to use disciplined observation to make classes 'disappear' into status groups with the advent of 'modernization' processes.

[13] See Habermas, *The New Conservatism: Cultural Criticism and the Historians Debate* (Cambridge, Mass.: MIT Press, 1989).

[14] See Weber, *Methodology of the Social Sciences*, pp. 34–39 for 3 notions of 'progress' and why both technical progress in the utilization of means and 'progressive differentiation' and emergent complexity fail to meet any sensible notion of political and administrative progress.

[15] Whitfield, *op. cit.*; Gough and Olofsson, *op. cit.*; Marquand, *op. cit.*; Dryzek, *op. cit.*; Craig, *op. cit.*; Foster and Plowden, *op. cit.*; Hellinger and Judd, *op. cit.*

central analytic for a minimally adequate understanding of the situation.

Habermas' attempt to improve the public sphere, and public control over state and governmental decision-making, addresses the mainsprings of our Western value systems in ways that cannot be discussed at greater length here. Suffice it to say that his concern about discourse and its relation to truth claims, validity claims, claims of principle and claims of competence establish a standard which rises too high above what most or all of us can meet as creators of discourse, reason, morality, collectivity and history. It is therefore highly unlikely that our institutions will get us to the desired point without significant, even world-historical, modifications in their fabric, texture and sense. Unfortunately, the present regression of thinking, sense and value on the matter of the relation between state, capital, democracy and society demonstrates this all-too-clearly.[16] Nevertheless, one must acknowledge that the very presence of intense concern about the issues by more and more members of the public since the mid-1990's could help establish new constructive and critical attitudes toward residual tendencies to deference in these societies. That these attitudes might eventually manifest themselves in and through electoral and other public and social processes hostile to, rather than supportive of neo-conservatism, is always possible, however unlikely. The recent acquiescence of vast majorities in the United States and the United Kingdom in President Bush's ill-advised 'war' against the Taliban and Afghanistan is at the very least a significant step backward that all-too-readily confirms such skepticism. It turns its back on the very international institutions that the Americans and British, among others, were at such pains to create and support in order to deal with such 'crimes' when they occurred less than a decade ago in the Balkans and elsewhere.

Habermas' proposal for improving communicative competence in order to save and extend the public sphere against the threat of its co-ordination into the systems world requires the very communicatively competent people that it needs to bring into being as a precondition for achieving the desired goals. The increased concern over

---

[16] Wilson, 'Science, Critique and Criticism: the "Open Society" Revisited', *On Critical Theory*, edited by John O'Neill (New York: Seabury press, 1976), pp. 205–230; Wilson, *Political Management* (Berlin and New York: Walter de Gruyter, 1984), especially chapters 7–12.

social, economic and political issues that neo-conservatism's very failures are helping to generate may constitute evidence that Habermas' prescription, while by no means historically necessary in an objective sense, may be *more* likely as a consequence of precisely these developments. On the other hand, for many the issue is what real individual citizens in these societies can do *now* to address the inability of their elites in the professions, the private sector and governments to achieve a resolution of the matters in dispute in the present circumstances.[17] A basic premise, here and throughout, is to work with who we are rather than assume we are other than we are in terms of our willingness to talk, listen and achieve consensus in the real present. In this endeavor, critique, as opposed to mere criticism, remains of central significance.

Perhaps it is only a matter of time before the people realize that it is not them or their institutions whose legitimacy is being challenged by present events and circumstances but rather the legitimacy of capital and its institutions. Although this text has emphasized the distinction between capital, public and social institutions, frequently in harmony though often at loggerheads, the point has been to underscore the significance of history and time in explaining how capitalism and representative democracy came together in various Western mixed-system nation-states. We are at a critical juncture with regard to the imperative need for public and social control of both political leaders and the institutions of capital through the structures, processes and mechanisms of representative democracy and the representative capacities of bureaucracy. Many argue that we need a corporatist style 'steering system' directed by political leaders in the interests of one or another form of 'industrial policy' if nation states are to behave like firms in their search for international 'comparative advantage' and overcome the presently unbalanced and one-dimensional drive to globalization. But this can only happen if publics acknowledge the limits of mass participation as a unilateral solution in favor of supplementing, and even complementing, it with more institutionalized modes, particularly bureaucratic representation.[18]

[17] Compare my analysis of sites for 'responsible politicization' in *Political Management* to the actual and possible role for 'bureaucratic representation', particularly of general public and social interests, in *Bureaucratic Representation*.
[18] See generally Wilson, *Bureaucratic Representation*.

The long accepted view in traditional 'bourgeois' parties that the elected member should be permitted considerable discretion because, after all, he or she possesses superior expertise, experience and/or judgment is being challenged frontally. This is occurring largely in response to what general publics believe to have been significant mishandlings of the public trust, whether based on issues of competence, ethics and morality or communicative interaction.[19] It is probably true that people are expecting too much of nation-state governments in capitalist democracies, particularly given the allegedly 'objective' realities of globalization and the 'new competitiveness'. Nevertheless, there is a growing sense that there is no rational basis or justification for accepting the claims of most of our political leaders most of the time, whether for reasons of trust, competence, commitment or sincerity. That so much of this public malaise is manifesting itself in discussions of 'the economy' and even capitalism itself is what points to a practical agenda around questions of the legitimacy of capitalism and those who support it.

There continues to be strong concern about the past and present profligacy of governments which appear to spend without regard to debts and deficits, yet this in itself is often the essence of a neo-conservative agenda that uses such myopia to encourage a public *retreat* from the public sphere. However, these tactics are increasingly being challenged by concerns about trust and competence that relate more directly to those anti-public and anti-social sector parties which have governed through the 1980's and 1990's to great fanfare but so little real accomplishment. It is now conceded that debts and deficits have been brought under control through balanced growth, and that their causes, far from being the fault of the social sector, are a function of foregone taxes, bad loans with government backing, bank, corporate and consumer debt, and bankruptcies, receiverships and administrations. Recipients of foregone taxes and other modes of privileged treatment by governments who were expected to invest in these economies did quite different things with their profits in the case of the private sector and with their taxes, loans and other bor-

[19] *Ibid.*, especially chapter 3. On rational justification, C. West Churchman, *The Challenge of Reason* (New York: McGraw Hill, 1968). On trust, Niklas Luhmann, *Trust and Power* (New York: John Wiley and Sons, 1979); Luhmann, *Social Systems* (Berkeley: University of California Press, 1995), sections on trust; and Adam Seligman, *The Problem of Trust* (Princeton: Princeton University Press, 1997).

rowings in the case of governments.[20] Infrastructure building and rebuilding, far from taking place in the ways needed, and often promised, in these societies, has either not occurred at all, or has been so seriously delayed as to exponentially increase costs while jeopardizing public safety and welfare. Public and social institutions have been so severely devastated as a result of neo-conservative neglect and misallocation of revenues and spending priorities that an *increase* in annual deficits may be required in order to put in place the infrastructure on which reduction of the fiscal debt depends in the future.

The issue of the legitimacy of capitalism thus arises out of neo-conservatism's elemental hostility to the institutions of the people in favor of those of capital, reflected in what has actually transpired in these societies as a consequence of commitment to these policies. While it has long been suspected that the theory of motivation that governments have employed in order to justify preferential taxation (or non taxation) of capitals was at base ideological and self-serving, the past and present period of neo-conservative political dominance has demonstrated it graphically and unequivocally. Instead of investing these profits in private sector infrastructure to achieve restructuring goals in the countries at issue, they have all-too-often either been 'consumed' or invested 'offshore' in circumstances which have justified mobility or flight by pointing to the expectation of superior returns on investment. Meantime, neo-conservative governments have clearly, often openly, permitted the institutions of the government, and the power and influence which they command because of their sovereign principal legitimacy, to be ransacked by private interests in the name of public necessity.[21]

By lending their credentials and status to a more direct co-optation of public capital than the people in general would ever have acceded to were they aware of what was taking place, these anti-public and anti-social governing parties have actually aided and abetted capital flight. Along with this has gone the devastation of the very public

---

[20] Hardin, *Privatization Putsch*; Sclar, *op. cit.*; Shipman, *op. cit.*; Kuttner, *Everything for Sale*.

[21] Thomas Collins and John Wingard (editors), *Communities and Capital: Local Struggles against Corporate Power and Privatization* (Athens, Georgia: University of Georgia Press, 2000); Blau, *op. cit.*; Kreml, *op. cit.*; Saskia Sassen, *Losing Control?: Sovereignty in an Age of Globalization* (New York: Columbia university Press, 1996); Thomas Dye (editor), *The Political Legitimacy of Markets and Governments* (Greenwich, Conn.: JAI Press, 1990).

and social infrastructure that must be continuously renewed and updated if these societies *and many of their capitals* are to become or remain 'globally competitive'. The emerging public critique of these political parties and the capitals they have served, under the guise of a public trust, must be based not only on disillusionment with their claims to principle, to good faith, or even to competence, but with *capitalism itself* as a globalizing phenomenon. This includes most prominently its demands for or expectations of continued rights of mobility, flight and a full power of disposition not available to other factors of production, like that provided to capital by NAFTA and the emerging FTAA. Beyond the shadow all this casts on whether capital can be treated as the private property of its apparent 'owner(s)', there is the matter of the obvious (*and increasing*) dependence of capitals on the nation-state in general and their own country of origin or headquartering in particular.

As citizens in advanced capitalist societies become more and more aware of this dependence and interdependence between capitals and governments in representative democracies, the veil is lifted from some of the more outrageous ideological props on which capitalism's legitimacy continues to rest, however tenuously. This by itself should help to restrain the tendencies to 'cowboy capitalism' so characteristic of capitals imbued with their own sense of rectitude and further fortified with one-sided recipes favoring deficit and debt reduction at any price alongside privatization and 'free trade'. Arguments against government 'intervention' are suffering a similar fate in the public mind as many contemplate the all-out attack on public and social sectors by those only too willing to benefit from continuous government largesse and special treatment. This has taken many forms, including: subsidies; tax liens and expenditures; contracts and subcontracts; beneficial regulation; and, increasingly, direct and continuous assistance in an international marketplace governed by the rules of 'global competitiveness'.[22]

Awareness of this hopefully will have serious implications for the alleged zero-sum relationship between the individual and society that has been a mainstay of capitalist ideology and a key element in neo-

[22] Jeffrey Gates, *Democracy at Risk* (Cambridge, Mass.: Perseus Publishing Co., 2000); Jenkins, *op. cit.*; Philip Morgan (editor), *Privatization and the Welfare State: Implications for Consumers and the Workforce* (Aldershot, U.K.: Dartmouth Publishing Co., 1995); Gordon Laxer, *Out of Control: Paying the Price for Privatizing Alberta's Liquor Board* (Ottawa: Canadian Centre for Policy Alternatives, 1994).

conservatism's litany of legitimacy. It is almost inevitable that as publics become progressively more aware of themselves as such, their collective self-conception, and that of their institutions *vis à vis* those of capital, will begin to change, perhaps radically. Durkheim's positive conception of individualism and personhood, for better or worse, begins to intrude itself more concertedly on the collective consciousness of our age, one in which the people are increasingly aware of themselves as collective, intermediate group and individual *resources*. Formulated more precisely by reference to the three traditional 'factors of production', the people are beginning to see themselves as *public (and social) capital*, thereby qualifying and updating the labor theory of value which political economy has honored mainly in the breach rather than in the observance.[23] In all of this there is, above all else, a controlling irony.

It is as a result of the movement to higher and more complex levels of the world system on the part of capitals and their respective nation-states that this often-exponential increase in collective self (and other) consciousness has come about. At the same time, the public has become aware of the ideological and doctrinal nature of a good deal of what passes for the defense of capitalism and its claims to legitimacy, including the examples cited but certainly not exhausted by them. The idea, for example, that nation-states themselves become totally or sectorally like *firms* presupposes a strong state and, in representative democracies, public presence, and a great deal of co-ordination and dependence and interdependence as political, economic, social and cultural issues are blurred and become subject to more and more overlap. To date this concept of public self and collective consciousness has not yet passed beyond national state cultures, at least where the dominant capitalist states are concerned, but the mobility and transmigration of peoples and cultures, for whatever reason, can be expected to alter this.[24]

[23] Durkheim, *op. cit.*, especially Book II, Chapter 3, 1, p. 287 and *supra.*, discussing the progressive 'abstraction' of the collective conscience as the division of labor spreads, leaving 'a larger place for individual variability' as a consequence. For analysis of value theory and the labor theory of value before and after Smith, see Ronald Meek, *Studies in the Labor Theory of Value*, second edition (London: Monthly Review Press, 1967, 1956); Ian Steedman et al., *The Value Controversy* (London: Verso, 1981); and Anwar Shaikh, 'Marx's Theory of Value and the Transformation Problem', in Jesse Schwartz (editor), *The Subtle Anatomy of Capitalism* (Santa Monica, California: Goodyear Publishing, 1977), pp. 106–139.

[24] Gianaris, *op. cit.*

The message that capitals, especially large corporate capitals, should be receiving as a consequence of these altered mind-sets is that the people increasingly understand that they in fact do constitute the essence of public capital. This means that they know that they are, at least to some extent, and unavoidably, a resource for capitals and for others who also live off this particular 'factor of production' in a direct and continuous way. But this realization carries with it a price, and is part of a larger, more enduring bargain that can and will be enforced, at least in capitalist democratic societies, if not elsewhere. Extraction of conspicuously more value than is created, particularly in consequence of present globalizing opportunities for 'offshore' profits and windfall opportunities, makes the public all too aware of the additional price it pays by its failure to articulate and achieve consensus with publics in other countries and cultures on these and related matters.[25] At first this mainly occurs between direct 'competitors' in high value-added markets for goods and services. But in time it begins to dawn on publics that capital flight is rarely if ever in the interest of the generations of exploited labor whose value is the price to be paid for the economic and technological development of the 'Third World' and its integration into the 'global marketplace'.

They now begin to realize that no public or social interests are necessarily served by capital flight, so the possibility that improvements in communicative technologies will assist and complement heightened awareness and consciousness begins to become a more realistic one, and even perhaps a likelihood in the emerging circumstances. Nevertheless, the implications of taking seriously the obligations that publics put themselves under when they seek through representative democratic mechanisms to take charge of the processes of public, social and economic policy-making by their governments suggests that a head-on collision with the institutions of capital and their supporters is almost inevitable. The tension between capitalism and democracy, maintained in recent history as a tenuous equipoise in the way Offe in particular has pointed out, increasingly seems to require a significant realignment. This is largely as a result of the

[25] See Schor, *The Overworked American*; Schor, *The Overspent American*. On consensus with citizens and publics in other countries and cultures, see especially Pippa Norris (editor), *Critical Citizens: Global Support for Democratic Government* (New York: Oxford University Press, 1999).

behavior and actual performance of neo-conservative parties, governments and leaders over the last twenty-five years.[26] Even capital flight and everything that is being appealed to in order to assert its absolute necessity may not be enough to overcome these recent developments.

In one sense, it is clear that the citizenry is in the process of repudiating the notion that a governing party, regardless of how it runs its electoral campaign, can be permitted to govern by attacking directly and frontally the institutions of the public and society once in power. Thus the idea-in-practice of an anti-public, or even an anti-social, political party can only be carried so far, particularly when these attacks and the policies which result from them are seen to favor, almost in zero-sum fashion, the institutions of capital. To be sure, it is still acceptable to pillory and dismiss governments for profligate spending and for poor performance of what are believed to be public as well as non-public functions. But the idea, once countenanced, that governments can carry out a responsible public mandate by simply cutting back public and social sector activity through the elimination, curtailment, contracting out or privatization of services, functions or benefits without any concern for infrastructure is thoroughly unacceptable. Citizens are beginning to realize that when governments say they are 'going out of business', it all-too-often means they have decided to go *into* business with the institutions of capital, on the assumption that the people will support this line of action on their part, once elected. The representation of citizens can rarely, if ever, be so conveniently, and hypocritically, collapsed into the role of customers.

That this was indeed the case in the 1980's was made abundantly clear by the success that neo-conservative parties had in persuading the people to associate public and social spending with the consumption of the value (or value-added) created by the private sector and nothing more. Resuscitating marginal utility theory about the public and social sectors in this new guise could only work, however, if citizens believed that government downsizing, contracting out and privatizing would lead to infrastructure commitments by the private sector outside the traditional three areas reserved for

[26] Claus Offe, 'Competitive Party Democracy and the Keynesian Welfare State: Factors of Stability and Disorganization', *Policy Sciences*, Volume 15, No. 3 (April 1983); Offe, *Contradictions of the Welfare State* (Cambridge, Mass.: MIT Press, 1985).

governments in *laissez (nous) faire* thinking. Not only did this not transpire; governments themselves stopped investing in those key sector areas where they had both jurisdiction and responsibility. The result is everywhere before us in the form of devastated public, social *and private* sector infrastructures in many or most of those advanced countries that have suffered for too long under the rigid orthodoxy of neo-conservative parties, leaders and governments. Meantime, private interests and many capitals simply took the money that should have been earmarked for these functions and either ran or hid.

A whole host of allegedly objective and rational decisions about deficits and debts and the economy generally are now revealed to have been based in choices which were themselves dictated mainly by ideology rather than reality. With these choices went the arbitrary foreclosure of other approaches to managing the key variables of the economies of these countries, many or most of which had been successfully employed in the past.[27] A choice was made to restrict the functions of central banks to monetary policy and management, which permitted a far greater percentage of the money to be lent by private banks at significantly higher rates of interest. A choice was made to disaggregate significant elements of the so-called public debt, which took the form of massive transfers to the private sector in order to attack social programs, health care and all levels of education and even training as its cause. A choice was made to use the strategy of privatization in order to transfer *healthy and successful* economic activities being carried out in the public sector into private hands, backing up any difficulties that might arise from this new status with government guarantees and bailouts at public expense.[28]

A similar process occurred when neo-conservative governments chose to back up, almost always at direct taxpayers expense, bad loans to domestic and international 'clients' by the chartered banks. A choice was made to turn the institutions of government over to the active promotion and protection of private and special interests. This took place either directly by preferring the institutions of capital to those of the people, or indirectly by allowing the latter institutions to become either the temporary property of these interests, or a 'window of opportunity' for further investment and privatization. Most significantly, a choice was made to make the tension

---

[27] Warburton, *op. cit.*; Harless, *op. cit.*

[28] Hardin, *Privatization Putsch*; Hardin, *The New Bureaucracy.*

between deficits and infrastructure requirements into a zero-sum game, thereby treating serious unemployment, in clear contrast to inflation, as a relatively unimportant matter. This was prosecuted under the guise of the difference between 'real' jobs created by 'the market', and the (allegedly) temporary work generated by governments that simply increases the deficit to no long-term useful purpose. Since real jobs could only be created by the 'private' sector, this all-too-often meant no jobs, that is, no real jobs in the form of occupations and careers. Under the pretense of helping societies avoid the plague of temporary work generated by government bureaucrats and their wasteful schemes, neo-conservatism has underwritten a plague of part-time, contractual work suited to the worst instincts of capital.[29] This was thoroughly compatible with the view that the movement to such work was itself an objective phenomenon rather than a choice made by the private sector in order to escape its responsibilities to its employees through its obligation to contribute to various publicly and socially designed and supported programs.

In all of this a conspicuous 'sleight of hand' has occurred on the matter of the relationship between deficits and debts. Not only has the debt been disaggregated so that certain parts of it can be attacked on ideological grounds, as noted. This has been carried out while ignoring the fact that private debt in a given nation-state is part of both the overall debt and its arbitrary rather than objective servicing costs through interest charges. Consumer debt has been disaggregated from private debt in order to perpetrate the rank hypocrisy that families and householders should spend, borrow and consume beyond their means, while the nation-state, in contrast, is dubbed a 'household' that must ideally be run without deficits and debts.[30] Finally, the one-armed commitment to monetary policy without fiscal policy over the past two decades or more has meant that we now face a future in which it may be necessary for governments to scri-

[29] Chorney, Hotson and Seccarecchia, *The Deficit Made Me Do It* (Ottawa: Canadian Centre for Policy Alternatives, 1992); McQuaig, *Shooting the Hippo* (Toronto: Viking, 1995); Nelson, *Post-industrial Capitalism: Exploring Economic Inequality in America.* (Thousand Oaks, California: Sage Publications, 1995); and Leah Vosko, *Temporary Work: the Gendered Rise of a Precarious Employment Relationship* (Toronto: University of Toronto Press, 2000).

[30] See Schor, *The Overspent American*; Blau, *op. cit.*; Philip Morgan, *op. cit.*; R. Berthoud and E. Berthoud, *Credit and Debt: the PSI Report* (London: Policy Studies Institute, 1992); Ford, *op. cit.*

ously *increase* deficits. This will be required in order to create and develop the public and social sector infrastructure neglected so conspicuously by neo-conservative governments in their haste to high-jack public investment in the society and its economy for private purposes. In addition, substantial public sector incentives and supports to encourage infrastructure development *in the private sector* will be required in order to compensate for the consequences of endorsing the thoroughly bankrupt theory of capitalist motivation which informed the policies of neo-conservatives over this period of time.

The link between these observations and the legitimacy of capitalism could hardly be drawn in bolder relief than by considering the bases of this legitimacy and how they relate to the thinking of Habermas and others regarding the need for public control and the conditions under which it might occur. Attention to the issue of communicative competence, however utopian the rationality requirements in Habermas' formulation, not only provides a useful framework for addressing contemporary problems bearing on the relationship between capitalism, the nation- state and representative democracy. Practically, it may well be manifesting itself at the more everyday-life level to an ever-increasing extent as publics become more consciously aware of themselves in terms of their needs, expectations, and rights and powers as public capital. This in turn will motivate them to give vent to these rights and powers when politicians in particular, but also bureaucrats, professionals and capitals and their supporters, fail to honor their obligations and responsibilities. This tendency cannot help but be reinforced by the knowledge that they are less and less likely to be acting alone when they give vent to these concerns in the present wasteland of neo-conservative hypocrisy and broken promises.

To be sure, this increasing collective self-consciousness is occurring in tandem with what publics still largely accept as an objective process of 'global restructuring'. Nevertheless, their skepticism is beginning to manifest itself in heightened awareness of and concern about the (if anything) *greater* indispensability of national state governments and public and social sectors for capitals. The concern of corporate capitals in particular to be free of such dependence and control so they can participate in the 'new competitiveness' that is emerging from this process is sounding less and less sincere, and for good reason. The public's awareness of its role, indirectly as taxpayers, consumers, and workers and directly and continuously as public capital tied in various ways to the institutions of capital in their respective societies, serves to underscore what the new competitiveness means. It depends for its success on unfettered mobility, the right of flight and a proprietary private power of disposition over capital understood as private property. While they may sometimes acquiesce in the fact that these are, after all, non-negotiable 'rights' of capital, publics are nevertheless determined to extract truth, commitment, accountability and competence not only from their elected leaders but from those in positions of corporate power.

The framework discussed here has sought to address issues in a way which shows how it is and why it is that publics have less and less choice but to become involved as they become more and more aware of themselves as public capital. It is the way that capital, with what Lindblom calls its delegated responsibility for running the economies of the nation-states in question, extracts and co-opts value which is then appropriated privately using the vehicle of public capital as the essence of a nation's wealth which is of central concern. It speaks more than anything else to the need for a balance between the institutions of capital and those of the public and society, one that does not attempt to play the latter two off against one another to the distinct advantage of the first.[31] The problem for capitalism and its legitimacy is that recent events are leading the people toward modes of resolution in the public sphere that could very well jeopardize not only the status of capitalism but its performance in the emerging world system. On the whole, however, this must be viewed as a necessary and unavoidable response to the excesses of the recent past, a past that is increasingly being seen, as it indeed must be, to have been the result of *choices* rather than objective and impersonal events beyond human control.

It is of more than passing interest to note that Habermas' distinction between the life-world and the system world fails to fit into the 'above' and 'below' schemas which have been so influential in academic thinking over the past two centuries in Europe and North America. We can readily appreciate the parallel sense that distinctions like superstructure and substructure (Marx), de-enchantment and rationalization (Weber) and symbolically mediated interaction and systems of rational purposive action (Habermas) make for the

[31] Lindblom, *op. cit.*, chapters 6, 12, 13, 22.

reasons already suggested. Yet it is the *relationship* between the life-world and the systems world which only underscores the point that the life-world as such is neither above nor below in this formulation. Indeed, it is the very absorptive power of the life-world itself, one which only changes its fundamental values in slow and deliberate ways, that poses clear limits to the extent to which systems rationality can in an objective sense penetrate and redefine this world. The fact that individuals and groups so often allow non-rational considerations to override 'rational' ones is itself a clue to both the non-rational reality of institutions and the necessarily self-serving ideological and class aspects of capital in the contemporary world.

This in turn raises the spectre of publics and citizens whose perceptions of their needs, rights and expectations are complemented by what they view as their heightened knowledge and sophistication in matters economic as they take shape in everyday life in these societies. Giving publics such a one-sided lesson in economics over the past twenty-five years and then being seen to be above practicing what they have preached has not been, and probably will not be, a salutary experience for neo-conservatism and its supporters among capitals. Often this was effectively beyond capital's control because it sincerely believed in the tenets being proffered as objective instruction, however much in a marketing mode. On this point a significant majority of the citizenry could be consistently expected to agree, at least in the initial phases of the economics lesson. What they will no longer tolerate, however, is the rampant hypocrisy, corruption, lies, greed and obsession with power and status for its own sake of their elected, appointed and scheduled leaders and officials. This is particularly true when such conduct takes the form of irresponsible, untrustworthy and incompetent instruction both at their own expense and to the one-sided advantage of capital, rather than the mutual advantage of capital and the people who are its central and indispensable resource.

In the final analysis, however, it is difficult to dispute the claim that the legitimacy of capitalism is to some extent independent of any of its practitioners in capitalist nation-states today. However central capitalism has been in creating the systems world of instrumental and formal rationality, it is also a fundamental element in the life-world in these societies. This is why it is one of the keys to understanding the institutional matrix, *the culture*, of advanced industrial societies. Indeed, it makes sense to speak of a culture of capitalism with core characteristics that have served to define the trajectory of Western development for at least two centuries now.[32] It is equally accurate to call capitalism an institutional system in its own right because of the way it has penetrated so many levels of our collective unconscious in its transfiguration of the meaning of life in the West, and elsewhere as well. In effect, and somewhat surprisingly, capitalism turns out to be responsible for generating and sustaining, if not legitimizing, some of the most consequential *traditions* of our culture, in particular a bias toward what does and what does not constitute rationality and reasonableness.

Nevertheless, the issue of capitalism's legitimacy can never be taken completely for granted, at least not in a representative democracy where people are becoming increasingly conscious of themselves as powerful *because* they are the indispensable resource for capital. Emerging responses to the recent period of neo-conservative excess in many capitalist societies only underscores this point, while it demonstrates how important it is to maintain the bargain between the institutions of capital and those of the public and society. In this endeavor parties, leaders and politically elected governments, as well as institutional bureaucracies in the three sectors, are the central actors. This means that issues like trust, competence, care and commitment to process must now be honored in the observance rather than the breach more than has been the case in recent memory. Failing to do this is fraught with serious consequences, and even immediate ones, particularly where referendums and other techniques of direct democracy have been brought into force to complement electoral and bureaucratic representative processes. It is almost a truism to say that capitalism can only work if the people who are its central resource continue to acknowledge its legitimacy and agree to function as public capital in a balanced equation in which they too give advice and instruction.[33]

Having become suspicious of the claim that there is really only one economics lesson and that they have not yet learned it, the people

---

[32] Hollingsworth and Boyer (editors), *Contemporary Capitalism: the Embeddedness of Institutions*; Hopkins and Wallerstein, *The Age of Transition: Trajectory of the World System, 1945–2025* (London: Zed Books, 1997); Stewart Clegg and S.G. Redding (editors), *Capitalism in Contrasting Cultures* (New York: Walter de Gruyter, 1990).

[33] Niklas Luhmann, *Trust and Power* (New York: John Wiley and Sons, 1979); Luhmann, *Social Systems* (Berkeley: University of California Press, 1995), discussions of trust; and Wilson, *Bureaucratic Representation*, especially chapters 3–5, 8.

have begun to function as the practical economists that most economists fear and despise in the real world. The irony here is that in the most bizarre possible way the people as practical economists are the creation of those very neo-conservative parties and leaders who are now suspected of incompetence, guile, corruption and insincerity on the grand scale. This is not unrelated to the fact that the twenty-five year period during which the people have been taught to both fear and be preoccupied with economic questions and issues has carried with it, almost against their individual wills, an exponential increase in their collective consciousness of themselves. In this rendition, they increasingly see themselves as a collective body with powers and rights, rather than a mere aggregate of concatenated individuals, *precisely because* they know they are an indispensable resource for capital.[34] It is too early to know how this head-on collision will turn out, but it is already abundantly clear that capitalism's legitimacy will depend as never before on the ability of its practitioners to learn from the people as workers, citizens and publics as well as in its more established passive roles as consumers and spectators.

[34] Thereby turning the direction of Durkheim's *op. cit.* collapse of the collective conscience into positive occupational individualism around on itself, precisely because neo-conservatism no longer even pretends to offer either it or the solidarity on which it was/is based as a viable option in capitalist democracies. Compare to Pippa Norris, *op. cit.*

CHAPTER THIRTEEN

CAPITALISM AFTER POSTMODERNISM

This study has been conceived and carried out as a critique of political economy in its guise as a legitimator of real world economic, political and social practices, particularly in its contemporary 'neo-conservative' variant. At the same time, it has attempted to integrate into this critique important insights and concerns from law, political science and the theory of institutions, particularly public, social and democratic institutions. The purpose was to reassert the contemporary significance of Adam Smith's conception of the wealth of nations en route to an updating of Marx's labor theory of value reformulated as the theory of public capital. While this theory was stated and addressed, it was not developed in detail; this effort will be the purpose of a subsequent text.[1] Instead, the present study has attempted to lay out the parameters of a critique of neo-conservative economic, political and social thinking, one which reveals its manifest hypocrisy while undermining its claims to greater practicality, relevance and good sense. This critique has included most prominently its claim to be free from the very ideological and doctrinal reflexes of which it has so often accused the liberal and social-democratic left.

In this sense, it constitutes an attempt to resuscitate and, to some extent, redirect the efforts of liberal and social-democratic thought by providing a new conceptual focus, albeit one written mainly within the framework of political economy and its critique.[2] Far from accepting the view that organized capitalism once existed and is now coming to an end, it addressed the ways that capital is already using, beginning to use or soon must use the nation-state. The purpose of such uses is to realize new and distinct processes whereby public capital, and the value that it produces or can be expected to produce,

---

[1] Tentatively titled *State Legitimacy and Capital Sector Growth: Instruments, Transfers and Uses of Public Capital to Private Ends.*

[2] See H.T. Wilson, *The American Ideology*; and Wilson, *Marx's Critical/Dialectical Procedure.*

is co-opted to private purposes.[3] The function of neo-conservative political economy, not surprisingly, is to provide advance or concurrent legitimation for the exercise of these very modes and processes. This is directly related to developments whereby economic activity of all types is either becoming more globalized and internationalized in its own right, or becoming more dependent on such developments. In contrast to the claim that organized capitalism and its dependence upon and interdependence with the nation-state is coming to an end, this study has attempted to show that capital's adaptation of this established relationship to new conditions is both urgently sought and in the process of taking place.[4]

Postmodern analysis often deconstructs such thought and thinking into mere discourses unconnected in any necessary way that can be documented to the concerns it claims to address. As long as this goes no further, we are left with a picture of the intellectual and cultural world as a series of variously overlapping, competing and conflicting discourses which at any given time and place serve to define the language games of a particular discipline or intellectual culture.[5] Commitment to one or another 'paradigm candidate' is accepted and understood to be unavoidable, while progress is seen to lie in conceptual, methodological and practical innovations between subdisciplines and specialties within any two (and occasionally more) paradigm candidates.[6] But some postmodernists have bitten the bullet and taken the leap into nihilism which was always available to this and allied views of the relation between knowledge and reality. Having accepted that there are many forms of discourse, it has gone on to label them equal in the sense of being equally worthless. Adorno realized that this was not only an expression of rage, directed pre-

---

[3] See Claus Offe, *Disorganized Capitalism* (Cambridge, Mass.: MIT Press, 1985); Scott Lash and John Urry, *The End of Organized Capitalism* (Cambridge: Polity Press, 1987).

[4] Sigrid Quack, Glenn Morgan, Richard Whitley, *National Capitalisms, Global Competition and Economic Performance* (Philadelphia: John Benjamins Publishing, 2000).

[5] Ludwig Wittgenstein, *Philosophical Investigations* (New York: Macmillan, 1953), discussions of 'language games' and 'form of life'.

[6] Michael Polanyi, 'The Republic of Science', *Minerva*, Volume 1 (1962), pp. 54–73; Herminio Martins, 'The Kuhnian "Revolution" and its Implications for Sociology', *Imagination and Precision in the Social Sciences*, edited by J.J. Nossiter, A.H. Hanson and Stein Rokkan (London: Faber and Faber, 1972), pp. 13–58; Mattei Dogan and Robert Pahre, *Creative Marginality: Innovation at the Intersections of the Social Sciences* (Boulder, Colorado: Westview Press, 1990).

eminently at the realization that concepts cannot absorb their objects and thereby achieve an identity with them, but that, as such, it is always and everywhere the hallmark of idealism.[7]

Not surprisingly, the argument that all paradigm candidates are equal in their worthlessness has become the basis for postmodernism's assumption of the mantle of the dominant paradigm! Deconstruction and discourse analysis, in and through their unseemly combination of nihilism and idealism, achieve their newfound, but hopefully temporary, status as the arbiter of textual sense, meaning and value by becoming the quintessential discourse of mediation in their own right. *They are the dominant discourse whose essence is the belief that discourse doesn't really matter!*[8] The ultimate irony here is that by saying or implying that discourses don't really matter, that all discourses are equal, postmodernism realizes a reconciliation between that rage at and worship of identity which is the hallmark of idealism, now as before. But the price paid for such nihilism and pessimism, already implied, is only heightened by the fact that its exponents rarely if ever take their intellectual and cultural pronouncements seriously in their everyday lives. Postmodern deconstruction, it turns out, is a heavy industry across a vast range of disciplines, where its refusal to take the substantive critique of political economy and allied disciplines seriously virtually guarantees its practitioners a privileged position with neo-conservative funding agencies, university administrations and governments.

This study is clearly and unambiguously opposed to such pretence and posturing. Not the least of the reasons for its resistance is that the sense and implications of such nihilism, far from being only conceptually impoverished and disappointing, are, as a consequence of this, of the greatest danger to both theoretical and practical improvement. Postmodern deconstruction puts thought, knowledge and intellectual culture right where neo-conservative forces defending the so-called new political economy would wish it to be: destitute of commitment and confidence and in free fall. This serves to aggravate severely already existing problems of dependence on corporate

[7] Theodor Adorno, *Negative Dialectics* (New York: Seabury Press, 1973), pp. 22–24 and *supra*. 'Idealism as Rage'. Also see Martin Jay, *Adorno* (Cambridge, Mass.: Harvard University Press, 1984), but especially Jay, *Downcast Eyes: the Denigration of Vision in Twentieth Century French Thought* (Berkeley: University of California Press, 1993), a major inspiration for the critique of postmodernism in this and other chapters.

[8] Alex Callinicos, *Against Postmodernism* (Cambridge: Polity Press, 1989).

and state authorities for funds and related support to carry out research and scholarly work which defends the people while at the same time endorsing heightened reflexivity toward and awareness of the power of capital. These latter concerns and commitments are thereafter reduced to obsolete, futile or meaningless instances of 'rights discourse' and 'economism', when it is the postmodernists themselves who are aiding and abetting neo-conservative efforts to co-opt the rights, powers and public capital of the people by surrendering to nihilism. Meantime, they garner an increasing share of the funding available for research and scholarship in the arts, literature and (now) social and political thought.

While it is difficult to believe that this is a coincidence, one should not really be surprised by this development. What is surprising, however, is the speed and comprehensiveness with which deconstructionist practices have so thoroughly infiltrated the discourses of political economy and its critique. The idea that postmodernism, in the person of Lyotard, Baudrillard and others, has rendered obsolete discourses from what is admittedly a Western (and Northern) tradition of political economy and its critique and critical theory can now be viewed in a different light. In effect, it can now be seen to perform a clear, positive function in and for the emerging reality of a globalizing and internationalizing capitalism, one that is not at all apparent from its billing.[9] Postmodernism's charge of theoretical obsolescence against Marxian and critical thinking, and the superiority of deconstructionist analyses which allegedly follows from it, constitutes an increasingly successful intervention in the ongoing dialogue between supporters of the institutions of the people and those who support the institutions of capital *on the latter's side*. As such, it assists, albeit unintentionally, neo-conservatism's efforts to persuade publics that there really is only one economics lesson, and that both Marxian and critical theory and Keynesian and neo-Keynesian practice, can always be counted on to get it wrong.

We hardly ever even begin to really communicate with one another in what is rapidly becoming a set of irrelevant, abstract, even silly

---

[9] J.F. Lyotard, *The Postmodern Condition: A Report on Knowledge* (Manchester: Manchester University Press, 1984); Lyotard, *The Postmodern Explained* (Minneapolis: University of Minnesota Press, 1992); Jean Baudrillard, *For a Critique of the Political Economy of the Sign* (St. Louis: Telos Press, 1981); Baudrillard, *The Mirror of Production* (St. Louis: Telos Press, 1975).

games of momentary conceptual fad and fashion in social and political theory and in the social sciences. But it is the fad and fashion of nihilism in the sheep's clothing of postmodern deconstruction that is most disturbing because of the combined sense of futility and exclusivity which its all-knowing dismissal can so often engender. It is a pall cast over the proceedings, a very chill wind whose increasing influence in our society and culture bespeaks grave portents for the future. Its very determination to misunderstand the meaning of 'going to the root of things' puts it in the position of unintentionally defending those 'practical' people who similarly deny the value of and need for discourse to ends it can hardly even begin to understand.[10] In the late 1920's and early 1930's, Karl Mannheim drew attention to what may well constitute a *fin de siecle* phenomenon not dissimilar to this, when it happened approximately one century ago, in his seminal text *Ideology and Utopia*. This study led to a series of 'clarion calls', in which Mannheim issued dire warnings throughout the 1930's and 1940's until his premature death in 1947.

For him the problem constituted nothing less than a retreat by social and cultural intellectuals away from critical analysis in general and the critique of political economy and the social, behavioral and administrative-managerial disciplines in particular. Such retreat has happened many times before, so we cannot treat it as a unique event. Mannheim argued that in such circumstances intellectuals either allied themselves with one or another class or retreated into language, concepts and the examination of the epistemological and methodological principles of their respective disciplines.[11] The point here is not to argue that history is repeating itself in any precise way. It is rather that Western modernity seems to be characterized by cycles of intellectual response and reaction to thought, society and life which include *ennui*, frustration and exhaustion, alliances with one or another class and preoccupation with language, concepts and epistemological and methodological foundations.[12] Mannheim's point was not that there was no room in social and political theory and

---

[10] For example in Marshall Berman, *All that is Solid Melts into Air: the Experience of Modernity* (New York: Viking/Penguin, 1988, 1982).

[11] Karl Mannheim, *Ideology and Utopia: An Introduction to the Sociology of Knowledge* (London: Routledge and Kegan Paul, 1954); Mannheim, *Structures of Thinking* (London: Routledge and Kegan Paul, 1982).

[12] See Matei Calinescu, *Five Faces of Modernity: Modernism, Avant-Garde, Decadence, Kitsch, Postmodernism* (Durham: Duke University Press, 1987).

the social sciences for the examination of language, concepts and epistemological and methodological principles or any value in doing so; on the contrary. He was concerned instead that the people who did this were becoming the arbiters of what counted in their respective disciplines, a situation not dissimilar to what is occurring today.

By comparison to the wave of Keynesian and neo-Keynesian economics and social sciences between 1930 and 1970 which preceded the onset of present trends toward post-this and post-that, this development is most disconcerting. At least in the former case there was an implicit, when not explicit, critique of earlier conservative practices favoring a more direct co-optation of public capital by those institutions of private capital in the state legal and constitutional apparatus supporting this practice. Alongside this went a far more sophisticated understanding of the necessary role of government and the public and social sectors as the guarantor through legal, electoral and bureaucratic processes of the rights and powers of the people expressed through their own institutions. It was in this sense that sociologists like Merton and Parsons could view the empirical, methodological, conceptual and theoretical 'progress' of all the social sciences, including economics, as a moving, seamless web indicative of a more systematic grasp of the relations between society, polity, economy and culture.[13] This process of development, in turn, was viewed as a solid and positive portent for the future, of the United States in particular, and of the non-communist developed world in general.[14]

Following the Vietnam War, the so-called 'oil crisis' and the rise of the EU, Japan and the rest of the Pacific Rim, many of these assumptions and projections had to be altered, in some cases significantly. U.S. interference in the Annam region after 1955 culminated in a war which was not financed by raising taxes, causing confidence in the dollar to collapse, and with it the entire basis of the post-War Bretton Woods Agreement, pegging the price of gold to the U.S. dollar. Combined with this, there has since been a series of global redistributions of power and capital, several of them of the

[13] Merton, *op. cit.*; Talcott Parsons, *The Structure of Social Action* (Glencoe: Free Press, 1937); Parsons, *The Social System* (Glencoe: Free Press, 1951).

[14] This new 'manifest destiny' was addressed critically by John Goldthorpe, in 'Theories of Industrial Society: On the Recrudescence of Historicism and the Future of Futurology' (Varna, Bulgaria: World Congress of Sociology, June, 1970).

greatest importance. The U.S. has become both the largest debtor nation and the most powerful economy in world history, mainly because conservative economists advising Reagan said that debt didn't matter and could be readily recouped through economic growth. In the absence of this growth, the indebtedness that was progressively accumulating was co-opted for private, and only occasionally if at all for public, consumption rather than investment in infrastructure.[15]

In the United Kingdom and elsewhere, massive propaganda supported a view of the public debt as the fault of unions and social entitlements, with privatization and free trade the solution to this problem, alongside 'competitiveness' and a more 'global' outlook. This in turn was seen to justify a far more direct and continuous co-optation of public capital that largely coincided with the collapse of public and social institutions. The net result in all cases, the U.S. included, was a debt situation at least as serious as the one that had caused so much alarm, coupled with a decade or more of serious inattention to problems of social, educational, cultural and even private sector infrastructure. Capitals, particularly entrepreneurs, inventors and small business persons, as well as other members of the public, have been (and continue to be) thoroughly demoralized by the persistence of this state of affairs. Having made public, governmental and social institutions so vulnerable where they have not eliminated (or privatized) them altogether, many capitals now seem surprised that these institutions are often too weak to rise to the challenge. Even though this *tour de force* could only have been accomplished with the aid and support of anti-public and anti-social political parties whose leaders were often naive, incompetent or corrupt, the results are there for all to see and therefore impossible to deny.

Apart from the direct consequences for subsequent generations of the serious cutbacks in funding for public and higher education,

[15] Benjamin Friedman, *A Day of Reckoning: the Consequences of American Economic Policy under Reagan and Afterwards* (New York: Random House, 1988). The other side of this conundrum was the near total dependence of American capitals on 'work and spend' consumption, as discussed by Schor, *The Overworked American*; and Schor, *The Overspent American*. George W. Bush's ideologically astute claim that there was still a large surplus, but that he was putting it in the hands of the American people rather than the government, presupposed, prior to September 11, 2001, that American taxpayers would consume it rather than either save it or use it to pay down *their* debts.

resulting in privatization and support for more 'practical' or 'strategic' programs of study, there is the longer-term impact on the university of the resulting demoralization and lack of public sector commitment. The fact that publics and society at large often still fail to see any direct tie between social, educational and cultural infrastructure development and a nation's prosperity is something that all political parties are continuing to use to their advantage in decisions about funding and support. Even in the face of international reports which cite infrastructure maintenance and improvement as responsible for 60 to 70 percent of a country's ability to be 'globally competitive', governments, aided and abetted by private consultants, lobbyists and trade associations, continue to treat such expenditures as of secondary importance.[16] The resulting demoralization has been a central reason for both the collapse of academic and intellectual resistance to and critique of neo-conservatism and the rise of postmodern deconstruction. This alongside the seeming inability of Keynesians and neo-Keynesians in particular to find their voices and respond effectively to neo-conservatism.[17]

Seen from the vantage point of present retreats and rationalizations like those already cited, the Keynesian and neo-Keynesian impact on economics, the social sciences and related disciplines was clearly a lesser evil in retrospect. Abatement of the ongoing dialogue between traditional and critical theory in its many and varied guises was inspired to a considerable extent by Lyotard's view that the essence of postmodernism is its refusal to entertain any and all meta-narratives. This has left us with the prospect of a continuing state of theoretical free fall that can only benefit forces espousing more allegedly 'practical' and 'strategic' approaches and solutions.[18] With the effective silencing of Keynesian and neo-Keynesian voices in a number of social, political and cultural disciplines, as well as in economics, has gone an attitude on the part of the new neo-conservative elite which is barely distinguishable in several important respects from that of the postmodernists.

In both instances, it is the refusal to entertain meta-narratives which characterizes such thinking. Whether the discourse beyond

---

[16] See particularly *World Competitiveness Reports*, where the role of infrastructure is more readily acknowledged.

[17] Wilson, *Bureaucratic Representation*, pp. 110–112.

[18] Lyotard, *The Postmodern Condition*. See Stephen Best and Douglas Kellner, *Postmodern Theory: Critical Interrogations* (Basingstoke, U.K.: Macmillan Education, 1991).

discourses is the objectively correct way of reading a text or the objectively correct way of understanding the economic situation, both point to a concept and practice of beginning which claims to be beyond dependence upon, or even indebtedness to, thought and theories separate from it. Having said this, Keynesians and neo-Keynesians have often been unable to respond effectively (if at all) to neo-conservative attacks on their stewardship of the economy, polity and society in the developed Western countries. This is largely because their responses have almost always been framed in far more academic, technical and intellectual language than what now passes for public enlightenment about the proper role of government *vis à vis* the so-called 'private sector'. The point here is that there is no such thing as either an objective reading or an objective understanding of the economic situation because in both instances there are meta-narrative pre-understandings, whether they are acknowledged or not.

An important indicator of similarities between neo-conservatism and post-modernism is their attitude toward the fact-value dichotomy and its relation to the social function of the intellectual.[19] For both neo-conservatives and postmodernists this dichotomy is an academic/intellectual construction that fails to make sense of a reality which it is incapable of capturing. Neo-conservatives speak of common-sense approaches and the 'household', while disparaging the idea that capitalism is a real state of affairs, however elusive and complex, for which the sovereign nation-state is at least as central as was the case in the past. Postmodernists attack the dependence of such views and understandings on the meta-narrative in general, and on one or a few meta-narratives in particular. Postmodernists make conceptual common cause with neo-conservatives, it turns out, not only in their view of the obsolescence of the modern social intellectual that Mannheim discussed in *Ideology and Utopia* and elsewhere. Both also believe that in allegedly being beyond 'modernity' we are therefore not only beyond industrialization but beyond capitalism, socialism and history as well.

Daniel Bell's *The End of Ideology*, subtitled 'the exhaustion of political ideas in the fifties', has been recognized increasingly as one of the most important anticipations of the present movement and those

[19] On the location of this distinction in a 'hierarchy of dichotomies', see H.T. Wilson, 'Time, Space and Value: Recovering the Public Sphere', *Time and Society*, Volume 8, No. 1 (March 1999), pp. 161–181.

allied with it in the ways suggested. Thirteen years later, in 1973, Bell published *The Coming of Post Industrial Society*, which solidified his concerns regarding ideology with a discussion about the emerging economic and technological order.[20] Advanced industrial society, he argued, was on the verge of changing beyond recognition the modern activity that we call capitalism, ironically enough about the same time that new ideological support for 'old fashioned' capitalism was beginning to emerge in North America, Western Europe and the British Commonwealth. The reason for identifying capitalism as a set of social, political and cultural, as well as economic practices in this study was to show its inherent flexibility with regard to major tenets like profit maximization, which have changed little, if at all, since the political economists, Marx and Weber discussed them.[21]

Bell's third book in this series, *The Cultural Contradictions of Capitalism*, attempted to take advantage of commonsense understandings of 'contradiction' in both academia and daily life by presuming that such a state of affairs must be temporary and must lead to a clear resolution.[22] Marxian and critical theory have always held that contradictions, even where correctly perceived and understood, are of the essence of all complex social phenomena rather than an aberration. It is precisely the absence of holism, historicism and a structural focus and approach which makes it difficult, if not impossible, for the commonsense attitude to life and living to see this. No less significantly, it also explains the intolerance of academics and intellectuals committed to either traditional theory and empirical method or to postmodernism toward the claim that contradiction is a fundamental property of reality, a dynamic force in social, political and economic affairs.[23]

That this necessitates a commitment by the intellectually minded to maintaining the tension between the search for correspondences and identities while acknowledging that the reconciliation it presup-

[20] Daniel Bell, *The End of Ideology: On the Exhaustion of Political Ideas in the Fifties*, revised edition (Cambridge, Mass.: Harvard University Press, 1988, 1960); Bell, *The Coming of Post Industrial Society: A Venture in Social Forecasting* (New York: Basic Books, 1973).

[21] Weber, *Economy and Society*, Volume I, Part 1, chapter 2; Weber, *General Economic History*; Clegg and Redding (editors), *Capitalism in Contrasting Cultures* (New York: Walter de Gruyter, 1990).

[22] Daniel Bell, *The Cultural Contradictions of Capitalism* (New York: Basic Books, 1976).

[23] Wilson, *Marx's Critical/Dialectical Procedure*, pp. 85–90, 101–102, 107–113, 140.

poses is impossible has always been what most clearly separated those committed to critique from virtually everyone else. Failure or refusal to maintain this tension leads one either into identity thinking or into the belief that nothing can be known, thus that all concepts and ideas are equal in their worthlessness.[24] Neo-conservatives opt for an identity posture best characterized by the assumption that reality is clear, non-contradictory and obvious, therefore that there is one economics lesson and one text. Postmodernists opt for an alternate set of assumptions and what is nothing less than a flirtation with nihilism, if it is not nihilism itself. They do this by failing to distinguish between meta-narratives, saying that their job is to refuse to entertain them, no matter what they say and what they claim. To be sure, this ignores, as noted, their own unacknowledged meta-narrative, one which has appeared and reappeared in modern Western intellectual culture on several occasions and with a consistent, if unpredictable, regularity.

How does one overcome the unavoidable perspectivism of the social intellectual, asked Mannheim in *Ideology and Utopia*? His answer was premised on the view, itself inspired by Weberian problems arising out of the fact-value dichotomy, that one must be clear on the 'correct' or proper functions of the social intellectual. This necessitated overcoming the tendency, already noted, for intellectuals to either become 'attached' to one or another class or to preoccupy themselves with language, concepts or the epistemological and methodological precepts of their respective disciplines. The key to the emergence of the new 'unattached' intellectual that Mannheim believed was so urgently needed was commitment to the priority of *wissensoziologie*, the sociology of knowledge. This new discipline, which Mannheim believed would be the key element in bringing about more responsible social and political study and research, required that intellectuals not only focus on understanding the social mainsprings out of which thought and theories arise, that is, the socially determined nature of all knowledge claims. They must also address the epistemological consequences of and problems raised by the sociology of knowledge itself.[25]

---

[24] Adorno, *op. cit.*

[25] Mannheim, *Ideology and Utopia*; Mannheim, *Structures of Thinking*. See John Heeren, 'Karl Mannheim and the Intellectual Elite', *British Journal of Sociology*, Volume 22, No. 1 (March 1971), pp. 1–15.

While much of Mannheim's discussion in *Ideology and Utopia* is thoroughly compatible with a reductionist approach to knowledge which seeks to 'explain' or make sense of knowledge claims by reference to biography and socialization, the second task at least sought to address the limitations of this approach. It was to be subject to scrutiny epistemologically and in other ways, thereby making criticism, even critique, not only possible but legitimate. Apart from the fact that Mannheim himself rarely practiced the sociology of knowledge he had encouraged in *Ideology and Utopia* in subsequent publications, there is another issue. There is a thin line between extreme skepticism and nihilism, the claim that nothing can really be known and the view that all concepts and theories are equally worthless and therefore that everything is permitted. The second task of the sociology of knowledge, alongside Mannheim's own intellectual activity after 1929, is what would stop the new discipline from sliding into nihilism, both in principle and in practice. The unattached intellectual, so understood, was allowed to be critical rather than simply 'standpointless'.[26]

'Recent reports of my death in the press have been greatly exaggerated' reported Mark Twain, a comment that is equally appropriate as a response to postmodernists who claim that industrialization, and capitalism and socialism, have been superseded. Alongside this insistence on post-capitalist and post-industrial society and culture a more recent event has come to pass, accompanied by intellectual anticipations of and responses to it, which gets less notice in North America than it does in Western Europe and elsewhere. The collapse of the former Soviet Union and its satellites in Eastern Europe is an event that is (incorrectly) believed to have transpired because of the steadfastness and resolve of American and European neo-conservatives rather than for internal reasons related to cultural conflict and the limits of totalitarian power. In effect, neo-conservatives and their supporters have argued, on the whole successfully, that communism was defeated by capitalism rather than by long repressed desires for representative democracy, civil liberties and cultural freedom of expression.

---

[26] Mannheim, *Man and Society in an Age of Reconstruction* (London: Routledge and Kegan Paul, 1940); Mannheim, *Diagnosis of Our Time* (London: Routledge and Kegan Paul, 1947); Mannheim, *Freedom, Power and Democratic Planning* (London: Routledge and Kegan Paul, 1951); Mannheim, *Essays on the Sociology of Knowledge* (London:

Reference to the collapse of the Soviet Union indicates yet another point of common ground linking neo-conservatives and postmodernists. This observation is directed less to this event in its own right than to the way it has been used to argue for the exhaustion, eclipse and irrelevance of both Marxism and socialism. While neo-conservatives take credit for this 'victory' in their role as supporters of capital and capitalism, postmodernists give them indirect aid and comfort by arguing that both capitalist and socialist discourses are little more than the flip side of one another. In so doing they effectively support the elision of seventy-five years of Bolshevik practice with the thought of Karl Marx, even if they do not intend to do so.[27] Neo-conservatives want to equate Marxism with past Soviet practice preparatory to extending their ongoing take-over and dismemberment of public and social institutions in Western democracies. Postmodernists provide effective support by saying that both discourses are part of modernity and modernism and therefore similarly irrelevant and obsolete.

When such support is combined with the effective muting of Keynesian and neo-Keynesian voices and ideas as a critical response and alternative to neo-conservatism the jaded contours of the debate become clear. This is only underscored by the success of neo-conservative efforts to link Marxian thought not only to failed Soviet practice but to the so-called Keynesian welfare state, social democracy and socialism. It is only when one realizes that the Soviet Union was a *pre-capitalist* rather than a post-capitalist social formation that one is able to appreciate why the collapse of the Soviet Union *confirms* rather than disputes Marx's analysis of capitalism. Arguments about which form of capitalism and representative democracy will be undertaken in Russia in particular only serve to underscore Marx's developmental logic regarding the historical priority of capitalism to socialism. This in contrast to the view that one can choose either a capitalist or a socialist path coming out of 'traditional society' into

---

Routledge and Kegan Paul, 1952); Mannheim, *Essays in Sociology and Social Psychology* (London: Routledge and Kegan Paul, 1953); Mannheim, *Conservatism: A Contribution to the Sociology of Knowledge* (London: Routledge and Kegan Paul, 1986).

[27] This is not far from Karl Popper's attack on Aristotle, Hegel, Marx, Mannheim and (later on) the Frankfurt School in *The Open Society and its Enemies* (London: Routledge and Kegan Paul, 1945); Popper, *The Poverty of Historicism* (London: Routledge and Kegan Paul, 1957; and Popper, contributions to *The Positivist Dispute in German Sociology*, edited and introduced with other essays by Theodor Adorno (London: Heinemann, 1976).

modernity, an interesting, if severely flawed, idea but not one in any way attributable to Marx.

The haste to engage in any and all forms of intellectual legerdemain in order to 'prove' that capitalism, and more specifically organized capitalism, has either come to an end or that its end is imminent is supremely remindful of Marxist (not Marxian) and Soviet forecasts between 1930 and 1980. Why is everyone in such a hurry, and how does one explain the fact that so many different groups seem to have what amounts to a vested interest in making this claim? One observation would suggest that 'capitalism' as an organizing topic of study, and particularly of critique, is something both neo-conservatives and postmodernists would prefer to see disappear altogether, however different their reasons for this may be. Another derives from this and would note the increasingly central role of linguistic and literary studies in postmodernist analysis and their not surprising preference for a focus on textuality rather than more social-scientific and social-theoretical concerns about the relation between knowledge and social, political and economic practice. Instead of critical concepts like 'capitalism' being less amenable to the charge of obsolescence and irrelevance than many or most others, such a charge is more useful to neo-conservatives than anything else postmodernists could possibly muster.[28]

This is evident from Lash and Urry's *The End of Organized Capitalism*, which often seems to confuse the literary and linguistic analysis of concepts and texts with the material reality of key forms of social, political and economic interaction central to capitalism as a historical and contemporary phenomenon.[29] Even if one were to support Hilferding's arguments about the central role of finance capitalism and the circulation of capital as discussed by Marx, one would be hard pressed to dispute the following point. It is all-too-often precisely the inability of corporate capitals to organize effectively in the international and global arena which leads them to seek ongoing alliances, assistance and support from national states and supranational and international bodies. Thus, while it may be true that cap-

[28] Ben Agger, *Fast Capitalism: A Critical Theory of Significance* (Urbana and Chicago: University of Illinois Press, 1989).

[29] Scott Lash and John Urry, *The End of Organized Capitalism* (Cambridge: Polity Press, 1987). A significant modification of this view of organized capitalism was provided by the authors in *Economies of Signs and Space* (London: Sage Publishing, 1994).

ital on its own often has trouble organizing, this does not mean that it cannot organize *even more effectively* through direct links of dependence and interdependence with legal, governmental and public authority. Indeed, the success of strategies for co-opting public capital demands that private capitals become progressively more, rather than less, institutionally embedded in the matrix of governmental, public and supranational and international bodies present or emerging on the world scene. Alongside the devastation of public, social, legal and constitutional institutions which represent the public and society rather than capital, we thus see an accumulation of new forms of dependence on and interdependence with state and other public bodies *in addition to already established capital sector powers and prerogatives.*

In contrast to a focus on capitalism which resists the tendency to allow 'globalization' to become a post-industrial, post-capitalist and post-socialist concept-cum-reality, postmodernists focus on 'culture', in particular the role of 'cultural logics'. This is put forward to invalidate any argument which would assert the persistence and central significance of common forms of capitalist practice which are global, organized and effective. But this denies the flexibility inherent in the different forms that profit maximization, now more than ever before, can take, while it permits yet another concept more compatible with literary and linguistic studies to supersede the analysis of globalization as an indisputably capitalist phenomenon in all its guises. It is in this sense that postmodernism sponsors a view of deep reading as a form of denial, if not one of rage, as noted earlier. For implicit in such ways of going about the activity of thinking and understanding is nothing less than a potentially (when not actually) nihilistic meta-narrative about the world and our ability to have a knowledge of it, however provisional such knowledge must necessarily be.[30]

This brings us to the final obsession with what is alleged to be 'post' in the postmodernist arsenal, namely, the (mostly) hidden assumption about the end of history. The essence of this claim is that we are on the verge of entering, or have already begun to enter, a post-historical period characterized by a globalization process that is not only beyond ideology, industry, capitalism and socialism. It is

[30] Adorno, *op. cit.*; John O'Neill, *The Poverty of Postmodernism* (London: Routledge, 1994); O'Neill, 'The Time(s) of the Gift', *Angelaki*, Volume 6, No. 2 (August 2001), pp. 41–48.

beyond both the structural and holistic analysis so central to the critique of political economy and critical theory and the concern about the relationship between knowledge and reality which is the foundational justification for any and all meta-narratives.[31] One of the most important studies which, oddly enough, is used to support this total view of what will (or has already) become obsolete with the emergence of the new order is Marshall Berman's *All that is Solid Melts into Air.* This book is significant because it looks at the institutions and practices of modernity and reduces them to 'a mode of vital experience, the experience of space and time.' For Berman, modernity is a 'paradoxical unity, a unity of disunity' which 'pours us into a maelstrom of perpetual disintegration and renewal, of struggle and contradiction, of ambiguity and anguish.'[32]

Berman, who believes that postmodernists 'have developed a paradigm that clashes sharply with the one in [his] book', takes his title from Marx, who concluded that modernity requires one to participate in a world in which 'all that is solid melts into air'.[33] What we have here is postmodernist impatience with and intolerance toward contradiction as a necessary, even essential, property of modern (capitalist) life and living, coupled with a determination to resolve it into a final, finished state of affairs through abolition of reflexivity and critique. Yet one constantly has to combine critique and criticalness with a residual commitment to both the intellectual history of modernity and the sociology of knowledge if one wishes to address constructively the questions: Why postmodernism (and derived 'posts') and Why now? This study has suggested how some parallel sequences of events in recent history may be important clues in explaining the emergence and popularity of postmodernism. It has also stressed the need to begin with at least the hypothesis that intellectual activity,

---

[31] Francis Fukuyama, *The End of History and the Last Man* (New York: Free Press, 1992); Fukuyama, *The Great Disruption: Human Nature and the Reconstitution of the Social Order* (New York: Touchstone, 1999).

[32] Berman, *All That is Solid Melts into Air: the Experience of Modernity* (London: Verso, 1983).

[33] Berman, *op. cit.* quotes Marx in one of his least analytical moments in the early paragraphs of the *Manifesto of the Communist Party*, I 'Bourgeois and Proletarians', 18th paragraph, for his title, thereby confusing the experiential capacity of those in and of modernity with its capacity for complex solidity, both organizationally and institutionally speaking. For one source of the reference, see Lewis Feuer, *Marx and Engels: Basic Writings on Politics and Philosophy* (Garden City, New York: Doubleday Anchor, 1959), p. 10.

and, in particular, certain world-views of this sort, may be cyclical in nature, or at the very least a periodic response to a given type of situation or set of circumstances.

Let us conclude by making four observations about what might account for post modernism's flirtation with nihilism. The first is that a major inspiration for the critical intellectual in social, political, cultural and economic studies for at least a century has been Karl Marx. To the extent that anybody accepts or takes seriously the preposterous proposition that his ideas are 'exhausted' in their own right or have been invalidated by the performance of the Soviet Union, that person will be suddenly absent of intellectual and critical moorings which may be very difficult to replace. Confusion of this sort can create an intellectual crisis for a large number of people, the moreso where such invalidation carries with it the Popperian view that the entire edifice of critique based in a commitment to Marx's critical/dialectical procedure is similarly implicated.[34] Postmodernism's response to this is to simply legislate capitalism and socialism out of existence as obsolete 'modernist' concepts and to dismiss Marxism as an obsolete discursive form possessing no enduring value in light of the new circumstances.

A second observation not unrelated to the first is the fact that the university in Western capitalist democracies is in the process of significant structural transformation. In its attempt to serve the two contrary masters of political and economic correctness, it has found itself without clear moorings from either the public or the private sector. This has been consistently aggravated, as noted, by the inability or refusal of publics to see the crucial tie between higher education as a whole and the renewal and improvement of essential infrastructure in the capital, as well as the public and social, sectors. Attempts to serve the interests of both political and economic correctness have led to the institutionalization of wanton hypocrisy in decisions about admissions, grades, advancement and the role of preferential criteria in the face of cutbacks, downsizing, privatization and the attempt to demonstrate practical and 'strategic' relevance even when such a posture is thoroughly inappropriate. When to this one adds the prospect of intermittent contractual employment as the only alternative to unemployment for Ph.D's in the disciplines most relevant to postmodern analysis, particularly if the individuals concerned

[34] Popper, *op. cit.*; Baudrillard, *op. cit.*

are alleged to be 'over-represented' in a given university department, faculty or program, one can understand how such developments can engender a sense of futility, frustration and rage.

A third observation is that the exponential dependence of both universities and intellectuals of all types on the computer and other forms of automated-electronic technology, alongside the gradual displacement of libraries and books by networks, microchip storage and specialized informational, bibliographical and research programs has begun to supplant the university as a space of talk and action in its own right. Administrators and programmers acquire far greater power and influence under the new and emerging arrangements while intellectuals become spatially (if not socially) isolated. Ties outside the university and across national boundaries become more and more important relative to the time one is required to be on campus for other than pedagogical and administrative purposes. As a result of the global and homogeneous nature of this more direct dependence on technology, intellectuals begin to doubt the role of thought and thinking relative to hardware and software acquisition and knowledge.

These three observations as to what might account for the post-modern attitude should not lead us to ignore one which must be addressed even though it is more vague and less defined than the others. In the midst of everything else that has been mentioned, there is a global redistribution of wealth that is going on apace, not so much between nation-states as between and among capitals all over the world. The actual form that this process of 'globalization' is taking is usually hidden from view, most often in the rhetoric and media hype asserting that it is nations rather than classes that are competing with one another across national and supranational boundaries.[35] The reasons for this, however indisputable, do not negate the overall impact this process of redistribution is having on the confidence of Western intellectuals in their own institutions. After all, what better justification could there be for a sense of frustration and despair, coupled with the desire to be beyond what is causing it, than a scenario in which the West takes all the blame and gets none of the credit for the process of modernization itself?

[35] Even before the terrorist events of September 11, 2001, the possibility, even likelihood, that the neo-conservatism/neo-liberalism grip on globalization would become uncoupled was suggested by Michael Hardt and Antonio Negri in *Empire* (Cambridge, Mass.: Harvard University Press, 2001).

Standing behind all of this is the specter of Max Weber no less than that of Karl Marx. Weber bemoaned the very likelihood of the success of world capitalism, by which he understood the linkage between the sovereign national state, capital and modern science-based technology, because he believed that it would denude life of all meaning. Weber's lament at the turn of the last century harbors a Nietzscheian refrain just this side of nihilism, which Weber clung on to and at the same time resisted with all his strength. One sees this clearly in the 'Science as a Vocation' essay in particular, as well as in the introduction and concluding pages of *The Protestant Ethic and the Spirit of Capitalism.* Perhaps it is the two vocation essays by Weber which, in the final analysis, provide the best counterpoint to postmodernism, concerned as they are with the ambiguities and contradictions of life under capitalism, the central social, political and cultural, as well as economic, phenomenon of Western modernity.[36] It is against the backdrop of Weberian pessimism that social intellectuals still have to rise to the occasion, rather than assisting in the massive, and consequential, self-confirming prophecy that contemporary postmodernism now threatens to become.

[36] Weber, 'Science as a Vocation', *From Max Weber: Essays in Sociology* (New York: Oxford University Press, 1946), pp. 129–156; Weber, 'Politics as a Vocation', *Ibid.*, pp. 77–128; Weber, *Protestant Ethic and the Spirit of Capitalism* (New York: Scribners, 1958).

INDEX OF NAMES

INDEX OF SUBJECTS